OBAMA
THE JOURNEY COMPLETED -
NEVER PROMISED A ROSE GARDEN

GYE NYAME
Supremacy of God

FREDERICK MONDERSON

SUMON PUBLISHERS

i

SuMon Publishers
PO Box 160586
Brooklyn, New York 11216

fredsegypt.com@fredsegypt.com
sumonpublishers.com@sumonpublishers.com
blackfolksbooks.com@blackfolksbooks.com
blackegyptbooks.com@blackegyptbooks.com

ISBN - 978-1610230568
LCCN - 2016900808

In the "Tribute to Professor George Simmonds," 'Unsung Hero,' Dr. Fred Monderson sat at the feet of his heroes, Brother X, Michael Carter, Dr. Leonard Jeffries, El Hombe Brathe, Dr. Lewis, Prof. George Simmonds, Dr. ben-Jochannan, Sister Camille Yarbrough, Etc.

2012 Commemorative Presidential Print
Presented to Frederick Monderson
By President Barack Obama and the Democratic National Committee

There's Bo, the President's dog, frolicking in the White House Rose Garden.

To Frederick,

On behalf of Bo and myself, please accept our gratitude and thanks for your leadership and support at this critical juncture in American history.

[signature] Bo 🐾

In a rare yet playful mood, Mr. Obama pets his dog Bo perhaps on way to an important meeting.

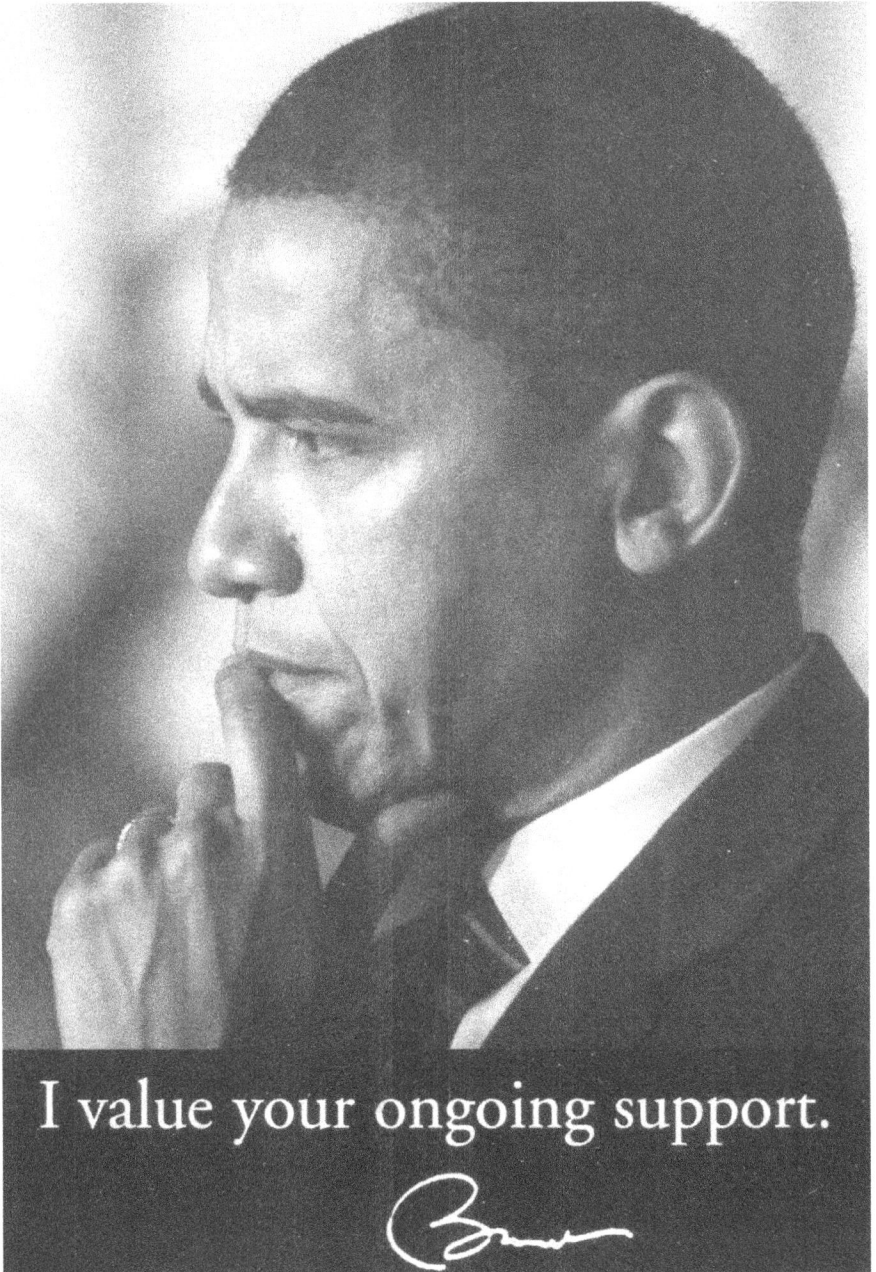

I value your ongoing support.

View of one of Mr. Obama's pensive moods, expressing and recognizing support of persons who "lifted him up" during those "challenging times."

Portrait of President Barack H. Obama unveiled at Rev. Al Sharpton's invitation to speak at NAN's Dr. King Affair.

Frederick, the journey ahead is going to be long. And it is going to be hard.
But know that is how change always happens in this country. And if we keep
showing up, if we keep fighting the good fight,
then eventually we get there. We always do. — *Michelle Obama*

PRESIDENT BARACK OBAMA

Dear Frederick,

As a gesture of my gratitude for your friendship and support, I hope you will accept the enclosed piece of artwork, which features the White House Rose Garden.

This beautiful spot provides a peaceful oasis just outside of the Oval Office for me. Often, this historic garden is also the site for the signing of significant pieces of legislation. I thought it appropriate to present this to you considering the successes that you and I have been able to achieve over the past three years since my inauguration.

32 million formerly-uninsured Americans will have access to the healthcare they need. We are successfully pursuing the terrorists who assaulted our nation, while also handing Iraq back to its people. We have reformed Wall Street. And while America was losing 700,000 jobs each month three years ago, we have steadily reversed this trend and have seen 22 months of private sector growth and the creation of more than 3 million new jobs.

We both know that these changes weren't easy. This progress was possible because of you, because you didn't stop believing. You stood up and made your voice heard. You kept up the fight for change long after the election was over.

But it is all at stake in this election. The very core of what this country stands for is on the line — the basic promise that no matter what you look like, no matter where you come from, no matter your station in life, this is a place where you can make it if you try. The notion that we're all in this together, that we look out for one another — that's at stake in this election.

It is critical for our nation that Democrats win up and down the ticket, at all levels … from the White House and Congress, to statehouses and courthouses around the nation. And to do this, we urgently need your ongoing support.

Again, thank you for all that you have done for the Democratic Party and for me. I hope that I can continue to count on you.

Sincerely,

President Barack Obama

To Frederick,
Our success is due to your dedication, friendship, and support. We thank
you from the bottom of our hearts.

VICE PRESIDENT JOE BIDEN
WASHINGTON, DC

Dear Frederick,

On behalf of President Obama and myself, let me express our sincere gratitude for the support and friendship you have provided us over the past four years ... during our historic 2008 campaign and then in the first three years of this Administration.

As a small token of our appreciation, a personalized photograph of the President and me has been enclosed along with this letter. Whenever you see this photo, please let it serve as a reminder that we are grateful for everything you have done for us and for the Democratic Party.

I hope we can count on your ongoing support over the coming year as we face off against the Republicans in Congress, who are road-blocking important economic initiatives such as the American Jobs Act. For the sake of our nation, we cannot allow the Republicans to play political games with our nation's economy and the lives of everyday Americans.

Our Party also needs your ongoing support as we move into a truly critical election year. It is vital to our nation's future for the Democratic Party to re-elect President Obama, hold onto the Senate, to regain a majority in the House of Representatives, and to win in state and regional elections around the nation.

I urge you to please take a moment to read the enclosed letter from Congresswoman Debbie Wasserman Schultz, the Chair of the Democratic National Committee. Debbie will update you about the current political situation, and let you know what needs to be done to ensure a Democratic victory in 2012.

Again, thank you for your ongoing friendship, your support for our Administration, and for your leadership within the Democratic Party.

Sincerely,

Vice President Joe Biden

DEMOCRATIC NATIONAL COMMITTEE
430 SOUTH CAPITOL STREET, SE • WASHINGTON, DC 20003 • 1-877-336-7200 • WWW.DEMOCRATS.ORG

CONTRIBUTIONS OR GIFTS TO THE DEMOCRATIC NATIONAL COMMITTEE ARE NOT DEDUCTIBLE
AS CHARITABLE CONTRIBUTIONS FOR FEDERAL INCOME TAX PURPOSES.

x

After eight bruising years of guiding the American ship of state, Barack H. Obama has essentially relinquished leadership of this moral and philosophic battleship many have labeled "the last hope for humanity." Want to recount some of the "rough stuff," he faced, look inside **OBAMA - THE JOURNEY COMPLETED** - since **Obama NEVER PROMISED A ROSE GARDEN**.

Never in the history of the nation's Presidency has an individual faced such challenges in the form of "friendly" and "enemy fire." Important, Mr. Obama has not received credit for his outstanding role in rescuing the American economy, saving the auto industry, reducing the nation's reliance on foreign energy, generating more clean energy initiatives, advancing the cause of women and speaking out on controversial issues. Unquestionably, Republican and "Tea Party" players have encouraged and generated a great deal of racial animosity and disrespect towards Mr. Obama and the institution of the Presidency during his tenure as Head of State, Commander-In-Chief, and Chief Diplomat. All criticized his policies with great vehemence and been extremely obdurate in opposition to his every legislative proposal; yet, he achieved so much, viz., Lilly Ledbetter, Credit Card and Student Loan Adjustment, Dodd/Frank financial and economic regulation, Climate Change initiatives, Iran Nuclear Deal, Asian Trade Deal, Removing key players from the battlefield in the War-On-Terror, the Cuba Initiative, "Race to the Top," encouraging mothers to return to College while boosting the role of Community Colleges as part of an effort to upgrade American teaching methodology in the key areas of education and choosing to be "My Brothers' Keeper" even recognizing "Same Sex Marriage."

His policies have not simply saved jobs of "first responders," teachers, and others in the auto industry; national unemployment rates have dropped to its lowest levels in a decade with the private sector adding many millions of jobs in a 72-month consistent job growth period and nearly 20 million persons been assured Affordable Care Act's health care protections. Wages have risen and poverty is down. Still, the depths of the inherited malady is still not fully explained to the

American people duped by previous administrations; and no scandal taints Mr. Obama's Presidency.

President Mr. Obama has shed light on and provided relief on the issue of undocumented immigration. He served not as a "Black President" but as an American President because he wanted to unite America and move it forward. Still, those in unrelenting opposition have added seeds of disharmony, discontent, disrespect, division, and particularly racial animosity since day one, while skillfully blaming Mr. Obama for wanting to "change the Constitution." In this strategy, not sufficient attention was paid the divisive role of those spewing "One term president" hatred; "Worse than slavery;" "Stupid;" "Waterloo;" "You Lie;" "Send Obama back to Kenya;" "Gangster government;" "take our government back;" a Pastor praying for Obama's death as his parishioner came out as a Black Protester with Guns, and the disgusting "Birther Charade" of Donald Trump. All this, the "Cool Ruler" took in stride affirming "Politics is a contact sport" and these are only "Good Ole Boys" acting out. However, only history will tell if Mr. Paul Krugman's assessment that "Obama is the greatest President ever" is absolutely correct. Nevertheless, given his mandate, Mr. Obama's objective was to rescue and protect his beloved nation while charting a path into the future that reduces America's reliance on foreign energy, create credible scientific opportunities for the nation's young minds and to his critics he admonished as T.D. Jakes put it: A giraffe was grazing at treetop level and along came a tortoise who hailed, "How's it going?" "Great," replied the ruminant. "And you?" "It's hell down here. All I can see and smell is garbage and foul odor." "Well, come up a notch and enjoy the green foliage and healthy air among the Blue skies." This is what Mr. Obama offered his critics and opponents who choose to remain in "Tortoiseville" as he sought clean and creative paths for America's future in a non-racial or environment of equality and opportunity.

fredsegypt.com@fredsegypt.com
SuMonPublishers.com@SuMonPublishers.com

Dr. Fred Monderson is an African historian, conducts Tours to Egypt, a retired Professor and Public School teacher who taught American History and Government. He can be reached at (917) 808-7096.

OBAMA THE JOURNEY COMPLETED - NEVER PROMISED A ROSE GARDEN

THE TABLE OF CONTENTS

FREDERICK MONDERSON

OBAMA THE JOURNEY COMPLETED - NEVER PROMISED A ROSE GARDEN

FREDERICK MONDERSON

OBAMA THE JOURNEY COMPLETED - NEVER PROMISED A ROSE GARDEN

1. BEN CARSON, SERIOUSLY?
By
Dr. Fred Monderson

Recently, a Washington lawmaker described the Affordable Care Act maliciously dubbed "Obamacare," as "the most dangerous law in American history." This week, at a social conservative gathering, the famed and now retired neurosurgeon from Johns Hopkins Hospital Center and member of the conservative Heritage Foundation, Dr. Ben

Carson, described "Obamacare as worse than slavery." Tragic! In a visit to a South American Republic this writer overhead a taxi driver railing at another motorist, "I know you bought your license, but at least learn to drive!"

"Change will not come if we wait for some other person or some other time. We are the ones we've been waiting for. We are the change that we seek." **Barack Obama**

Dr. Carson is clearly a highly skillful and successful surgeon. However, his comments regarding the Affordable Care Act initiative set forth by President Obama and now law reflects either an abysmal ignorance of African/American history and race relations in this country or a severe psycho/cultural pathology which impels him to seek his "thirty pieces of silver" in the form of approbation from powerful white supremacists who fear and hate President Obama.

OBAMA THE JOURNEY COMPLETED - NEVER PROMISED A ROSE GARDEN

Inasmuch as lawmakers are enormously wealthy, the lawmaker in question may have bought, or inherited, his seat while still being ignorant of American history. Dr. Carson, on the other hand, may have been too busy conducting brain surgery to have truly studied American slavery, as well as its psycho/cultural aftermath, to make such a reckless, perverse comparison. Let us not forget that Malcolm X reminded us, "The slave master used overseers and the method of divide and rule to control the slaves!" Of course, Willie Lynch was the master manipulator of slave management. In an earlier version of today's developments, the Republicans used Michael Steele, the first Black Chairman of the Republican Party to attempt the defeat of President Obama. He was a dismal failure and was subsequently fired. Whether Ben Carson is a "Judas Iscariot" or not only time will tell! Nevertheless, in the record of the oppressor; lawmakers especially, have historic ties to odious legislation that terrorized and victimized significant segments of the African-American population. Dr. Carson, one of perhaps very few Blacks afforded a platform at the ultraconservative Family Research Council's meetings and probably at several other such gatherings, raises questions as to his motivation, purpose, audience and intent, as well as his knowledge of history, certainly of Black History! It is thus appropriate that a mini-history lesson be used to enlighten these individuals like Dr. Carson and others on some of the "most dangerous laws passed in American history!"

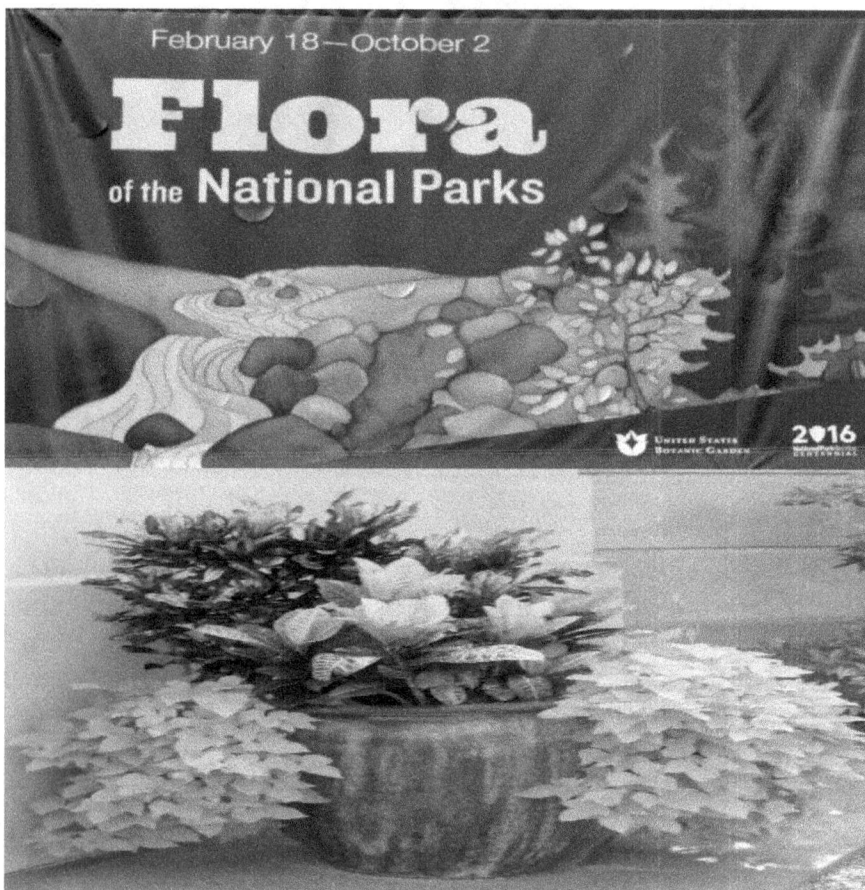

Perhaps in his narrow-mindedness, what the Congressman meant refers to are times when the law as applied to all Americans is dangerous but when applied to African Americans it is not! Nevertheless, in Dr. Carson's case, he certainly knows medicine but does not fully realize that a Black Republican, people of his hue, *a la*

OBAMA THE JOURNEY COMPLETED - NEVER PROMISED A ROSE GARDEN

Michael Steele, J.C. Watts, Allen West, Alan Kees, Herman Cain, "who all sat by the door," ultimately found the inner portals closed. Thank goodness, most have their professions on which to fall back. In the minds of many Black people especially in that rant against "Obamacare," Dr. Carson has certainly fallen from grace and many young students who were inspired by his "gifted hands," must now wonder whether psyche and spirit have been impaired!

FREDERICK MONDERSON

The intent of this essay is to show, some of the most odious laws, sketched below, which proved to be infinitely more oppressive and dangerous as applied to African-Americans in this country, more than the Affordable Care Act as law. This meaningful and comprehensive health care law is designed to address the needs of millions of Americans who have no medical coverage and can only rely on the immediacy of Emergency Room care. Two things can thus be considered in this case. The article in *The New York Times* of October 6, 2013, referenced the hundreds of millions of dollars this Anti-Obamacare movement is collecting and disbursing. It speaks to the disinformation it spews and the insidious gathering and individuals involved behind this movement and its sinister aims.

Given that speakers are paid a fee for their presentation, it is fair to ask whether Dr. Carson is but one recipient of this money-mill. Second, the article mentions the thousands of persons being trained to extend the task of "informing the public about Obamacare." Granted, some policy laws as huge as Obamacare may have some faults in their initial roll-out, obstacles are expected. However, these "pseudo-patriots" such as Dr. Carson, however, are not interested in repairability but in destruction. Which great idea has not had setbacks before being perfected? Surely we can name Medicare, Social Security, the conquest of space, even formation of the Union of the United States which is still in process, after nearly two and a half centuries, to perfect itself! Most importantly, it is not inconceivable that there may be much misinformation in the anti-Obamacare strategy, but the **Affordable Care Act** was a principal issue in the Obama Campaign Platform. It was passed by Congress, upheld by the Supreme Court twice and is the law of the land. Even more important, it is hardly likely to be repealed despite now some 50 attempts by House Republicans to repeal this historic piece of federal legislation! In this 2016 Presidential election, while Hillary Clinton wants to correct any deficiencies in the law, Donald Trumps does not want to repair the measure, but to repeal and start again. Who knows how long such a health care challenge will take to arrive at a similar status as the current Affordable Care Act, given nearly 20 million persons have registered for it.

OBAMA THE JOURNEY COMPLETED - NEVER PROMISED A ROSE GARDEN

In school, youngsters are reminded that even the brightest students dropout; and that even the most brilliant people sometimes say dumb things! Dr. Carson certainly knows medicine but his understanding of the forces and realities of history is a failure. Perhaps, in his present mental state, if this was an operation his patient would probably come out seriously impaired. When Vice-President Dan Quayle mis-spelled potato as p-o-t-a-t-o-e he disappointed a great many. Likewise, when Dr. Carson stood with the Conservative Family Research Council and pronounced that President Obama's Affordable Care Act, maliciously called "Obamacare," was the "worse law since slavery," not only did he disappoint untold numbers of adult Blacks, but his status as an icon to many young Blacks took a severe hit! As for this writer, as an American, I feel I must share my thoughts on this misguided statement. Particularly, because similar ones have been expressed among people who have either conspired with or have been funded by surreptitious individuals who plotted to disrupt, subvert and/or obstruct the orderly function of the United States government under the legal administration of President Barack Obama, twice elected by a majority of the American people. For such actions, persons are thus guilty of treason!

OBAMA THE JOURNEY COMPLETED - NEVER PROMISED A ROSE GARDEN

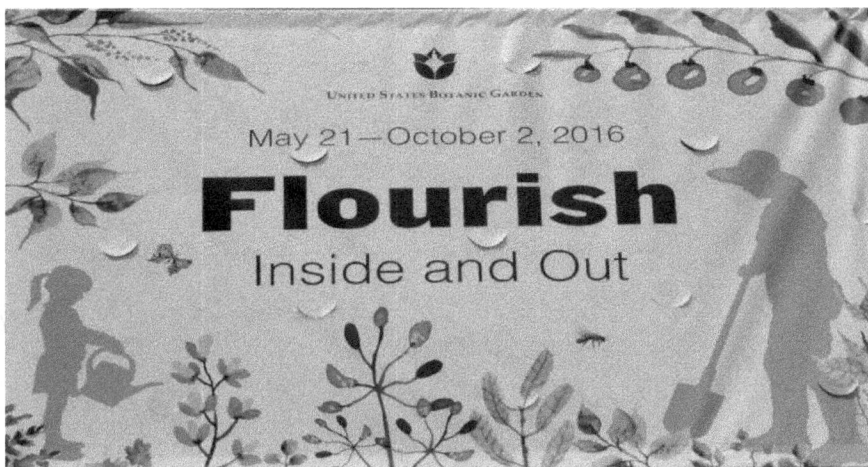

Let me then first point out some milestones in American History, whether under de-jure legislative process or de-facto practice, that have been hall-marks underscoring the notion of "the Ugly American." In this vein, it would be helpful to separate Pre - and Post -1863 *Emancipation Proclamation* issues to establish the context in which Dr. Carson, especially, is not only ignorant, but perverse, malicious and spiteful. This is sadly predictable, considering his alignment with a conservative heritage mindset that reeks of association with historical terrorist activities against Blacks in America. It is an established fact that after President Obama's 2008 victory, Senator Mitch McConnell publicly boasted, "I intend to make Barack Obama a one-term President." Morgan Freeman, the Academy Award winner, appearing on CNN's Piers Morgan, asserted that the Senator's statement was "blatantly racist!" Freeman's comments also would be apt regarding Dr. Carson's statement.

FREDERICK MONDERSON

OBAMA THE JOURNEY COMPLETED - NEVER PROMISED A ROSE GARDEN

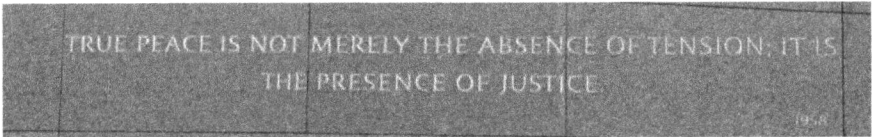

TRUE PEACE IS NOT MERELY THE ABSENCE OF TENSION; IT IS THE PRESENCE OF JUSTICE

Now, history has shown that to secure Southern support for acceptance of the initial United States Constitution, the founding fathers established the **3/5ᵗʰ Clause** or the **Compromise of 1787**, in which enslaved Africans were counted as "three fifths" of a White person or to have 5 Blacks counted as 3 Whites. Let us also remind Dr. Carson that many a "founding patriot" sent slaves to fight for America's freedom in the Revolutionary War; that one free Black, Crispus Attucks was the first to fall in the fight for America's freedom. This means that among America's first patriots was a Black Man, a bona fide hero!

Eli Whitney's 1793 Cotton Gin, a U.S. Government Patent opened floodgates of the enslaved despair requiring an increasing work force to not simply tend cotton but also tobacco and other features of the slave economy.

The **Compromise of 1820** was also called the **Missouri Compromise**. It stipulated, among other things, that Maine would be admitted to the Union as a "Free State," and Missouri as a "Slave state." The remainder of the **Louisiana Purchase** (1803) would not become a slave state.

FREDERICK MONDERSON

OBAMA THE JOURNEY COMPLETED - NEVER PROMISED A ROSE GARDEN

Following the **Compromise of 1820**, in 1832, the **South Carolina Nullification Act** forced President Andrew Jackson to dispatch federal troops to check the rebellious action of this leading practitioner of African debasement through public examination and commerce in Africans considered chattel. Nearly 250 years later, Jesse Jackson pointed out, South Carolina; home state of former Senator Jim DeMint, who now heads the Heritage Foundation; on whose website Dr. Carson's photo is prominently displayed; and this Senator who wanted to create President Obama's "Waterloo;" that the state he represented supported 36 state prisons and 1 state college. It is not surprising in such a former "rebellious slave state," that Blacks are the principal occupants of its state prisons and hardly represented at its state college or other such institutions of learning. It is noteworthy in this day and age, after Dr. Carson had spoken, Dylan Roof killed 9 African-Americans at prayer in a church while the rebellious South Carolina flag, long the symbol of that state flew proudly over the state

17

house. Governor Haley, a Republican, pushed to have the flag removed, perhaps she remembered Amritsar.

OBAMA THE JOURNEY COMPLETED - NEVER PROMISED A ROSE GARDEN

Among its many mandates, the **Compromise of 1850** not only sought to establish north/south, free state/slave state regional balance, but established the **Fugitive Slave Laws** in which, then legalized and empowered slave catchers rounded up, oftentimes, both free and enslaved Blacks who runaway but were returned to southern servitude. Sometimes they were returned from the North to Black slave owners who were often active participants in a system of inhumanity that brutalized and debased the bodies and souls of untold numbers of other African people held in bondage through judicial and administrative fiat.

FREDERICK MONDERSON

OBAMA THE JOURNEY COMPLETED - NEVER PROMISED A ROSE GARDEN

Black Codes were the legal mechanisms by which enslaved Blacks were dehumanized, controlled and psychologically and often physically emasculated in a system of exploitation that generated great wealth through the plantation culture for principally southerners in the "lynching states." Perhaps, not surprisingly, in the 2012 election, the Republican candidate Mitt Romney won all the southern states with history of lynching and slavery's horrors. So much for the "New South!"

FREDERICK MONDERSON

OBAMA THE JOURNEY COMPLETED - NEVER PROMISED A ROSE GARDEN

In 1857, Chief Justice Roger Taney issued the **Dred Scott Decision**, a ruling that Dred Scott, an enslaved African-American seeking his freedom, was not a citizen and could not bring suit in a United States Court. Even more, this apologist for slavery further ruled, that based on American history, this enslaved "Black man is not a citizen and has no rights which a White man must respect!" Dr. Carson also ought to be aware, even after his outlandish disparagement of President Obama's most important legislative accomplishment; that of a Black man held in the highest esteem by untold millions of African and other people worldwide; there would be at least one conservative heckler in that group he was addressing, who would have shouted "The Nigger has spoken!" Perhaps it would be, "The Nigger Doctor has spoken!" Then again, while "his camp" has previously thought the President of the United States, Barack

FREDERICK MONDERSON

Hussein Obama is a "Nigger," perhaps in his misguided mind, Dr. Carson may also have thought, though he has "probably moved inside the door," he is not a "Nigger." But somewhere along the line he will be reminded that he is a "Nigger," especially if his strategy as a tool of presidential debasement, does not work!

OBAMA THE JOURNEY COMPLETED - NEVER PROMISED A ROSE GARDEN

Abraham Lincoln was very intelligent; a great man and President who realized, "a house divided against itself cannot stand;" and as such, he put his heart, his administration and his life into the **Emancipation Proclamation**. This bold and courageous act paved the way for the **Civil War Amendments** - 13th, legally ended slavery; 14th, gave citizenship to individuals born or naturalized in the United States; and the 15th, which empowered Black men with the legal status to exercise the franchise. However, under cover of law, these legislative milestones were often assaulted and desecrated by southern conservatives who were the "powers that be" who were architects of "Jim Crow" practice. These then were part of a most terrifying period in American history the historian Professor Rayford Logan called "the Nadir," because of the perennial perpetuation of horrific acts of terror in lynching, intimidation, tar and feather, share crop peonage, denial of the right to vote and hold office, all committed against Blacks.

FREDERICK MONDERSON

OBAMA THE JOURNEY COMPLETED - NEVER PROMISED A ROSE GARDEN

That conservative movement, to win political control of the "prostrate South" during and after Reconstruction, formed "white redeemers" such as the Ku Klux Klan, White Citizens Council, Knights of the White Camellia, etc., and began to systematically terrorize Blacks effectively instilling fear and other measures to disfranchise them. In conjunction, Southern conservative lawmakers enacted the "Grandfather Clause," which ruled that "If one's grandfather had voted previously then one could vote." This strategy as a tool instilled fear and helped exclude Blacks from the polls since their enslaved grandfathers could not have voted before the 15th Amendment of February 1870. The "Grandfather Clause" was repealed in 1915 because of its inequity and as a pillar of "Jim Crow" practices. A legal requirement that Blacks pay a "Poll Tax" to vote was instituted and they were required to take a "Literacy Test" which some with advanced, even doctors degrees, could not pass because of the political skullduggery manipulating educational requiring machinations to voting. All these shenanigans employed contributed to a *de facto* and *de jure* "Jim Crow" state of affairs across the south especially in which ex-slaves were relegated to second class citizenship or no citizenship, and were perennially victims of "terrorism at will." Meanwhile, the "White Primary" became the order of the day, precluding Blacks from running for elected office and enabling Whites to control the political process! That sacred American objection, "Taxation without Representation applied here. All of this occurred while the federal government pandered to the whims of arch conservatives, irrespective of the party to which they belonged.

FREDERICK MONDERSON

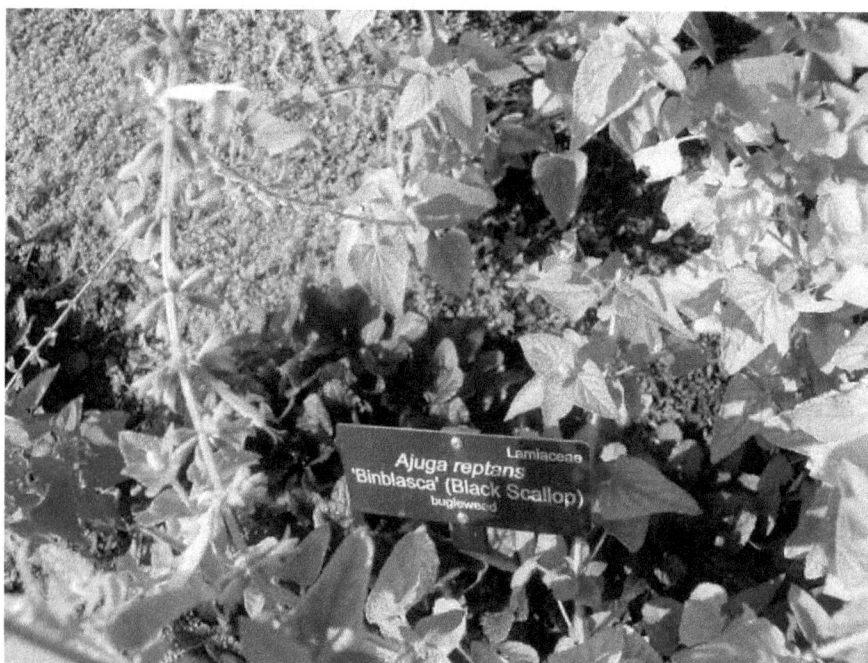

OBAMA THE JOURNEY COMPLETED - NEVER PROMISED A ROSE GARDEN

Many of those events and circumstances culminated in the 1896 Supreme Court ruling of *Plessey v. Ferguson* that established a "Separate but Equal" rule, which was, in actuality, "Separate and Unequal." This significant ruling particularly affected the education of young children, sometimes for Ten dollars spent on a white child's education, only one dollar was spent on that of a black child's. This inequity under cover of political and social practice particularly enabled state enforced residential segregation that bred lynchings and other forms of terror and violent acts including murder of Black men, women and children. So much so, a few years ago in 2011, a CBS 60-Minutes program, investigating a Civil Rights case of murder in which the principal perpetrator was still alive, yet no one was talking but the victim's family, revealed more than 100 unresolved Civil Rights murders. The report also pointed out, in order to run for and hold political office across the South, individuals had to belong to or espouse the policies of the "lynching states" terrorist ideology. Thus, in that environment and under cover of state law and politics, racially motivated mob violence, lynchings and murder were never seriously challenged in territory under conservatives' control. In 2015, *The New York Times* published an article detailing nearly 4000 killings of Blacks from 1870 to 1950 in several southern states, avowedly Christian, and where the investigator wanted to place a marker as a reminder of this tragic phenomenon in American history.

OBAMA THE JOURNEY COMPLETED - NEVER PROMISED A ROSE GARDEN

Under existing "unjust laws" in the Post-Reconstruction era, especially in the South, Black-Americans were denied the fundamental rights of the United States Constitution. Among others, these included "Exclusion from Jury Duty," "Denial of Freedom of Speech," "Voting Rights," and the "Right to Assemble." They were also excluded from union jobs until, on the eve of World War II in 1941, A. Philip Randolph, a Black activist labor leader, threatened to "March on Washington!" In response, President F.D. Roosevelt took some action and the Congress of Industrial Organizations, sister arm of the American Federation of Labor, began enrolling and facilitating the hiring of Black workers. At the end of World War II and having succeeded President Roosevelt, President Harry Truman desegregated the armed forces because Blacks had served gloriously to defend this nation as they had in every war in which American has ever been engaged. Even more importantly, a pivotal catalyst that may have influenced the racist behavior of America was probably the "winds of change" sweeping the post-war world especially in the colonies.

In 1954, Thurgood Marshall, long in the vineyards of challenging laws oppressive to Blacks, was able to successfully argue *Brown V. Board*

OBAMA THE JOURNEY COMPLETED - NEVER PROMISED A ROSE GARDEN

of Education of Topeka, Kansas that, in fact, overturned *Plessey v. Ferguson*. This significant legal victory forever changed America although racism and discrimination changed its *modus operandi* but still essentially remained the same, if not becoming worse. Lest we forget, however, the movement for change was led by a number of individuals who took a stand against the "Bull Connors of the South," the Klan and the ensuing hatred and racial insanity they represented, certainly aided by institutional racism. This profound movement was led by leadership stalwarts as Reverend Shillingsworth, Martin Luther King, Rev. Abernathy, Harry Belafonte, Rosa Parks, Kwame Toure (Stokeley Carmichael), Fannie Lou Hamer, Malcolm X, Reverend Lowery, Jesse Jackson, Andrew young, and Viola Liuzzo, Andrew Goodman, Michael Schwerner and the many "freedom Riders" among others who stood up to preserve the American Dream and paid a price. Today these courageous leaders and martyrs would be tremendously surprised, if not sickened, by Dr. Carson's stunning remarks since, in American politics, it has always been, "Where you stand is where you sit and where you sit is where you stand!" Congressman Charlie Rangel explained that the Anti-Obamacare Movement was predicated and driven by hatred for President Obama, a Black male and, therefore, one would have to wonder how Dr. Carson, also a Black male himself, could align himself with persons filled with such conservative and racial venom!

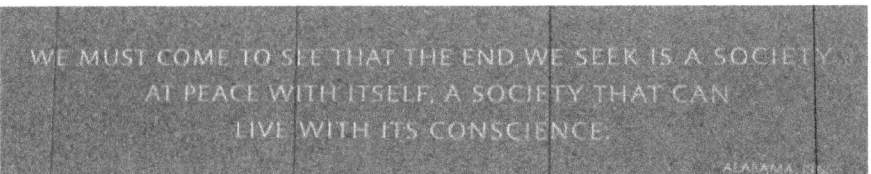

WE MUST COME TO SEE THAT THE END WE SEEK IS A SOCIETY AT PEACE WITH ITSELF, A SOCIETY THAT CAN LIVE WITH ITS CONSCIENCE.

ALABAMA

FREDERICK MONDERSON

OBAMA THE JOURNEY COMPLETED - NEVER PROMISED A ROSE GARDEN

FREDERICK MONDERSON

Gerrymandering was essentially a Republican creation though Democrats have also practiced it. Yet, it encouraged and ably assisted voter suppression particularly before and after the 1965 Voting Rights Act. Presidents Kennedy and Johnson's "Great Society" which supported the **1964 Civil Rights** laws and the **1965 Voting Rights** law required a provision which insisted that the voting law must be extended every 25-year period in order for them to remain effective. In an interesting development, despite Dr. Ben Carson "sitting at the king's table, eating his meat," and having climbed to the pinnacle of his profession to make that outlandish proclamation; if the Voting Rights law expires, given recent Republican controlled statehouse efforts to suppress the Black vote, Dr. Carson and his children and grandchildren will not be able to vote! However, and even more important, it is evident that the group with whom Dr. Carson is comfortably aligned, the Republicans were accused of innumerable and unimaginable skullduggery on election day at the last two Presidential elections and all under cover of law. Even more, despite their treasonous planning to subvert the government, no one was arrested. They lost before and will lose again as their record stands serenely blemished!

OBAMA THE JOURNEY COMPLETED - NEVER PROMISED A ROSE GARDEN

FREDERICK MONDERSON

Let us not forget, Sarah Palin who, to make political points in her losing 2008 effort running for president, accused President Obama of "palling around with terrorists." As early as 2013 and today in 2016 she is like a spent comet lost in the great void of the political cosmos; even teaming with or "Palling around" with Ted Nugent racist and profound dis-respecter of President Obama. Notwithstanding, the record reveals only after 2012, and by theoretical reconstruction, that after the 2008 presidential election, a group of rich and powerful Republican individuals got together and planned to subvert Mr. Obama's Presidency. This formed the fundamental strategy of the Republican Party going forward. In conjunction with the shenanigans of the nascent "Tea Party" movement and Republicans blocking every legislative initiative of President Obama, such behaviors earned them the "Party of No" badge of dishonor and plummeted the Republican controlled Congress rating among the American people! Some people have rightfully called this behavior treason because these persons plotted to subvert the legislatively constituted United States government under the leadership of the first African-American President Barack Hussein Obama.

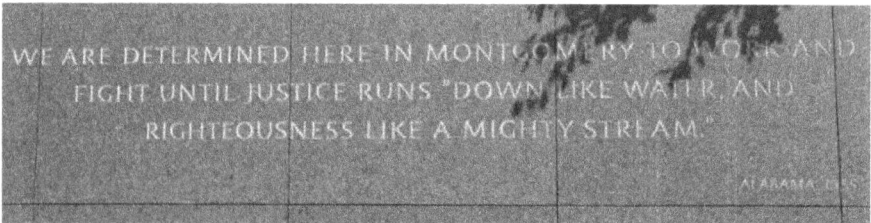

WE ARE DETERMINED HERE IN MONTGOMERY TO WORK AND FIGHT UNTIL JUSTICE RUNS "DOWN LIKE WATER, AND RIGHTEOUSNESS LIKE A MIGHTY STREAM."

What happens in the dark ultimately comes to light and though only visionaries could see such early treasonous machinations; *The New York Times* of Sunday, October 6, 2013, front page and p. 18, article entitled "A Crisis Months in the Making" exposed the repeated strategy after the 2012 election and named names. It did not take intellectual genius to realize the same 2008 actors and anyone who is or was of substance in Republicandom, were very much involved and were now exposed in this article. Ed Meese, a named principal "conspirator," was United States Attorney General under President

OBAMA THE JOURNEY COMPLETED - NEVER PROMISED A ROSE GARDEN

Ronald Reagan. In as much as his name surfaced in this article, many realized it established continuity of nefarious, some say racist, treasonous, Republican activity for 2008, possibly decades in the making and even down to today. Since many of these old and new conservative activists, articulated a "take no prisoners legislative strategy" and who planned and executed behaviors intended to subvert the will of the American people expressed by the second election of the President of the United States, they should, in fact, have been arrested for their treasonous behavior. The elders have often said, "Show me your company and I will tell who you are!" It is clear that Dr. Carson is quite at home with individuals implicated in treasonous words and deeds against the legally elected government of the United States and a presidential position to which he aspired but failed. Seeking to remain relevant, he aligned with Donald Trump whose "super-Nova" is at "cliff's edge." Sadly and perhaps this deluded individual feels that his Republican pals will hold moderate tones in his presence as they berate other African-Americans!

Dr. Carson ought to awake from his misguided slumber and recognize the world has become aware and several millions of Africans worldwide are outraged and feel strong revulsion for him. This is because of his disgusting distortion and omission of the historical record by his shameful, subjective assault upon a public policy set forth by President Obama which is intended to support the human rights of people lacking medical care making it more affordable and hence more accessible to millions of Americans who for the longest had been denied that right.

FREDERICK MONDERSON

OBAMA THE JOURNEY COMPLETED - NEVER PROMISED A ROSE GARDEN

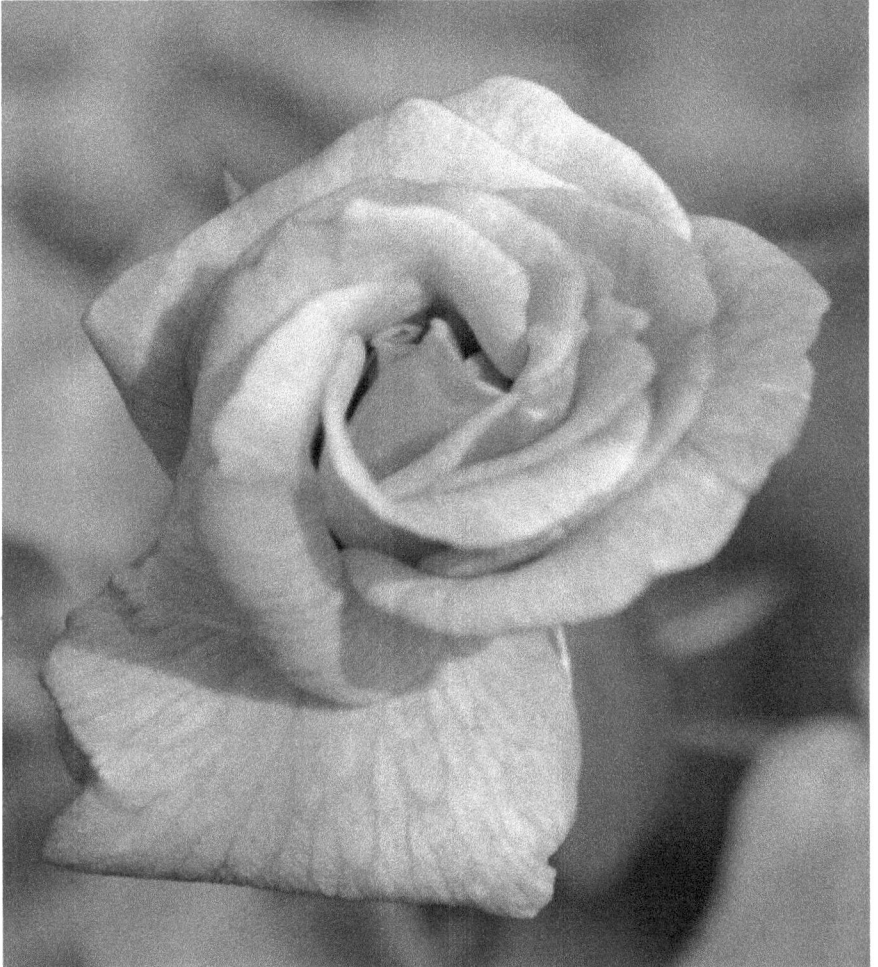

This self-negation of Dr. Carson, a physician and a person of African descent is unfortunately not necessary. It was prevalent during slavery, for the slave owner would instill the illusion among the "house slaves" that they were more valued than the "field hands." This practice induced and created a class within a caste resentment among the enslaved. Predictably, it encouraged betrayal of each other in order to find favor from the slave owners. Are people like Dr. Carson currently in 2016 likewise? Such persons, whether Rev. Mark Burns or other religious "poverty pimps" who openly pander for the "thirty pieces of silver" available to them in the form of approbation by the powerful and callous of heart in the USA? They must be recognized, identified and placed within the station of their current reality, which is correctly political oblivion.

"If you're walking down the right path and you're willing to keep walking, eventually you'll make progress." **Barack Obama**

OBAMA THE JOURNEY COMPLETED - NEVER PROMISED A ROSE GARDEN

2.   OBAMA AND LEADERSHIP
By
Dr. Fred Monderson

Of all American presidents demonstrating outstanding leadership in challenging times, perhaps none has faced more difficulties than Barack Obama. Granted each President faced serious challenges, for example, George Washington and foundation of the nation; Thomas Jefferson and the Louisiana Purchase and Barbary Pirates; James Monroe and his Doctrine; Abraham Lincoln and Secession and Civil

FREDERICK MONDERSON

War; Franklin D. Roosevelt and Depression, needing a "New Deal" leading up to World War II; Dwight Eisenhower and the Korean War; Ronald Reagan and the Cold War; and George W. Bush stung by September 11, 2001; but none, in time perspective, has faced the challenges meted out to President Obama considering the calamitous situation he inherited at home and abroad. Thus, contrary to misguided belief fed by insidious propaganda, Mr. Obama had demonstrated exemplary leadership. Nevertheless, perhaps only people with a Hubble Telescopic vision can see, understand and appreciate his accomplishments and this is what makes his tenure as the 44th President so exceptional.

"The future rewards those who press on. I don't have time to feel sorry for myself. I don't have time to complain. I'm going to press on."
Barack Obama

OBAMA THE JOURNEY COMPLETED - NEVER PROMISED A ROSE GARDEN

George Washington and the "founding fathers," in establishing the new nation, its instruments and institutions, seeking survival and sustainability viz., the constitution endowing institutions and a variety of powers to make the system work was indeed a formidable challenge. Yet, with the exception of a few Tory loyalists, everyone was rooting for the success of the President and his men to make the new nation a credible venture. Upon realization that Jefferson's Louisiana Purchase not simply tremendously expanded the physical borders of the nation with the promise of the potential for great economic prosperity in both free and slave sections of the economy, many of the vast majority of movers and shakers and aspiring property owners, hailed Mr. Jefferson for the nation's extraordinary good fortune now that the Haitian Revolution under Toussaint L'Ouverture had forced Napoleon to bequeath that great largess to America for some $15 million, less than the price of some New York City apartments these days. Thus, Jefferson's work in writing the Declaration of Independence and launching the new nation, together with the Louisiana Purchase endeared the nation to support his presidency especially in his challenge to the Barbary Pirates.

OBAMA THE JOURNEY COMPLETED - NEVER PROMISED A ROSE GARDEN

FREDERICK MONDERSON

Following cessation of hostilities in Europe ending the aftermath of the French Revolution and Napoleonic Wars; and in America, the War of 1812, the "Second War for Independence" against Britain that ended in 181; James Monroe faced the horde of European imperialists seeking to regain their "New World" recolonization following the defeat of Napoleon in Europe. Again, this bold move that created a lucrative economic market for the US in Latin America was hailed as a great leadership strategy especially since it was backed by the power of the British naval might.

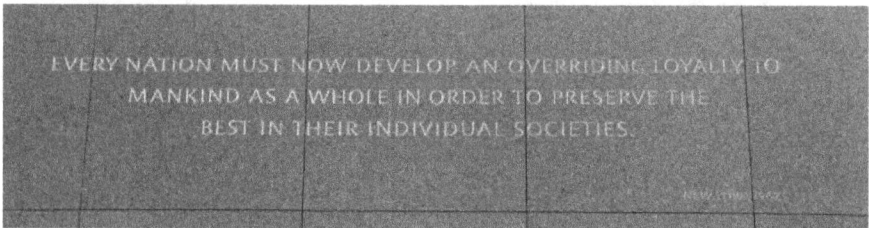

EVERY NATION MUST NOW DEVELOP AN OVERRIDING LOYALTY TO MANKIND AS A WHOLE IN ORDER TO PRESERVE THE BEST IN THEIR INDIVIDUAL SOCIETIES.

With a nation divided culturally, economically and politically, beating of the potential drums of war, secession and actual war, the loyalists supported Mr. Lincoln and hailed his leadership at a time of great distress for the nation. Winning the day, or war, outlining a plan to bind the wounds of conflict and heal the nation then unfold a plan towards a path of economic development, Mr. Lincoln was seen as a genius. Losing his life as he did, his greatness was amplified.

Franklin D. Roosevelt was elected in 1932 on a "New Deal" promise as the nation sweltered under the trials and tribulations of the Great Depression. In a "damn the torpedoes, full speed ahead" attitude, Mr. Roosevelt challenged the nation from "Captain to Cook," to rescue his beloved land initiating untold numbers of programs, in a "If one does not a work, try another" mindset as frame of reference. Ahead of his time in recognizing the aspirations of all Americans, viz., labor, immigrants, power companies, Blacks, women, FDR pressed ahead with his "alphabet programs" until finally challenged by the "9 old men" of the Supreme Court. Men of vision and tenacity are seldom stopped in their tracks but either walks around or through obstacles. In time, even the Supreme Court came around and with lots of help

OBAMA THE JOURNEY COMPLETED - NEVER PROMISED A ROSE GARDEN

from being drawn into World War II, Mr. Roosevelt pulled the nation out of the Depression placing it on a path of economic prosperity with untold economic and other safeguards in place to meet new and emerging, particularly, economic challenges.

FREDERICK MONDERSON

The size of the Roosevelt Memorial in Washington, D.C., is indicative of the expansiveness of the man's thinking and actions wherein all people lent their shoulders to his wheel as he rescued his nation from the clutches of its most catastrophic challenge initiated in the Great Depression. His vision and leadership set the stage for unparalleled transformation of the nation. It is no wonder Presidents Lincoln and Roosevelt proved to be Mr. Obama's greatest role models.

OBAMA THE JOURNEY COMPLETED - NEVER PROMISED A ROSE GARDEN

Dwight Eisenhower, a general in World War II became President from 1952-1960 and had to contend with the Korean War and also the communist threat in the Cold War. He was well liked and Americans rallied to his efforts to readjust in wake of the realistic military dynamics of the post-World War II and Korean conflicts.

FREDERICK MONDERSON

President John Kennedy came and left early but he transformed the Office of the Presidency and the nation and its image on the world stage. In meeting Khrushchev's challenge in the "Cuban Missile Crisis," not only did President Kennedy diffuse the potential consequences of a nuclear conflict but he exemplified American resolve when "all the marbles" were at stake. This martyr's death emboldened his successor Lyndon Johnson to masterfully bring into legal fruition Mr. Kennedy's "Great Society's" vision. This work in progress resulted in the **1964 Civil Rights Act** and the **1965 Voting Rights Act** that changed the nation in the most unimaginable manner.

OBAMA THE JOURNEY COMPLETED - NEVER PROMISED A ROSE GARDEN

Though he denied being "a crook," Richard Nixon created foreign policy masterpieces in establishing détente with China and Russia that were significant first steps in Ronald Reagan's path to glory in confronting the Berlin Wall's divide. Nevertheless, Ronald Reagan the actor and governor of California certainly endeared himself in the minds and hearts of the American people though a career that spanned several decades. As President, this public capital proved favorable in acceptance of his social and economic policies and his military build-up that resulted in collapse of the Soviet Union as they tried to match his level of military preparedness. So much so, no modern President received as enormous posthumous recognition as Ronald Reagan in his extensive funeral and naming of airports and public buildings in his honor. His 11th Commandment, "Thou shall not criticize a fellow Republican" became enshrined in American and Republican political lore and his aura continues to radiate from the shrine of his memory as Republican "wanna-bes" seek to exploit mileage of his blessings through association with Mrs. Nancy Reagan, identification with the

FREDERICK MONDERSON

Reagan Library or curry-favoring to Reagan's lieutenants and even exploiting the notion through "I was in the room with Ronald Reagan" saying.

OBAMA THE JOURNEY COMPLETED - NEVER PROMISED A ROSE GARDEN

Pulling all the strings that got him into the White House, George Washington Bush lulled the nation into a false sense of security that Al Qaeda exploited in effectuating their 9/11 plan of an unprecedented attack on the homeland that killed thousands. It was foolish that conspiracy theorists blamed Mr. Bush for concocting the attack. Notwithstanding, he cherished his respect for history given his being named after the first George Washington and the significance of his oath to uphold the office. That he made some faulty decisions, as a human being this is understandable, owing to poor advice and faulty intelligence. Some have argued Sadam Hussein's attempt on the life of the Senior Bush prompted George to invade Iraq after the

Afghanistan "Shock and Awe" blitz. Nevertheless, the reality of two wars, the Bush Tax Cuts for his "base," a Prescription Drug Plan that was unpaid for as well as skull-duggery speculation in banking, runaway Wall Street downward spiral recklessness and the unchecked housing market as a result of lax regulation brought America to the brink of economic disaster and failed-state status. Now, having laid low at the end of his tenure, Mr. Bush is being rehabilitated through "exploitation of his good side." Nonetheless, the goodwill endeared to these great presidents, elected twice, did not include endowing such benefits upon Barack Obama.

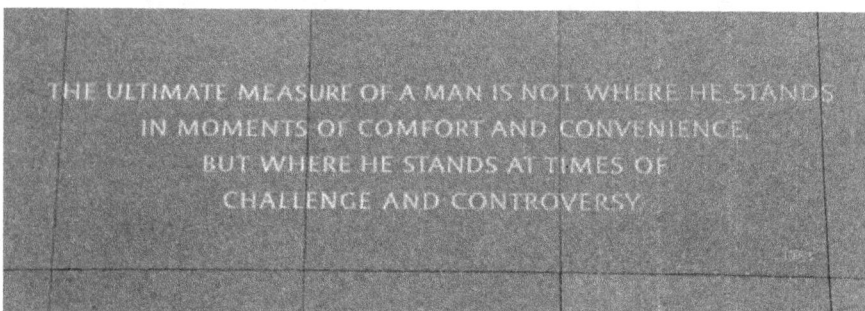

THE ULTIMATE MEASURE OF A MAN IS NOT WHERE HE STANDS
IN MOMENTS OF COMFORT AND CONVENIENCE,
BUT WHERE HE STANDS AT TIMES OF
CHALLENGE AND CONTROVERSY.

With Mr. Obama, we have "a horse of a different color!" He broke the mold of 43 white-only male presidents. None of the former presidents had risen from the humble beginnings of Barack Obama, struggled to acquire that "Million Dollar White man's education" from Columbia and Harvard, "done business white but married black" and possessed the tenacity and wherewithal to challenge for, campaign and win the Presidency of the United States. As such, a credible argument can be made; losers wanted to shift the responsibility for the nation's calamity and so acquiesced in Mr. Obama's victory in hopes to benefit from his cleaning out the "messy stables." However, in a nation of contingency planning from day one, if not before, elements probably hatched the plan to create his demise as he first tackled the problems, created constructive solutions and moved the nation away from the brink of economic collapse and mounting disrespect on the world stage. Then, Mitch McConnell and his "Mandate" happened.

OBAMA THE JOURNEY COMPLETED - NEVER PROMISED A ROSE GARDEN

FREDERICK MONDERSON

Despite his years in Congress, Mitch McConnell does not seem capable of single-mindedly originating his "I intend to make Barack Obama a one-term President" mantra. He must have had input, followed orders to hatch such a seemingly brilliant yet flawed, outwardly racist statement and assignment! "Original as it may seem, one has to wonder if he is actually capable of writing his own material even though he seems to have tried doing a good job executing the plan."

From that day one seedling planted in the nucleus of the anti-Obamaites temple, a forest of ill-will germinated as countless off-shoots vied with each other to disrespect, threaten and block Mr. Obama's every legislative initiative designed to aid the broad masses

OBAMA THE JOURNEY COMPLETED - NEVER PROMISED A ROSE GARDEN

of the American people. Republicans removed their focus from doing the people's business to insuring Mr. Obama's tenure as President is a failure. Connecting the dots, it is evident racial animus has been a catalyst for all such behaviors. After all, right thinking people always queried whom did they want "To take our country back from?" The interesting thing about Barack Obama is his demonstrating exemplary cool-headed leadership as he chooses to see the "boys will be boys" nuisance as just that and he earnestly seeks to execute the requirements of his oath of office. Nevertheless, and fighting on two fronts, he has remained relentless in keeping the wolves at bay, struggling to rescue the American economy despite "front and back fires" scorching his path. This unending sabotage is not by "angels with dirty faces" but "devils with clean faces!"

FREDERICK MONDERSON

OBAMA THE JOURNEY COMPLETED - NEVER PROMISED A ROSE GARDEN

After all, according to a major front-page write-up in *The New York Times*, certainly after the 2012 election but more probably about the 2012 victory, an influential group of Republicans met and planned to treasonably sabotage Mr. Obama's term in office. However, his extraordinary leadership style successfully navigated the Republican legislative and non-governmental organizations' quagmiric minefields.

FREDERICK MONDERSON

OBAMA THE JOURNEY COMPLETED - NEVER PROMISED A ROSE GARDEN

Mr. Obama's deliberative style, his tremendous self-preparation and familiarity with all the issues, unrelenting search and dispatch of Osama bin Laden; that Wall Street has tripled its worth under his watch; passage of Lilly Ledbetter law; and Obamacare with some 17 million registered for its privileges today, 11 million private sector jobs have been added during his presidency, two wars were ended, and the Somali Pirates are now "unemployed," these are remarkable accomplishments. So much more attests to Mr. Obama's leadership skills and style. Unlike many who shoot first then sort later, Mr. Obama first deliberates in his leadership style. When Senator John McCain thought of military action in Eastern Europe, Senator Obama responded, "I have spoken with my advisors and we need to study the situation some more." This deliberation prevented American military involvement attesting to leadership skills. In Libya, Mr. Obama was accused of "leading from behind" but no American lives were lost. Since, many foreign policy issues have and continue to unfold testing Mr. Obama's leadership.

FREDERICK MONDERSON

In the new episode of the downed Malaysian Airliner over the Ukraine Airspace, many persons want to instantly blame Russia under Mr. Putin's leadership. Rather than outright accuse Mr. Putin, President Obama has had a number of subordinates hint at Russia's complicity as Mr. Obama sorts out the intelligence. Rather than come right out, Mr. Obama's deliberative strategy connects the dots before outright laying the blame for the tragedy at Mr. Putin's doorstep. In this and so many ways, Mr. Obama exemplifies extraordinary leadership.

OBAMA THE JOURNEY COMPLETED - NEVER PROMISED A ROSE GARDEN

"We, the People, recognize that we have responsibilities as well as rights; that our destinies are bound together; that a freedom which only asks what's in it for me, a freedom without a commitment to others, a freedom without love or charity or duty or patriotism, is unworthy of our founding ideals, and those who died in their defense." **Barack Obama**

3. TED CRUZ: "FRAUD" or PATRIOT?
BY
Dr. Fred Monderson

Sometime ago a commentator dubbed "President Obama the most dangerous man in America," but because Mr. Obama was re-elected proved this hyperbole wrong. Then Congressman Allen West, because

OBAMA THE JOURNEY COMPLETED - NEVER PROMISED A ROSE GARDEN

of his too-hot-to-handle outlandish approach earned the description and the voters quickly dispatched him. Now, Texas Republican Senator Ted Cruz seems immensely qualified for this indubitable title. If so, and the two above examples are applied to predict Mr. Cruz's political future, even the Hubble Telescope cannot spot a presidential election and thus rejection given his aspirations to even higher office. However, whereas New York's Republican Peter King's labeled the Senator "a fraud," more than likely he will go the way of politicians rejected by the electorate; yet he remains the darling of those 20% of supporters who remain dinosaurs in a rapidly changed world.

"Understand, our police officers put their lives on the line for us every single day. They've got a tough job to do to maintain public safety and hold accountable those who break the law." **Barack Obama**

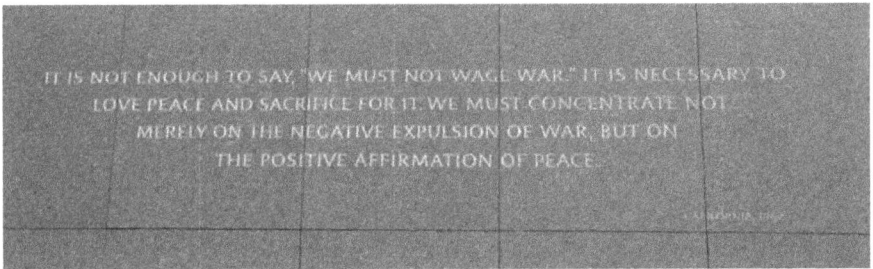

Commentators keep pointing out, it's becoming clear, Senator Ted Cruz is an enigma, some say tremendously intelligent, but more important one still has to wonder how he hoodwinked the people of his state or is he simply trumpeting conservatism as a mantra for election in that neck of the woods. Then again, his antics since coming to Washington has exposed the nature of the man whose aspirations are to be "king," but more and more he seems heading into a political cul-de-sac. Yet, without question, in a culture such as ours, individuals in politics especially, overwhelmingly enjoy home state or ethnic popularity. However, in the case of Senator Cruz, it's been pointed out, though they may have voted for him, a majority of Spanish speaking individuals particularly from his home state have

FREDERICK MONDERSON

found fault with his brinksmanship style and revolted, saying he does not now speak for them! Nonetheless, in the Senate and nation's current undertaking that he has been personally implicated in setting the "match to burn down the Capitol barn," a number of actions question his capability of being more than a local leader, much more, "Presidential timber." That is, having led the charge, not in his lane but in another, to shut down the government, his shameless display in front of the veteran's memorial, whether he served or not, is indicative of the antonymous nature of the man. Nevertheless, let's seek to characterize the Senator from Texas.

OBAMA THE JOURNEY COMPLETED - NEVER PROMISED A ROSE GARDEN

1.   The state of Texas, seeming to struggle to field leaders of the caliber of a Lynden Baines Johnson, later President, chose Ted Cruz to be its junior senator. Ethnic pride may have attracted that state's Hispanic population to overwhelmingly vote for Mr. Cruz. That being so, many are bewildered by the actions of his first significant roll-out that ignited a firestorm damaging the welfare, well-being and image of the United States, at home and abroad.

2.   A verse in a popular song by the calypsonian Mighty Sparrow reads, "Hurried Birds make Crooked Nests!" In many respects, with limited political experience Senator Cruz chose to hurriedly ascend to the pinnacle of Republican leadership. Rather than being a rising leader, some believe he is a rising demagogue who exploits situations for his own benefit despite the consequences of his reckless behavior.

3.   Without question, prominent Republicans have plotted; some say conspired in a treasonous manner, to subvert the efforts of the Obama administration and to make his Presidency a failure. A publicly stated case in point was Senator Mitch McConnell's boast, "I intend to make Barack Obama a one-term President!" Now, *The New York Times* article of Sunday October 6, 2013, front page, details actions, organizations and individuals involved in "A Crisis Months in the Making," designed to **Stop Obamacare**! The enormous sums mentioned in the money-mill strategy, principally funded by the billionaire Koch brothers and the great number of individuals and organizations involved lead reasonable people to suspect theirs was a single focus and possibly part of an orchestrated effort to prove the overall Obama agenda a failure.

OBAMA THE JOURNEY COMPLETED - NEVER PROMISED A ROSE GARDEN

4.   In the Presidential Debate of 1984, Mr. Reagan accused his opponent Walter Mondale of being young and thus less experienced! Mr. Cruz was probably recruited by his backers, despite his inexperience, to stop Obamacare, by any means necessary. In this undertaking, even if he had to shut-down the government and force the American nation on to the precipice of uncertainly irrespective of the consequences, Mr. Cruz thought his actions justifiable.   The damage partly done, some *lu lu* terms have been used to describe the Senator and his "Tea Party" collaborators in the House who "picked a fight they could not win" and "Cruz and the hardliners plotted." Their actions were "very, very damaging" to the American nation. Their acrimonious division was "irresponsible," tantamount to "sabotage," even "disappointing" to many people; and "a disaster for the

Republic!" Some confessed his divisive strategy caused "Republicans to shoot at each other."

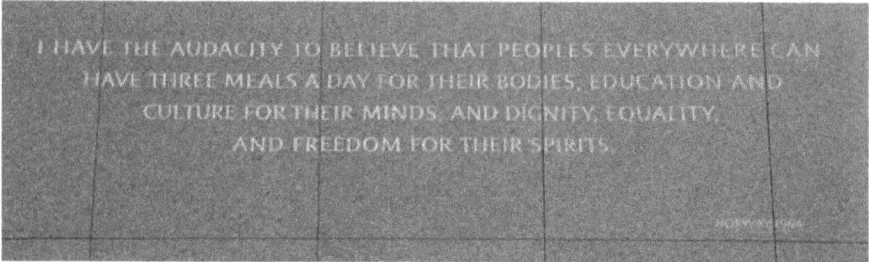

I HAVE THE AUDACITY TO BELIEVE THAT PEOPLES EVERYWHERE CAN HAVE THREE MEALS A DAY FOR THEIR BODIES, EDUCATION AND CULTURE FOR THEIR MINDS, AND DIGNITY, EQUALITY, AND FREEDOM FOR THEIR SPIRITS.

5. Senator Cruz has entered the vortex of a "Losers' Gallery," all victims of Barack Obama and he has yet to learn from their defeat. From the time he launched his 2008 Presidential campaign, Mr. Obama faced and vanquished the very best the Republican Party could muster despite the great financial sums committed to his defeat and even the tom-foolery they demonstrated in attacking his wife. But when he looked into the camera and warned, "If you're watching, lay off my wife," he was not playing with those acting as "spoiled children."

OBAMA THE JOURNEY COMPLETED - NEVER PROMISED A ROSE GARDEN

6.   Mr. Obama had to contend with the "Tea Party" Movement's shenanigans perhaps originating from the lab of an evil scientist whose seed-germ of racial hatred found fruition among raw-renk racists who had infiltrated the ranks of legitimate protesters seeking to alleviate issues festering for decades in American government. To this day the "Tea Party" "Ball and chain" racism is evident and Cruz's favored membership leaves no doubt as to his possible mindset and political philosophy. When Mr. Cruz teamed with *Freedom Watch's* Larry Kylon at the closed World War II memorial, amidst the Confederate Flag and insisted the President of the United States "get off his knees" and "Put down your Koran" this was not leadership, this was lunacy, practiced by persons, perhaps escaped from an insane asylum.

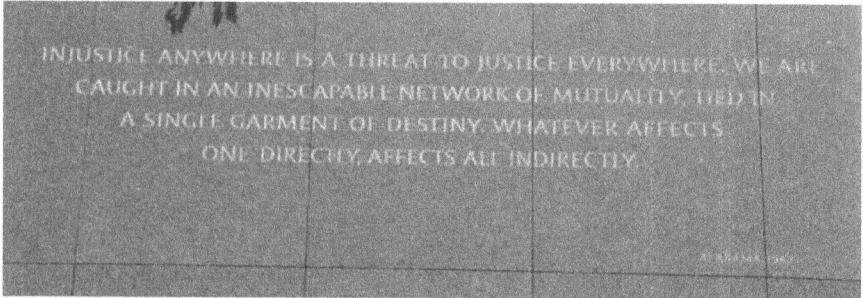

INJUSTICE ANYWHERE IS A THREAT TO JUSTICE EVERYWHERE. WE ARE CAUGHT IN AN INESCAPABLE NETWORK OF MUTUALITY, TIED IN A SINGLE GARMENT OF DESTINY. WHATEVER AFFECTS ONE DIRECTLY, AFFECTS ALL INDIRECTLY.

7.   Some six years ago, along came Barack Obama, who, in a patriotic manner and seeking to find solutions to problems in a nation driven to the brink of calamity, he was confronted by a racist behemoth rapidly expanding and carrying along descent folks in a camouflaged protest now seen as part of a grand strategy doomed to failure. The behemoth at full blast, Mr. Obama was attacked for being a Black man with temerity and courage to run for the Presidency; being unpatriotic by not wearing a flag pin on his lapel; not a citizen, though born in Hawaii the "Birthers" have questioned; an opportunist named "Joe the Plumber" coined the phrase socialism and a socialist label was attached to the bright young aspirant to the highest office in the land. Even more, Mr. Obama was accused of being a Muslim and depicted in the most ridiculous and disgusting caricature. The desperadoes first accused him of being a "Wrightist Christian" then a practicing Muslim, but this got no place. This was a foregone issue and for Mr. Cruz and company to foolishly try to make capital of Mr. Obama being Muslim was downright dumb, stupid, and childish.

OBAMA THE JOURNEY COMPLETED - NEVER PROMISED A ROSE GARDEN

Not only did "Joe the Plumber," who was endorsed for Congress by Allen West fall to "Mr. Obama's plunger," but others in the "Losers Gallery" such as opportunistic, "I can see Russia from my porch" Sarah Palin; and "God told me to run," "In Libya and now in Africa,"

FREDERICK MONDERSON

"Gangster Government" Michele Bachmann; "Poison the Well" Rick Santorum: and "I will be the nominee" Newt Gingrich, all could not touch Mr. Obama! To these we may add, "Binders of women" and "Corporations are people too" Mitt Romney; and "I want to see the wounds" of his "Birth Certificate" Donald Trump; as well as "I will engage the Black community" Michael Steele and "Blitz" Herman Cain, all "circus criers" in their own right. These were all vanquished and their careers, with the exception of John McCain, now hang in the extremely large "Trophy Room" of Barack Obama.

When the Greeks entered Ancient Egypt, the Egyptians told them, "You Greeks are but children." Unfortunately, "youthful" Ted Cruz did not learn from these historic failures and choose to challenge Barack Obama. However, driven by an obnoxious political philosophy articulated by bigoted, vicious and narrow-minded people afraid of change and long associated with an odious past in American history; these insurgents, who not only attacked the President, but also did the unthinkable in shutting down the American government and driving the nation again to a financial brink, were actions perhaps more damaging that the recent fiscal cliff fiasco. So much so, even Republicans are finding Mr. Cruz's actions repugnant.

OBAMA THE JOURNEY COMPLETED - NEVER PROMISED A ROSE GARDEN

FREDERICK MONDERSON

8.   It is sad; those persons this Texas "Pied Piper" as chosen to lead seem lacking a historic memory and lack of a futuristic vision. It is hardly likely that the American people will choose Mr. Cruz to be their global spokesman after his reckless performance. However, in their "spin" Cruz and his "Tea Party" allies tried to blame the President for the Shut-down and resulting developments that embarrassed and inconvenienced so many as well as the name and image of America. In fact, they dared him hoping he would give in to their blackmail but Mr. Obama stood tall and firm. He was thus being bullied by "Tea Party" hooligans and, intelligent and determined as he is; he read Senator Cruz's "hole card" and guess what, the Senator folded, leaving his group to moan, lick their wounds and perhaps learned a lesson "Don't mess with Barack!" The Republican brand may have suffered irreparable damage because of Mr. Cruz's actions!

OBAMA THE JOURNEY COMPLETED - NEVER PROMISED A ROSE GARDEN

"I don't care whether you're driving a hybrid or an SUV. If you're headed for a cliff, you have to change direction. That's what the American people called for in November, and that's what we intend to deliver." **Barack Obama**

FREDERICK MONDERSON

4. CRUZ, OBAMA AND HEALTH CARE REFORM
By
Dr. Fred Monderson

Republican opposition to the **Affordable Care Act**, the singularly important legislative achievement of President Obama, has been long-standing from day one; that is after his 2008 election victory. Then, the law was perniciously christened "Obamacare" and later publicized in the most prolific manner as "disaster" and finally later a "train wreck." As a principal thrust of Republican strategy, a great deal of funds have been allocated and people trained and

OBAMA THE JOURNEY COMPLETED - NEVER PROMISED A ROSE GARDEN

deployed to emphasize great negativity about the law, all this under the guise of "educating the public." A keen observation about the two principals, Senator Ted Cruz and President Obama, is the manner in which they each describe the law. In a recent Press Conference on Monday October 21, President Obama consistently described the law by its proper name, *Affordable Care Act*; while, Senator Ted Cruz, also in an interview conducted by Dana Bash, CNN's National Political Correspondent and shown on Candy Crowley's *State of the Union*, Sunday October 20, 2013, consistently described the law, nearly a dozen times, as "Obamacare," and not once by its proper and legal name. This is clearly contempt and disrespect for the man and the law, especially from a "Lawman!"

"Change will not come if we wait for some other person or some other time. We are the ones we've been waiting for. We are the change that we seek." **Barack Obama**

FREDERICK MONDERSON

As things stand and especially with the looming shutdown of the government fiasco to hopefully "defund Obamacare," concerned persons should take another look at Senator Ted Cruz (R. Texas) who succeeded Senator Kay Hutchinson. After "a lengthy 10-month career in the Senate," clearly it seems Mr. Cruz's egotistical desire to be Republican leader exposes his philosophy, and when it comes to President Barack Obama it is not really political or ideological, it is racial, racist! Equally, the problem with "Obamacare" it not that it is a "train wreck," a popular Republican refrain, but that it represents **Obama**! The man himself embodied in his Blackness along with his family in the White House is what unnerves those who espouse conservative right wing ideology, some have seen as a "lunatic fringe." These people in America speak of "Heritage," but it seems actually a Heritage encased in the appalling experiences and mentality of slavery, lynching, terrorism and its resultant discriminatory and

OBAMA THE JOURNEY COMPLETED - NEVER PROMISED A ROSE GARDEN

racist social and psychological scarification. This state of mind is what President Obama intends to move his nation beyond, but as we know, old ideas die hard!

FREDERICK MONDERSON

As such, any reasonable person listening to Senator Cruz will probably realize his ideas insistently as they are about "Obamacare," are not original but he seems to be parroting his handlers' views. The problem with Cruz, he is the "wrecking ball," the "train wreck"! As such, if Senator Cruz is the face of and represents the future ideology of American leadership we must begin praying hard and loud for the Republic because it is not simply heading over the fiscal and other cliffs, but across the edge of global human experience, decency and existence. After all, such adamant objection to the law, at least, dates to former Senator Jim DeMint's insisting on "Obama's Waterloo," and he may still be stoking such fires from his new leadership of the Heritage Foundation.

OBAMA THE JOURNEY COMPLETED - NEVER PROMISED A ROSE GARDEN

FREDERICK MONDERSON

So we ask; can intelligence be devoid of reasonable practical thinking? For example, in the recent 2012 Presidential Election, former Speaker Newt Gingrich has often been described as "The most intelligent man in the room." Well, we saw what happened to him after he declared, "I'll be the nominee!" Now, we're being told how intelligent Mr. Cruz is. A very appropriate question is whether he is a "Newt Redux." That is, given Mr. Cruz's "Obamacare is a train wreck" mentality, it may be only a matter of time before his speeding fireball jumps the track. Yet, it is thus amazing how one interview can teach so much. That is, given the legislation in question is entitled "Affordable Care Act" and this highly intelligent Senator in his interview not once in a dozen times used the legal name and Mr. Obama consistently in the same number of times used the correct legal title gives an indication of the dis-informative nature of the

OBAMA THE JOURNEY COMPLETED - NEVER PROMISED A ROSE GARDEN

Republican strategy and how persistently constructive Mr. Obama really is.

> IF WE ARE TO HAVE PEACE ON EARTH, OUR LOYALTIES MUST BE COMPREHENSIVE
> RATHER THAN SECTIONAL. OUR LOYALTIES MUST TRANSCEND OUR RACE,
> OUR TRIBE, OUR CLASS, AND OUR NATION, AND THIS MEANS
> WE MUST DEVELOP A WORLD PERSPECTIVE.

We must remember; *The New York Times* article expressed how many persons were engaged by the more than 20-named conservative organizations involved in this fight and that they are actively training thousands to educate people about facts of the health care law. However, in as much as these people were so much against the law, **Affordable Care Act**, it stands to reason they could only spread disinformation about the measure to sow negativity and dislike for a legislative effort designed to help millions of Americans who are now without health care and desperately need the afforded protections.

On the other hand, President Obama gave a Press Conference and explained some dynamics of events surrounding the Affordable Care Act's roll-out that has been plagued with problems. The bumpy beginning has been described as having "glitches," "kinks," even "bugs," but no one was more disturbed about its problematic failure than Mr. Obama himself. Nevertheless, in a dozen or more instances, he correctly named the law Affordable Care Act and not once "Obamacare." A laughable example of the same confusion can be seen in "What's in a name!" When some persons were asked "Do you like the Affordable Care Act," they responded yes, it is good! When asked, "Do you like Obamacare?" they said "No, it is bad." To repeat, the source of this confusion can be seen explained in *The Times* article that mentioned thousands of young people were being trained and sent across the country to "explain Obamacare;" when in fact, these propagandists are spreading disinformation to ensure the law fails despite its purpose.

FREDERICK MONDERSON

OBAMA THE JOURNEY COMPLETED - NEVER PROMISED A ROSE GARDEN

Fast forward to 2016 Presidential campaign, a Senator Rubio spokesman was asked his stance on Rowe v. Wade. His first response was, "It's the law of the land!" Though conservatives oppose the intent of this law, the gentleman did not vacillate but straightforwardly stated, "It's the law of the land." Well, so is the Affordable Care Act!

After all, using "Obamacare" as their principal focus, President Obama said, the "Republican signature idea was to shut down the government" if they could not get their way and will now "go harder with the website woes." But, the President reminded, "this battle was not waged around a website," and insisted, "but so millions of

Americans can get affordable care." Of course, customers can by-pass the website and apply by phone or contact centers specifically designed for walk-in assistance.

OBAMA THE JOURNEY COMPLETED - NEVER PROMISED A ROSE GARDEN

Mr. Obama took the time to explain and despite the spewing negativity, he provided a more positive spin about the Act and even with the underlying conditions, the Affordable Care Act offers "new benefits and protections," some never knew they had or exercised. He explained pre-existing conditions are covered; children can stay on their parents' health insurance plans until age 26; seniors accrue saving on their prescription plans; women will get mammograms and free birth control through their employer plans. All this is because the Affordable Care Act created competition where there was none. Now insurance companies must compete, but they will still get new tax credits.

Erik "chilling" within the Garden environs.

OBAMA THE JOURNEY COMPLETED - NEVER PROMISED A ROSE GARDEN

Mr. Obama further pointed out Healthcare.gov was visited 20 million times. The belief is, if 3-7 million young people enroll, 6 in 10 persons can get covered for less than $100.00 per month. This has been called a balanced risk pool. However, unless the technological problems are resolved, the same young people needed to keep costs low may not sign up. As such, down the road, a lackluster risk pool will drive up costs. Nevertheless, December enrollment for January 1 coverage is still do-able. Even still, since open enrollment ends in March, enrollment may pick up as time moves on! Notwithstanding, so far, some 500,000 consumers submitted completed applications that are now being checked and processed. Pressing the positive image and benefits of the health care law, President Obama reiterated:

> I OPPOSE THE WAR IN VIETNAM BECAUSE I LOVE AMERICA. I SPEAK OUT AGAINST IT NOT IN ANGER BUT WITH ANXIETY AND SORROW IN MY HEART, AND ABOVE ALL WITH A PASSIONATE DESIRE TO SEE OUR BELOVED COUNTRY STAND AS A MORAL EXAMPLE OF THE WORLD.

1. The product is good!
2. Health insurance is good and it saves money.
3. The demand is there;
4. People are thrilled;
5. Women can buy insurance for premiums same as they had before;
6. They can secure insurance for maternity and preventive care.

Addressing the initial problems, Mr. Obama further pointed out, "The law is more than a Website. The essence of the law is working just fine." He admitted problems in the roll-out and that experts are working 24/7 to fix them. Yet, he reminded persons, it is only 3-weeks into a 6-month open-enrollment period. Most important, however, he reassured, because the law is good, "The insurance plans will not run out, will not sell out." And, insisting that "Health Care is not a privilege but a right to enjoy," President Obama promised "I intend to deliver on this pledge." Informing that the website is not the only way to purchase insurance, he also mentioned other avenues off-line where persons could download an application fill it in and mail it. There are also call centers where real people, **Navigators**, will answer all questions at 1-800-318-2596, within a time frame of 25-minutes for an individual and 45-minutes for a family. Individual states are also conducting their own programs to assist the application process. Equally, many Republican controlled legislatures are "opting out" to participate which means they are depriving their people of a legal right. Fact is, when such things as "costs" are mentioned, many states with Republican controlled leadership are opting out and these potential registered people may help in reducing costs.

OBAMA THE JOURNEY COMPLETED - NEVER PROMISED A ROSE GARDEN

Next the President implored the anti-Obamaites to "stop rooting for its failure because Medicaid and Medicare individuals want this insurance." The bottom line is, he stated: "Health Insurance is good; prices are good; it's a good deal; and people are signing up to buy this insurance that will give them medical security."

FREDERICK MONDERSON

All this notwithstanding, contrary to the views Mr. Obama expressed about the virtues of the Affordable Care Act, Senator Cruz could not find anything positive about it and keeps repeating his negative spin on the law. His stance, somewhat manufactured, is reminiscent of Congressman Ron Paul's 2012 answer to the question, "Can you name one good thing President Obama has done?" In response, this Congressman, supposedly a "paragon of liberal Republican virtues" studied long and hard and could not think of one single good thing Mr. Obama has done to benefit the American people. Not the Lilly Ledbetter, equal pay for women, law; Rescue of the Auto Industry which their workers acknowledged; bail out of Wall Street and aiding the Banking Industry's significant rebound from the 2008 mess; instituting new financial and economic policies under Dodd-Frank;

OBAMA THE JOURNEY COMPLETED - NEVER PROMISED A ROSE GARDEN

put in place efforts to reduce pollution and reliance on foreign oil sources; Credit Card and Student Loan reforms; Aid to States to retain teachers, firemen and police officers; Negotiating and ending the wars in Iraq and Afghanistan; getting Osama bin-Laden and decimating Al Qaeda's top leadership; efforts to compensate Black farmers; enabling mothers to return to college, and much more. Either Mr. Paul was getting forgetful, having selective amnesia, or he was parroting the negative mantra that not only earned Republicans the "Party of No" label, but in their subsequent post-shutdown slide gets voted unfavorably by two-thirds of the American people. Now, we see Mr. Cruz following in these same footsteps.

FREDERICK MONDERSON

He has divided his party and had them "Shooting at each other."
Representative Peter King (R - New York) thinks him "a fraud" and
wants to "neutralize him." His fool's errand of leading the charge to
shut down the government and inconveniencing untold numbers of the
American people, soiling America's image abroad with his
brinksmanship; and even unintentionally enabling China to voice
concerns about American global leadership, has earned Mr. Cruz great
enmity by many Americans; but still he wants to be president.

OBAMA THE JOURNEY COMPLETED - NEVER PROMISED A ROSE GARDEN

Thus, in evaluating Cruz, Obama and Affordable Care Act, the first is bad for America; the second is good; and the third is even better!

"There is not a black America and white America and Latino America and Asian America -- there is the United States of America,"

OBAMA THE JOURNEY COMPLETED - NEVER PROMISED A ROSE GARDEN

5.   KANYE - "Black is Beautiful"
By
Dr. Fred Monderson

The **New York Daily News** front page headline of October 30, 2013, and p. 3 reads, "Kanye - Disses Michelle and Pres - THE WEST ZING says he and Kim are the TRUE first couple." It is interesting how the colorful article describes the rapper as "Idiotic," "Jackass," "Ego-maniac;" "Total ass;" "Dope;" "Loudmouth;" and "Deranged."

FREDERICK MONDERSON

To this one could add "Nut!" Poor Kanye, this fella does not get it! In all fairness, he can use a little pushback.

"The future rewards those who press on. I don't have time to feel sorry for myself. I don't have time to complain. I'm going to press on."
Barack Obama

Kanye West needs to realize, first, there is a tremendous difference between class and crass. The article quotes him as saying, "Nobody is looking at what (President) Obama is wearing. Michelle Obama can't **Instagram** a pic like what my girl **Instagrammed** the other day. It wasn't about the suit; it was about the girl!" If you will, Mr. Obama dresses reasonably well but he carries his worth in his head. In another context a commentator described the President as "frighteningly well-prepared" for his many and profound duties as Chief Executive of the United States. Equally, for any Black man to accomplish what he has; twice; is truly the mark of a brilliant mind. Even more important, his intellect, developed tremendously as a Columbia and Harvard graduate, has for nearly 8-years, befuddled untold numbers of Republicans and some Democrats, the most powerful individuals in America, even on the world stage, good, bad and indifferent. Mr. Obama is a thinker, a doer, an intellect, a man who walks and dresses well and holds a large stick! Good or bad, around the world, he is the most talked about man, black or white!

OBAMA THE JOURNEY COMPLETED - NEVER PROMISED A ROSE GARDEN

Michelle Obama doesn't **Instagram**. She probably tweets sometimes. She is a classy lady, married to a gentleman and the mother of two beautiful young girls resident in the nation's White House, and the American people have recognized her as their First Lady. The President does not go around as a mendicant seeking recognition for Michelle! This beautiful, legally trained, balanced fashionista is a star; who, on the world stage, representing this nation, has often been described as President Obama's most lethal weapon particularly when deployed among the globe's most powerful, financial and political in the most cultural and social settings. This natural dynamic is easily accomplished without having to show her exposed backside! After all, she is a well-respected married woman whose husband is madly in love with her and they have been so for many years. Kanye's "girl" is just that, as he grovels on his knees, and showers her with a rock more than likely will last longer than his intended marriage. In his case, he does not realize there is a big difference between a girl and a happily married lady who needs to do it only one time.

FREDERICK MONDERSON

OBAMA THE JOURNEY COMPLETED - NEVER PROMISED A ROSE GARDEN

Mr. West says further, "And, collectively we're the most influential especially with clothing." Interesting that, every time I see Mr. West paraded in that faded blue jeans with the knees exposed, as if it's the only one; I often say to myself, "With all his millions doesn't Kanye have a decent pair of pants. Perhaps I ought to send him a pair of my trousers." Then again, this buffoon does not realize he is an entertainer, a fiddler, who must sing and dance and make outlandish statements for people to laugh. Before the rock and after the baby, **Talk Show Host** Wendy Williams told her audience, "He's not good enough for her." So, Mr. West is out there groveling to show how good and genuine he is! He must, however, remember, there is a record in whose tracks he is following. As such, he is saddened when his "girl" does not get the recognition he alone thinks she deserves.

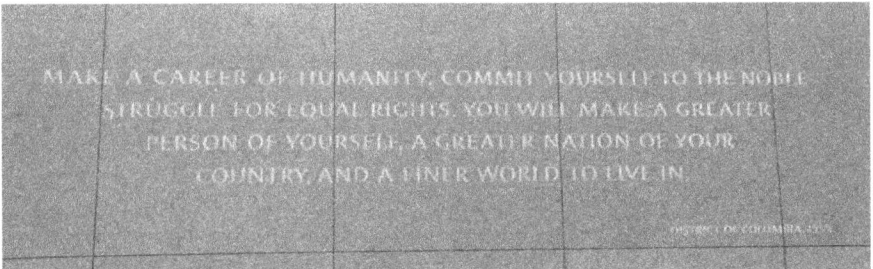

Regarding the public display, the article continued, "West was referring to his fiancée's recent look-at-me **Instagram** photo that seemed almost an ad for her prodigious post-baby butt."

FREDERICK MONDERSON

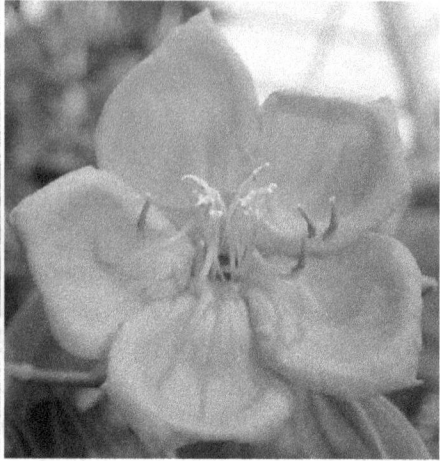

Since she came under public scrutiny, all comments have been made were about Michelle's arms because she works out regularly. Not a word has been said about her butt because only her husband has seen it. Men often make pin-up images of exposed butts, examine, even pat them daily and with Hubble-like invasive scrutiny count how many pimples are there!

OBAMA THE JOURNEY COMPLETED - NEVER PROMISED A ROSE GARDEN

Even further, Kanye West says he and Kim have "more culture influence than President and First Lady Michelle Obama" because the wife of the most powerful man can't **Instagram** selfies of her booty like the rapper's 'girl' can. Well, there are all kinds of culture, from glitter to gutter. There's the 3:00 PM tea with the Queen of England culture, for example, where Michelle bowled over the monarch. Everyone knows "Kan-Kim" can't touch that, so his "culture influence" is orchestrated baloney! As a student, my Professor Leonard James often said, "The more monkey climb the more he exposes himself!" In this case, the more Mr. West opens his mouth, to comment not sing; he is showing how little and inconsequential a man he truly is!

FREDERICK MONDERSON

I BELIEVE THAT UNARMED TRUTH AND UNCONDITIONAL LOVE WILL HAVE THE FINAL WORD IN REALITY. THIS IS WHY RIGHT, TEMPORARILY DEFEATED, IS STRONGER THAN EVIL TRIUMPHANT.

Only time can expose charlatans like Mr. West. When he broke out with the crack, "George Bush does not care about Black People" he fooled a lot of people. His attempt to soil the image of Barack and Michelle will back-fire tremendously. Reasonable people are of the view, when, across this country, happily married Black couples especially sit with loved ones in their church pews on Sunday morning, it's easy to see them mirroring the image of the first couple Barack and Michelle Obama who exemplify "Black Love" and "Black is Beautiful." Those strong Black men, head of their households are upstanding heroes to their young children and communities. And their beautiful wives, whether as deaconesses, in the choir, on the organ, simply ushers, or in pews, without question, they see Michelle Obama and other dignified Black women as Coretta Scott King, Betty Shabazz, Murlie Evers, Ollie Mc Clean, Amy Jacques Garvey, Queen Mother Moore, Delores Blakeley, Mitta Monderson, all as role models to admire and emulate! Mr. West truly has no idea, that "Black is Beautiful!"

OBAMA THE JOURNEY COMPLETED - NEVER PROMISED A ROSE GARDEN

FREDERICK MONDERSON

"That's what the American people called for in November, and that's what we intend to deliver." **Barack Obama**

OBAMA THE JOURNEY COMPLETED - NEVER PROMISED A ROSE GARDEN

6. GOVERNORS
JINDAL and CHRISTIE
"Running"
By
Dr. Fred Monderson

Appearing on **CNN** and in responding to a question, Louisiana's Governor Bobby Jindal stated, "The Next President should be a governor. Obama did not run anything" before he was elected. As a result, he has not been able to govern effectively! This statement is so characteristically Republican, except for the "Governor" bit. Interestingly, George Bush was Governor of Texas and his administration was considered a failure! Yet, such a view, in its fundamental ramifications is at the heart of the myriad problems plaguing this nation. Perhaps the concept is best explained in the following analogy. President Obama is piloting a canoe, albeit a large one, in deep waters. As he frantically bails water soaking its bottom, individuals sitting behind him constantly and stealthily dip their buckets in the surrounding waters and empties them into the sailing vessel. Putting it another way; from day one President Obama has done everything possible to clean-up the diplomatic, economic, financial and social mess he inherited from two administrative terms of Republican leadership. In this dynamic, Republicans have undertaken a superhuman full-court press to sabotage his efforts, so his tenure in office will be considered a failure. Their intent has been, "Stop Obama!" From What? Rescuing the nation? Are Republicans on Al Qaeda's payroll? In their blind rage, not only have they earned the indubitable distinction of being "The Party of No," but Republicans have failed in this quest to effectively sabotage the President's agenda while harming the American state and sullying its diplomatic and observed image abroad. Governor Jindal, for his part, is staking his optimistic intention to be a candidate for the Republican nomination for the 2016 Presidential election. We know another Governor Chris Christie of New Jersey has the same ambition. What is interesting, however, using Jindal's yardstick, both these governors have "baggage" that will be issues their opponents, first Republicans and later Democrats, will seek to exploit as we approach the 2016 national election, and their candidacies are advanced.

"We've persevered because of a belief we share with the Iraqi people - a belief that out of the ashes of war, a new beginning could be born in this cradle of civilization. Through this remarkable chapter in the history of the United States and Iraq, we have met our responsibility. Now, it's time to turn the page." **Barack Obama**

OBAMA THE JOURNEY COMPLETED - NEVER PROMISED A ROSE GARDEN

Perhaps Governor Jindal may have forgotten but "he was running Louisiana" when Hurricane Katrina devastated New Orleans. Much has been said, written and documented about this disaster and his failed response. The question of improperly buttressing the levees in a highly Democratic and Black Ward was seen as a major cause of the resulting calamity. The slow and ineffective response of the Bush Administration has also been seen as contributing to the suffering, the rising death toll, and the loss of property and business value. Nonetheless, the iconic image of President Bush, airborne above the flooded city will always remain imbedded in the memory of both victims and observers alike. Even more important, in such an emergency that warrants a visit from the President of the United States, it stands to reason Governor Jindal was in that aircraft with Mr. Bush! Thus, he can share in the notoriety of the insensitive gesture, the slow and ineffective response as well as the displacement and the long-standing neglect, and equally exile of many citizens from that state. In many respects, the destruction of the city not only disrupted the Democratic preponderance of New Orleans but the economic strength of many businesses and that of its residents, primarily Blacks who suffered damage beyond repair.

Governor Christie, on the other hand, invoked the irony of his party, the Republicans, when he praised President Obama for his rapid response, the deployment of **FEMA** administrators and even greeting Mr. Obama on his visit to Sandy ravaged New Jersey. Coming as it

113

did, on the eve of the 2012 Presidential election, some were angered by Christie cozying up to Obama and others thought this had a significant impact, perhaps creating the difference, in the President's defeat of Governor Mitt Romney. Fact is; either Christie is a good politician or a good actor. Then again, the governor could be both a good politician and a good actor. However, given the situation, Mr. Christie played *real politik*! His state was devastated and though a Republican, when a Democratic President came calling, offering help in this emergency, he placed the needs of his citizens above all else. He did not "Sell his soul to the devil;" he utilized the available federal assistance promised his state. All this notwithstanding, an important indictment can still be leveled against both Governors Jindal and Christie, who ran their state, and this has to do with the question of poverty.

In the case of Governor Jindal, a recent report has shown, as an example, East Carroll Parish in his state of Louisiana, was described as "the most unequal place in America." There, a resident, Delores Gilmore, mother of two sons, sent them out of state because of the wide income inequality gap in the state. If this is because of economic inequity there must also be social inequity, for while 75% of public school children, mainly comprising African Americans graduate; 100% of Private School, mainly Caucasian kids, graduates from high school. There may very well be other social inequities such as unemployment, health care accessibility, shopping, driving or walking while Black, issuing of tickets to raise revenue, and all that goes with being Black and/or poor, in the state run by Governor Jindal. In the case of Governor Christie, there is a current Ad on television pointing out that poverty in the state is at an all-time high. The Ad also makes

OBAMA THE JOURNEY COMPLETED - NEVER PROMISED A ROSE GARDEN

reference to the "governor gutting" the "same sex bill" among other problems plaguing the state. Yet, in retrospect, some believe the Sandy response was executed to bamboozle New Jersey residents. This is particularly so since at the first opportunity Governor Christie got, he returned to pummeling the president. Another example below serves to show how "calculating" Governor Christie really is, at times, never mind the "Bridge-gate" mess.

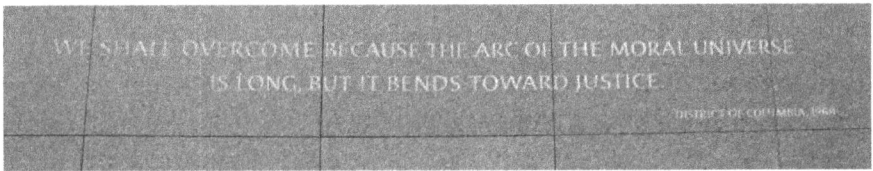

WE SHALL OVERCOME BECAUSE THE ARC OF THE MORAL UNIVERSE IS LONG, BUT IT BENDS TOWARD JUSTICE. DISTRICT OF COLUMBIA, 1968

After the death of Senator Lautenberg (**D-NJ**), the governor had a chance to appoint someone serve out the remainder of Mr. Lautenberg's term. As a Republican governor he could have, and in most cases, a Republican could have been appointed senator. For a short time, the governor did such. However, he did call for a special election. Now, the African-American Mayor of Newark, New Jersey, Cory Booker had expressed an interest to become Senator in the expected general election in 2014 when the governor is also up for re-election.

FREDERICK MONDERSON

Often Malcolm X would emphasize the significance and potency of the Black vote! In fact, he has said, the Democratic and Republican electorate is so equally divided, Blacks determine "who goes to the White House and who to the dog house." Given such, they can also do the same and create a challenge for the governor. As opposed to the Republican appointed to fill the senate seat out of the remaining term of office thereby enabling Cory Booker to seek the office when the governor is on the ballot and with the mayor energizing large numbers of African voters in that historic election, the governor preempted such and called for a special election. This may seem ordinary but it was calculated. Well, African Americans turned out *en masse* to elect the Mayor as Senator. That meant the governor, in his mind, had nullified the Black vote for September 2014. Then again, nothing is written in stone. Nevertheless, returning to Governor Jindal's original contention, of "run" or "running" something, no matter what is said, does not guarantee success, fairness or the desire and intent to aid the aspirations of all the people no matter their social standing. It goes without saying; politicians are only interested in being elected and being re-elected. As such, they more often pay attention to the wealthy that can bankroll their aspirations rather than the poor who generally remain at the bottom of the social ladder. Of course, the brilliance of Barack Obama trounced the concept by appealing to the masses to make those $4.00 and $6.00 donations.

As he carried this brilliant, concerned strategy to its most useful effectiveness, clear-sighted commentators recognized many interesting things about President Obama the likes of narrow-minded Republicans are unable to grasp. First, Mr. Obama's intellect and skills preceded the run for the presidency and despite the assistance from so many; the man, his energy and vision is essentially what

OBAMA THE JOURNEY COMPLETED - NEVER PROMISED A ROSE GARDEN

dictated the outcome. Second, from time immemorial kings and rulers have had advisers who were masters in their particular domain, whether religious, political, economic, military or social, and they provided this expertise as requested. Their advice was weighed and became factored into a particular decision on a specific issue. In executing his job responsibilities, Mr. Obama simply followed tradition, as every preceding American president has done, chose the best advisers and made the crucially important decisions to rescue the nation's future Republicans had driven into the ditch. Third, as the racists in and out of the Republican Party pummeled Mr. Obama, rather than respond angrily in tit-for-tat acrimony, he deployed that infectious smile, and like Mighty Sparrow sang, "Ah stay, Ah stay, but ah planning still!" He was so successful, Mr. Obama was able, "with no experience" to pull the nation back from the financial and fiscal cliff, pass legislation to guarantee women equal pay for equal work, institute far reaching economic and financial reforms in Dodd/Frank, create projects for infrastructure repairs, ending two wars in Iraq and Afghanistan, challenge Somali Pirates, and outfox Osama Bin-Laden while decimating top operatives in his organization. All this Mr. Obama accomplished while the Republicans not only blocked every legislative initiative he proposed but at every turn they pilloried him and shamefully disrespected not simply the man, but more important the institution of the Presidency.

Thus, in contradiction to Governor Jindal's contention, skill, daring, courage, honesty and effective work ethic, and sensitivity to the needs of the people as well as excellent support in unending effort are the hall marks of good government. Thus, not having "run anything" is not necessarily a handicap for effective and efficient leadership and administration going forward.

"My parents shared not only an improbable love, they shared an abiding faith in the possibilities of this nation." **Barack Obama**

OBAMA THE JOURNEY COMPLETED - NEVER PROMISED A ROSE GARDEN

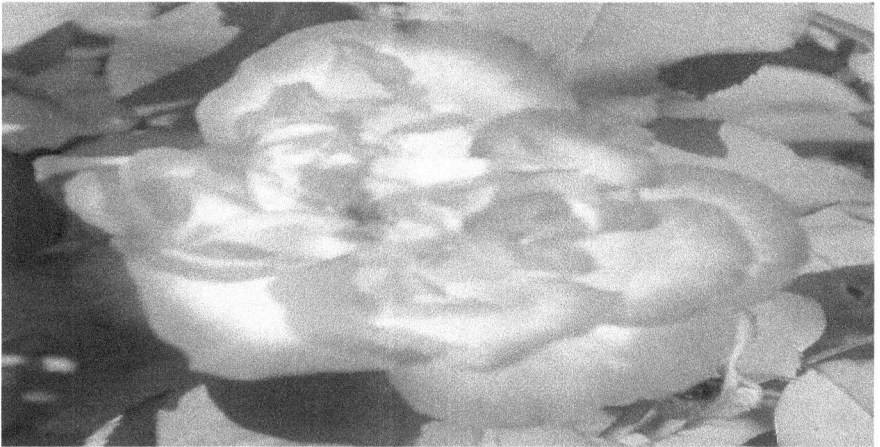

7. "END OF NEGOTIATIONS"
By
Dr. Fred Monderson

"Atta boy Mr. President!"

Recently CNN's Talk Show Host Piers Morgan, in questioning Senator John McCain mentioned Speaker John Boehner's exasperation on the House floor while reiterating his statement to the President regarding negotiations on the "government shutdown" and the impending "debt ceiling" debacle, to which Mr. Obama's response was simply "They'll be no Negotiations!" What persons such as Mr. Boehner and Republicans especially "Tea Party" members of Congress must realize, every action or statement persons make are part of their historical record and later time can become an issue. Naturally, persons must wonder at the President's response to the Speaker at this challenging and crucial time in the American experience but events of the past relationship hold the answer.

119

FREDERICK MONDERSON

"We cannot continue to rely only on our military in order to achieve the national security objectives that we've set. We've got to have a civilian national security force that's just as powerful, just as strong, just as well-funded." **Barack Obama**

There is no question Republicans were incensed at Mr. Obama's 2008 victory over Senator John McCain. From that time, every effort was utilized to insure the President's term was a failure and he not be re-elected in 2012. Considered judgment is that upon his first election, a group of powerful individuals got together and plotted, some say conspired, to do whatever in their power to bring about a failure of his Presidency. As fate would demonstrate in the perennially unfolding contradiction, plotting against Mr. Obama, as they were, in reality these "patriots" were in fact sabotaging the greater interest of the American state, the American people that he, Mr. Obama represented as the constitutional leader of the nation.

Even more sinister, given the symbolic significance of Mr. Obama being the first African-American to hold the highest office in the land; a source of great pride to African-American people, enslaved and though constitutionally free, were historically the victims of the most insidious terrorist activities perpetrated by groups of whites who got together, plotted and orchestrate the most vicious forms of inhumane treatment and racial discrimination that denied the humanity of the enslaved; and even after the inhumanity of the Slave Trade and Slavery; the fact Mr. Obama is married to a black woman and head of a beautiful family in residence at the White House, that great symbol of American constitutionality and stability, undergirded the contempt and hatred the plotters held for this man of resolute vision, fortitude, tenacity and courage, as he truly executed the responsibilities of the office he was elected to serve in. Yet, Mr. Obama was a good sport, seeming to say, "I know you 'good ole boys' are out there in the bushes, in the dark, plotting my failure, but it's my constitutional responsibility nevertheless to protect you," that is why he confessed "I know politics is a contact sport!" Even more that, "American politics is tough!"

OBAMA THE JOURNEY COMPLETED - NEVER PROMISED A ROSE GARDEN

As such then, 110% of Republicans arrayed against every legislative, social or political effort Mr. Obama favored, proposed or worked to bring about. Those who could help bring change poisoned the minds of those who could not. It is equally an interesting fact of American political and social historical reality that sinister groups have the uncanny ability to metamorphose like a chameleon with the same intent of racial or class oppression in actuality. So much so, history has shown we get a planter class of slave-holders influencing laws and employing slave catchers to uphold Fugitive Slave Laws; the creation and perpetuation of *de jure* and *de facto* Jim Crow's odious practices; the insidious birth of the Ku Klux Klan and White Citizens Council mentality effectuating an unrelenting series of terrorist practices in the "lynching states" of the South and elsewhere which, not incidentally, all voted Republican in the 2012 national elections. It is interesting that these areas provided the "seed germ" and "groundswell" for manifestation of the "Tea Party" movement, born in the cauldron of racial venom and opposition to Mr. Obama and his policies designed to rescue the American nation after the last Republican administration had "driven the car into a canyon" not ditch with policies that led to two wars in Afghanistan and Iraq; banking and housing failures; massive unemployment; tremendous declines on Wall Street; enormous suffering on Main Street; and devastation on such "back streets" entities as "Katrina," just to name a few of their created maladies.

FREDERICK MONDERSON

OBAMA THE JOURNEY COMPLETED - NEVER PROMISED A ROSE GARDEN

Which brings us to Mr. Obama's vision to save his nation through enlightened policies designed to rescue the auto industry, banks, housing, first responders, educators, creating a clean air environment; creation and use of more effective energy resources; efforts to reduce reliance on foreign oil while championing Republican signature stance on defense and simultaneously executing the war on terror, downsizing the nation's involvement in Iraq and Afghanistan, even combating Somali Pirates and "un-American activities" especially at home despite the many threats to his life!. As he battled these challenges Mr. Obama had to contend with the prosecution of Senate Minority Leader Mitch McConnell's blatantly publicized and racially inspired statement, "I intend to make Barack Obama a one-term president." Naturally, Mr. McConnell was not sufficiently honest to say he was following orders but wanted to give the impression he had hatched and undertaken the immense talk on his own volition! Nevertheless, in fooling himself and the people, his mission was a failure. However, he did make waves along the way.

To recall, in one past episode of negotiations with the President regarding legislative activities on budget and debt ceiling issues, Mr. McConnell left those talks in a thousand-word photographic description showing a beaming "I got that Nigger" thumbs up expression signal to his puppeteers. The same could be said of Speaker Boehner, who, in similar style disrespected the President by not returning his phone calls and ultimately, wearing a smug smile and puffing his ubiquitous cigarette, then stated after similar negotiations,

FREDERICK MONDERSON

"We got 98% of what we wanted!" Nonetheless, in the interest of the nation's well-being and in a somewhat fatherly manner, Mr. Obama allowed these "spoiled children" to have their way. However, in that long-memory with which he pursued Osama bin-laden and Al-Libby, master terrorists, as the present "government shutdown" and "debt ceiling" stalemate loomed, Mr. Obama invited the same two political actors to the White House in a later chapter of the ongoing saga and scolded them, then said, "They'll be no negotiations because you will not hold me or the American people hostage." Little did we know, these "good ole boys" were acting, if not under orders, then in concert with individuals as demonstrated in *The New York Times*, Sunday October 6, 2013, p. 1, 18 an article entitled "A Crisis Months in Planning."

As such, when the Minority Leader of the Senate and the House Speaker recently left the White House meeting with Mr. Obama, two radically different manifestations were demonstrated. First Senator Mitch McConnell had lost his smiling "I got that Nigger thumbs-up" smug signal to whom he knew was his viewing audience. This time it should have been, "The Nigger got me thumbs-down," but he head-bowed ashamedly and hurriedly entered his waiting black SUV and

OBAMA THE JOURNEY COMPLETED - NEVER PROMISED A ROSE GARDEN

departed as seen on TV. Mr. Boehner, on the other hand, essentially said, "We received 98% of what we wanted" but was visibly incensed as he stood in front of the cameras on the White House lawn.

To recall, when "Blade" told the vampire, "I'll catch you later" and he did at the movie's end, Mr. Obama must have thought after the first episode and as he played golf with the Speaker, "I'll have something for you later" and he did.

For the longest, American policy has been, "we do not negotiate with terrorists and hostage takers." For all practical purposes, the President felt Republican actions certainly bordered on such anathematic behavior and he vowed not to give in this time without a fight!

FREDERICK MONDERSON

"We, the People, recognize that we have responsibilities as well as rights; that our destinies are bound together; that a freedom which only asks what's in it for me, a freedom without a commitment to others, a freedom without love or charity or duty or patriotism, is unworthy of our founding ideals, and those who died in their defense." **Barack Obama**

OBAMA THE JOURNEY COMPLETED - NEVER PROMISED A ROSE GARDEN

8.   SURPRISE! THEY'RE DISRESPECTING THE PRESIDENT!
By
Dr. Fred Monderson

The President's team described Republican behavior in the shut-down and debt-ceiling fiasco as those of "extremists," "terrorists." All of a sudden, in response, these "big boys" began crying the President was playing foul! Remember when tough guys would enter a bar and order a "Double Scotch on the Rocks." Today, sometimes these Republican "tough guys" often say, "Can I have a water, please!"

FREDERICK MONDERSON

The **Oxford American dictionary** defines Extremist as "A person who holds extreme or fanatical political or religious views."

The **Oxford American Dictionary** also defines terrorist as "A person who uses or favors violent and intimidating methods of coercing a government or community."

"Understand, our police officers put their lives on the line for us every single day. They've got a tough job to do to maintain public safety and hold accountable those who break the law." Barack Obama

The New York Times article of October 6, 2013, which is turning out to be the clearest conduit into the Anti-Obamaites minds-eye view and working has enlightened us to their "By Any Means Necessary" modus operandi. This "Bull-in-A-China-shop" recklessness has led the nation down Ted Cruz's strategy that "could not, would not and did not work," according to the Senate Republican leader Mitch McConnell. It is generally acknowledged, leaders set examples and standards their followers or members must adhere to or are called to answer. After all, from day one, Senators McConnell, DeMint and many others have admirably demonstrated the most toxic attitude and behavior toward Mr. Obama. So, it is not surprising Republican rank and file have worn well their coat of disrespect as it relates to challenges to the President of the United States whom the American people have unanimously chosen twice to represent them.

The fundamental reason why the "Tea Party Tail" wags the "Republican Dog" is because that movement was born out of a cauldron of racial hatred fed and perpetrated by a conservative heritage and legacy falsely believing in the inequality of man dictated by skin color. The story is told of a "White Guy who married a Black woman." All his friends got on his case, asking "Why did you marry this Black Woman?" He simply replied, because "Black don't crack!"

The fact is, none in Republican leadership had the gumption to say, "Sure we are ideologically and politically opposed to the President

128

OBAMA THE JOURNEY COMPLETED - NEVER PROMISED A ROSE GARDEN

and his political party, but our efforts must still be bolstered by high moral and ethical standards" That is to say, for example, while we may dislike Mr. Obama for whatever reason, we respect the office he holds and *ipso facto*, we respect him. Comparatively speaking, it's like we tell our citizens, respect the police officer's uniform more so than the man! I'm not saying don't respect the man! We respect and give way to an emergency vehicle's flashing light or the siren of an ambulance whether we know there is a patient within. Unfortunately, this civility is alien to Republican behavior toward President Obama, particularly as manifested in those disgusting facial expressions and behaviors of Reps. Issa and Chavetz. We notice!

Perhaps a more global example may suffice. At the height of the French Revolution, when the movement had turned against itself, the Englishman Edmund Burke in his book *Reflections on the Revolution in France* (1792) wrote, "The only thing necessary for evil to triumph is for good men to say nothing." Thus, as the "Tea Party Movement's" tail began to grow towards initially wagging the Republican dog, their leaders of substance turned a "blind eye and ear" to this behavior. In the movie **Matrix**, when one of the main actors or characters Neo finally reached "Machine City" and "faced the face," he boldly stated, "The program Smith has grown out of control and you can't stop him. Only my efforts can do so!" This was Republican behavior towards President Obama. Out of control!

FREDERICK MONDERSON

It is so with the conundrum facing the Republican Party's mantle, the "Tea Party" members have lashed out left and right and are now threatening their own members, its leadership and rank and file, who no longer dance to their music. Well, if they could unleash such "friendly fire," against their own, imagine the enmity they have consistently spewed towards President Obama. Of course, good Americans have said we will not accept this disrespect of our President and the office he holds. However, in the highly unlikely probability that "Tea Partiers" succeed to the Presidency, having sullied the office so much; one wonders do they have any shame left and how will they clean the shamefully stained environment.

1.   A commentator recently said after Congressman Joe Wilson told the President "You lie" during the State of the Union Address in the House Chamber, he raised one million dollars donation the next day. Naturally when called to the mat for this disrespect of the President, Mr. Joe Wilson wanted to meet personally with Mr. Obama to deliver his apology. Who knows if he wanted to further insult the President to his face? Mr. Obama said, "No, send the apology in the mail." Even more important even though Mr. Wilson was "sorry" in all probability he did not return the million dollars contributions.

OBAMA THE JOURNEY COMPLETED - NEVER PROMISED A ROSE GARDEN

2.   Coming out as a shiny new penny, as she did in the 2008 presidential campaign, Sarah Palin was very visible in the first wave of "Tea Partiers" whose vile criticism of Mr. Obama was cause for astonishment. Today, the time has told for this faded political glory who sought to be a factor in New Jersey's recent Special Election to fill Senator Lautenberg's vacant seat. The result is failed history.

3.   A study in contrast pits youth and age. On the one hand, Megan McCain has repeatedly said, "I like President Obama. I'm praying for him!" On the other hand, in the initial Health Care Reform brough-ha-ha, former South Carolina Senator Jim DeMint, had said on CNN, "I like the President but he has faulty numbers. If we stop him, it will be his Waterloo." Well, he failed and so left the Senate to head the Heritage Foundation. Under his leadership this organization was mentioned among the treasonous conspirators after the 2012 election of President Obama. In all probability, the team of recycled actors and organizations mentioned in the article were also at work after the 2008 election. Given Senator DeMint's Health Care backlash of the President, it is inconceivable to divorce him from his associate Senate Minority Leader and highest ranking Republican McConnell who made this blatantly racist statement, "I intend to make Barak Obama a one-term president." In many respects both senators who failed in their quest more than likely can be numbered among the 2008

131

treasonous conspirators from whence they received their marching orders.

4. It is interesting that Donald Trump did not "fire" the "Birther Queen" who led him on the humiliating "fool's errand." Then again, as a "circus crier" Mr. Trump as an entertainer relished in noise making fanfare but knows the House does not always win! His most disrespectful disgustingly characteristic feat, having failed the "Birth Certificate test," he asked to see the President's school transcript. How low can you go, and this man wants to be president! It is thus fitting for citizens to ask to see Mr. Trump's birth certificate and school transcript.

The District of Columbia War Memorial, just opposite Dr. King's Memorial in view of the Tidal Basin.

These are just a few samples of persons disrespecting the President of the United States. Some have argued this demeaning behavior is because Mr. Obama is Black! Yet, people of this persuasion fail to realize "black" gives vigor, fortitude and tenacity to the nation's "step!"

OBAMA THE JOURNEY COMPLETED - NEVER PROMISED A ROSE GARDEN

"In the white community, the path to a more perfect union means acknowledging that what ails the African-American community does not just exist in the minds of black people; that the legacy of discrimination - and current incidents of discrimination, while less overt than in the past - are real and must be addressed." **Barack Obama**

FREDERICK MONDERSON

9.   PRESIDENT OBAMA'S LEGACY I
By
Dr. Fred Monderson

Recently, on Candy Crowley's program "State of the Union" on CNN, Senator Diane Feinstein indicated "President Obama's legacy has not yet been written." Perhaps it's not to whom you speak that determines the response to such a contention! That is, whether it's the man in the street or academics, even political operatives be they Democratic or Republican, and particularly among the latter "straight leg" or "Tea Party" a fuller answer is warranted. Nevertheless, according to visionaries, from the inception of his Presidency Mr. Obama has been writing his legacy, but whether some people have accepted such is another story. Notwithstanding, President Obama fits the classic characterization of a man who "walks softly and carry a big stick." In this case, however, he also "thinks before he acts," a characteristic lacking in many politicians.

134

OBAMA THE JOURNEY COMPLETED - NEVER PROMISED A ROSE GARDEN

"There is probably a perverse pride in my administration... that we were going to do the right thing, even if short-term it was unpopular. And I think anybody who's occupied this office has to remember that success is determined by an intersection in policy and politics and that you can't be neglecting of marketing and P.R. and public opinion."
Barack Obama

Mr. Obama's legacy began when he chose to become a candidate for the highest office in the land. The composite nature of his successful campaign was not simply unique, for its strategy, intensity and overall performance, but its ability to attract a broad cross-section of the populace as volunteers, tech-savvy young people, even convincing "the small man" of his important role in this sweep of history, gets premium billing in Mr. Obama's legacy.

FREDERICK MONDERSON

That Mr. Obama successfully withstood the calculated and orchestrated attacks of nefarious individuals, *a la* "Joe the Plummer;" a nascent "Tea Party;" the "Birther Brigade" and its top operatives, viz., the "Birther Queen," Donald Trump, Michele Bachmann, and other "enlightened saboteurs;" even politicos including "Waterloo" Jim DeMint; "You lie" Joe Wilson; and "Go for the Kill" Billy Crystal; etc.; and this does not discount false "men of the cloth" who pray for the President's death. Still, to emerge successfully as the President in 2008 bodes well for Phase I of Mr. Obama's legacy. To repeat, this victory, "to fight his way back" in 2012, despite the opposition, assures a strong legacy of substance in membership of the "twice elected Presidents" club.

To have orchestrate the nation's recovery from the devastating economic and monetary malaise existing within his first term's "first

OBAMA THE JOURNEY COMPLETED - NEVER PROMISED A ROSE GARDEN

100 days;" weather the grave situation of unemployment, bursting housing bubbles, bank failures and an automobile industry in crisis; deteriorating infrastructure of roads, bridges, schools, tunnels, ports, airports; and even more significant the nation's enormous reliance on foreign sources of energy is certainly a legacy package and having put the nation on a corrected course of action is commendable. Not only was the nation's image badly besmirched abroad but this was repaired, though there are persons who hate America and Americans irrespective.

FREDERICK MONDERSON

As the nation's chief diplomat, the President's image abroad is equally important for great nations have relations with all other nations. Certainly, in the "go it alone" age Mr. Obama's predecessor had created, much work was needed to repair America's relations abroad. Add to this two wars in Iraq and Afghanistan as well as the ubiquitous

OBAMA THE JOURNEY COMPLETED - NEVER PROMISED A ROSE GARDEN

war on terror, Mr. Obama had to deal with nuclear proliferation by Iran and North Korea; China's economic expansion and its consequences as well as the need to reassure America's allies and friends, the future held great promise.

"I consider it part of my responsibility as President of the United States to fight against negative stereotypes of Islam wherever they appear." **Barack Obama**

FREDERICK MONDERSON

10. OBAMA AND EXECUTIVE ORDER
By
Dr. Fred Monderson

When President Obama issued his Executive Order regarding the immigration status of young immigrants brought to this country illegally by their parents, this act engendered great enmity by Republicans who never liked him to begin with and have vacillated on immigration reform though several influential Republicans favor some form of comprehensive legislation. As such, a cliché spoken by Secretary of State Hillary Clinton is a good barometer of Mr. Obama's opponents' behaviors. Mrs. Clinton once said, "If President Obama walked on water," former U.S. Ambassador to the U.N. under President Bush, "Bolton would say it's because he could not swim!" To examine this statement further reveals a lot about Mr. Obama's opponents. To "walk on water" is an extraordinary feat. Only one man in history has been able to execute this phenomenon, and he had divine connection. For Mr. Obama to accomplish the necessary far reaching legislation to "fit this bill" means he is exceptional, possibly possessing a tincture of divine essence himself. Given the history of

OBAMA THE JOURNEY COMPLETED - NEVER PROMISED A ROSE GARDEN

Republican obstructionism relative to this legislative agenda, therefore, his actions, activities, accomplishments must be of a higher standard and aided by divine guidance; yet, in every iota Mr. Obama's efforts never matches up to Republican expectations. Whether this is purposeful or not, Republican behavior is a nefarious and demonstrated fact! Even the killing of Osama bin Laden and dismantling of his terror network, for the most part, could not garner much praise from Republicans who only blinked momentarily then closed their eyes. The "blink" was necessary otherwise people would see Republicans for the real hypocrites they truly are. Fact is, they "clapped with one hand."

"In the end, that's what this election is about. Do we participate in a politics of cynicism or a politics of hope?" **Barack Obama**

Now, that there was precedence in the issuing of an Executive Order and that this was Mr. Obama's first did not matter! Recently, some "What's his face" lawmaker, Senator Charles Grassley, said Mr. Obama, a constitutional scholar, was "stupid!" Imagine! A Doctor of Law, Constitutional scholar, graduate from two of the nation's finest Ivy League Universities, Columbia and Harvard, President of the Harvard Law Review and an individual possessing all the temerity and wherewithal to campaign successfully to become President of the United States, twice, "beat the Supreme Court twice," appoint two Supreme Court Judges, accomplish legislative and policy gains as he has, is "stupid." Equally, that he is a "tyrant" for leading not following seems more reflective of the person making the statement, for only a stupid individual could see such as he gazes in the mirror.

FREDERICK MONDERSON

Nevertheless, this *ad hominem* claim is in keeping with Republican pernicious "bloopers." Remember "You lie" Wilson; "Waterloo" and "faulty numbers" DeMint; "the President should be ashamed of himself" Congressman; and the McConnell Mantra, "I intend to make Barack Obama a one-term President!" What Republicans need to do is borrow the Hubble Telescope to see; rather Yogi Berra's "observe;" that they are dealing with a very intelligent, astute, strategically savvy-minded individual not only at the pinnacle of power but at the top of his game and preparing for the future!

Much has been said about President Lincoln and the issue of slavery and Secession but at a time when the nation's fabric was torn asunder, Mr. Lincoln issued the Emancipation Proclamation which was itself an Executive Order. His Order insisting Confederates should be tried in federal courts that was eventually overturned, constituted a decision of a leader not afraid to take action in face of legislative sloth and inaction. Nevertheless, this latter measure was overturned by the Courts. Faced with the calamity of the Great Depression and stymied by the "9 old men," President Franklin D. Roosevelt issued Executive Orders to inaugurate many programs to get the nation moving forward. In modern times, Presidents Nixon, Reagan, Clinton and George W. Bush issued Executive Orders. Some issued multiple such orders, especially Ronald Reagan, Republican darling and "King of Executive Orders." Nevertheless, that this was Mr. Obama's first and few other Executive Orders and in keeping with the "Party of No" objection to the President's every action, Republican opposition to the decision granting reprieve to immigrants who fit the discussed

142

OBAMA THE JOURNEY COMPLETED - NEVER PROMISED A ROSE GARDEN

category, is not surprising; it is disgraceful. However, an explanation of what constitutes an Executive Order is in order.

In *The American Political Dictionary* Jack Plano and Milton Greenberg (8th Edition, 1989: 169) define an Executive Order as, "A rule or regulation, issued by the President, a governor, or some administrative authority, that has the effect of law. Executive orders are used to implement and give administrative effect to provisions of the Constitution, to treaties, and to statutes. They may be used to create or modify the organization or procedures of administrative agencies or may have general applicability as law. Under the National Administrative Procedure Act of 1946, all executive orders must be published in the *Federal Register*." They further state its significance (1989: 169) in as much as, "The use of executive orders has greatly increased in recent years as a result of the growing tendency of legislative bodies to leave many legislative details to be filled in by the executive branch. The President's power to issue executive orders stems from precedents, custom, and constitutional interpretation, as well from discretionary powers given to the President by Congress when enacting legislation. This trend will likely continue as government involves itself further with higher complex and technical matters."

On Jack Cafferty's CNN program, in answer to a question some two years ago, someone noted, "The 2012 election began on November 4th, 2008." Thus, given the methodology of Republican strategy towards Mr. Obama's administration, the "McConnell Mandate" and "lone wolf" legislators' attacks on the very being of the President and Presidency; these people cannot yet comprehend the superior nature of the mind they are in contention with who stays ahead and continues to befuddle their pack. For example, for some three and a half years Mr. Obama has tried to govern effectively in the interest of the American people, and though he reached out to create bipartisanship legislation it has been to no avail because of a predetermined treasonous plot to sabotage his administrative agenda. He was accused of "dividing the nation" yet, look at "Donald Trump's behavior" if this is not divisiveness, what is! Yet, he was still able to accomplish significant legislative successes in the interest of the American people. Many of his followers wondered, after the manner Republicans treated

OBAMA THE JOURNEY COMPLETED - NEVER PROMISED A ROSE GARDEN

Mr. Obama, in Spike Lee's words, "When is he going to take off the gloves?" Now, as Republicans boasted of the one billion dollars they will raise to defeat Mr. Obama, the President finally began to deploy his strategy, emphasize the power of incumbency and building and strengthening coalitions among significant voting blocks, viz., Blacks, women, gays, immigrants, Hispanics, Native Americans, labor, etc. In response to such actions, Republicans have accused him of playing "dirty pool!" Well, a close look under Republican fingernails will reveal the "pool chalk" accumulated over their years of "spinning dirty pool!"

The Red Cross Headquarters building.

To recall, after the "Debt Ceiling" debacle, Senator Mitch McConnell was shown smiling giving his now famous "I got that Nigger in the White House Thumbs up" signal; Speaker John Boehner refused to return Mr. Obama's phone calls but met with the Press and later, smoking, boasted "We got 98 percent of what we wanted." Nonetheless, people wondered, why is the President allowing "minions to think they're whales!" Then a *New York Post* political cartoon featured President Obama looking through the White House window as the New York Yankees relief pitcher Rivera approached asking himself, "I wonder why he sent for me!" Thereafter, "Gentleman Jim" Obama invited "Smoking Boehner" to a game of golf. As these gentlemen teed off in their golfing shorts, and as he putted at the 12th Hole, the President looked at Boehner and thought, "Don't worry, I've got something for you, Mr. Speaker!"

After the Osama bin Laden compound raid by Seal Team Six, the *Post* again featured a political cartoon showing Mr. Obama instructing the team, "The next compound you will raid will be Trump Towers!" After the "Gang" of Karl Rove, the Koch Brothers, the TD bank official and other Super PACs boasted, "We will raise one billion dollars to defeat Obama" the President said, "Oh yes, well employers must pay for Women's Contraceptives." From the "Bully Pulpit" he preached, "Gays should be allowed to marry to protect the rights of people in long term relationships," which the NAACP termed "a Civil Rights issue." As Chief Executive, he challenged the Supreme Justices to rule on his challenge to the many features of Arizona's immigration law and his own Health Care Reform measure. To protect his Attorney General Eric Holder from a Republican "witch hunt" over "Fast and Furious" the President exerted "Executive Privilege" that Plano and Greenberg (1989: 169) defined as, "The right of executive officials to refuse to appear before or to withhold information from a legislative community or a court. Executive Privilege is enjoyed by the President and those executive officials accorded the right by the President. No legal means by which executive privilege could be denied to executive officials existed for many years, but in 1974 the Supreme Court established a landmark precedent (*United States v. Nixon*, 418) U.S. 683 [1974] by unanimously ordering President Richard M. Nixon to release recorded tapes with allegedly criminal information on them that eventually led to his resignation." The significance of this action is explained further by Plano and Greenberg (1989: 169) where, "Executive Privilege in the American system is claimed as an inherent executive power under the constitutional separation of powers and on time-honored tradition. Although the right of the President to refuse to appear before congressional committees is generally unchallenged, the issue remains as to whether his major advisers should enjoy the same privilege. The right of Congress to obtain information for the

OBAMA THE JOURNEY COMPLETED - NEVER PROMISED A ROSE GARDEN

lawmaking process and to investigate for possible impeachment actions, and the right of the courts to hear and decide cases involving executive officials, clash with the President's right to function as the head of a coordinated branch of the national government. Critics charge that executive privilege is often invoked to deny the American people information critical of executive policies."

Ronald Reagan had said of Walter Mondale, "I will not, for political purposes, exploit my opponent's youthful age and inexperience." Now, in the 2012 political climate, as the Junior Senator from Florida, Marco Rubio, became intoxicated with hearing his name mentioned as a possible Romney Vice-President nominee, he started "pussyfooting" over an immigration bill Romney had decried in his "immigrants should self-deport," insult during the Primaries. The President, as Commander-In-Chief, soared like the American Eagle, legal and otherwise; fired on the "Rebels' Camp" by issuing his new Immigration Executive Order, forcing Senator Rubio to abandon his idea. Mr. Romney argued Congress should offer a permanent solution but given his past stance and the House objection to Mr. Obama this was not going to happen at this time. Thus, Mr. Obama's discretion in issuing an Executive Order ahead of Republican slothful stall, at least this decision temporarily eased the agony of the young immigrants.

Instantly in their confused state of shock, Republicans cried "foul," deploying their tired pliant, the President is again "playing dirty pool!" Imagine, after their nearly four years of unrelenting assaults on every legislative initiative, attacks on his integrity, leadership and judgment, these people forget they're dealing with the most powerful man in the world, the President of the United States and leader of the Western Alliance. Somehow Mr. Obama seemed to remind his opponents, "The circus may be in town, but I'm actually the ringmaster of Washington, DC."

All this notwithstanding, Ralph C. Chandler and Jack C. Plano in *The Public Administration Dictionary* (1982: 249-50) provide insights into the history of the Executive Order and its historic use that states: "The earliest executive orders were neither numbered nor issued in any standard format, and there was no requirement for official notices or publication. As the mechanism became more formalized, however, a chronological numbering system came into use in 1907, and all earlier orders were assigned numbers. The Federal Register Act of 1935 required all executive orders of general interest to be published in the Federal Register, with a later act requiring publication of all executive orders. Executive Order Number 1 was issued by President Abraham Lincoln in 1862. It concerned the establishment of military courts in Louisiana. Since that time, executive orders have been used in a wide range of policy areas, depending on the president's personal values and his perception of his constitutional responsibilities."

Even further, the authors explained, "Beginning in the 1960s, executive orders were used more and more in controversial social and political policy areas. They were frequently issued as a result of recommendations made by task forces and special committees, which were first introduced by the Kennedy administration as new policy-making groups. Once a president has decided to make an authoritative policy statement, there are a number of factors involved in the decision to use an executive order, as opposed to some other means of proclamation. First, there must be a strong public demand for solution to a given problem. For example, Executive Order Number 11491 was issued in 1969 by President Richard M. Nixon in response to growing federal employee discontent over the limited provisions for public sector labor relations contained in Executive Order Number 10988, which had been issued in 1962. Second, the president must consider whether there will be funding for, and enforcement of, the directive. Both factors are crucial to the success of an executive order. Third, the president must consider whether Congress or the courts will effectively address the policy needs he has in mind. If they will act, perhaps he does not need to act. Neither Congress nor the courts seemed inclined to deal with discrimination in public housing in the early 1960s. Executive Order Number 11063 was therefore issued by President John F. Kennedy in 1962, setting the official national policy of nondiscrimination in federally assisted housing. Executive Orders are subordinate to statuary law, to decisional law by the Supreme Court, and even to the legislative intent of Congress. An executive order can be declared invalid by the courts if it conflicts with any of these 'laws of higher authority.'"

To this they explain (1982: 250-510) the significance of the measure, "The executive order is an important policy-making tool which is more flexible and adaptive than statuary law. It allows an opportunity to experiment with programs at the federal level without full-scale congressional involvement. The availability of the executive order serves a safety-valve function as part of the overall system of checks and balances. If a critical issue gets bogged down in Congress, the executive order is a mechanism available to fill a policy void until a statuary decision can be made. Some critics object to a president's use of the executive order, considering it a usurpation of legislative power."

Organization of American States Headquarters.

Now, after Mr. Romney told the President to "start packing" and the Republican camp has been "writing his Obituary," flexing his muscle of incumbency, Mr. Obama, like John Paul Jones reminded everyone, "'Surrender, I have not yet begun to fight'" for the interest of all the American people, my considered vision for this great nation and that my children and grand-children will have a better and brighter future resulting from the environmental, educational, immigration, clean-energy and humanitarian policies I enact. If I have to, I will bring Congress along, reluctantly or otherwise, into a clearer understanding of our combined responsibilities to all the American people because our system is 'of the people, by the people and for the people' that is the one hundred percent not just the one percent."

150

OBAMA THE JOURNEY COMPLETED - NEVER PROMISED A ROSE GARDEN

After 6 years of Republican obduracy, two years of "Tea Party" influence in the House, untold challenges to Mr. Obama's legislative agenda, he has nevertheless moved the nation forward.

As things stand today, and in as much as congress has failed to provide Health Care coverage to some 50 million Americans; Congress has stalled on filling administrative leadership positions; sheriffs and other state leaders have targeted immigrants; there are un-ending challenges to the sanctity of the vote, etc., Mr. Obama as Chief Executive and leader of the American people, will go ahead and issue Executive Orders to serve the best interest of the nation.
This he has promised, the opposition be damned!

"Now you have a choice: we can give more tax breaks to corporations that ship jobs overseas, or we can start rewarding companies that open new plants and train new workers and create new jobs here, in the United States of America." **Barack Obama**

FREDERICK MONDERSON

A tree planted in honor of Dr. Martin Luther King, Jr.

11.   OBAMA: WORSE PRESIDENT? PHOOEY!
By
Dr. Fred Monderson

In a Quinnipiac University poll, President Obama was named the "worse President since World War II!" Naturally, skeptics need to query the nature and type of questions asked and the people consulted to arrive at the conclusions stated. Equally, the conscious level of those polled must be taken into consideration. Accordingly, "30% of persons" questioned felt Mr. Obama was the worse President! Apparently, this poll is conducted perennially and the last time it was conducted, in 2006, was two years into President George Walker Bush's second term. At that time, he was voted the worse in this category! Without question, there was "much on his plate." However, many believe what Republicans, especially, are saying about President Obama is what they say about Black people period! Considering his situation, be that as it may, we must remember, even Mr. Obama must remember, Malcolm X has said, "You're not catching hell because you're an American. You're not catching hell because you're an Elk. You're catching hell because you're Black!" After all, Vice-President Biden was right in saying, Republicans are "trying to put you back in slavery!" Fact is; assessing contemporary developments; state-house voter disenfranchisement, etc., dye-in-the-wool racists cannot comprehend the magnificence of Mr. Obama's thinking capacity. He is well educated, very intelligent, compassionate, a humanitarian, far-sighted, historically conscious and cool under fire. So with him on the 20th floor, 1st floor Republican activists and occupants cannot conceive such brilliance in a Black man!

"You have young men of color in many communities who are more likely to end up in jail or in the criminal justice system than they are in a good job or in college. And, you know, part of my job, that I can do, I think, without any potential conflicts, is to get at those root causes." **Barack Obama**

The parallel is simple as T.D. Jakes tells it. A giraffe was feeding at the tree top, enjoying the cool breeze, young, fresh greenery and staring into the promise of the clear blue skies yonder. Along came a turtle enquiring, "How're you doing?" Looking down, the giraffe answered, "Great, the view is wonderfully spectacular. And You?" The turtle responded, "Looks like a terrific mess. All I see down here is garbage and the smell is awful." The giraffe responded "You should steep-up and get a better view!" Fact is; both gave honest answers to their situation. However, while Obama grazes in tree top sunlight, breathing fresh air, his detractors are in turtledom!

Nevertheless, before we consider the questions, it is interesting to note some factors regarding the state of the nation under Mr. Bush's watch which Mr. Obama inherited and masterfully addressed as President!

First of all, 2006 was five years since the "second attack" on the World Trade Center on 9/11/2001, resulting in the "shock and awe" response visited on the Taliban in Afghanistan! The Taliban harbored Osama

OBAMA THE JOURNEY COMPLETED - NEVER PROMISED A ROSE GARDEN

bin Laden, leader of Al Qaeda, who was "at war with America," and credited with the attack. The year 2006 was also 3 years into the invasion of Iraq that ultimately toppled Sadam Hussein, resulting in nearly 5,000 American military deaths and thousands more injured. This does not include Coalition forces and Iraqi casualties, military and collateral, and the trillions of dollars spent in a war Americans considered useless, wasteful and ill-considered.

The significant players in the Bush Administration included Vice President Dick Chaney, Donald Rumsfeld as Secretary of Defense, and Condoleezza Rice as National Security Adviser who ultimately replaced General Colin Powell as Secretary of State. Based on the information supplied him, Mr. Powell testified to the Security Council of the United Nations that Sadam Hussein possessed weapons of mass destruction (WMD) with a launch capacity that was very rapid. He was even tied to purchasing uranium from Niger in West Africa to make his weaponry more effective. However, while both wars ensued, a number of interesting variables began to surface and in total proved much of this intelligence was considered faulty, if not purposefully deceitful.

Significantly, as it turned out, Mr. Chalaby, an Iraqi national who had written a book on *Ancient Egypt* was an "American friendly," who fed them inside information about Sadam's armaments. As it turned out, "Chalaby had this thing against Sadam," and targeted the Americans at him using purposely faulty intelligence. Notwithstanding, when the "stuff hit the fan," Chalaby fled to Iran, at that time an enemy of Iraq.

Apparently and second, evidence indicates, Sadam Hussein had tried to assassinate Mr. Bush's father, President Number 41, in Kuwait; so, Mr. Bush, President Number 43, was rather eager to get back at Sadam! The crafted web of deceit revealed even more details. Vice-President Dick Chaney was shown to be connected to Halliburton, a contractor company doing business in Iraq with great financial success. Even more important, it was persuasively argued, Iraqi oil would pay for the expense of the war, though this too proved misleading! Equally significant, however, as the occupation unfolded, General Shinseki informed Congress it would require some 500,000 troops to garrison Iraq but he was ridiculed and so, the conflicts revved up in face of Iraqi insurgency and the same happened in Afghanistan, though the deaths were not as numerous but still significant.

In as much as the American leadership initially raised the question of Sadam's intentions, the international community remained skeptical and so, "Mr. Bush chose to go it alone." In response, the international community took a dim view of America, thanks to the impetuosity of Mr. Bush, "the warlord!" This reality stained America's foreign relations image for the rest of Mr. Bush's term! One American woman was overheard saying in the Cairo Museum, "It has gotten so we don't want to say we're Americans because all Bush wants is war!"

OBAMA THE JOURNEY COMPLETED - NEVER PROMISED A ROSE GARDEN

UNITED STATES
DEPARTMENT OF AGRICULTURE

Dedicated as a Living Reminder in Memory
of the Victims of the Holocaust
by Secretary Dan Glickman

May 2, 2000

Yom Hashoah, Day of Remembrance

Franklin D. Roosevelt Red Bud from a seed collected
at President Roosevelt's "Little White House."

At home, the economy was in serious disarray. There were bank failures; Wall Street numbers dropped precipitously and the DOW fell to near 6500; high unemployment became the order of the day losing some 600,000 to 800,000 jobs per month; the automobile industry was

FREDERICK MONDERSON

in crisis; the nation's infrastructure had begun to crumble; an energy crisis unfolded; foreclosures were up, new housing starts were down; teachers and first responders' jobs were on the chopping block; and with unemployment up and taxes down, state and local governments faced challenging realities. Now, in this bleak moment in America's history, Senator Barack Hussein Obama, from the great state of Illinois, declared his candidacy for the Presidency and the rest is history, literally and figuratively!

After a grueling and well-orchestrated and successful campaign, possessing a beautiful wife, two lovely daughters and a wonderful mother-in-law, like a bright-eyed and bushy-tail knight whose hair was still black, Mr. Obama stepped on to the national and world stage to rescue his nation! Just as Jim Santorum would confess after his failure in 2012, "lots of things get said in a campaign;" Mr. Obama felt "the many lights" of this great nation would forget the campaign rhetoric leveled against him, come together, put their shoulders to the wheel, help to "remove the car from the ditch," and move the country nation forward. However, this was not to be! Nonetheless, Mr. Obama and his excellent team of advisers set about to tackle the myriad foreign and domestic challenges facing the nation, many believed, was in a near failed-state status! Still, rather than condemn his adversaries, Mr. Obama politely but confidently confessed, "Politics is a contact sport" and considered these persons "Good ole boys just acting out!"

OBAMA THE JOURNEY COMPLETED - NEVER PROMISED A ROSE GARDEN

Continental Hall and home of the Daughters of the American Revolution.

Facing the future with a positive attitude, one of the first and significant acts of a new president is to venture abroad, let friends and enemies get a taste of the new executive and lay out a view of the path he intends to pursue. This Mr. Obama did wonderfully well. Even more significantly, he astutely "deployed his better half," "Mighty Michelle," who not only wooed the world but provided the cover for him to win allies, put enemies on notice and addressed the fundamentals of the two wars. He then dispatched a new envoy to the Middle East and pivoted towards strengthening a foothold in Asia for defense and economic realities manifesting in this new century. All this was very well executed.

Next on the domestic front, the president sought to review and strengthen the nation's financial and fiscal policies and practices with a view toward overhauling the monetary system and this resulted in Dodd/Frank legislative policy; tackling foreclosure problems and other housing issues; rescuing the auto industry; bailing out the banks;

placing a moratorium on impending firing of teachers and first responders such as police officers and firemen; establishing protections for women under the Lilly Ledbetter Act; proposing a more equitable arrangement for student loan debt and easing credit card rates; tackling climate change and global warming; creating incentives for more efficient domestic energy systems and creating initiatives for education excellence. Meanwhile his wife Michelle and Vice-President Joe Biden's wife Jill became active advocates for veteran families faced with the challenges of two wars.

Unbeknownst to all but a few, the sinisters were at work! While it did not become public until *The New York Times* reported in October 6, 2013, a treasonous group had met and planned a concerted, many pronged campaign designed to sabotage the tenure of the first Black President! Perhaps as the point man, and intoxicated by the glare of the cameras, Senator Mitch McConnell laid it bare, as if speaking for his team, "I intend to make Barack Obama a one-term president!" True to his boast and in subsequent negotiations as Senate Minority leader, after an important meeting, the Senator gave his now famous or infamous "Thumbs-up" code symbol signaling to "his people" "I got that Nigger!" However, it's common knowledge, racist hue mentality held, "A Nigger occupies the White House."

It is hard to believe, high up as he is, Speaker Boehner, did not know of the treasonous Republican meeting even if he did not participate. The "conspiracy" existed certainly from 2008 to 2012, so Boehner's denial is perhaps farcical! Still, he did disrespect Mr. Obama by not

OBAMA THE JOURNEY COMPLETED - NEVER PROMISED A ROSE GARDEN

returning his phone calls amidst important negotiations. Even more significant, this "representative of the people" certainly helped hold the nation and Mr. Obama hostage in the Debt Ceiling Debate and later symbolically boasted "We got 98% of what we wanted!" This is incredible, for to get 98% of any pie means all others got crumbs to nothing!

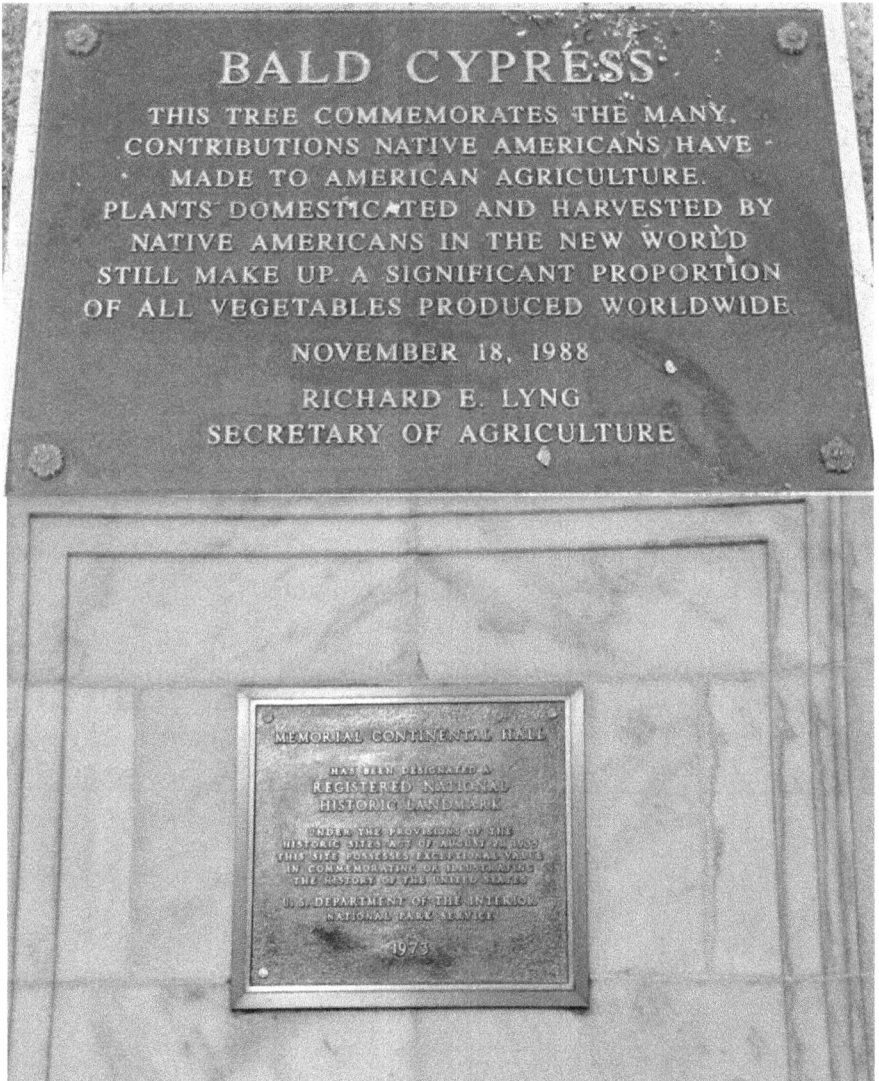

FREDERICK MONDERSON

Today, Mr. Obama's record speaks for itself. He ended and wound down the wars in Iraq and Afghanistan. He gets credit for killing and disposing of Osama bin Laden and severely curtailing the aspirations of Somali Pirates. He represented the United States very well at the funeral for Nelson Mandela in South Africa. The economy has rebounded well! Some 9 million new jobs have been added in the private sector so far during Mr. Obama's tenure. Rising from 6500 when he took office in 2008, to 17,000 today, the **DOW** has experienced a vibrancy unimagined even in "good times," in fact, its historical. The week of July 4, 2014, 300,000 jobs were added. Some even joked, "Knowing Mr. Obama would celebrate Independence Day; Republicans called up Hurricane Arthur to rain on Mr. Obama's parade!" Notwithstanding, on a more serious note, concerted attention is being paid to climate change, a clean air environment and infrastructure repair jobs. Emphasis is also being placed on all aspects of transportation, even thoughts of creating a high-speed rail system with trains to improve cross-country commute.

Incentives have been offered for innovations in clean energy, better and longer lasting batteries and cars are moving towards cleaner emissions and better gas mileage. Even Black farmers have been compensated for their long-standing suit against the government!

OBAMA THE JOURNEY COMPLETED - NEVER PROMISED A ROSE GARDEN

In education, Mr. Obama created "Race to the Top" to improve performance; issued incentives for parents to return to college; and he bolstered Community Colleges to lay a foundation for technical education in preparing for the future. Still more seriously important, Mr. Obama conceived of an answer to address the nearly 50 million Americans without health care. He campaigned on this issue in two elections, legislated the **Affordable Care Act** that withstood a Supreme Court challenge amidst acrimonious negative propaganda publicity, and despite technical problems in the health care system roll-out, more than 8 million Americans have signed-up for the insurance protections, so far. Its unimaginable what the results would have been if Republicans had put their shoulders to the "Obamacare wheel!" With some luck and superb administrative vigilance terrorist attacks on the homeland have been prevented. In fact, a popular T-shirt has a Logo that reads: "Homeland Security: Fighting Terrorism since 1492!" As such, some have considered this nation, the birthplace of terrorism for Ku Klux Klan and Knights of the White Camellia, etc., and their "Jim Crow partners'" behaviors towards African-

Americans during the 19th and 20th Centuries which can certainly be considered classic cases of terrorism.

The list enumerated above and much more Mr. Obama achieved despite a Republican "Party of No" actively committed to block-every legislative initiative he proposed. Consider the Affordable Care Act was voted against 43 times in the House of Representatives controlled by Republicans and not 1 Obama initiated jobs bill got through. Who's working for the American people? Coupled with this subjective campaign *The Times* article named some 20 right-wing groups that were formed and well-financed, also the training of untold numbers of young people to "provide information about Obamacare," which in fact is nothing but efforts to defame Mr. Obama and his work. So much so, Senate Majority Leader Harry Reid decried the exorbitant spending by saying, "They're trying to buy America but it's not for sale!" Sorrowfully, the President confessed, "All they do is talk about me and block my every effort."

The mentality of persons such as the "McConnells" and "Boehners" and their backers who consider Mr. Obama is "A Nigger out of place!" Hence, they must and will do everything in their power to defame him and poison the minds of Americans so a negative perception will linger. Important too, many Democrats do not stand up for Mr. Obama! Malcolm X called them "Dixiecrats!"

OBAMA THE JOURNEY COMPLETED - NEVER PROMISED A ROSE GARDEN

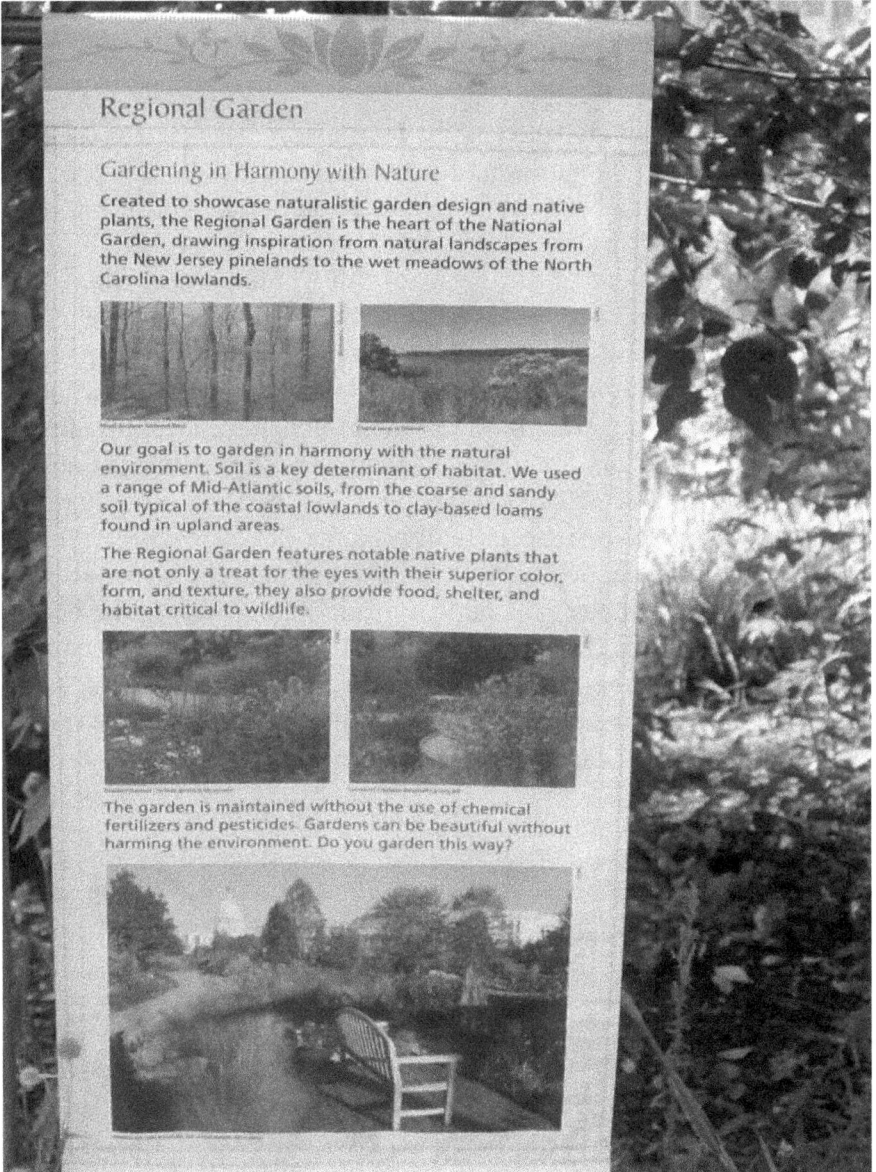

Most important, enquiring minds wonder whether the Poll asked did Mr. Obama's race play a role in the negative result. After Donald Trump's "Birther Charade," and the many threats, the fact is in both the 2008 and 2012 election Mr. Obama won by a margin of 53-47 percent of the vote. He lost all the "Lynching States" of the South and thus the 30% number is down from the 47% who would never vote for the Black man.

Nevertheless, when it comes to the use of Executive Action on part of the President, Mr. Obama was elected to lead the nation. If legislative elements block his every action, he must act on behalf of the people and therefore, Executive Action gets his agenda moving. While the Poll seemed to indicate Mr. Reagan, Bill Clinton and Richard Nixon scored better than Mr. Obama one has to wonder whether a blind man conducted the poll. History has shown Bill Clinton worked the "Monica Lewinsky matter" in the White House while Hillary was in the next room; Richard Nixon resigned in disgrace after imploring "I am not a crook!" As for Ronal Reagan, for long he was an actor on radio, screen and television shaping his persona in a world of Hollywood many believe is really "make believe." Still, President Reagan, while he deployed "Star Wars" and blew wind at the Russians, their empire was actually tottering. However, he changed his hairstyle and lied about the Contras! More importantly, however, Mr. Reagan was the master of Executive Action, employing it more times than any other president. Therefore, to significantly question Mr. Obama's use of Executive Action in contrast with Mr. Reagan is actually laughable!

The fact is; Mr. Obama is a humanitarian who put people ahead of politics, has been faithful to his wife and kids and intellectually stands as a Gulliver to his Lilliputian challengers. Nevertheless, all things being equal, objectivity trumps subjectivity, which makes the Poll results questionable at best, defaming and destructive at worst. Equally, it is strange how Republicans supply ideas to the terrorists who hate America. These people watch the American news on television. And, Mr. Obama tarries on for what else is new!

BRADFORD PEAR TREE
(PYRUS CALLERYANA BRADFORD)
AN ORNAMENTAL SHADE TREE DEVELOPED BY
U.S.D.A. SCIENTISTS
PLANTED MAY 2, 1966
BY
MRS. LYNDON B. JOHNSON
ORVILLE L. FREEMAN, SECRETARY OF AGRICULTURE
VA. & MD. 4-H CLUBS
IN BEHALF OF NATIONAL BEAUTIFICATION
REPLACED MAY 2, 1987

UNITED STATES
DEPARTMENT OF AGRICULTURE

DEDICATED TO THE BRAVE MEN AND WOMEN OF THE UNITED
STATES DEPARTMENT OF AGRICULTURE WHO
SERVED THE UNITED STATES OF AMERICA
THROUGH MILITARY SERVICE IN TIME OF ARMED COMBAT.

DEDICATED BY: EDWARD MADIGAN,
SECRETARY OF AGRICULTURE

AUGUST 9, 1991

FREDERICK MONDERSON

Finally, in a recent press conference on an impending uptick of American involvement in Iraq, the Chairman of the Joint Chiefs, General Dempsey, spoke with a fearlessness and conviction that expresses sheer confidence in his Commander-in-Chief. Such

OBAMA THE JOURNEY COMPLETED - NEVER PROMISED A ROSE GARDEN

steadfast composure as the general demonstrated in his leader fails the methodology, assessment and intent of the Quinnipiac Poll!

"We need to internalize this idea of excellence. Not many folks spend a lot of time trying to be excellent." **Barack Obama**

FREDERICK MONDERSON

12.   "SUEING THE PRESIDENT"
By
Dr. Fred Monderson

As a thinking person, I read with great interest Jeremy W. Peters' article in *The New York Times* of July 31, 2014, p. A 15, entitled "House votes to Sue Obama for Overstepping Powers." This is a move many think is a slap in the face of not only Mr. Obama but of America in general and foreign observers see not just "Political theater" but actors vengefully "Crying at the circus." Even more important, from the time Mr. Obama assumed the Presidency Republicans have, with impunity, disrespected the man and the Office of the President in the most shameful manner exposing their most vile racial attitudes. One of this writer's professors has always exclaimed, "The more monkey climbs, the more he exposes himself!" As such, and in their climb, Republicans have grossly exposed their true selves relative to their anti-health care stance which is antithetical to human decency and against the interest and aspirations of the 99 percent, certainly the 50 million uninsured American persons!

OBAMA THE JOURNEY COMPLETED - NEVER PROMISED A ROSE GARDEN

"We worship an awesome God in the Blue States, and we don't like federal agents poking around our libraries in the Red States. We coach Little League in the Blue States and have gay friends in the Red States." **Barack Obama**

The burden of leadership is great requiring men and women of magnanimous potential and resolution who are dedicated to the pursuit of the highest good for the betterment of humanity, irrespective of whom they lead. A good example is underscored in the following: On the one hand, while President Harry Truman long ago admonished, never mind the backdrop, "We must build a new world, a far better world, one in which the eternal dignity of man is respected." On the other hand, Maulana Karenga, author of Kwanzaa, equally admonished, "It is our duty to bring good into the world through our thoughts and actions." So, based on recent events, and based on the pronounced wisdom of these two thinking giants, the reader is asked to evaluate whether Mr. Obama or Republicans have been and are, working towards bringing the American nation's philosophical principles of wisdom and goodness into reality in order to better the lot of humanity.

Nevertheless, to begin at the article's end, Representative John Lewis, Democrat of Georgia, called the Republican resolution, "A shame and a disgrace" and that "It has no place on this floor." Contrast this with the statement of Representative Jeff Duncan of South Carolina, "who summoned the story of Adam and Eve in explaining how men, because of their 'inherent infallibility,' could not be trusted with too much power;" this is a sentiment he said the Founding Fathers expressed. Equally, the expression "As Christian men of the day, they understood that since the Garden of Eden, man has fallen" is, in his view, a true representation of the issue, now as then.

FREDERICK MONDERSON

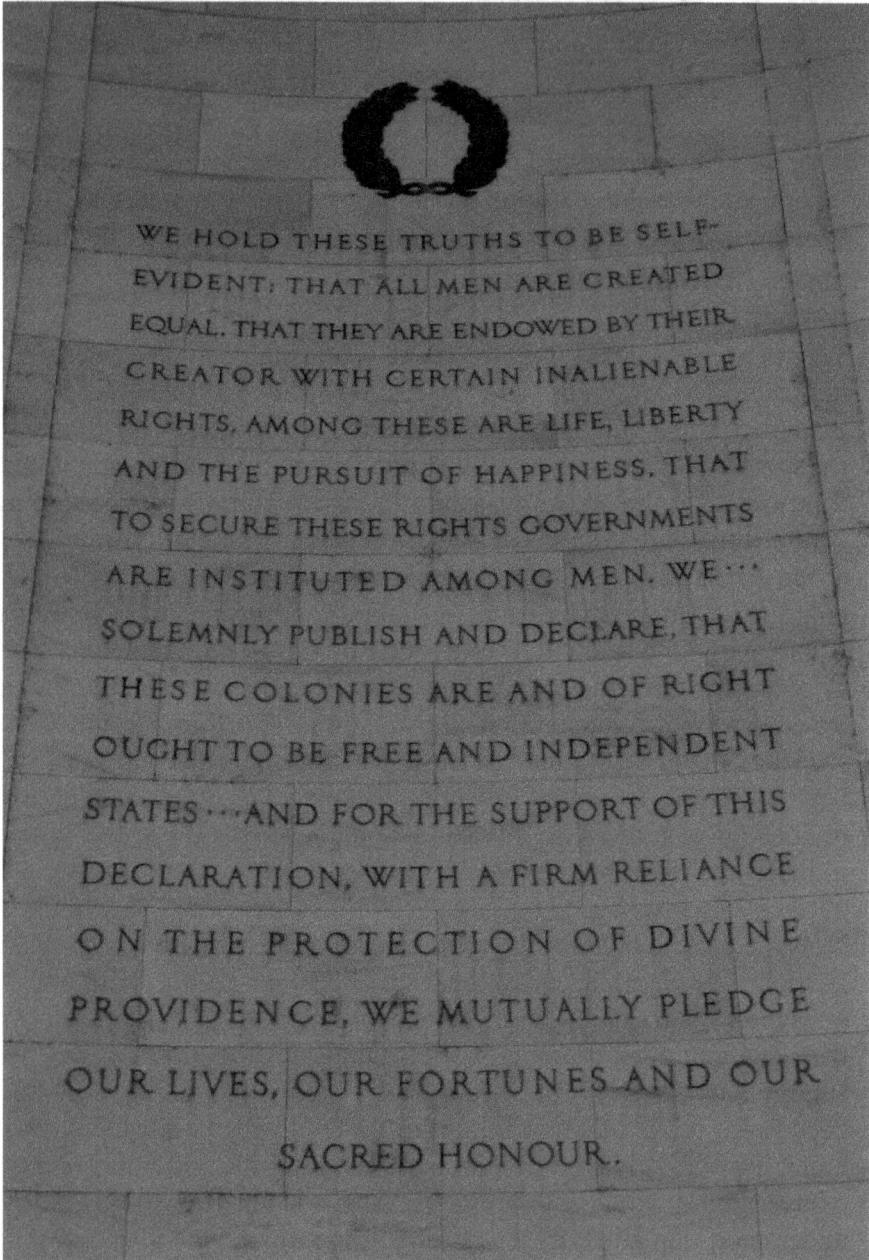

WE HOLD THESE TRUTHS TO BE SELF-EVIDENT: THAT ALL MEN ARE CREATED EQUAL. THAT THEY ARE ENDOWED BY THEIR CREATOR WITH CERTAIN INALIENABLE RIGHTS, AMONG THESE ARE LIFE, LIBERTY AND THE PURSUIT OF HAPPINESS. THAT TO SECURE THESE RIGHTS GOVERNMENTS ARE INSTITUTED AMONG MEN. WE··· SOLEMNLY PUBLISH AND DECLARE, THAT THESE COLONIES ARE AND OF RIGHT OUGHT TO BE FREE AND INDEPENDENT STATES···AND FOR THE SUPPORT OF THIS DECLARATION, WITH A FIRM RELIANCE ON THE PROTECTION OF DIVINE PROVIDENCE, WE MUTUALLY PLEDGE OUR LIVES, OUR FORTUNES AND OUR SACRED HONOUR.

Naturally, there are some who still believe their jaundiced view is the truth and that is all there is to it. Sadly, this is not so, nor is the Republicans hostile view of Mr. Obama and the world, correct.

172

OBAMA THE JOURNEY COMPLETED - NEVER PROMISED A ROSE GARDEN

History, as Malcolm X reminded us, has always been "a good teacher." In searching for truth, we can look at a very good example from the French Revolution where amidst the ghastly repercussions, the Englishman Edmund Burke in his *Reflections on the Revolution in France*, 1792, wrote, "The only thing necessary for evil to triumph is for good men to do or say nothing." Thus, all good people must condemn this unconscionable behavior which leaders in the House of Representatives of the United States of America have demonstrated against the nation's leader, its Chief Executive, who is of African descent! Republicans, led by Mitch McConnell of Kentucky obstructed every action of sensible *policy initiative* the President proposed principally because of the color of his skin and that he belongs to a different political party. Coming to light years later, it was determined, on the very day of President Obama's first inauguration, several high-ranking Republican members of the House in conjunction with others, pledged themselves to insure that Obama is a one-term president; that he does not get a "win." Since the House controls funds of the nation, their pledge was/is an act of treason because of the inherent intent and implications of this action.

Of major importance, in that age of revolution extolling the dignity of the human spirit based on the logical notion of the "Fatherhood of God" and the "Brotherhood of Man," such high ideals were enunciated in sacred documents as the **Declaration of**

173

FREDERICK MONDERSON

Independence, the **U.S. Constitution** and the **Declaration of the Rights of Man**.

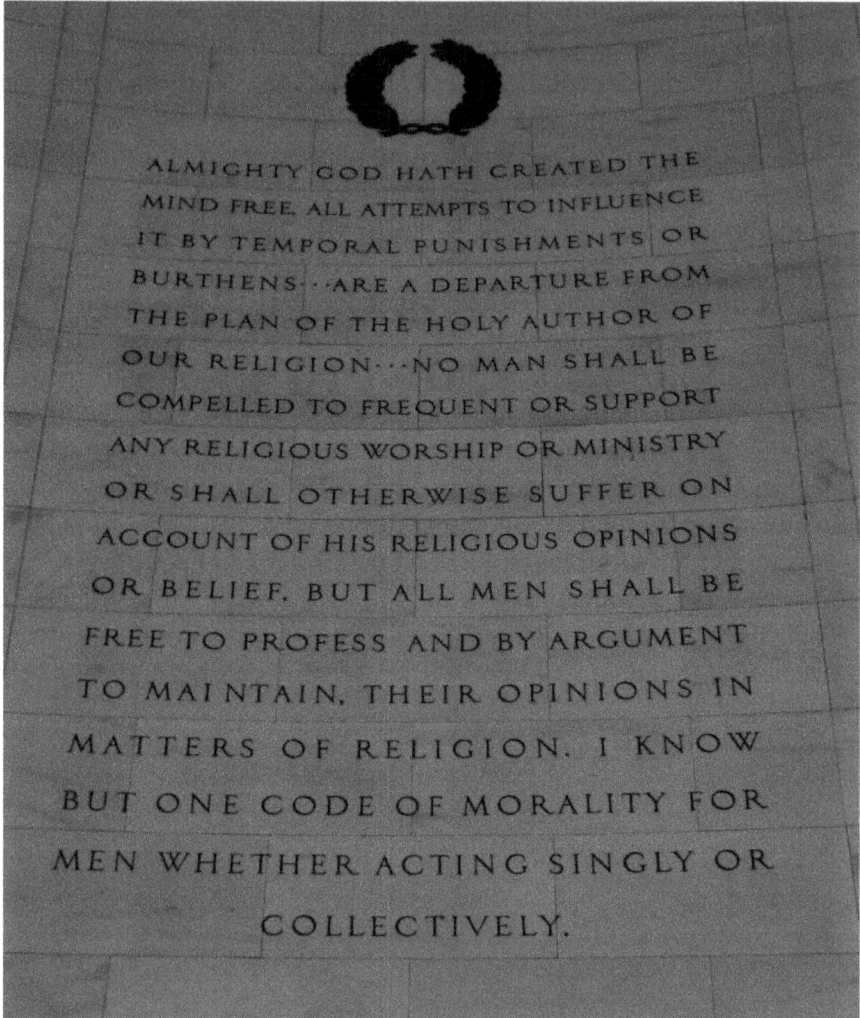

ALMIGHTY GOD HATH CREATED THE MIND FREE. ALL ATTEMPTS TO INFLUENCE IT BY TEMPORAL PUNISHMENTS OR BURTHENS···ARE A DEPARTURE FROM THE PLAN OF THE HOLY AUTHOR OF OUR RELIGION···NO MAN SHALL BE COMPELLED TO FREQUENT OR SUPPORT ANY RELIGIOUS WORSHIP OR MINISTRY OR SHALL OTHERWISE SUFFER ON ACCOUNT OF HIS RELIGIOUS OPINIONS OR BELIEF. BUT ALL MEN SHALL BE FREE TO PROFESS AND BY ARGUMENT TO MAINTAIN, THEIR OPINIONS IN MATTERS OF RELIGION. I KNOW BUT ONE CODE OF MORALITY FOR MEN WHETHER ACTING SINGLY OR COLLECTIVELY.

These writings are considered in most of Western European and American culture to be cornerstones of right and just treatment of all humanity. However, as history has shown, while events unfolded, in that Christian Western World, Baron Montesquieu author of *Spirit of the Laws* was forced to write, owing to the practiced behaviors of his day, regarding treatment of African peoples, "Either we are not Christians or the Negro is not a man!" He was, however, not referring

174

OBAMA THE JOURNEY COMPLETED - NEVER PROMISED A ROSE GARDEN

simply to the behaviors of Frenchmen, themselves engaged in the Slave Trade and Slavery, but including their European counterparts the British, Dutch, Portuguese, Brandenbergers or Germans, and the Americans who perpetrated and were major participants in that dastardly and ghastly determined "Crime against Humanity," which lasted for nearly four hundred years. This laceration and/or genocide of the human spirit, body and mind, as W.E.B. DuBois documented, has claimed 100,000,000 lives lost to Africa, with resulting psychological trauma which has scarred both the perpetrators and the victims of that horrible experience.

It must be constantly recalled that the Preamble to the Declaration of United States Independence declares, "We hold these truths to be self-evident that all men are created equal and are endowed by their creator with certain unalienable rights to life, liberty and the pursuit of happiness." However, in contradiction on that day, the Founding Fathers held in bondage fellow human beings they considered chattel, in a *de jure* and *de facto* state of existence equated with dogs, horses, pigs, chickens, cows, viz., all property! The unalienable "Right" of the African peoples to liberty was, thus, alienated.

The record further shows, that the august House of Representatives today under Republican and "Tea Party" control, which voted to bring suit against President Obama for executing the responsibilities of the Office of the President is acting in a similarly reprehensible manner. This despicable act is but a continuum of the refusal of whites to concede the rights of African peoples, even if one of them is President of the United States of America. In the time of the "Founding Fathers," this House had voted to elevate Mr. Obama's and his wife Michelle's ancestors to the status of 3/5 of a person. Today many believe that "A Nigger in the White House," is still the 3/5 of a person for which their white ancestors voted in order to ratify the Constitution and give slaveholding states, such as South Carolina, political representation in the then new system of United States government.

In today's climate, as Republicans psyched themselves before taking this historic vote to bring suit against President Obama, the South Carolinian Tom Rice spoke of the "tyranny of King George III (Mr. Obama)" wherein, "At the end of the bloody revolution, the last thing they needed was another king; they wanted freedom… Our forefathers paid dearly for that freedom." To hear the Representative of South Carolina speak today would make even the great American desert shed tears! South Carolina, Oh, South Carolina, cauldron of slavery, perpetuator of untold anguish and misery, *who would not let Our People Go*! If "Our forefathers paid dearly for that freedom," what price did African-American forefathers, fore-mothers, and their children pay against whom your ancestors committed such unspeakable horrors and who, centuries later, are still paying for the true meaning of that freedom and equality Republicans and their cohorts boast so loftily about. When Tom Rice pontificates about "our forefathers paid dearly for that freedom," he is in the continuum of his ancestors who (a) does not consider Blacks to be fully human; (b) sees President Obama as "Just another Nigger who is out of his place and must be returned to his rightful place." (3) entertain the warped notion, "blacks are inherently inferior in the natural order and must be so in the social order." Thus these perpetrators of racial animus and insensitivity rationalize and justify sub-standard treatment to the Black -American citizen.

OBAMA THE JOURNEY COMPLETED - NEVER PROMISED A ROSE GARDEN

c. People of his hue, flaunt the law, the Voting Rights Act and the 14th and 15th Amendments by seeking to politically disfranchise Blacks and the poor.

What astute analysts and commentators who examined Republican behavior of lately have come to recognize, there are code words that are used which distinguish the President from "Them" or the "Others," even "Our" or "Us!"

Example, when Mr. Boehner asked, "Are you willing to let anyone tear apart what our founders have built?" or, especially the South Carolinian, whose state; the largest slaving entity among the *Ante Bellum* states and which Jesse Jackson, among many other things, once accused of having 36 state prisons, mostly peopled by Blacks, and 1 state college; home of "Waterloo" Senator Jim De Mint; even Republican "You lie" Joe Wilson; even when Mr. Rice use terms like "Our forefathers paid dearly for that freedom," and more "We cannot stand by and watch the President shred Our constitution," their intent is not simply a moral malady, it is unconstitutional so that these people mean to vilify and exclude "The Nigger in the White House" despite his fully earned and accomplished position; and his role model as father, husband, hero and citizen to untold millions at home and abroad.

FREDERICK MONDERSON

GOD WHO GAVE US LIFE GAVE US LIBERTY. CAN THE LIBERTIES OF A NATION BE SECURE WHEN WE HAVE REMOVED A CONVICTION THAT THESE LIBERTIES ARE THE GIFT OF GOD? INDEED I TREMBLE FOR MY COUNTRY WHEN I REFLECT THAT GOD IS JUST, THAT HIS JUSTICE CANNOT SLEEP FOREVER. COMMERCE BETWEEN MASTER AND SLAVE IS DESPOTISM. NOTHING IS MORE CERTAINLY WRITTEN IN THE BOOK OF FATE THAN THAT THESE PEOPLE ARE TO BE FREE. ESTABLISH THE LAW FOR EDUCATING THE COMMON PEOPLE. THIS IT IS THE BUSINESS OF THE STATE TO EFFECT AND ON A GENERAL PLAN.

Somehow, and unhappily these "little men," have psychologically transposed themselves back to the founding days of the Republic and see slaves as now living in the big house and they the whites occupying the slave shacks! That false and prejudiced mindset is molded from an equally false perception of reality and is fundamental to every attempt to undermine the President's legislative agenda. Many believe the Republicans seem to have forgotten their history and the sustained venomous antagonisms towards Mr. Obama, his candidacy and time in office, are disgraceful facts. That is why, "Five

OBAMA THE JOURNEY COMPLETED - NEVER PROMISED A ROSE GARDEN

Republicans voted not to sue the President on Wednesday. Paul Brown of Georgia; Scott Jarrell of New Jersey; Walter B. Jones of North Carolina; Thomas Massie of Kentucky; and Steve Stockman of Texas" because as "good men" of moral stature they voted their conscience not the Republican "party line." They wanted to essentially divorce themselves from the "rebels," especially the lynching states' representatives. Nonetheless, the gentleman politician that Mr. Obama is has precluded his "firing on the rebel camp." Instead, he turned their animosity into positive energy fueling his work ethic "when they go low, he goes high," while he prioritized for the public good and even if he has to continue using Executive Action, he will. Whatever, and since economic trends are improving, come November, Republicans will regret this action and spiral out into space like the lost and irrelevant Sarah Palin whose "lips are dripping with words of Impeachment!"

Never forgetting her "Thumpin," Sarah Palin's behavior is reflected in reminiscence of "elder wisdom" which held, "When goat *do do* wants to roll it looks for the highest ground and the slightest breeze!" Nevertheless, all should remember Mr. Obama's appeal on behalf of the American people which is to, "Stop hating all the time. Come on. Let's get some work done together." All this, amidst reports the recent economy has been robust in its performance with untold numbers of jobs being added. In a meeting with the public to explain this new development, Mr. Obama reminded all that: "The decisions that we made to rescue our economy, to rescue the auto industry, to build the economy on a new foundation, to invest in research and infrastructure, education - all those things are starting to pay off." Placing icing on that cake, the President added, "Imagine how much further along we'd be, how much stronger our economy would be, if Congress was doing its job, too."

Notwithstanding, as the disgraceful scenario unfolded, most balanced individuals will admit; this action to sue the President is a "stunt" designed to energize the Republican base for the upcoming 2014 general election using repeal of the Health Care Act as a motivator. The strategy and facts are clear to persons with a wide understanding of how ideas are formulated into American law. They understand Mr. Obama conceived the long-standing idea of health care reform to address the lack of health care insurance for some 50 million Americans; he campaigned on the issue in a winning 2008 presidential bid; the act withstood a challenge in the Supreme Court as well as being a significant issue in the 2012 campaign, all this while the Republican controlled House of Representatives voted 43 times to repeal an act that still stands! More importantly, the act is helping many among that 50 million who will vote, the Republican base energized, notwithstanding. Today they have voted more than 50 time to repeal and this is what Donald Trump's main objective is.

OBAMA THE JOURNEY COMPLETED - NEVER PROMISED A ROSE GARDEN

When the Health Care Act was introduced, the Republican full court press criticized the system for its technological errors. In time, when this was fixed and its success became manifest, like a recurring decimal Republicans scrambled to find relevance in their strategy, which has been principally *ad hominem* attacks on the President. After all, having failed to make Mr. Obama a one-term president; failed to fully block every legislative initiative he proposed, suing him became the only duck as a substitute for an eagle.

When the article is examined further, a glaring number of contradictions are evident. Besides Senator Ron Johnson of Wisconsin and Senator Rand Paul of Kentucky who were among those who sued the President, Mr. Boehner's suit and Sarah Palin advocacy as another opponent of Mr. Obama, such actions can be equated with the pugilist "Gunboat Johnson" in that old "3 Stooges" movie. "Gunboat" had 50 fights, lost 49 and tied the 50^{th,} though he spent six weeks in the hospital recuperating. Thus, "Lipstick on a Pig" Sarah Palin, especially who "was never even a good Vice-President candidate" will never forget the "Thumpin" Mr. Obama put on her candidacy in 2008. Now, having exhausted her entire arsenal of anti-Obama ammunition she has stumbled upon a new word, "Impeachment." This former politician whose mantra had been, "You don't go to a gun fight with a broom" which explains her frame of reference, still struggles to be relevant as she spirals uncontrollably into the great cosmic void of political irrelevance. Still, she fails to recognize how formidable an opponent Mr. Obama truly is and hopelessly fails to realize how irrelevant she herself is.

Mr. Boehner, on the other hand, is caught between the rock of his party's hard-core hawks and opposing a formidable opponent in Mr. Obama. Mr. Boehner still recognizes though he refuses to admit, certainly in public, President Obama is no ordinary adversary!

OBAMA THE JOURNEY COMPLETED - NEVER PROMISED A ROSE GARDEN

FREDERICK MONDERSON

"My family, frankly, they weren't folks who went to church every week. My mother was one of the most spiritual people I knew but she didn't raise me in the church, so I came to my Christian faith later in life and it was because the precepts of Jesus Christ spoke to me in terms of the kind of life that I would want to lead." **Barack Obama**

OBAMA THE JOURNEY COMPLETED - NEVER PROMISED A ROSE GARDEN

13.   "OBAMA'S WAR IN IRAQ"

By

Dr. Fred Monderson

The lead Editorial of the New York *Daily News* of Saturday August 9, 2014, p. 22, entitled "Obama's War in Iraq" is disturbingly misleading, consistent with the perennial impugning of President Obama as Commander-In-Chief of the Armed forces of the United States. The article begins with a questionable title and ends in disparagement, sadly seemingly ignorant of the true realities of the situation in Iraq and the world today, his approach to the issues, and Mr. Obama as a thinking leader and President.

"Our higher education system is one of the things that make America exceptional. There's no place else that has the assets we do when it comes to higher education. People from all over the world aspire to come here and study here. And that is a good thing." **Barack Obama**

The reason the title, to begin with, is false is simply because America has fought a number of wars, yet none has been associated, title-wise, with an individual or president! Perhaps only the Hollywood produced movie **Hart's War**. This nation fought the "French and Indian Wars (1756-1763);" the "Revolutionary War (1776-1783);" "War with the Barbary Pirates (1803-1804);" "War of 1812: Second War for Independence (1812-1815);" "War with the Seminoles" but not Andrew Jackson's (1819); "War with Mexico (1844-1845)" in which Sonny Carson ancestor Samuel Carson fought and died; "Civil War (1860-1865)" - How Civil was it? "Spanish-American War (1899-1902);" "World War I (1914-1918) 'To save the world for democracy';" "World War II (1939-1945) 'Serving as the arsenal of democracy;" "War against Communism (1946-1986);" "Korean War (1952-1953);" Viet Nam War (1958-1975) - or, Police Action;" "Invasion of Grenada (1986) 'To save American medical students';" "Gulf War I (1991) to stop Sadam Hussein in Kuwait;" "Afghanistan War (2001-Present) 'Shock and Awe' to get Osama bin-Laden;" "Iraqi War - Gulf War II (2003-2011) 'to find the Weapons of Mass Destruction.'" We could add the "War on Poverty (1960s)" and the "War on Drugs (1970-1999)." Now Republicans are talking about "A War on Women (2013-2014)" and blaming President Obama! These people will not accept blaming George Bush for Afghanistan and Iraq, yet they would blame President Obama consistent with their "Anti Obama positions and rhetoric."

OBAMA THE JOURNEY COMPLETED - NEVER PROMISED A ROSE GARDEN

The acceptable general consensus has been to blame individuals for policy or military mishaps but not the crisis, certainly not at its inception stage because this negativity colors the message! In as much as this President has been so maligned, obstructed with at every turn and yet, been so successful in legislative action and economic policy and practice, energy, etc., the perception of leadership should not be an issue, certainly not exploited for political purposes. Let's face it, leadership is about decision making. If 60% or 65% of a leader's decisions are successful, in many respects, he has surpassed the threshold in successfully operationalizing the art of the possible.

Description on the Cornice of Union Station.

FREDERICK MONDERSON

Equally, since President Obama has been photographed with and utilizes his Advisory Council, viz., Vice President Joe Biden, National Security Advisor Susan Rice, Joint Chiefs, Secretary of Defense, etc.; we thus see, in a complex world decisions are not easily arrived at. As an example, Lt.-General William Mayville, Jr., Director of Operations for the Joint Chiefs in a press conference on Monday, August 11, 2014, said in response to a question, "We're studying and assessing the situation" in order to "offer options to the President." As such, it stands to reason every decision is made with serious consideration and though the President gets the last word, it is ultimately based on sound judgment as his expert advisers see and frame the issues for his decision. Importantly, there has not been a "wholesale resignation" from his "Think Tank;" the costs of military engagement has decreased; Americans are not dying *en masse* across the globe; allies have maintained their relationships with America; and most nations still see America as leader of the free and humanitarian world. As such, the state of reality certainly defies distorted perception of the president's leadership.

Sometimes constructive criticisms are helpful while a leader addresses the myriad issues. However, when the criticisms are "Prejudiced" by political and other considerations, especially without providing meaningful alternative suggestions, then the criticisms become *Ad Hominem.*

OBAMA THE JOURNEY COMPLETED - NEVER PROMISED A ROSE GARDEN

Yet, the article speaks of the "umpteenth example of this passive President's chronic unwillingness to take stronger or strategic action until a moment of crisis forces his hand." Even further: "It was in 2011 that Obama, having failed to negotiate a status-of-forces agreement with the newly independent Iraqi government, shortsightedly pulled all troops out of the country." Naturally, the *Daily News experts* were in the room and at the table of negotiations! Importantly, we must consider restrictions Iraqis placed on the Americans that President Bush set the date for withdrawal! Perhaps such a strategy was designed to get the Americans out of Iraq. Let's not forget the trickery of another Iraqi who supplied false "evidence of WMD." Who knows what role Iran played? Given Al Maliki's unchecked treacherous behavior in his "ethnic cleansing" and rush to reward his tribal allies, can we wonder at Obama's actions?

These complicated dynamics become clearer given an old adage which holds, "There are no permanent alliances, only permanent interests." The Iraqi Prime Minister Al-Maliki's behavior is one example. That is, having gained the national office and with the Americans out of Iraq, he began removing all but his tribe from leadership in government and the military. This certainly created conditions for the successes of Isis' militants since others in the military felt they had nothing to fight for under Maliki. Former Senator and Secretary of State Hillary Clinton distancing herself from the President is another example by blaming Obama for the setback in Syria. But, the rejected builder's stone can one day become the structure's cornerstone.

Nonetheless, in a broader view, the article affirms the president "Frames the mission in humanitarian terms," then "All should applaud American air drops of basic life sustaining stuff - and the application of targeted force to save innocent lives." Par for the course! Give America credit for humanitarian actions but impugn Mr. Obama, his military and which is a hallmark of Republican political posturing.

The article climax ends by saying, "Waiting to act until inaction is no longer morally defensible is not a doctrine. Pain avoidance is not a strategy." From the inception of his presidency, Mr. Obama has been

OBAMA THE JOURNEY COMPLETED - NEVER PROMISED A ROSE GARDEN

proactive from Lilly Ledbetter to pursuit of Osama bin-Laden and Somali Pirates to clean air and energy self-sufficiency strategies. The only difference is he studies the issues fully rather than plunge heedlessly into situations most nations shy away from.

Description on the Cornice of Union Station.

"We have an obligation and a responsibility to be investing in our students and our schools. We must make sure that people who have the grades, the desire and the will, but not the money, can still get the best education possible." **Barack Obama**

191

FREDERICK MONDERSON

14.   BARACK OBAMA:
THE GREAT VISIONARY
By
Dr. Fred Monderson

Every once in a great while a visionary comes along whose passion, intellectual fortitude, work ethic and great appeal to the masses endears him or her to a great many people over time and great distances. Barack Hussein Obama is one such individual whose visionary capabilities has mesmerized the American people causing them to trust and ultimately elect him to be President of the United States of America, a position of tremendous influence throughout the

OBAMA THE JOURNEY COMPLETED - NEVER PROMISED A ROSE GARDEN

world. This likability has helped those who have felt victimized by American policies and practices, whereby the visionary has created the environment enabling him to blunt the enormous anti-Americanism that had developed over many years.

"If the people cannot trust their government to do the job for which it exists - to protect them and to promote their common welfare - all else is lost." **Barack Obama**

Everyone, in and out of Iran seemed pleased that the upcoming election reflected the democratic process at work and that the people would get a chance to elect those who most represent their ideas. The debates and other election actions bode well for progress in Iran as the world watched. The thing conspicuously absent in the debates was the mention of America, the "great Satan." Within two days some 80 million votes were counted and the winner declared. The people took to the streets to protest what they seem to rightfully believe, the elections were stolen. In the United States, Republicans especially began criticizing President Obama for not speaking out about the Iranian government's responses to their people protesting about their election results.

The visionary character of President Obama coupled with the input from his team of wise men determined he would not comment on developments on the street in Iran. In as much as the name of America was not a part of the election nor was it being mentioned in the streets, the United States should guardedly monitor developments on the ground but maintain a balanced approach. Republicans on the other hand, wanting a more forceful response began criticizing the President for not speaking out on the election results. Senator John McCain, as is customary, publicly labeled the election results a fraud. This "shoot from the lip" attitude of his is characteristic of the expressions he voiced when Russia invaded Eastern Europe and he spoke out while Senator Obama consulted with wise men and officials familiar with foreign security issues, before he spoke. Similarly, while the President took a cautious approach to the developments, in his first speak about the election results, the Ayatollah Khomeini blamed America and Britain and Israel for interfering even though the US had not done so. Therefore, it seems President Obama's cautiously neutral stance was really the best way to go so as to maintain America's non-involvement in Iranian developments.

Thomas Jefferson in his *First Inaugural Address* on March 4, 1801 stated: "But would the honest patriot, in the full tide of successful experiment, abandon a government which has so far kept us free and firm, on the theoretic and visionary fear that this government, the world's best hope, may by possibility want energy to preserve itself?"

The visionary nature of President Barack Obama seems to have surfaced as early as his first graduation from Columbia University with the man believing some force was helping to shape his destiny. Graduating from Harvard University Law School, that same guardian spirit seems bent on directing his path and led him to Chicago rather than Wall Street for visions of the future may have seen the ultimate mess that would surface there later while Mr. Wonderful would still be there to come to their rescue.

OBAMA THE JOURNEY COMPLETED - NEVER PROMISED A ROSE GARDEN

15.   SPEAKER BOEHNER'S SUIT
BY
DR. FRED MONDERSON

This is not about Speaker Boehner's well-pressed suit, which is very likely tailor made. However, to read that House Speaker John Boehner, along with his Republican and "Tea Party" associates plan to sue President Obama on his use of Executive Orders is remindful of the *New York Daily News* front page reply to Donald Trump's response to the City of New York $40m settlement to the "Central Park Jogger 5" case; "Just-Ass." As the people's representative leading the House of Representatives, Mr. Boehner has presided over a Republican led chamber that passed no bills of substance, shut the government down, held the nation hostage in a Debt Ceiling standoff, personally disrespected the President of the United States by not returning his phone calls and virulently attacked Mr. Obama from "Pillar to Post." Then when negotiations did take place he boasted, "We got 98% of what we wanted." This boast is tantamount to robbery. The Republicans, of which Mr. Boehner is a principal leader has blocked every legislative effort on part of the President, and besides, by the Grace of God, only in most cases his use of Executive Power has enabled Mr. Obama to constructively conduct the people's business which is his chief responsibility as the principal representative of the entire nation.

Recently a Republican lawmaker made the news by stating "If we criticize Mr. Obama they will say we are racists." Who is this gentleman and where has he been these many years? When did he arrive?

From his initial declaration for the Presidency in 2008, Mr. Obama has been the victim of the vilest racist treatment reminiscent of the anti-bellum mentality that characterized the South. Who could forget "Lipstick-on a pig" Palin whipping up crowds at "Tea Party" gatherings that elicited responses as "Kill the Nigger" which became the cry of the day; yet she did not have the decency to say "No" to such extremes! Let us not forget "Waterloo" DeMint; "You Lie" Wilson in the same chamber Mr. Boehner presides over; Bachman and Trump flogging the "Birther" dead horse. Even more important, the clearly expressed intent of Senator Mitch McConnell, "To make Barack Obama a one term President" was actually a smoke-screen for a more sinister and treasonous intent of a conspiracy to sabotage Mr. Obama's Presidency after the 2008 election. Why? Because we now have "a Nigger in the White House." While visionaries read this play before it actually unfolded, Republicans mining the legislative field for much of Mr. Obama's first term, by its end, even skeptics had begun to smell the odorous nature of Republican sinister and racist intent. Today, much of their behavior is camouflaged in "Code Words."

OBAMA THE JOURNEY COMPLETED - NEVER PROMISED A ROSE GARDEN

Very much in its tradition of "scooping" important news stories, *The New York Time*s bombshell article of October 6, 2013, p. A 1, revealed the 2012 plot of high echelon Republican operatives and their backers who planned to waylay Mr. Obama's campaign for re-election. The article revealed nearly two dozen political organizations either already in existence and others formed to "train operatives and disseminate information" about Mr. Obama's **Affordable Care Act**, under the guise of informing the public about its demerits. Interesting, the name of Mr. Ed Meese, Ronald Reagan's Attorney General was one of the principals. At that high level of political discussion it stands to reason Mr. McConnell and Mr. Boehner were very probably privy to all goings on. However, for the most part, 2012 was, in all probability a re-mix of 2008 and given Republican disdain for Mr. Obama, while the plot was revealed about the treasonous gathering in the former year, it stands to reason the same actors were probably involved from the inception in 2008.

FREDERICK MONDERSON

Description on the Cornice of Union Station.

Now, since it was Mr. Obama's responsibility to move the nation forward and he was being sabotaged at every turn by a predetermined agenda, some have argued was racially motivated, he had to take matters in hand and issue Executive Decisions whenever he saw the need, since Congress adopted a sloth approach to its responsibilities. Naturally, we must consider the considerable efforts to make Mr. Obama's Presidency a failure and he was still able to effectuate and manage significant change across the nation's social and economic as well as its demographic landscape, all in the interest of the American people. Equally, keeping his eyes on the prize, he wound down two wars, effectively wounded the Al Qaeda movement, contained the war on terror, nullified the Somali Pirates and changed the world's perception of America. All the while Wall Street and the Dow nearly tripled as compared to when he took office. Unemployment was seriously reduced, and across the significant barometers of social progress, the President was able to move the nation forward. Some of this was achieved through the use of Executive Orders.

OBAMA THE JOURNEY COMPLETED - NEVER PROMISED A ROSE GARDEN

An Executive Order is generally issued when the Executive Officer, a President or Governor, is hindered by some opponent and so orders the action commenced. In the case of President Obama, whose appointments to fill important posts, judicial and otherwise administrative, which have remained unfilled because of the Republican controlled House of Representatives and their potential to block other than an "up and down" vote, Mr. Obama issued such orders of appointment when Congress was not in session. Generally, such appointments only last until the legislative body returns. An assumption would hold, once in the position, the returning legislative body would confirm such. Reason may prove this to be the case. However, as in the case of President Obama and the virulence of the Republicans nit-picking along the way, the struggle to acquire one victory, after so many defeats, has been non-stop.

Ralph C. Chandler and Jack C. Plano in *The Public Administration Dictionary* (New York: John Wiley and Sons, 1982: 249-250) define an Executive Order as: "A formal and legally binding presidential policy directive to be followed by members of the executive branch of the federal government. An executive order is an instrument used by the President of the United States to exercise the limited and delegated authority of the executive branch. There is no statute that defines the term 'executive order.'" Despite their obstructionism, and many believe it is because of race, "Republicans behave as if Mr.

FREDERICK MONDERSON

Obama invented" the "Executive Order." The earliest executive orders were neither numbered nor issued in any standard format, and there was no requirement for official notice or publication. As the mechanism became more formalized, however, a chronological numbering system came into use in 1907, and all earlier orders were assigned numbers. The Federal Register Act of 1935 required all executive orders of general interest to be published in the Federal Register, with a later act requiring publication of all executive orders." In fact, it was a Republican who "invented the Executive Order."

OBAMA THE JOURNEY COMPLETED - NEVER PROMISED A ROSE GARDEN

FREDERICK MONDERSON

Accordingly, Chandler and Plano (1982: 250) explained: "Executive Order Number 1 was issued by President Abraham Lincoln in 1862, it concerned the establishment of military courts in Louisiana. Since that time, executive orders have been used in a wide range of policy areas, depending on the president's personal values and his perception of his constitutional responsibilities. Beginning in the early 1960s, executive orders were used more and more in controversial social and political policy areas. They were frequently issued as a result of recommendations made by task forces and special committees, which were first introduced by the Kennedy administration as new policy-making groups. Once a president has decided to make an authoritative policy statement, there are a number of actors involved in the decision to use an executive order, as opposed to some other means of proclamation."

"No other country in the world does what we do. On every issue, the world turns to us, not simply because of the size of our economy or our military might - but because of the ideals we stand for, and the burdens we bear to advance them." **Barack Obama**

OBAMA THE JOURNEY COMPLETED - NEVER PROMISED A ROSE GARDEN

16. FIGHTING OBAMA
"Tooth and Nail"
By
Dr. Fred Monderson

In response to President Obama's decision to use Executive Action on Immigration reform because of Republican failure to act, Speaker Boehner publicly announced his intent to fight Mr. Obama "tooth and nail!" So what is new! Mr. Boehner and his Republican colleagues have fought Mr. Obama "tooth and nail" from day one! They blocked his every legislative initiative, encouraged a climate of hatred and disrespect to be heaped upon this President of the United States and not a Republican leader has had the "testicular fortitude" to say No!

FREDERICK MONDERSON

Mr. Obama is a citizen and a man! However, he is not only a citizen but he is an African, American, hero! No one should forget it!

"That's the good thing about being President; I can do whatever I want." **Barack Obama**

Everyone is aware, Mr. Boehner and Republican leadership and rank and file as well as their "A to Z Associates" have fought Mr. Obama and his policies not so much because of ideological political differences but because he is a Black Man! Such actions were predicated through national and political leadership, because Mr. Obama dared to unlock the Presidential chamber and reveal its secrets long accessible only to white men dating even anterior to the foundations of the Republic.

Description on the Cornice of Union Station.

It needs be emphasized, in all his pronouncements on controversial issues such as the use of Executive Action to bring about a policy decision, Mr. Obama has consistently emphasized his action will be within the legal power granted him. Yet, despite their refusal to act on this important issue, Republicans have falsely saber-rattle that the President is breaking the law and making his own laws, even functioning as an Imperial President. For example, the audacity of Rep. Michele Bachmann, in run-up to the 2012 election in which she

OBAMA THE JOURNEY COMPLETED - NEVER PROMISED A ROSE GARDEN

played-up a hypocritical line, "God told me to run;" even accused Mr. Obama of running "a gangster government" in Washington, D.C! Imagine this woman of questionable abilities among a litany of mediocre leaders who have distorted Mr. Obama's leadership, intent and patriotism, while simultaneously underestimating his resolve as a giant resisting, in fact, out-foxing, his Lilliputian opponents perennially disposed to mischievous behaviors as well as creating a climate for others to act threatening and disrespectfully.

Perhaps Mr. Boehner is the only one not aware or refuses to recognize how many of his allies, intentional or otherwise, have been fighting Mr. Obama "tooth and nail" from day one. If we discount John McCain, Sarah Palin, Mitt Romney, Eric Cantor, Jim DeMint, Allen West, Rick Santino, and of course Michelle Bachmann, not to mention "Joe the Plumber" and a "Tea Party Movement" born in a cauldron of racial hatred; then we can start with Mitch McConnell, newly elected Senate Majority Leader.

FREDERICK MONDERSON

Mr. McConnell's two greatest aspirations in life have been, first, "to make Barack Obama a one term president," in which he failed!

OBAMA THE JOURNEY COMPLETED - NEVER PROMISED A ROSE GARDEN

Second, even more longstanding, to become Senate Majority Leader in which he has since succeeded, but the question remains, can he become a true leader and effectively legislate in the interest of the broad masses of the American people or is he too tied to special interests who probably crafted his initial aspiration of undermining Mr. Obama's Presidency?

Given, Mr. Obama "cooked the small fry" listed above, if we begin with the "tooth and nail fight," we recall Mr. McConnell's original statement was not only deemed racist but his intent was later exposed as part of an insidious conspiracy to undermine Mr. Obama's legislative agenda and his Presidency. Given what happened after the 2009 election in January 2009 that was exposed after the 2012 election in *The New York Times* newspaper of October 6, 2013, and given Republican behavior as late as 2014, can Mr. McConnell see the "folly of his evil ways" and work to move the nation forward in cooperation with and under the President's umbrella in the interest of the broad masses of the American people. Then again, since leopards do not change their spots, and recalling the glare in Mr. McConnell's eyes after that meeting when he gave that now infamous "thumbs up" to his "handlers" or "fellow conspirators," silently indicating "I got that Nigger," can we expect a "conversion on the road to Damascus" for Mr. McConnell. However, we must never forget, Mr. Obama is the President and many should await his next "tell all" book!

Yet, despite the "tooth and nail" mantra as Republicans have fought Mr. Obama's legislative agenda; under threat of being sued; and impeached for doing his job; he can still boast Lilly Ledbetter, securing a settlement with Black farmers; despite absence of a Congressional jobs bill, infrastructure repairs and nearly 10 million private sector jobs created on his watch when previously the nation was losing some 500,000 to 800,000 jobs per month, this is remarkable progress. All this attests to the ineffectiveness of Republican obstructionism against a president conscious of his responsibilities and acutely aware of his place in American history as he scaled their obstructionist barriers. These accomplishments were not, however, in isolation for not only did Mr. Obama rescue the auto industry and redeem the integrity of this critical segment of the American economy but he did so against acute Republican obstruction. Bailing out banks and other financial institutions was a prudent and correct strategy that has enabled Wall Street to prosper whereby the DOW has tripled its overall value from the time of Mr. Obama's ascendency to the Presidency to today. An effective energy policy has enabled gas prices to drop to their lowest levels in more than a decade; and it should also not be missed that education initiatives such as recognizing the role of community colleges and funding such ventures is enormously futuristic; as well as, credit cards rates and college loans adjustments and incentives for parents to improve their educational skills combined with clean energy requirements and sound economic and financial regulatory policies in addition to environmental concerns, have all been a priority for Mr. Obama's Presidency.

Description on the Cornice of Union Station.

What more can be said about Mr. Obama's signature legislative accomplishment? It is an idea whose time has come because of the needs of a broad swath of the American populace in need of health care security. To recall, perceptively Mr. Obama saw the need, formulated a health care agenda, campaigned on it, have it withstand the tumultuous and acrimonious critical debate, was challenged in the United States Supreme Court twice and ruled upon favorably by this august body; yet, a Republican controlled House of Representatives voted more than four dozen times to repeal the Affordable Care Act derisively called "Obamacare."

OBAMA THE JOURNEY COMPLETED - NEVER PROMISED A ROSE GARDEN

The American people should be very careful of what it asks for in 2014 as they may get it over the next two years. Knowing full well Republican objection to the **Affordable Care Act**; yet, Americans voted to give Republicans control of both Houses of Congress. Many believe this is a license to sabotage the health care act that has been helpful to so many people so far.

Two things can be noted here. As Paul Krugman has stated in "Obamacare Hits a Pothole," *The New York Times* Friday October 28, 2016, p. A 27: "Health reform had two big goals: to cover the uninsured and to rein in the overall growth of health care costs - to "bend the curve," in the jargon of health policy wonks. Sure enough, the fraction of Americans without health insurance has declined to its lowest level in history, while health costs growth has plunged: Since Obamacare passed Congress, private insurance costs have risen less than half as fast as they did in the previous decade, and Medicare costs have risen less than a fifth as fast." Even further, "The way the exchanges were supposed to work was that both healthy and less-healthy people would sign up, providing insurers with a good mix of risks that let them offer reasonably priced policies. Broad participation was supposed to happen because the law requires everyone to have insurance - the "mandate" - or face a penalty. Buying insurance was supposed to remain affordable because the law provides subsidies for middle- and lower-income families, ensuring that health costs don't become too large a share of income." Without question many states under Republican governorship refused to participate, all in cooperation with the "Stop Obama" mandate, very likely dating back to Mr. McConnell himself. This has been the "dropped anchor" as Mr. Obama sailed the ship of state. So Mr. Krugman asks, "Can the current problem be fixed? He responds as follows:

"As a technical matter the answer is clearly yes. Strengthen the mandate; expand the subsidies; close the loopholes that have allowed some insurers to bypass the exchanges; take a more active role in setting standards and reaching out to families to make them aware of their options. Some states are doing much better than others, and it wouldn't take a lot of money to expand best practices to the nation as a whole. The trouble is that Congress would have to vote to spend that money. So unless Democrats manage to take the House (unlikely) or Republicans are willing to cooperate in the public interest (even more unlikely), the easy fix that's clearly in sight will have to wait for a while. So, is the latest health care news disappointing? Yes. Is it catastrophic? Not at all." Hence, it's all about an "Obama win!"

Given all that is said, Mr. Obama was elected President and he has the authority of a Veto. We have to wait and see how genuinely American Republicans act or whether they are unalterably tied to Mr. McConnell's initial aspiration, long a Republican goal.

"I believe marriage is between a man and a woman. I am not in favor of gay marriage. But when you start playing around with constitutions, just to prohibit somebody who cares about another person, it just seems to me that's not what America's about. Usually, our constitutions expand liberties, they don't contract them."

"I miss Saturday morning, rolling out of bed, not shaving, getting into my car with my girls, driving to the supermarket, squeezing the fruit, getting my car washed, taking walks." **Barack Obama**

OBAMA THE JOURNEY COMPLETED - NEVER PROMISED A ROSE GARDEN

17.   OBAMA AND COMPROMISE
By
Dr. Fred Monderson

Throughout the election campaign, among Senator Obama's strong suits was the ability to build consensus and with this compromise could be considered a twin attribute. Upon assuming the Presidency, Mr. Obama set about proposing and pushing legislation in Congress and this involved compromise in all such fights. For example, within a relatively short time after his inauguration President Obama submitted an 800 Billion plus spending bill to Congress. With the democratic majority in the House of Representatives the measure was generally passed without one supporting Republican vote. In the

FREDERICK MONDERSON

Senate, on the other hand, with some compromise three Republicans crossed the aisle to join the Democrats and passed a bill of a lesser sum of 785 Billion. In many other situations in his relation with Congress, President Obama compromised to get his way. For instance, as the Chief Legislator, the President would submit the broad framework of a piece of legislation and ask Congress to flush it out with the necessary compromises to create a bill he could sign when it reaches his desk.

All this notwithstanding, the notion of compromise has had a tremendous history in American politics, stemming from the early days of the Republic; however, it remained a viable alternative to grid-lock on Capitol Hill. Technically, the year 1787 has had more compromises than any other year in American history and government, ever.

The first significant compromise in 1787 had to do with the slave trade. In England, focus on abolition of the trade became magnified in the Somerset Case pursued by Granville Sharpe in which Chief Justice Mansfield ultimately ruled in the interest of "positive law" that "English soil is too sacred to permit slavery." This came in response

OBAMA THE JOURNEY COMPLETED - NEVER PROMISED A ROSE GARDEN

to British plantation owners practice of taking their slaves from the West Indies back to England to live more socially elevated in their homeland. By 1787, thanks to the work of abolitionists Clarkson, Buxton, Sharpe and others petitioned Parliament through resolutions to outlaw the slave trade. As the new American nation began wrestling with its political dynamics in formulating the United States Constitution, this foreign activism spread to America and the slave trade became a national issue. That is, 'What to do about it?'

Jack C. Plano and Milton Greenberg's *The American Political Dictionary* New York: Holt, Rinehart, and Winston, Inc., (1962) (1989: 29) offers commentary on the commerce and slave trade compromise generally considered: "An agreement reached at the Constitutional Convention of 1787, giving the national government power to regulate foreign commerce, requiring the consent of two-thirds of the Senate to treaties, and prohibiting the national government from taxing exports or interfering with the slave trade until 1808." The significance of this is stated as: "A substantial number of people opposed ratification, but strong opposition to the Constitution rapidly dwindled after its adoption. The Anti-federalist group, however, became the supporters of Thomas Jefferson, whose views on the nature of the Union, as distinguished from those of Alexander Hamilton and other Federalists, continue to be influential and controversial in American politics today. The Anti-federalists were also known as "Democratic Republicans" and, in time, evolved into the "Democratic Party."

FREDERICK MONDERSON

OBAMA THE JOURNEY COMPLETED - NEVER PROMISED A ROSE GARDEN

"We have an obligation and a responsibility to be investing in our students and our schools. We must make sure that people who have the grades, the desire and the will, but not the money, can still get the best education possible." **Barack Obama**

18.   OBAMA - THINKER!
By
Dr. Fred Monderson

From the time of his ascendency as a senator then candidate for the Presidency, Barack Obama has been victimized through criticisms of his inexperience, inaction and failing to follow through. In the 2008 campaign, first the Democratic challenger Hillary Clinton coined the inexperience label. She claimed Mr. Obama's foreign policy inexperience makes him unable to answer the "3:00 AM Phone Call;" and as such, places the nation's safety in jeopardy through inexperienced leadership.

"We have an obligation and a responsibility to be investing in our students and our schools. We must make sure that people who have the grades, the desire and the will, but not the money, can still get the best education possible." **Barack Obama**

OBAMA THE JOURNEY COMPLETED - NEVER PROMISED A ROSE GARDEN

One of the drawbacks of the Democratic process, the "weaknesses" party challenges raise and emphasize are the exact issues the opposing party candidates amplify in the next round of the campaign. This conundrum faced Senator Obama as his fellow senator and Republican opponent in the 2008 presidential campaign John McCain chose to emphasize in his strategy which turned out to be a losing proposition. The cumulative result of these many failed strategies was recognition of Barack Obama as possessing a tremendous work ethic but most important he being a clear-headed thinker who gets results.

As the onslaught against Mr. Obama unfolded in the 2008 campaign with the Pied Piper "Joe the Plumber" playing a prominent role, a growing number of disaffected Americans hoodwinked by the emerging "Tea Party Movement," we now know was "funded surreptitiously by big money interests;" players such as "Lipstick on a Pig" Sarah Palin galvanized by "Maverick" shibboleths whipped crowds assembled at meetings into "over the top frenzies" that targeted Mr. Obama in unkind caricature.

FREDERICK MONDERSON

"We need to steer clear of this poverty of ambition, where people want to drive fancy cars and wear nice clothes and live in nice apartments but don't want to work hard to accomplish these things. Everyone should try to realize their full potential." **Barack Obama**

19. "OBAMA, DOIN' TOO MUCH!"
By
Dr. Fred Monderson

There is an old cliché, "Damn if you do, and Damn if you don't" and the attitude of this 'wide brush' painting has emerged as a consistent strategy critics of President Obama have employed to seedling his path with negativity as he wrestles with the myriad of problems facing the nation. Claiming that Obama is 'Doin' too much,' his critics, principally Republicans, have tried to box him in by having to defend his good work, but this approach has not been effective because these adversaries have grossly underestimated their opponent. This is evident in the 'Thumpin' he administered his opponents in the recent Presidential election and the program he instituted to rescue the nation, from the quagmire 8 years of Republican Administration rule created.

"I'm no longer just a candidate. I'm the President. I know what it means to send young Americans into battle, for I have held in my arms the mothers and fathers of those who didn't return. I've shared the pain of families who've lost their homes, and the frustration of workers who've lost their jobs." **Barack Obama**

Hitting the ground running, a number of President Bush Executive Orders were, with great speed, overturned. In his effort to reduce the nation's dependence on foreign sources of energy he encouraged the development of wind energy. He supported development of hybrid electric cars with advanced batteries, while insisting that carmakers reduce emissions and has favored experimenting with clean coal energy. Staying busy, the President appointed a number of "Czars," such as "Urban," "Car" and "Stimulus" designed to keep track of how the region, industry or money is doing.

OBAMA THE JOURNEY COMPLETED - NEVER PROMISED A ROSE GARDEN

Bureau of Engraving and Printing "the Money" Building.

Underestimating the intellectual brilliance of Barack Obama and the quintessence of "team Obama," caused the Republicans the election. Even more important, as the President ignores his critics, he goes about pursuing his program underscoring his success and the failure of his opponents' strategy. This is reflected in the changing realities and the American people's positive assessment of Obama and negative assessment of the Republican opposition.

The wonderful thing about President Barack Obama is that while he recognized his adversaries and their criticisms, he ignores them and goes about his business pulling new plans and ideas out of his symbolic "hat." Important to note, ignoring the opposition is a very potent remedy in dealing with all types, particularly problem people. There is an interesting story of "ignoring" told about His Excellency Haile Selassie, Emperor of Ethiopia, who came to America to attend some important state function in 1954, with the British Queen Elizabeth in attendance. In as much as he had been on the throne longer than the Queen, protocol dictated during the preliminary introduction into the social setting, Haile Selassie preceded the Queen. Naturally, within the social-racial constraints of pre-civil rights movement in American society, this protocol arrangement played well in the Black community.

In follow-up to the Emperor's visit, a Black newspaper sent an African-American reporter to Ethiopia to interview the king. Upon arrival at the Audience Hall, he thought he saw a regal figure sitting on an elevated throne at the rear of a very large room. On entering he was informed of protocol for proceeding. He was to stop, kneel at each of three cushions placed one before the other, as he got closer to the throne area. In his eagerness and perhaps American arrogance, he simply kicked these aside and approached the king. There was still some distance between him and the throne, but there was a figure seated there. Yet, as the reporter tried to speak to the person, he got no response. Puzzled, he was not sure if it was a statue or a real person because he could see no movement of the seemingly "cold figure." The next day there was a reception at the palace and the reporter, bent on getting his story, was there, so he "snaked" his way towards the monarch and forcefully reached to touch Selassie, only to realize he was entangled with a real person who seemed as "cold as a statue." Meanwhile, the king seemed to be looking for help from his assistants, as if to say, "Get this clown off of me." Point of moral, he got the Selassie stare, cold shoulder and silent treatment!

OBAMA THE JOURNEY COMPLETED - NEVER PROMISED A ROSE GARDEN

FREDERICK MONDERSON

Who knows if Barack Obama ever heard of this incident but when it comes to ignoring his critics and opponents, he does a very good imitation of Emperor Selassie as he Obama goes about his work of thinking, proposing and following through on programs and plans to carry out his mission.

Recently I met an elder, Mr. McPherson and asked him, "Sir, what do you think of this Obama thing?" He replied, "The President is doing a very good job. He doesn't want to get in a direct confrontation. They are criticizing him at every turn but he is not talking, ignoring them, just going about his business." Such an attitude, demeanor, is indicative of a very confident man, but also one who understands the gravity of the task before him. I am reminded of something General George Patton said sometime in 1944, before the invasion of Normandy. When many officers at a meeting seemed too self-assured and were underestimating the Germans, General Patton cautioned that despite what appeared an impending victory, "We could still lose the war!" This is the same way with President Obama, who feels he has no time for idle-chatter and counter-productive speculation and negative vibes but must keep working. He realizes "We're not out of the woods as yet." Despite the positive showing of the economy, Wall Street rebounding, housing starts are up despite the foreclosure situation, efforts to get stimulus shovel ready projects are proceeding, plans to assist the auto industry, get the financial system past the bank stress-test and get credit flowing, and all the rapid infusions of capital into the financial system that may not give the expected rapid returns; still, there is much more work that would need to be done. Therefore, Obama is keeping his pedal to the metal!

OBAMA THE JOURNEY COMPLETED - NEVER PROMISED A ROSE GARDEN

Perhaps the thing that sets the Obama Administration apart from that of the Republicans in Congress and their allies in the print and electronic media, is the fact he is probably smarter than them and this may be the reason he defeated them in the last election. In addition, because he is serious and deeply concerned about the American condition and takes his job seriously, he is not about letting up. This attitude underscores the nature of the man, his brilliance and perhaps with a view to the future, that is, his re-election and how history will record his efforts at this critical time in American history. Good luck Barack, you're not 'doing too much,' perhaps only you can see there needs to be more done. After all, many still do not realize the gravity of the situation you inherited.

FREDERICK MONDERSON

"I just miss - I miss being anonymous." **Barack Obama**

OBAMA THE JOURNEY COMPLETED - NEVER PROMISED A ROSE GARDEN

20.   OBAMA AS EDUCATION REFORMER
By
Dr. Fred Monderson

Like so many of his creative approaches to problems in the American social and economic body-politic system, President Obama now turns to address the problem of education, an important issue upon which the future of America will depend heavily. Significantly these issues will bear on the grand design to not simply rescue America from the quagmire it has steadily slipped into over the last decades, but keep to keep the nation competitive in a fast changing world. Throughout his campaign Mr. Obama assessed the state of education, viz., instruction, facilities, personnel, strategies, remuneration, creativity, vision and the role and responsibility of government to provide the funding and moral support to elevate American education to a pinnacle that serves as a beacon and pace setter to empower tomorrow's leaders and the nation's future research and development. This way, in the partnership of educational empowerment America must remain a trendsetter in science, medicine, technology, social studies and behavioral mannerisms. However, while this ideal is attainable, it is far from current and in order that this becomes a reality there must be a concerted and meaningful partnership between government, educators, administrators, parents and students and the private sector which benefits the most must play its part. Notwithstanding, in order to achieve the best results, the political drama surrounding education must play itself out in the best interest of American education in general and the students' well-being and progress in particular. Again, this is why the public sector must play its part in encouragement, incentives, equipment and remuneration, for, after all, this sector is the principal beneficiary of American education.

"We welcome the scrutiny of the world - because what you see in America is a country that has steadily worked to address our problems and make our union more perfect." **Barack Obama**

Yet, while these ideals are worthy aspirations, the reality is that American education is in crisis for a number of reasons, primarily owing to the notion of social equality and adequate accessing as well as infusing the broad funding streams designed to encourage achievement and creativity from the many who could better the lot of all. Because America is a great and expansive nation where the seedlings of great minds are first nurtured, then the requisite support ought to be given without emphasis on favoring one group or region over another. A very good example to underscore an analogy with regional financial disbursement can be drawn from the role and make-up of the military. Whether in peace or war, America draws its citizen soldiers equally from every city and state in the nation to serve in every branch of its services. This they do with distinction in performance of duty, sometimes giving life and limb. Equally too, whether the national Guard of the Army in general are first to respond to emergencies or catastrophes at home or abroad, viz., Katrina in Louisiana, Earthquake in Haiti or Ebola in West Africa; in fact, anywhere in the states, even being mobilized for combat overseas.

OBAMA THE JOURNEY COMPLETED - NEVER PROMISED A ROSE GARDEN

Therefore, similarly that dedicated service and recruitment for defense of the Republic, consideration for educational support ought to be equal regardless of person or region. This seems to be the ideal Senator, now President Barack Obama, preached and steadily seeks to achieve in order to correct the deficiencies and set the nation on a path that elevates and sustains America as a leader in the multiplicity of engines that drive the progress of modern civilization.

The fact of the matter, for some, American education is in the doldrums in segments of the inner cities, some rural areas and particularly among minorities. The path to this dismal state of affairs is long, studded with moments of brilliance and gloom, and for African-Americans the progress of the earliest educational initiatives of the flow and ebb will hopefully be followed by more flow than ebb.

FREDERICK MONDERSON

"I know that campaigns can seem small, and even silly. Trivial things become big distractions. Serious issues become sound bites. And the truth gets buried under an avalanche of money and advertising. If you're sick of hearing me approve this message, believe me - so am I.
Barack Obama

OBAMA THE JOURNEY COMPLETED - NEVER PROMISED A ROSE GARDEN

21. OBAMA'S STIMULUS AND DANCE OF LEGISLATION
By
Dr. Fred Monderson

Hypothetically speaking, as Senator Barack Obama winds-down his election campaign, his wonderfully organized and creative mindset not only focused on the dramatic requirements of the final full-court press to the tape recognizing the calamitous state of the economy, he began looking ahead with a stimulus strategy. Much of this was imbedded in his platform pledges and probably on election night perhaps after a two-hour rest and self-congratulatory accolades, he began tinkering with the grand plan he envisioned for rescuing the economy based on the parameters he had already outlined.

The Garfield Memorial with the Capitol Building to the right.

OBAMA THE JOURNEY COMPLETED - NEVER PROMISED A ROSE GARDEN

George Washington's Memorial in all its Glory!

With his major objective accomplished, President-Elect Obama next began more frequent consultation with the economic team he had put together and been meeting with, while along the campaign trail he began planning his economic strategy, framing the parameters of his rescue plan. Now, the "Shadow economic advisers" emerged into full-public recognition to support and give credence to Mr. Obama's strategy to deal with the full-blown and daily realization of the rapidly deteriorating American economy burdened with rising unemployment, collapsing housing market, the Wall Street mess and perhaps all influencing the world economic down turn.   Therefore, his economic agenda, spelled out in the stimulus package was now being flushed out by a team headed by Paul Volker, former head of the Federal Reserve System. Meanwhile, as Obama counts down to Inauguration and assuming the mantle of the Presidency, the economic quagmire worsened and elements of the critical public began clamoring for President-Elect Obama to step in and stem the bleeding economy suffering from higher job loss, more people filing for unemployment benefits, more foreclosures, turmoil on Wall Street, bank closures, not to discount suicides as the easiest way out.

In addition, trouble began to brew overseas and in respect for **No. 43** all Mr. Obama would utter: "There's only one President at a time."

President Bush, on the other hand, now having fully grasped the reality of his place in history, could only nod in appreciation that, at least Mr. Obama still afforded him the opportunity to gracefully exit the stage he occupied over the last eight years. Therefore, and recognizing Obama was a class act, Mr. Bush resolved to give

OBAMA THE JOURNEY COMPLETED - NEVER PROMISED A ROSE GARDEN

unqualified support to the transition team of his successor to make it as smooth as possible, so number 44 would get a head start to clean-up the mess number 43 made as steward of the nation. Meanwhile, the "sour grapes Republican Congressional delegation" began closing ranks, planning to lower the boom on Obama when he comes around seeking bipartisanship "pushing his economic stimulus bill."

There are several types of Bills or laws presented to the House of Representatives or Senate for consideration and debate before it passes to the President to sign it to become a law. There are public and private bills and these require the President's signature. Then again there are Joint Resolutions, Concurrent Resolutions and Resolutions that do not require the President's signature.

FREDERICK MONDERSON

OBAMA THE JOURNEY COMPLETED - NEVER PROMISED A ROSE GARDEN

William A. McClenaghan's *American Government* describes a **Bill** as: "A proposed law; a public bill applies to the entire nation; a private bill applies only to certain people or places." A **Joint Resolution** is, "A proposal for some action that has the force of law when passed; usually deals with special circumstances or temporary matter." A **Concurrent Resolution** is, "A statement of position on an issue, adopted by the House and Senate acting jointly; does not have the force of law; does not require the President's signature." A **Resolution** is a "measure dealing with some matter in one House; does not have the force of law; does not require the President's signature."

A money bill, such as the stimulus bill is a different matter. Accordingly, Article 1, Section 7 of the Constitution states, "All Bills for raising Revenue shall originate in the House of Representatives; but the Senate may propose or concur with amendments as on the bills."

The Constitution clearly states money bills can also originate from the Executive Branch or the Legislature through the House of Representatives. At the time, no one fully realized the depth of the financial crisis facing the nation. That being so, President Obama came into office with his plan as the conceptual framework was envisioned by the economic minds he was able to muster during the transition period.

Flower bed before the Capitol Building.

"We want everybody to act like adults, quit playing games, realize that it's not just my way or the highway." **Barack Obama**

OBAMA THE JOURNEY COMPLETED - NEVER PROMISED A ROSE GARDEN

22.   WOMEN
By
Dr. Fred Monderson

Much ink has been spilled and debate words uttered about the role of women in politics and as citizens enjoying the social amenities of being half of the nation's population and electorate. Even more important with certainty at least, their role as significant in the Presidential election has been discussed at length and this has helped to make women and women's issues an important topic in the recently concluded Second Presidential Debate between President Barack Obama and former Governor of Massachusetts Mitt Romney in which it was reported, they were playing to the all-important and pivotal female vote. So much so, as every such event creates an earmark that becomes a subject of discussion long after, again as women issues lingered, these candidates got more post-debate publicity. Whereas in the first debate between these two men, observers and commentators gave Mr. Romney a "win" because President Obama seemed lethargic and unprepared. In the second much anticipated debate, the President "came to play," and by some accounts, trounced Mr. Romney. Many commentators confessed Mr. Obama had come prepared, was more energized, knowledgeable and on point! However, they viewed Mr. Romney somewhat opposite, even attributing his "failure" to handling the "woman's issue."

"People of Berlin - people of the world - this is our moment. This is our time." **Barack Obama**

In the debate, when confronted with a women's question, Mr. Romney reflected on his choice of staff upon being elected Governor of Massachusetts. His staff was all male, probably all white but without women. Seeking to correct this, he claims, he contacted women's groups saying "Can you find me qualified women to be part of my staff." In response, he claims, he was supplied with "binders of women." Within minutes, this utterance, "Binders" and "Women" went viral on the Internet where all manner of "Cartoonish" creations flooded the airwaves. Days later, this strange women recruitment description remained a TV and radio talk show topic even among late night comics. Seems this mishandling did not go well with women who had additional "women's issues" with Mr. Romney. Thus, with the election considered, "Too close to call," it became a wait and see situation to determine if this will hurt him.

Conversely, when Mr. Obama assumed the Presidency; in fact, in the Transition Period, he came with his team of qualified women. So much so, at the time Mr. Obama was compared to other Presidents who had women in their cabinet. Thus, with women in high profile roles in his cabinet, in support, advisory and decision making roles, Mr. Obama further appointed two women to the United States Supreme Court. He ended up appointing Susan Rice as United Nations Ambassador and Hillary Clinton as Secretary of State.

OBAMA THE JOURNEY COMPLETED - NEVER PROMISED A ROSE GARDEN

FREDERICK MONDERSON

Reflecting on the social challenges his mother faced as reported and the business ceiling that limited his grandmother's aspirations notwithstanding her professional ability to perform functions in her job in a bank; Mr. Obama championed the cause of women by passing the Lilly Ledbetter Fair Pay Act as the first legislative action of his new administration. As stated, recognizing a woman's place is on the Supreme Court, he appointed two to the prestigious judicial body which was in keeping with his inherent belief in the equality of the sexes. However, it could very well be that the President chose the two women, their professional standing notwithstanding, but also their sensitivity to the legal implications of *Roe v. Wade* and the threat that continuously hang over this important legislation that is so significant in terms of giving women a choice regarding their bodies!

As a family man with a loving wife, two beautiful daughters and a darling mother-in-law, some of his closest advisers and inner circle people, Mr. Obama could be considered a "women's man," not a womanizer, if you will pardon the pun!

OBAMA THE JOURNEY COMPLETED - NEVER PROMISED A ROSE GARDEN

Memorial to Nurses who served in Viet Nam, beside the Viet Nam Memorial.

Within the "Don't Ask, Don't Tell" conundrum women were also an issue since Lesbians and transgender individuals were also counted in this group. The President believed women should get contraception medication from their bosses and he spoke to this effect. In such situations as his insistence on hiring of teachers; his proposing that women go back to college to further their education; certainly recognizing their important roles in family health when he passed Health Care Reform; and their roles as head of families when he extended the nation's safety net through the support of food stamps; Mr. Obama has always been conscious of the significant role women play in the society and he has supported them without question. However, because of Republican predisposition to oppose the President, every issue he proposed, especially women's issues, from their narrow viewpoint, they have had to and did oppose his position. Nevertheless, he can certainly claim to have "stood up for women" in his administration because of their importance and to expect large chunks of their vote is not unreasonable!

FREDERICK MONDERSON

Elders have always said, "If you want to know about 'eight' ask 'seven' and 'nine' because they lived next door!" Despite the glossy picture Mitt Romney paints of himself as Governor of Massachusetts, we must give credence to the thoughts of Senator John Kerry, a lifelong resident of the state and Governor Deval Patrick especially because the latter moved into to the office Governor Romney vacated. Mr. Kerry lived through the Governor's term and Mr. Patrick was forced to clean up after Mr. Romney. Sadly, he often explained what a mess he inherited but the Romney machinery seemed to blunt this important message from "nine" and "seven" about "eight."

"The Internet didn't get invented on its own. Government research created the Internet so that all the companies could make money off the Internet. The point is, is that when we succeed, we succeed because of our individual initiative, but also because we do things together." **Barack Obama**

OBAMA THE JOURNEY COMPLETED - NEVER PROMISED A ROSE GARDEN

23.   PRESIDENT OBAMA AND AFFIRMATIVE ACTION
By
Dr. Fred Monderson

President Barack Obama faces the challenge posed by the need for Affirmative Action in an age when its critics argue "America has elected an African-American President and hence in a post-racial society there is no need for Affirmative Action." However, such a position is highly debatable, for many people use the spurious argument that African-Americans are the sole beneficiaries of Affirmative Action and in their circular argument that brings us back to the election of President Obama, they believe there is no longer such a need. Yet, Affirmative Action benefits, besides African-Americans, women, firefighters, physically challenged individuals, and even veterans. Equally too, in some respects, we can probably recognize both "Public" and "Private" affirmative action. That is, we know what "*De Jure*" Affirmative Action is; "*De Facto*" Affirmative Action refers to certain groups of immigrants arriving on these shores being "Set-up" by "their established organizations and societies" that gives them a step or two ahead of "Natives" who do not enjoy or seem entitled to this "Leg-up." Therefore, aiming at one particular group in a pernicious assault, really affects a greater population. Even more important, the group singled out, despite what is said is in greater need of Affirmative Action today given Blacks are the last hired and first fired; their pay grades or scale is less than that of whites; their rates of unemployment, especially among the young, are higher than those of whites; their color is a prime element for suspicious actions of racial profiling, questionable character and abilities; bank 'red-lining in Black communities;' housing discrimination; victims of police brutality and random violence in "Black on Black crime;" even their being relegated as prolific candidates for the Prison Industrial Complex; and these do not exhaust potential and perennial victimization African-Americans are subjects of. To fully understand the dynamics of the situation facing President Obama one should be acquainted with Affirmative Action's meaning, origins and relevance.

"Even when folks are hitting you over the head, you can't stop marching. Even when they're turning the hoses on you, you can't stop." **Barack Obama**

Jack C. Plano and Milton Greenberg in *The American Political Dictionary*, New York: Holt, Rinehart and Winston, Inc., (1989: 260-261) explain, Affirmative Action is: "A plan or program to remedy the effects of past discrimination in employment, education, or other activity and to prevent the recurrence. Various federal and state statutes require affirmative action to redress past discrimination against or promote the employment of racial or religious minorities, women, handicapped workers, disabled veterans, veterans of the Vietnam era, and to some extent, the aged. Affirmative Action usually involves a work-force utilization analysis, the establishment of goals and timetables to increase use of underrepresented classes of persons, explanation of methods to be used to eliminate discrimination, and establishment of administrative responsibility to implement the program.   Good faith and a positive effort to remedy past discrimination must also be shown.   Affirmative Action is to be distinguished from antidiscrimination or equal opportunity laws, which forbid unequal treatment rather than requiring positive corrective measures.   In 1978, the Supreme Court held that Affirmative Action programs are valid, but that explicit racial quotas are prohibited."

FREDERICK MONDERSON

Plano and Greenberg (1989: 273-274) further equates "Equal Rights with Affirmative Action" in describing it as: "The movement to equalize the rights of men and women. Traditionally in American law, women have not enjoyed the same rights as men, and this has manifested itself in many areas of American life, including property rights, education, and employment opportunities. State laws vary widely, although many are protective of women rather than directly discriminatory. Women's suffrage led to a gradual narrowing of legal differences, but with increasing intensity since the 1960s, an extensive body of new laws and administrative regulations, as well as court decisions, has provided protection against sex discrimination. In March 1972, Congress proposed to the states a constitutional amendment that provided that 'equality of rights under the law shall not be denied or abridged by the United States or any state on account of sex.' The seven-year time limit for ratification expired in March 1979 and Congress, in an unprecedented move, extended the deadline to June 1982. Still, the proposal failed to receive the thirty-eight state legislative approvals necessary for ratification." It would be interesting to know how many would be considered under Republican control at the time.

Classic "Scout team" in their "Rice Paddy Glory!"

Affirmative Action is also equal to the notion of "Comparable Worth" and it certainly benefitted the Women's Liberation Movement. Thus, Plano and Greenberg sees the significance of Equal Rights in that: "The concept of equal rights has had a dramatic impact upon American life, equal to, if not greater than, the impact of changing race relations. Many constitutional authorities believe that changes already brought about on behalf of women's rights as well as liberal application of equal protection of the law concepts diminish the need for an equal rights amendment. Others note that an amendment will give rise to a host of constitutional problems relating to the traditional roles of men and women. The equal rights movement achieved two major victories in the 1960s - the passage of the Equal Pay Act of 1963, which requires equal pay for men and women doing similar work, and the Civil Rights Act of 1964, which forbids discrimination against women in hiring and other personnel policies. An end to sex discrimination in education was ordered by Congress in 1972 and the Equal Credit Opportunity act was adopted in 1974. A 1978 enactment prohibits discrimination against pregnant women in any area of employment. Pension rights of widowed homemakers and of working mothers who temporarily leave jobs to raise families were put under protection in 1984. In 1986, the Supreme Court declared sexual harassment to be unlawful sexual discrimination under the Civil Rights Act of 1964."

Korean War Memorial featuring a company on patrol

"I don't oppose all wars. What I am opposed to is a dumb war. What I am opposed to is a rash war." **Barack Obama**

OBAMA THE JOURNEY COMPLETED - NEVER PROMISED A ROSE GARDEN

24. PRESIDENT OBAMA AND CONGRESS
By
Dr. Fred Monderson

From the earliest days of the Republic, Presidents have struggled in their relationship with Congress, for after all, the Legislative body holds the purse strings to the economic road map the President sketches and tries to implement. This relationship is dictated by a number of factors depending on whether his party is in the majority of the 435 member body of the House of Representatives or the 100 members of the Senate.   Whether he can persuade some members of the opposition to cross the "proverbial aisle" and support him or whether his "coat-tail effect" can help incumbents or new candidates get elected; and the extent to which he can endorse, campaign for or raise money for local candidates who can win their race for Congress and then support the president's agenda as its presented to the lawmaking body for passage, are all important probabilities the President can affect.   Even more, the President's relationship with Congress is much more complex than simply economic matters for policy, appointments, security concerns, deployment of troops for military action overseas, protection of the environment, wild-life refuges, civil rights enforcement and protection and promotion of the general welfare and more, are all affected by the President's relationship with Congress.

"I opposed the Defense of Marriage Act in 1996. It should be repealed and I will vote for its repeal on the Senate floor. I will also oppose any proposal to amend the U.S. Constitution to ban gays and lesbians from marrying." **Barack Obama**

As a Congressional "insider" and having been a member of the Senate, President Obama had become acutely aware especially of these "upper house" workings. As the nation's Chief Legislator he probably built-up friendships and working relationships with colleagues and instantly began exploiting this knowledge in proposing and moving his agenda through this body, In the House of Representatives, he depends on his majority or sometime minority leaders and in the experiences and abilities of Rahm Emanuel, his Chief of Staff, himself a former member who was very familiar with House workings.

The role of Congress as an important entity in the American governmental structure was born in controversy and shaped to be a complimentary, yet, counterweigh or force to help yet, be a check on the President or Executive branch, and as such becoming too powerful in the political equation.

OBAMA THE JOURNEY COMPLETED - NEVER PROMISED A ROSE GARDEN

"Korean War Memorial" featuring a company on patrol.

In the period between realizations the Articles of Confederation was an inadequate document to forge a United States of America and promulgation of the U.S. Constitution, the issue of representation became a serious contention. Small states were fearful that large states would dominate the government and they would lose their individual identity. As the delegates to the Constitutional Convention wrestled with the issue, the "Virginia Plan," the "New Jersey Plan" and finally the "Connecticut Compromise" emerged with the latter exerting more influence on the structure and function of American government that emerged after negotiations and essentially determining what role Congress would play as the new nation was launched.

FREDERICK MONDERSON

OBAMA THE JOURNEY COMPLETED - NEVER PROMISED A ROSE GARDEN

The "New Jersey Plan" offered by William Patterson, proposed a unicameral or single legislative body or house, devised to revise rather than replace the Articles of Confederation. Robert C. Bone in *American Government* (New York: Barnes and Noble, 1977: 16) has explained: "While it retained the Confederation's single vote for each state and supremacy of the legislative branch (which would elect a plural executive) the "New Jersey Plan" greatly strengthened the powers of Congress. Its acts were to become the 'supreme law' over all state laws; and its powers were to be expanded to impose taxes and regulate trade." The "Virginia Plan" by James Madison, on the other hand, proposed the "establishment of a national government 'consisting of a supreme Legislative, Judiciary, and Executive.' The lower house of the legislature, 'elected by the people of the several states,' was to choose the upper house. The Judiciary was to be chosen by the legislature as a whole, as was a 'national executive,' with the question of whether the executive was to be single or plural left open. Roger Sherman proposed the "Connecticut Compromise," Bone (1977: 16) notes, that "provided for a House of Representatives based on proportional representation with the slave population of any state counted as three-fifths of its actual number. In contrast, the Senate was to be composed of two members from each state, to be chosen by the state legislatures."

More of the Korean War Memorial featuring a company on patrol.

Sherman's contribution to the structure of American government went beyond this framework impacting in two significant ways more than two centuries later. Sherman framed the debate and status of the Black man by "elevating" him to "2/3 of a man" and for two centuries his social relations in the society has been influenced by this philosophic and human relations inequity. Perhaps, even more meaningful, has been the notion of "compromise" in government for when opposing forces have been entrenched in their positions, the notion of compromise has helped to break the grid-lock to get legislation or the issue under consideration moving in the interest of all.

OBAMA THE JOURNEY COMPLETED - NEVER PROMISED A ROSE GARDEN

A recent and good example of compromise is seen with President Obama's Stimulus Bill presented to Congress within weeks after his inauguration. The issue seemed divided along party ideological lines with the Republicans in both houses seemingly unalterably opposed to the President and the Democrats' position on the Bill. Yet, three "moderate" Republicans broke ranks and compromised their party's obdurate stance to vote with the President in this one. Thus, as happened countless times when "horns were locked" Sherman's "Compromise" idea has helped to break the gridlock and move the issue forward.

FREDERICK MONDERSON

"It is time to put in place tough, new common-sense rules of the road so that our financial market rewards drive and innovation, and punishes short-cuts and abuse." **BARACK OBAMA**, Address to Joint Session of Congress, Feb. 24, 2009

OBAMA THE JOURNEY COMPLETED - NEVER PROMISED A ROSE GARDEN

25. PRESIDENT OBAMA AND WAR POWERS
By
Dr. Fred Monderson

Throughout its history America has fought many wars from the colonial conflict knows as the French and Indian Wars, through the Revolutionary War for Independence to the current wars in Iraq and Afghanistan that President Barack Obama has inherited. Only Iraq and Afghanistan and Viet Nam have lasted long enough (excepting World War II) to involve more than one President to be commander. Franklin D. Roosevelt's lengthy tenure covered World War II and he died in 1945 to be succeeded by Harry Truman at the war's end. Viet Nam, on the other hand, following the French defeat at Dien Bien Phu in 1954, first involved President Dwight Eisenhower in the 1950s, then John F. Kennedy, his successor Lyndon B. Johnson, then Richard M. Nixon and his successor Gerald Ford who saw America's involvement in Viet Nam end in 1975. Afghanistan and Iraq were begun by President George Bush (No. 43) and inherited by Barack Obama (No. 44). In times of war the President's powers are tremendously expanded because the lives of Americans are placed in danger and as Commander-in-Chief, he holds some responsibility for the safety of all Americans, whether in combat, morally or otherwise.

"In a global economy where the most valuable skill you can sell is your knowledge, a good education is no longer just a pathway to opportunity - it is a pre-requisite." **BARACK OBAMA**, Address to Joint Session of Congress, Feb. 24, 2009

Inasmuch as the Constitution has determined the President is solely responsible for foreign policy matters and the Supreme Court has reinforced this legality; up until Viet Nam, the Commander-in-Chief was the principal force behind deployment of troops abroad and waging war. The **War Powers Resolution** has sought to curb this power of the President by establishing guidelines on how he could wage war.

However, the Constitution specifically gives Congress the powers to declare war and establish protocols; though day-to-day waging of conflict is the President's. Article I, Section 8, Sub-sections 11-16 of the Constitution provides guidelines for Congressional authority in this matter. Congress has the power: "To declare war, grant letters of marquee and reprisal, and make rules concerning capture on land and water; to raise and support armies, but no appropriation of money to that use shall be a longer term than two years; to provide and maintain a navy; to make rules for the government and regulation of the land and naval forces; to provide for calling forth the militia to execute the laws of the Union, suppress insurrections, and repel invasions; to provide for organizing, arming, and disciplining the militia, and for governing such part of them as may be employed in the service of the United States, reserving to the States respectively, the appointment of the officers, and the authority of training the militia according to the discipline prescribed by Congress."

OBAMA THE JOURNEY COMPLETED - NEVER PROMISED A ROSE GARDEN

FREDERICK MONDERSON

Plano and Greenberg (1989: 521) define War Powers as: "Although defense and war powers are subject to constitutional limitations in the same way as other powers, they have been stretched to their limits during serious crises.   Presidents Abraham Lincoln, Franklin Roosevelt, and Harry Truman regarded the war powers as a special and undefined category of powers that can be exercised whenever the security of the nation is threatened.   Congress, the public, and the courts have generally accepted the primacy of the President's role and his exercise of vast powers during time of war.   Under conditions of modern warfare, the war powers include control over the domestic economy as well as the military phases of the conflict."

OBAMA THE JOURNEY COMPLETED - NEVER PROMISED A ROSE GARDEN

Congressional authorization was not applied to the first two conflicts, the French and Indian Wars (1756-1763) and the Revolutionary War (1776-1783). The French and Indian Wars were waged under colonial administration. Irving L. Gordon in *American Studies*: *A Conceptual Approach* New York: AMSCO School Publications, Inc., (1975) (1980: 67) explained the change from initial friendliness to subsequent hostilities between the white settlers and Native Americans (Indians). He states: "In notable cases, the Indians showed friendship to the first white settlers. In Virginia, Massachusetts, and New York, the Indians provided the settlers with food and helped them survive the early difficult years. In Pennsylvania the Indians signed a treaty with William Penn who, although he held a land grant from the British Crown, insisted that the Indians be paid for their lands. With time, European settlers became more numerous; they began to cheat and mistreat the Indians and to pressure them for additional lands. In Massachusetts the preacher and social reformer Roger Williams condemned colonial seizures of land without paying the Indians and insisted that the Indians, not the British Crown, were the rightful owners. Along the North Atlantic Coast, settlers and Indians fought each other in numerous "Indian Wars" in which both sides committed atrocities and brutalities. The settlers, sometimes aided by Friendly Indians, proved victorious. They decimated the hostile Indians and drove out the remnants, usually westward toward and beyond the Appalachian Mountains."

FREDERICK MONDERSON

Still more of the Korean War Memorial featuring a company on patrol.

Requirements made on the colonists by British authorities led to events that precipitated the Revolutionary War for Independence. Events such as the Proclamation of 1763 following French and Indian Wars hostilities which reserved lands west of the Appalachians for Native Americans, prohibiting settlements there and insisting settlers in these lands remove, began an activism that ultimately led to the Declaration of Independence (1776) and Revolutionary War (1776-1783), at the end of which the new nation was born. The governing council that prosecuted the war elected General George Washington, of "Fort Necessity" fame, who through trial and error and setback and success was able to defeat the British and assure the new nation's republic beginnings. A body of wise men crafted the United States Constitution that gave Congress and the President Powers to protect the nation from threats of a military nature.

OBAMA THE JOURNEY COMPLETED - NEVER PROMISED A ROSE GARDEN

FREDERICK MONDERSON

The next significant military engagement was the "War of 1812" waged against the British whose navy harassed American maritime vessels at sea, boarding these vessels and "impressing" Americans into British naval service. President Sam Adams, it is thought, badly managed this engagement, that at conclusion of hostilities the British got the better hand. All except the "Battle of New Orleans" in January, 1815, where General Andrew Jackson administered a resounding defeat on British forces, unknowingly, days after the armistice had been signed. This was the only honorable outcome of the war reflecting favorably on the American psyche.

In an age when America was in the throes of internal improvements, African-American struggles for freedom, reform movements, southern sectional rebellion under threats of Nullification and abolitionism, "Manifest Destiny" pronouncements pushed American expansion westward coming into conflict with Native-Americans out west, settlers and Mexicans out of which the Texas revolt of 1836 emerged. A decade later in 1845 Texas was admitted to the Union and this generally led to war with Mexico. These were events that the Constitution did not make provisions for but the philosophy of expansionism drew America into the conflict that ensued and as Irving L. Gordon (1980: 76-77) explained: "The admission of Texas was resented by Mexico and helped bring about the Mexican War. The United States was victorious and in 1848 acquired California and the American Southwest - together called the Mexican Cession. In 1853 the United States purchased from Mexico a small strip of land, now part of southern New Mexico and southern Arizona. This strip of land, containing a railroad pass through the mountains to California, was known as the Gadsden Purchase."

OBAMA THE JOURNEY COMPLETED - NEVER PROMISED A ROSE GARDEN

Korean Officers in Washington, DC inspecting the Korean War Memorial.

Following the Lincoln-Douglas Debates culminating in the Election of 1860 that Abraham Lincoln won, Southern states withdrew from the Union. The South considered Lincoln hostile to the institution of slavery and South Carolina having challenged the national government as early as 1832 in the "Nullification" movement, issued an Ordinance of Secession dissolving the bonds of the Union. Six other nations joined this rebel state and upon outbreak of hostilities four other southern states joined in rebellion. Irving Gordon (1980: 298) in commenting on Causes of the Civil War noted: "historians have long disputed regarding the causes - especially the primary cause - of the Civil War. Some have insisted that the primary cause was slavery as a moral issue. Others have focused attention elsewhere: (a) on the Constitutional issue - do states have the right to secede or are we one nation indivisible, (b) on political developments - the South's realization that eventually the North and Western support would secure control of the central government, (c) on fanaticism by extremists of both sides and on blundering leadership, (d) on

267

differences in civilization between a static South dominated by a planter aristocracy and a dynamic North reflecting democratic values, and (e) on economic differences between the South and North."

With the fate of the nation hanging in the balance Abraham Lincoln emerged as the principal figure in the Civil War and his generals were fully behind him. Comparatively speaking, however Barack Obama's critics may view him, his generals are equally behind him fully committed because they understand the issues, not the way politicians vying for the same seat often prognosticate.

OBAMA THE JOURNEY COMPLETED - NEVER PROMISED A ROSE GARDEN

The next significant military engagement was the War with Spain called the Spanish American War of 1898. Historians generally seek causes to all wars and in an age when the Industrial Revolution was sweeping America; the Close of the frontier now fully populated; and American Nationalism, these developments pushed the nation to further expansion and creation of an empire beyond its borders. This outward interest led to war with Spain as reflected in a number of engagements. We see the challenges and utilization of American presidential authority in World War I, World War II, Korea, Viet Nam, Grenada, Gulf War I, Iraq and Afghanistan and the challenges posed today by **ISIL (ISIS)** in Iraq as well as the complex situation that continues to build. This state of affairs has come to include Yemen, Somalia, Libya, and the emerging threats posed by Cody's "Army of God" in Uganda/Central Africa and Boko Haram in Nigeria. All these factors indicate the President must meet them being aware of possible Republican "back-stabbing." Nevertheless, as the Africans say, "the struggle continues."

"The answers to our problems don't lie beyond our reach. They exist in our laboratories and universities; in our fields and our factories; in

OBAMA THE JOURNEY COMPLETED - NEVER PROMISED A ROSE GARDEN

the imaginations of our entrepreneurs and the pride of the hardest-working people on Earth. Those qualities that have made America the greatest force of progress and prosperity in human history we still possess in ample measure." **BARACK OBAMA**, Address to Joint Session of Congress, Feb. 24, 2009

A classic example of Ionic capital colonnade.

FREDERICK MONDERSON

26. THE PRESIDENTS AND SLAVERY
By
Dr. Fred Monderson

It is amazing how significant events in the African-American experience seem to unfold within the term of certain Presidents' tenure that whether positively or negatively, conveys the true nature of various actors' beliefs and practices in the social, political, legal and cultural history of this nation. In the Kennedy and Johnson years, George Wallace voiced: "Segregation today, Segregation tomorrow, Segregation forever!" However, as the Civil Rights Movement escalated with pressures mounting on all sides, the true nature of racist obstructionism and callousness manifested. The will of the people, marshaled albeit with blood, sweat and tears in the street, retired those fossilerious persons and their beliefs for the most part to museum displays as curios of how we really were! During the Reagan Administration years; some say extremely right wing; artists and

OBAMA THE JOURNEY COMPLETED - NEVER PROMISED A ROSE GARDEN

activists led by Stevie Wonder mounted an unrelenting campaign to honor Dr. Martin Luther King, Jr., with a national holiday and whether reluctantly or not, President Reagan signed the bill into law to Make Dr. King's birthday, January 16 or the third Monday of the month, a national federal holiday. Now, the first African-American President Barack Obama has been elected, the United States Senate has reportedly passed a resolution apologizing for the nation's involvement in the institution of slavery that wrecked so much psycho-social trauma on the African persona enslaved in America. However, the deep lacerations into the enslaved African's psyche, his social and spiritual well-being has been so sever, the effects of discrimination and racism still manifests throughout the society work.

"I opposed the Defense of Marriage Act in 1996. It should be repealed and I will vote for its repeal on the Senate floor. I will also oppose any proposal to amend the U.S. Constitution to ban gays and lesbians from marrying." **Barack Obama**

FREDERICK MONDERSON

From the time of George Washington, presidents never made serious attempts to challenge the institution of slavery in its multi-dynamic functionality until, "The Program Smith got out of control," Abe Lincoln had to step-in. Fact is; we know so much of the economic benefits derived from a system in which the inhuman treatment, the emotional and physical scarification of both oppressed and oppressor not much thought has gone into the long term psychological impairment visited upon the same oppressed and oppressor. Even more, fact is, while the oppressed further swelters under the legacy of the institution of slavery, as represented in the psychological suffering transmitted in the affected gene pool but more particularly manifested in slavery's offspring institutional racism, more needs be done to

OBAMA THE JOURNEY COMPLETED - NEVER PROMISED A ROSE GARDEN

address this pathology. The perception that Black skin must be subject to the same unconscionable treatment from empowered Black Codes slave-catchers turned policemen who meet out brutality against Blacks in a shoot first then claim such actions were under claims of being fearful for one's life does not sell-well. We know a policeman's job is a dangerous one! Still, many sign up to be cops.

Embellishing the Korean War Memorial.

A policeman is trained, perhaps several times over a career. Pay, hours, vacation and retirement packages are all wonderful. He is given a pistol, a vest, a car with direct links with headquarters, as well as a partner with an enormous back-up potential. No doubt many policemen do a terrific job, but those who shoot first seem to manifest that ante-bellum security mentality of the same uncontrolled anger of the slave practitioner mentality and the underlings who enforce such.

"I've got a pen and I've got a phone - and I can use that pen to sign executive orders and take executive actions and administrative actions that move the ball forward." **Barack Obama**

FREDERICK MONDERSON

27. VISIONARIES AND HIIPPOCRITES
By
Dr. Fred Monderson

An old truism dictates "Where you stand is where you sit and where you sit is where you stand" which means since the "Tea Party" and Republicans are "married," and have progressed as the "Party of No," they must be characterized as being unpatriotic since they are single-mindedly focused on "the one not the ninety-nine percent" of Americans. As such, their ranks can be perceived as bloated by not simply visionaries and hypocrites but also opportunists. This has become clearly evident as the "winds of change" have begun to sweep across the nation and philosophically speaking "if it ain't tied down" it will be blown away. More correctly, as the winds blow away the smoke obfuscated by the political rhetoric of the last few years, the "king is really naked" except for the one per cent Band-Aid that covers the American special interest person. But, like old time wisdom has always held, "You can fool some of the people some of the time, but you can't fool all the people all the time," Barack Obama continues to execute the people's business as the oath of office dictated from Day One and no one will stop him from "this appointed task."

OBAMA THE JOURNEY COMPLETED - NEVER PROMISED A ROSE GARDEN

"Tonight, we gather to affirm the greatness of our nation - not because of the height of our skyscrapers, or the power of our military, or the size of our economy. Our pride is based on a very simple premise, summed up in a declaration made over two hundred years ago."
Barack Obama

No matter what has been said by whomever, Herman Cain, Et. Al. American history has been so inextricably intertwined, and "until justice rolls down like a mighty stream," all this has to be viewed from the prism of black and white. Not that white is loyal and black disloyal, all are in agreement; for while the general unemployment rate is 9.1 percent, black unemployment is 16 percent. Today white unemployment is 5 percent, yet Black unemployment is 10 percent. If you count black youth unemployment heading somewhere towards 40-50 percent, it asks the question "Why is this so?"

While some motorists and pedestrians even shoppers have been stopped and questioned while "driving, walking or shopping black," no motorist, pedestrian or shopper has been stopped while being similarly white. That is not to say there are no particularly ethnic perpetrators of criminal behavior for such persons are both black and white. But, who could countenance, criminal behavior whether from black or white criminals? Their victims can be optimistic or premeditated. Whatever, they are all victims of criminal behaviors.

In a recent Republican debate the question was raised about homosexual rights to which, one of the candidates answered and the audience responded in a hearty cheer. Another question to Texas Governor Rick Perry about the several hundred persons executed by that state to which Mr. Perry responded, "The people of Texas know the meaning of justice!" And, so they sent Ted Cruz to the United States Senate! The audience not simply cheered the man, even his answer, but especially the execution of so many people! Are we to believe Texas is such a violent state that it can foster such criminal behavior resulting in such drastic retribution? The world wants to know, were any of those executed innocent? The New York *Daily News*, Sunday October 9, 2011, reported on the death penalty and identified several persons, black and white, exonerated thanks to the new science of evidence examination. One person executed was deemed innocent but too late to save him. Another inmate, Troy Davis, even as he lay on the executioner's gurney, as a final act of penitence, confessed to the family "I did not kill your loved one!" Thus, many people believe the death penalty should be outlawed because it is not a deterrent to criminal behavior but does show the state demanding supposedly "an eye for an eye."

OBAMA THE JOURNEY COMPLETED - NEVER PROMISED A ROSE GARDEN

The great western novelist Louis Lamour painted a wonderful picture of Texas as an upstanding state, its people hardy but just, and the Sackets, a family of noble principles, who, when members had gone afar, confronted injustice and caught in a stand-off in the "old west," word would go out, a Sacket was hold-up against unsavory characters, send help and those "Noble Texans" would come to the rescue like the cavalry! However, in the movie, *The Great Debaters*, Denzel Washington stars as a Professor teaching young Wiley College students how to debate during the 1930s Depression era. One, actually two, episodes raise serious concerns.

FREDERICK MONDERSON

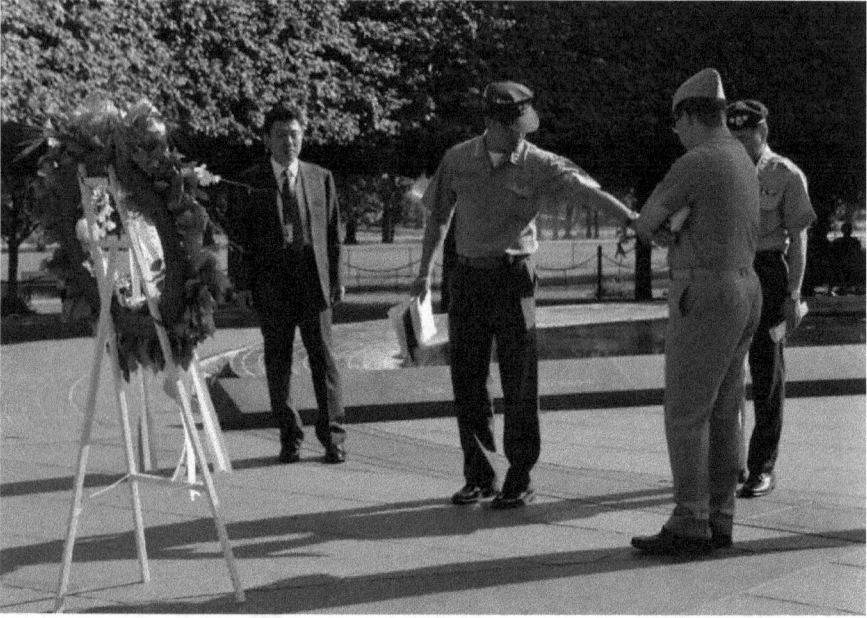

Korean Officers inspecting the Korean War Memorial.

In the first of these, the lead actor and three students, two males and a female are returning home one night. They come upon a scene, a roast, not a fish fry, nor a Marshmallow, but a "Nigger roast." That is, a Black man, hung and literally or actually being roasted on a fire surrounded by a screaming mob from which they were lucky to escape but that image of "Justice" could not be erased!

After a successful debate run, little Wiley College was invited to debate the powerful Harvard University debating team. "In trouble with the law" their coach could not chaperone and so the youngsters were on their own. The entire college and everyone in barbershops and homes listened to the radio as events unfolded debating the question "Whether unjust laws should be obeyed!" In climax, young Farmer brought the House down, when he flourished, "In Texas they lynch Niggers! No one was arrested; still we tried to peacefully protest."

Ida Wells used a white man's description of events to highlight one aspect of "Texas justice" and identified who came out and what impact events of "vigilante justice" had on those in attendance. The quote states: "The Negro rolled and tossed out of the mass, only to be pushed back by the people nearest hm. He tossed out again, and was roped and pulled back. Hundreds of people turned away, but the vast crowd still looked calmly on. People were here from every part of this section. They came from Dallas, Fort Worth, Herman, Denson, Bonham, Texarkana, Fort Smith, Arkansas and a party of fifteen came from Hempstead County, Arkansas, where he was captured. Every train that came in was loaded to its utmost capacity, and there were demands at many points for special trains to bring the people here to see the unparalleled punishment for an unparalleled crime. When the news of the burning went over the county like wildfire, at every country town anvil boomed forth the announcement."

In *The Black Book* by Harris, Levitt, Furman and Smith (1974), a picture on page 58 shows a Black man roasting on a bed of fire with dozens of well-dressed men gleeing over the ghastly scene. It is remindful of a somewhat similar image in the movie **Judge Dred** where Stallone cautions a young recruit about some men "pig-roasting a human" with claims they were going to feast on the victim. Also, on page 55-four Black men were hanging from a tree in evidence with a caption by the African-American poet Langston Hughes: "I've been a victim, the Belgians cut off my hand in the Congo, they lynched me in Texas."

When the issue surfaced about "Nigger Head Mountain" on Governor Rick Perry's farm, the media was quick to quote him as saying something to the effect, "In 1984 my father painted over the sign." The news reported, however, the sign was there while he was a State Senator, Commissioner and even Governor. A few months ago the news documentary "60 Minutes" did an episode about the murder of a Civil Rights activist in Mississippi. According to the FBI investigator there were 100 unsolved Civil Rights murders. The one they were pursuing revealed the killer was alive but no one was talking except the family of the murdered man. Nonetheless, an even more chilling revelation in the Documentary stated in essence, in the age of lynching of blacks, anyone who wanted to run for office had to be an active member of one of the terror groups, viz., Ku Klux Klan, Knights of the White Camellia, Red Shirts, etc., or had to espouse their views. Significantly, if any white man wanted to be important during those times he had to be associated with or essentially in support of lynching of Blacks! Thus, paint over is not the issue. The really important issue actually is how many "Nigger heads Rolled" on "Niggerhead Mountain," or how many blacks were lynched there and across Texas in that classic age of "American terrorism?" Again, are we to believe the mountain is a memorial to some great Nigger those people wanted to honor? No it was a "Lynching farm!"

View of Lincoln Memorial from downstream of the "Reflecting Pool."

An even more gristly account of "Texas Justice" is given as an example in Gilbert Osofsky's *The Burden of Race*: A *Documentary History of Negro-White Relations in America* (Harper Torch Book (1961) 1968) in which the chapter "An Era of Hate and Violence,"

OBAMA THE JOURNEY COMPLETED - NEVER PROMISED A ROSE GARDEN

Section 3 "Rule by Violence" where the journalist Ida B. Wells excerpted from her classic *A Red Record: Lynching in the United State*, 1892-1893-1894. Here she recounts the case of Henry Smith, a Negro, who killed a young child in revenge against her father who had mistreated him. She was critical of Bishop Allicus Green Haywood of the Methodist Episcopal Church whose description of the death stated, "First outraged with demoniacal cruelty and then taken of her heels and torn asunder in the mad wantonness of gorilla ferocity." Ms. Wells stated as follows: "Nothing is farthest from the truth than that statement, it is a cold blooded, deliberate, brutal falsehood which this Christian (?) Bishop uses to bolster up the infamous plea that the people of Paris were driven to insanity by learning that the little child had been viciously assaulted, choked to death, and then torn to pieces by a demon in human form. It was a brutal murder, but no more brutal than hundreds of murders which occur in this country, and which have been equally every year in fiendishness and brutality, and for which the death penalty is prescribed by law and inflicted only after the person has been legally adjudged guilty of the crime."

Close-up classic view of the Lincoln Memorial.

Those murders and the brutality of lynchings may be numbered among the nearly 4000 lynchings *The New York Times* article published in 2015 that were committed in several Southern states from

283

1870 to 1950. A marker is being considered for each such location but this has not gone over easily with owners of the land because who wants to be associated with "The atrocities we committed!"

Nevertheless, some may view Eric Cantor, House Majority leader as a visionary, simply because he realizes the power of the mob. After all, as the "Tea Party" pounded Barack Obama on his road to the White House and then to gain political respectability, its leaders may have toasted, "Raise your glasses with me Brothers and Sisters." As such, whether their storm included everything and the Kitchen Sink, Obama took it all, the gentleman that he is, continuing to defend the American system against such "white collar rebels."

Showcasing a place for outstanding Americans to have a say, beside the Lincoln Memorial.

"Our priority is to go after **ISIL**. And so what we have said is that we are not engaging in a military action against the Syrian regime. We are going after **ISIL** facilities and personnel who are using Syria as a safe haven, in service of our strategy in Iraq." **Barack Obama**

OBAMA THE JOURNEY COMPLETED - NEVER PROMISED A ROSE GARDEN

28.　　SHARPTON, TODAY
By
Dr. Fred Monderson

Returning to New York the weekend of August 17, 2014, "A Tabloid Headline" report indicated "Sharpton Slams Christie" for dancing while Ferguson burns! Sharpton, himself just returning from the City of Ferguson posed the question "Why have men of substance, seeking to become President not spoken out on Ferguson." However, as everyone has seen Rev. Sharpton vilified on TV, in Tabloid articles and "Letters to the Editor," people continue to wonder what motivated Sharpton's role in the Tawana Brawley Experience, to begin with. The shortsighted and prejudiced view is just that, for it undervalues the true measure of the man!

FREDERICK MONDERSON

"The thing about hip-hop today is it's smart, it's insightful. The way they can communicate a complex message in a very short space is remarkable." **Barack Obama**

In this situation, Al Sharpton did what any self-respecting gentleman would have done. He came upon a young woman, Black; who claimed she was raped by a bunch of men, White; one of whom committed suicide subsequently as indications pointed his way. Sharpton fought but was stained by the development of injustice generated by the behemoth of the law.

Today we recognize the word gentleman has lost its true meaning. Once upon a time, for example, the term "Southern Gentlemen" conjured up a mythical individual who even took his hat off when a lady passed. When we see the vitriol directed toward President Obama by "Southern Gentlemen" as Mitch McConnell; "Waterloo" Jim DeMint; "You lie" Joe Wilson; "Stupid" Senator Grassley; this notion is indeed mythical compared to Sharpton's commitment and steadfast resilience which is real! His "Damn the Critics" attitude, full-speed ahead activism is not inconsistent with Presidential steadfast determination lacking in these spineless "Southern Gentlemen."

Way back in 1941, after A. Philip Randolph spoke at a White House dinner decrying the practice of excluding Blacks from government jobs and threatened to "March on Washington!" President Franklin D. Roosevelt listened intently to the message, passed out cigars and after a long pause insisted, "Mr. Randolph, you want change? Go out there and make me do it!" That's the American way!

OBAMA THE JOURNEY COMPLETED - NEVER PROMISED A ROSE GARDEN

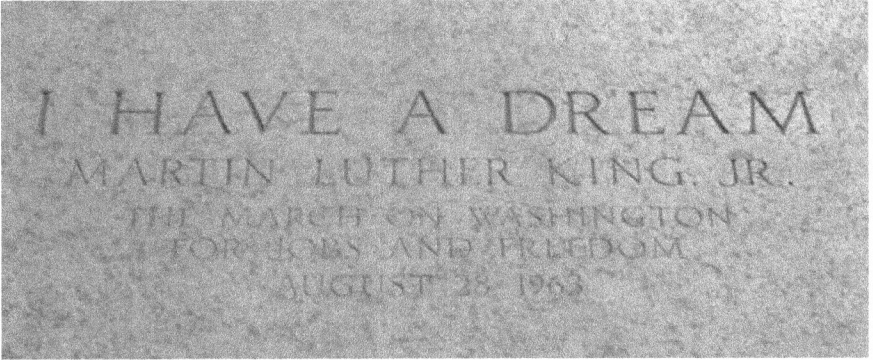

The problem with the Brawley affair is that Black women have little value in this society. They are, first of all, not considered beautiful. White women, on the other hand, are considered the epitome of beauty. Witness her lofty position displayed on all the walls as images in the Jefferson Building of the Library of Congress where no Black women are represented save as security guards. This is a classic example of the white woman as the symbol of beauty. Still, Michelle Obama can hold her own with the best of them.

FREDERICK MONDERSON

OBAMA THE JOURNEY COMPLETED - NEVER PROMISED A ROSE GARDEN

Remember "Dynasty" days on TV. In one episode, the heroine poisoned the hero at the end, and in the next frame of the TV ad the same woman, in real life, blonde hair and all, was shown as a symbol of beauty, pitching a hair product, as she threw her head and hair back.

Tawana Brawley and Sharpton were vilified for years. In that horrifying experience, the "powers that be" smashed the truth. In the "Central Park Jogger Case," the official contingent came in with guns blazing and ruined the lives and spirit of five young Black men. Donald Trump, in a full-page ad in *The New York Times* called for the death penalty for these young men. Years later, after the horrible treatment and incarceration, the five men they were judged innocent of the crime and awarded a settlement, Donald Trump had much to say, damning the youths, even objecting to the city's settlement. Still, too little, too late! There has been no apology for his recklessness,

Again, white over the Black woman dictates, glorify Bonnie with Clyde but vilify Assata Shakur and Joanne Chessamard. Not much of a stretch, but, the reason President Obama engender such racial enmity in his efforts to govern is because his father chose to "Marry not live with" his mother.

Nevertheless, from Bensonhurst to Brawley and Amadou Diallo to Sean Bell mirroring Eric Garner in Staten Island, New York, and Michael Brown in Ferguson, St. Louis; along the way, standing and marching shining the light of truth is a testament to Sharpton's involvement as a civil right leader whose vision has grown tremendously over the years. As such, Sharpton is unique. It was that uniqueness Bishop Washington saw in cultivating the boy preacher at 7 years of age. Rev. Jesse Jackson also tapped that youngster to head the Youth Division of Operation Breadbasket of PUSH.

This show of genius, notwithstanding, in their nefarious criticisms, many enquire, "Where is Rev. Sharpton's church?" Jesus did not have a church. However, he did castigate the hypocrites and money-changers in church. Sharpton's church is in the streets! Like Jesus, he calls out perpetrators of injustice and oppression and has paid a price, not just in words but in blood when he was stabbed in Bensonhurst. Yet, he forgave his assailant. This assault was not unlike that of Dr. King who told of the young white girl who wrote saying she prayed and thanked god the knife wound was only inches away from his heart. Sharpton too came within inches of leaving the Civil Rights Movement without a champion of courage, vision, tenacity and resilience, who stands up irrespective, yet pays a price in vilification.

In the journey that shaped the civil rights icon evident today, Sharpton dared to run for the Senate, Mayor and President, all the while cultivating the greater vision to see and understand the issues from the

OBAMA THE JOURNEY COMPLETED - NEVER PROMISED A ROSE GARDEN

"bird's eye view." In that Presidential bid, Sharpton, primarily a winner, proved a master of organizational institution building by establishing chapters of the National Action Network throughout the country. This is so evident at the organization's "Keeping the Dream" Convention in April of every year, as in 2016 where many boast of the voices they now have thanks to Al Sharpton's activism.

FREDERICK MONDERSON

Being human, Sharpton certainly has faults but who is without sin! More important, however, his activism shines light on and keeps issues of inequity and injustice on front burner status. Therefore, in lieu of any substantial individual standing up and calling attention to those important issues of Black concerns, Sharpton is the man! When he calls, many come running! In the Diallo protests, many "men of big affairs" lined up to get arrested. In the "Sean Bell shooting" incident he called and some 50,000 came to "Shop for Justice" in Midtown, the "Heart of Christmas." Partnering with Martin Luther King III, he spearheaded the 50th Anniversary "March on Washington" in 2013. And he continues to speak on the "Central Park Five" issue, the

OBAMA THE JOURNEY COMPLETED - NEVER PROMISED A ROSE GARDEN

"Tribute to Michael Jackson," "Prison violence at Rikers Island," the need for Prison Reform, the deaths of Trayvon Martin and Eric Garner at whose march he presided, and much, much more.

Oh, the Great Man, looking out from his Memorial Temple.

Therefore, in the final analysis, many are praying for God to protect and strengthen Sharpton for him to remain standing until "righteousness rolls down like a mighty stream" and "justice is meted out to all men" in equal measured proportions, irrespective.

FREDERICK MONDERSON

"With patient and firm determination, I am going to press on for jobs. I'm going to press on for equality. I'm going to press on for the sake of our children. I'm going to press on for the sake of all those families who are struggling right now. I don't have time to feel sorry for myself. I don't have time to complain. I am going to press on.

Barack Obama

OBAMA THE JOURNEY COMPLETED - NEVER PROMISED A ROSE GARDEN

29. "OBAMA: A BAD YEAR? NO!"
By
Dr. Fred Monderson

In *The Washington Post* of Sunday December 14, 2014, Chris Cillizza writer on "The Worse Week in Washington" wrote: "Congrats: President Obama, you had the worst year in Washington, again." Arguably this is another "hatchet job" on a good and decent leader swimming in a sea alongside 'gators, barracudas, and piranhas that see only his color, refuse to work toward rescue of the nation but choose to emphasize his failures they help engineer; not his brilliance they cannot duplicate and further refuse to recognize and accentuate his accomplishments, while incessantly trying to cut him off at the knees. Like so many others who see his glass half empty, in contradiction, many see that same glass three quarters full. Let's not forget, the former Republican Secretary of State Condoleezza Rice said on public television, "President Obama is a decent man doing the best for the country."

"We're not going to baby sit a civil war." **Barack Obama**

In his beginning this "hatcheteer" Cillizza stated: "The year began with Obama proposing a set of reforms to the National Security Agency, a result of on-going National Security leaks and ended with mid-term elections that saw his party lose its majority because of the President's unpopularity. In between were continuing challenges to the Affordable Care Act, America's re-entry into Iraq - a war the President had vowed to exit - and memoirs from former Cabinet officials questioning Obama's decision-making and judgment." This and much more was stated.

Who could forget the famous *Time Magazine* cover that "embellished O.J. Simpson's blackness?" In the same way, Mr. Bingo, the Illustrator for *The Washington Post* emphasized "Mr. Obama's color" and traditionally this has been to cast such subjects in a bad light. Why did the artist waiting on No. 45 to shout "Bingo" not color the "White guy" Dan Snyder - "Really Bad Year; the Secret Service men - "Bad Year;" and "Not so good year" Chris Christie! Governor Christie lightened his load by throwing his men under the bus, for after all, "The Buck Stops" with him who is responsible for the "Bridge Gate" wrong-doing notwithstanding! Today much of this is bearing fruit as the investigation and trial continues to picture him as tainted.

Naturally, on the next page, both writer and illustrator cast Mitch McConnell as having the "best year." It is said, for McConnell, it was the realization of a life-long dream, a not-insignificant accomplishment for a man who has been around politics since the 1960s. McConnell, like Harry Reid whom he will replace in the Senate's top job is not a flashy politician who surged through the ranks

OBAMA THE JOURNEY COMPLETED - NEVER PROMISED A ROSE GARDEN

in record time. He is a plotter and strategist of the highest order, a man who always has a plan and executes his relentlessly.

The "founding fathers" were called "freedom fighters" but today such persons are called "terrorists." Sure Mr. McConnell is not flashy. He did, however, flask that "Thumbs Up" sign to his handlers. "I got that Nigger in the White House!" These qualifications certainly place him high-up on the now exposed treasonous plot against Mr. Obama. That he is a plotter is no doubt. Too bad *The Washington Post* people don't read *The New York Times*, in particular its article in October 6, 2013, depicting the treasonous or seditious plot by which high ranking Republican operatives and their backers tasked to derail Mr. Obama's Presidency. Nearly 20 NGOs were named as being funded, their operatives trained and deployed to "educate" the public about the evils of Obamacare! Former Attorney General Ed Meese under Ronald Reagan was named in the article as a principal actor in the "treasonous" plot against the duly elected government of the United States of America under the leadership of President Barrack Hussein Obama. As such, every Legislative or Executive initiative Mr. Obama initiated was scrutinized by Republicans to determine its legality and to use Boehner's benchmark "98 percent," got blocked. Edmund Burke admonished, "The only thing necessary for evil to triumph is for good to do or say nothing." Were there no good Republican men or women when all this transpired that emboldened "B" and "C" actors took it upon themselves to pile on the disrespect and generate racial hatred towards Mr. Obama?

FREDERICK MONDERSON

An article on former Senator John Thompson was entitled as "When Politics Meets Art and Art Meets Politics." Consider this scenario! Given some ingredients, much remains "secret" or hidden, we must conjure the outcome.

OBAMA THE JOURNEY COMPLETED - NEVER PROMISED A ROSE GARDEN

Mitch McConnell "has been around politics since the 1960s." Who can count the deals he made, the toes he stepped on in his climb to accomplish his "lifelong dream of becoming Senate Majority Leader." Did he ever entertain the thought of becoming President? Traveling on the same train he very well could have been a protégé of Ed Meese in his striking days. Now, along comes Barrack Obama, an upstart African-American who "Surged through the ranks in record time." This is troubling to Ed Meese and his "Knights at Table" charged with "stopping Obama," resulting in undermining the Presidency, the well-being of the nation, and the welfare of the American people be damned! "Stop Obama by any means necessary!" Remember the sickening expression of the Naval Commander in "A Few Good Men" as the Chief confirmed Cuba Gooding had passed the underwater test.

Possessing seniority in the "Club," steeped in intimate knowledge of the workings of politics in Washington, Ed Meese recruited his combatants from the active field of powerful Republican operatives. From his office of high visibility as Senate Minority Leader, nearly 50-years in politics and may be obligated to Ed Meese for perhaps chaperoning him along the way; Mitch McConnell was probably the first chosen for this operation against the President of the United States perhaps particularly because of the color of his skin. Why should a Black man rule? One good thing the American system is how to reconstruct scenarios. Now, throw in "Waterloo" DeMint; a chunk of "Stupid" Senator Charles Grassley; add a little "You lie" Wilson; put in a pinch of block Allen West from the inner portals; while we're not sure about John McCain, let the uncontrolled, limelight seeking Sarah Palin earn her stripes, and don't trust "God told me to run" Michele Bachmann because our actions may not set well with "her boss," the divine! This plot is so ingenious; it should make stage play status "On Broadway."

However, given McConnell "failed in his famous goal 'to make Obama a one-term President,'" we have to agree the operation evidently began after the 2008 election and by the January 2009 Inauguration though revealed in 2013 after the 2012 election, the effort to work and rework the plan was probably ongoing. Equally, and given Mr. McConnell "is a plotter and strategist of the highest order, a man who always has a plan and executes it relentlessly;" a failure in his primary goal does not preclude a secondary objective. Hence, Mr. McConnell's "Party of No" well-choreographed track record of obstruction and blaming the other guy is finally rewarded by a hood-winked America public, aided by some failures on Mr. Obama's part, unrelenting legislative "Lilliputians trying to tie Gulliver" and the confessions of "insider foxes who cry sour grapes!"

After Dr. Murray was released from prison, having served time as a responsible party in the death of Michael Jackson, he began making statements about his closeness with the singer even mentioning his "fixing Michael's Caterer." That astute comic and radio and TV personality Steve Harvey who conceptualizes so readily and well responded, "Hell, he is shopping for a book deal!" Panetta and Gates certainly shopped for book deals in betraying the President's confidence in them. Say what you will of George Bush's defense Secretary, he would not have "rat on his boss." In all likelihood financial gain was their primary objective for they perhaps never donated the proceeds to favorite charities. They could not wait until Mr. Obama's term ended. These men could not spell loyalty nor could these supreme warlords, countenance "falling on their swords!"

OBAMA THE JOURNEY COMPLETED - NEVER PROMISED A ROSE GARDEN

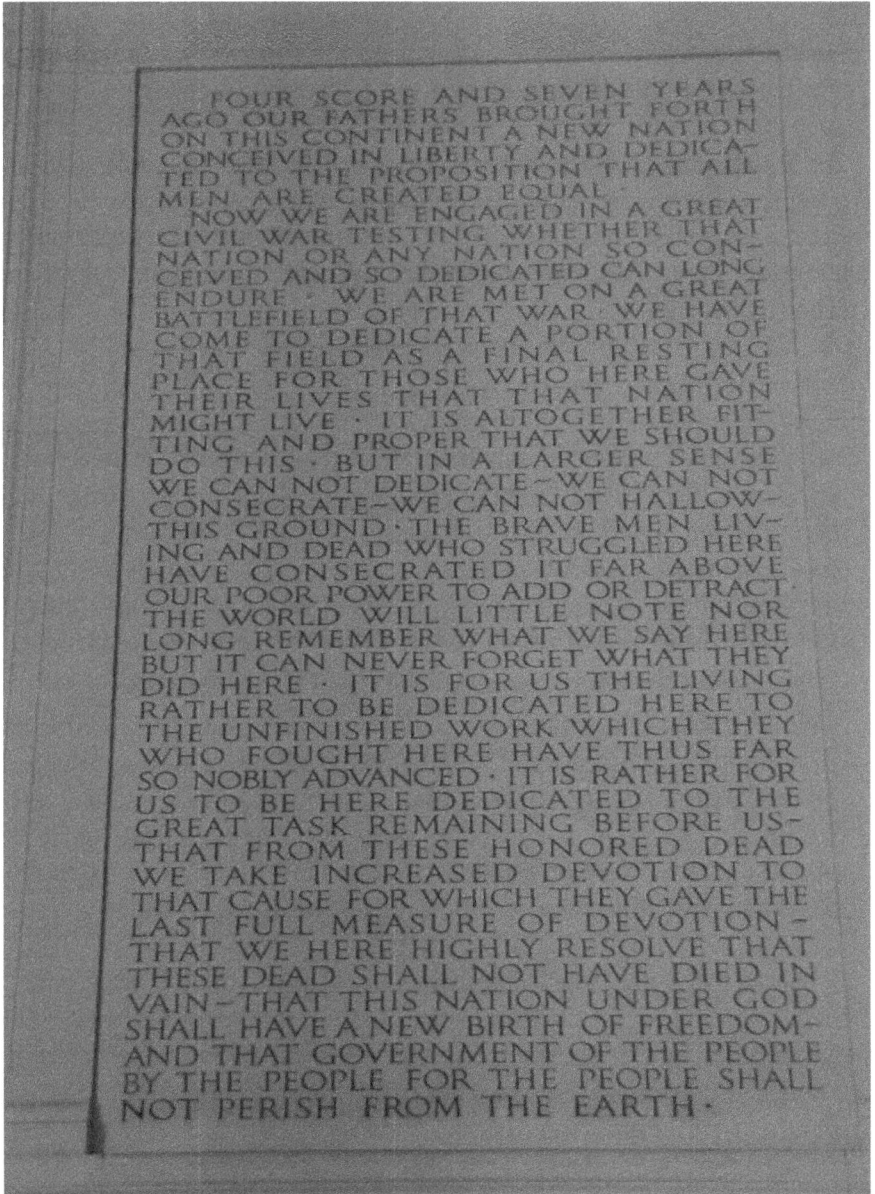

The famous Gettysburg Address in the Lincoln Memorial.

Thus, one of Obama's problems was choosing "kiss and tell" guys like Panetta and Gates whose autobiographies were nothing more than insider gossip. So much so, "By the next morning, Republicans were using those lines in TV Ads bashing Democrats as Obama clones." So what's new about Hillary? She started the route down the dusty trail and naturally could have refused the Secretary of State position that gave her the foreign policy credentials to be considered a credible 2016 candidate. Of the three "revealers," she is the only one as a potential candidate and for African-Americans who love this President, the jury is still out! Across the board, many should pay attention to a Biblical challenge, "Where were you when they crucified my Lord?"

Notwithstanding, "Sizzling" Chris Cillizza, continued to bash Mr. Obama expressing, "The revelation that the IRS was targeting Tea Party groups for special scrutiny; the Edward Snowden leaks about NSA surveillance and the botched rollout of Healthcare.gov to name three that happened in 2013." Equally, "Obama's longtime pledge to 'reset' relations with Russia was exposed as frighteningly naïve when President Vladimir Putin moved into Eastern Ukraine with impunity. Obama's response to Putin's aggression - Sanctions - was derided as using a spray bottle to put out a five-alarm fire." Even further, the "Dumb War in Iraq," the Rise of **ISIL**, the two turncoats and finally Mr. Obama's confession: "I am not on the Ballot. These policies are on the Ballot. Every single one of them!" Finally, that famous Faulkner's line, "The past is never dead. It is not even past" the author uses to characterize Mr. Obama's political fortunes in 2014, the Past keeps Complicating his Present - and Clouding his Future."

Separate rules are constructed for Mr. Obama! Mitch McConnell's racist statements in the past have not complicated his present nor clouded his future. Kentuckians voted for the bacon Mr. McConnell could bring home as Senate Majority Leader as opposed to his fresh opponent while ignoring his questionably unethical behavior.

Sure "Uneasy lies the head that wears the crown," but Obama's second jeopardy is his color, if not his first. Sure there is political opposition but political opposition worse than the Ferguson Police initial full-court press response to demonstrators is a low for this

OBAMA THE JOURNEY COMPLETED - NEVER PROMISED A ROSE GARDEN

country that boasts of being at the apex of the political food chain. Something stinks below.

Perhaps if the article's author had not ended the year before December 15, he would have realized some of the myriad accomplishments of Mr. Obama merit a more positive critique. After all, he gave McConnell nearly 60 years to climb the hill that Obama did to a higher hill in 4 years.

FREDERICK MONDERSON

By the actual Calendar year's end, the economy is better than good. Unemployment is down 26 percent with some 10,000,000 private sector jobs added even though Republicans refused to pass Mr. Obama's jobs bill. Somewhere in America gas prices may be lower than two dollars and Wall Street is looking very good with the DOW nearing 18,000, a height never before reached. That Putin fellow, well he is suffering from Obama's sanctions imposed after the invasion.

Boastful as Iran's façade is, it too is hurting from sanctions. Obama's incrementalism has worked. The Presidential historian Doug Brinkley characterized President Obama as one who "doesn't over-react."

A consensus now is that Obama's next book on 'The White House Years,' will perhaps be "Wisdom from My Father" warning to beware of snakes in the grass, or don't trust Washington shadows after noon, or is it 9:00 AM. Still, Mr. Obama is too decent a fellow to wallow in the mud. His opponents have already shown their shallowness.

OBAMA THE JOURNEY COMPLETED - NEVER PROMISED A ROSE GARDEN

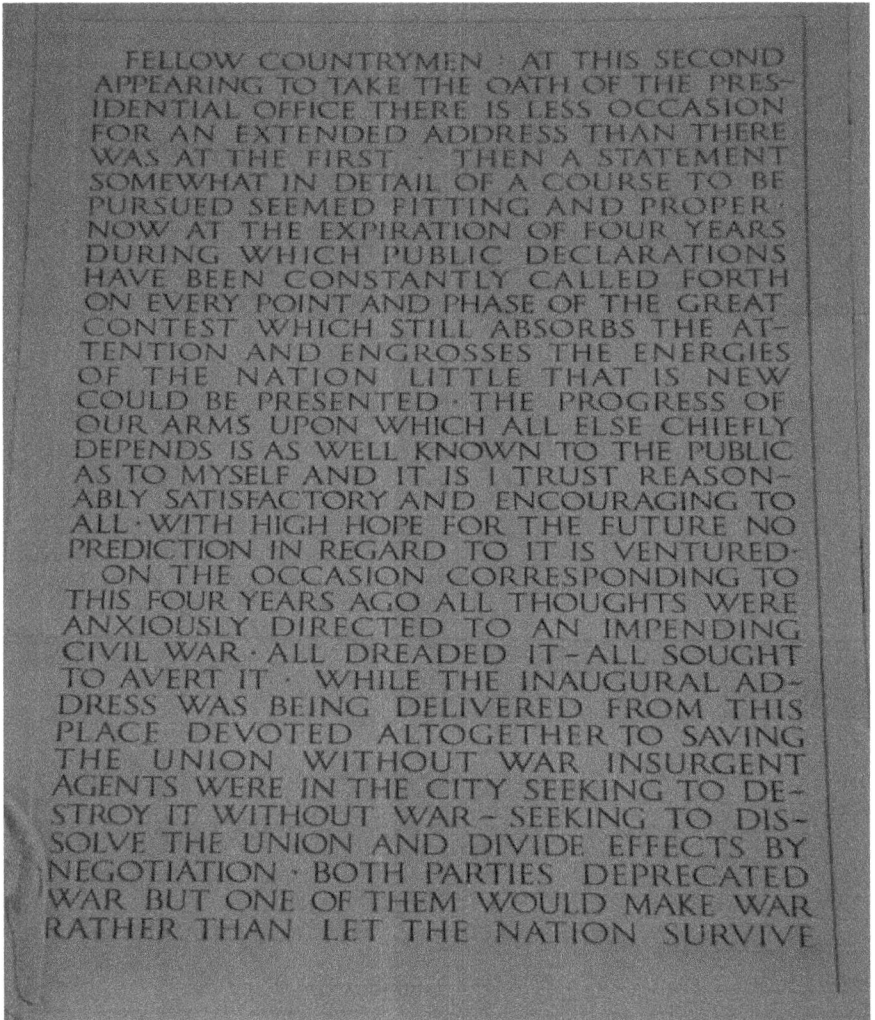

The famous Gettysburg Address in the Lincoln Memorial.

History must judge Mr. Obama favorably for his climate agreement with China; his new Immigration initiative; and the vision to see and courage to chart a new course with Cuba. If we could credit Republicans with winning the 2016 and 2020 Presidential elections this would have meant eight more years of failed Cuba policies. Meanwhile, Cuba continues to grow from Cub to Lion and the

305

ringmasters continue to diminish in size. However, Mr. Obama's Cuba opening is futuristic in its intent like so many other Obama initiatives will realign relations in the Americas and Western hemisphere. It has been described by the White House Correspondent Jim Acosta as "A major, major step forward." It's a pity the "Sizzle" missed the boat, I mean, did not get that e-mail.

The famous Gettysburg Address in the Lincoln Memorial.

"But what we can do, as flawed as we are, I still see God in other people, and do our best to help them find their own grace. That's what I strive to do, that's what I pray to do every day. I think that there's no doubt that as I see friends, families, children of gay couples who are thriving, you know, that has an impact on how I think about these issues." **Barack Obama**

306

30. A PRECIPITOUS TIME
IN HISTORY
By
Dr. Fred Monderson

People like Chris Cillizza and similar Republican sycophants have been so "Hubble-like focused" on the mole in President Obama's eye they miss the plank or, colonnade, within his opponents' front yard. That is, in their focused search for his forest they fail to see his trees. The nation is at a precipitous time in its history and the people who should make a difference are not paying attention as they pander to the money elite who contribute so much to their re-election "war chests." However, while Obama looks for and steers toward the calmer seas and clearer skies of a bright future, many "wolf in sheep clothing," or they are "sheep in wolf," either way, they keep looking to earth for the ground hog shadow to decide which way to go.

"What I worry about would be that you essentially have two chambers, the House and the Senate, but you have simply, majoritarian, absolute power on either side. And that's just not what the founders intended." **Barack Obama**

President Obama has been criticized for "leading from behind" while Republicans who have created minefields along the path he must travel hope to be rewarded in a political coup forcing the world to wonder at the American anomaly. For centuries Black veterans from Crispus Attucks, the thousands buried in the Brooklyn Navy Yard to today's soldiers serving at the farthest reaches of the American empire have all served with distinction. Many have given their lives, untold numbers disabled in service to defend the ideals of this nation. Now, after two centuries of such service an African-American becomes Commander-In-Chief by virtue of being elected President and Chief Executive. To challenge this reality, American racist with ante-bellum mentalities focus clandestinely, then in-clandestine, with unwarranted scrutiny on a decent man struggling to represent all the people in the American mosaic. A famous photograph show Mr. Obama among GIs in Iraq that included two Black soldiers on the top row of the enclosed structure. The gleam in their eyes begged that words be put in their mouths as: "After serving the nation for two centuries, it's time we were rewarded with a Commander-In-Chief who looks like us."

OBAMA THE JOURNEY COMPLETED - NEVER PROMISED A ROSE GARDEN

Today we celebrate the original "Tea Party" members as historic heroes but, truth is, they were considered criminals by the administering British power. Today's "Tea Party" movement is a different matter. Claims to identify with the historic group bears no merit because: (1) they were a colonial people and these are not. (2) They were being administered by a distant power and these are not. (3) The right of political representation was for the most part, being denied and this is not so today. (4) They were being taxed on foreign imports without commensurate representation while the nation today exports worldwide. (5) Trial by peer and other extenuating circumstances were a major issue but today we have trial by jury. (6) The nation was in the throes of a revolutionary movement and the British were not opposed to firing on colonists. Today, the only firing is on unarmed Black civilians. (7) Perhaps the only similarity of today's "Tea Party" with the "Tea Party" of the Boston harbor incident is as the British classified them then as "criminals." Whatever happened to "Impeachment for high crimes and misdemeanors?" Does the name Mitch McConnell ring a bell? How about Ed Meese?

FREDERICK MONDERSON

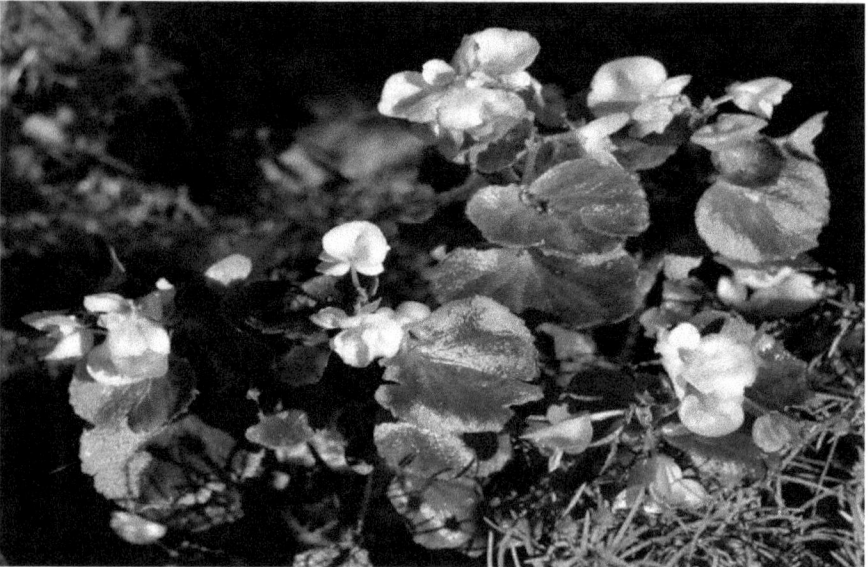

OBAMA THE JOURNEY COMPLETED - NEVER PROMISED A ROSE GARDEN

The New York Times article of October 6, 2013 named individuals and groups involved in a treasonous plot against President Obama's 2012 re-election campaign in a "Racist-gate" type conspiracy. Former Attorney General Ed Meese was named as a principal actor. While the dots were not connected sufficiently at the time of the 2008 election, two unmistakable facts are evident. First, there is Senator Mitch McConnell's public racist rant about "making Barrack Obama a one term President." If this is not "high crimes and misdemeanor" in high places of the government, what is? Second, if Ed Meese was active in the objective outlined in 2012, given McConnell's statement, it is reasonable to assume the "fix was in," giving his "marching orders" that proved a failure as applied to Obama's re-election. This, therefore, necessitated coming out of the closet for round two with the same failing results. This is a nation of contingency planning and to assume parts one and two just fell out of a hat is wishful thinking.

IF WE SHALL SUPPOSE THAT AMERICAN SLAVERY IS ONE OF THOSE OFFENSES WHICH IN THE PROVIDENCE OF GOD MUST NEEDS COME BUT WHICH HAVING CONTINUED THROUGH HIS APPOINTED TIME HE NOW WILLS TO REMOVE AND THAT HE GIVES TO BOTH NORTH AND SOUTH THIS TERRIBLE WAR AS THE WOE DUE TO THOSE BY WHOM THE OFFENSE CAME SHALL WE DISCERN THEREIN ANY DEPARTURE FROM THOSE DIVINE ATTRIBUTES WHICH THE BELIEVERS IN A LIVING GOD ALWAYS ASCRIBE TO HIM. FONDLY DO WE HOPE – FERVENTLY DO WE PRAY – THAT THIS MIGHTY SCOURGE OF WAR MAY SPEEDILY PASS AWAY · YET IF GOD WILLS THAT IT CONTINUE UNTIL ALL THE WEALTH PILED BY THE BONDSMAN'S TWO HUNDRED AND FIFTY YEARS OF UNREQUITED TOIL SHALL BE SUNK AND UNTIL EVERY DROP OF BLOOD DRAWN WITH THE LASH SHALL BE PAID BY ANOTHER DRAWN WITH THE SWORD AS WAS SAID THREE THOUSAND YEARS AGO SO STILL IT MUST BE SAID "THE JUDGMENTS OF THE LORD ARE TRUE AND RIGHTEOUS ALTOGETHER."
WITH MALICE TOWARD NONE WITH CHARITY FOR ALL WITH FIRMNESS IN THE RIGHT AS GOD GIVES US TO SEE THE RIGHT LET US STRIVE ON TO FINISH THE WORK WE ARE IN TO BIND UP THE NATION'S WOUNDS TO CARE FOR HIM WHO SHALL HAVE BORNE THE BATTLE AND FOR HIS WIDOW AND HIS ORPHAN – TO DO ALL WHICH MAY ACHIEVE AND CHERISH A JUST AND LASTING PEACE AMONG OURSELVES AND WITH ALL NATIONS ·

The famous Emancipation Proclamation Address in the Lincoln Memorial.

OBAMA THE JOURNEY COMPLETED - NEVER PROMISED A ROSE GARDEN

We must give Republicans credit for fore-seeing an Obama win! It would be naïve to believe the plot had no antecedent plan and discussion before November 2008. Just as *The New York Times* article was able to ferret out the 2012 treasonous plot, Chris Cillizza, instead of emphasizing "Obama's Worst Year" should have investigated the "Tea Party" origins and its links to the seditious movement. That is, what contacts were established, who financed the movement, who stoked the fires, and whether it is possible to inveigle anyone who would do a "Gates" or "Panetta" on the movement's inner workings? No one believes "Joe the Plumber" was an original thinker beyond pea-size proportions.

Just as 2012 NGOs were training operatives to "Educate the public" about "Obamacare" the same false propaganda mill may very well have been at work behind "Tea Party" gatherings, signage, but when "Lipstick on a Pig" Sarah Palin began to talk "Crosshairs" and provocateurs began shouting "Kill the Nigger," they tipped their hands. Was this the genesis of McConnell's thought and actions? Perhaps Cillizza could investigate and enlighten us.

That false and sinister propaganda mill that gave us the "Witch Doctor," "Palling Around with Terrorists," "Socialism" and the "Birther Movement" continued to stoke fires by pontificating about Obama changing the Constitution and the imminent race war. Yet, not one Republican of stature spoke out against the political persecution. Edmund Burke reminded, "The only thing necessary for evil to triumph is for good men to say nothing." Certainly, not Ed Meese, nor Boehner, DeMint, Palin, Trump or Grassley spoke out against the climate of racial hatred and disrespect brewing in the Republican cauldron, perhaps because they are stirring the pot! By Burke's standard, "these were not good men!" They would favor trillions for foreign wars but not a billion for health care to cover nearly 50 million Americans who lack this protection. Where is the patriotism fervor?

FREDERICK MONDERSON

OBAMA THE JOURNEY COMPLETED - NEVER PROMISED A ROSE GARDEN

Fast forward. When the recent CIA scandal broke, word is, they were afraid to inform Colin Powell about goings-on during his tenure for fear he would blow his stack. His credibility was already tarnished from the WMD presentation. So, in 2008, showing he had "bulls' balls," this "best of a bad lot" chose to endorse Barrack Obama over his party's standard bearers McCain and Palin. The treatment meted out to the Black candidate and ultimately President Obama was probably foreseen by Mr. Powell who chose not to be a candidate for the top job, indeed in his own right. This puts "Uncle Ben" in a precarious position, for as an "attack dog" on "Obamacare" he is yet to realize his "glass ceiling" is very not high.

FREDERICK MONDERSON

However, as the militias stacked up on armaments and helped the economy along with such spending, as well as their conducting regular drills in anticipation of a supposedly pending race war, Blacks remained reticent. They simply brought home their veterans from the wars in Iraq and Afghanistan who simply became observers. Some simply became forward observers as LURPS. Still the disrespect continued, the legislative sabotage ensued, and some in the public were "red Herring" into believing McConnell and Boehner's sun had set. Instead they were re-elected by propagating a stunt to sue the President and to "Impeach the Nigger in the White House!"

In all this Mr. Obama continued his appointed tasks. Wall Street was on fire with the **DOW** approaching 18,000; the auto industry had regained its market share in many respects; more than 11,000,000 new jobs were created by the private sector; the price of gas had plummeted; and the President acquired a climate change agreement with China. The good news - the President's party lost the 2014 mid-term election not so much because things were bad, which they weren't, but as his ship began to sink, the congressional rats he was ferrying began jumping overboard. Not a one chose to champion the cause and so Panetta and Gates proved super patriots while Snowden was considered a traitor!

OBAMA THE JOURNEY COMPLETED - NEVER PROMISED A ROSE GARDEN

Meanwhile, as Republicans licked their chops in anticipation of incoming power, after Trayvon Martin, their tunnel vision never saw Eric Garner, Michael Brown and Ferguson, Tamir Rice and Coleman happen. After a long train of such abuse the people took to the streets across the nation. It was not simply police callousness and failure to realize "Black Lives Matter" and even the Grand Jury failure to indict, but more important the escalating climate of racial hatred and disrespect manifesting against the White House to statehouses working to stir voter suppression, even to the outhouse all exuding a tremendous odor, and all afflicting the man in the street.

If the President could be disrespected in the House of Representatives by a Republican member and now Republicans will gloriously exercise power in both houses, with that power perhaps they should erect a "statue to Joe Wilson" as a testament to their folly. Perhaps Mr. Obama will sign such a bill exposing the nature of the Republican beast!

"We need to recognize that the situation in Ferguson speaks to broader challenges that we still face as a nation. The fact is, in too many parts of this country, a deep distrust exists between law enforcement and communities of color. Some of this is the result of the legacy of racial discrimination in this country." **Barack Obama**

317

FREDERICK MONDERSON

31.   OBAMA STRIKES BACK
By
Dr. Fred Monderson

Anyone familiar with the O.J. Simpson trial could tell after the Prosecution had put on and rested its case, Simpson was toast! Stick a fork in him. When Johnny Cochran died, at the Eulogy Al Sharpton said, "People believed it was OJ the world cheered but no, it was Johnny Cochran. For, when the Prosecution handed Simpson the ball,

OBAMA THE JOURNEY COMPLETED - NEVER PROMISED A ROSE GARDEN

deep in the end-zone, Cochran began running to "If the glove does not fit, you have to acquit."

"Where the stakes are the highest, in the war on terror, we cannot possibly succeed without extraordinary international cooperation. Effective international police actions require the highest degree of intelligence sharing, planning and collaborative enforcement."
Barack Obama

In the "Obama Saga," for years the opposition had been massing just beyond his perimeter after having sent some forty-odd sorties to unsuccessfully probe his signature legislative success, the Affordable Care Act. Now, reinforced in the successful 2014 Mid-Term Election, one night they sat partying before voluminous bon-fires. Peering over his barricaded fortifications Obama could see the glare, fearful of an imminent attack; "he fired a flare and opened with voluminous fire on the rebels' camp."

His first salvo was the new Immigration initiative designed to allay distress of some 5 million undocumented persons, mostly decent, hard-working individuals whose papers were not just right. A principal rebel leader John Boehner, assessing the now inflicted damages to his forces cried foul, retorting: "The President thinks he is above the law. I will sue him in a court of law." In a somewhat hypocritical posture General Boehner had overlooked the myriad, if not illegal, certainly morally, reprehensible acts his troops and their allies had perpetrated against the power that be. Across the nation and around the globe, even souls in Purgatory began to celebrate, "Obama had taken off the gloves!" In concert with the other rebel Commander Mitch McConnell they surveyed the damages and plotted their next move while Obama prepared the next salvo.

FREDERICK MONDERSON

OBAMA THE JOURNEY COMPLETED - NEVER PROMISED A ROSE GARDEN

By morning as the "rebels" were stirring, Obama fired another fuselage. This time it was the Cuba Initiative!

For more than half a century the nation had maintained an embargo on Cuba resulting from the 1962 Missile Crisis and its establishment of communism in the Western Hemisphere, some 90 miles off America's shores. By all standards, we had won the standoff. The Soviet Union withdrew and we imposed punitive measure on Cuba. As time passed and struggling to meet the imposed challenges, Cuba gained credibility for standing up to the "Colossal to the North." Interestingly enough, while the Soviet Union initially supported Cuba financially, circumstances forced the island state to creatively develop its inner strengths. Blocked from a forward thrust, the young regime stepped back then moved sideways.

A somewhat similar situation prevailed in the British West Indies. For many years after Independence their economies were tied to the principal and former colonial master, Britain. They celebrated their Christmas festivities with fruits imported from Britain. One day a wise ruler suggested: "Hey, why not make our fruit cakes from our locally grown produce?" This and other such initiatives changed the economic equation tremendously. No more shipping charges; no more insurance charges; no more product charges; no more left over fruit and this helped local farmers' bottom line. It saved the nation from exporting badly needed foreign currency. Recently, at Bourda Market in Georgetown, a shopper asked the young lady behind the counter, "What type of juice you have today?" She responded, "Cane juice, Sorrel, Cherry, Guava, and several others." This is culture and local economic shift.

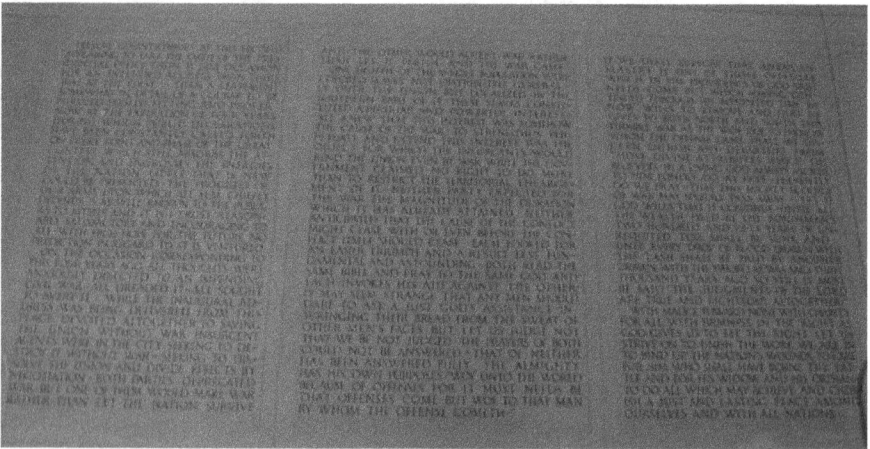

Full text of the famous Gettysburg Address in the Lincoln Memorial.

In the case of Cuba they evolved the greatest foreign mechanics of old style American automobiles. Following a doctrinaire societal policy they pursued a one-party political system with the government strictly controlling all facets of the state. Castro shipped "rotten eggs" to America and began cultivating revolutionary friendships among nations fighting for independence from "First World" countries supporting colonialist, settler and racist regimes. The nation began educating their youth to follow along the socialist path. Their schools produced doctors, engineers and other specialists born of the challenges placed on them. When called upon for material support to resist colonial aggression Cuba sent armed contingents to train locals and battle them. The West was now in a quandary. The embargoed

OBAMA THE JOURNEY COMPLETED - NEVER PROMISED A ROSE GARDEN

genii was now out of the bottle! Building more bridges, Cuba offered free medical and computer scholarships for students of poor nations. Her dispatched doctors were sometimes the only competent physicians manning local hospitals in Third World countries.

Cuba thrived on disasters. Oftentimes her medical and engineering teams were first to arrive in hard hit places. She was very early in West Africa battling Ebola. While not a member of the Organization of American States she certainly got communiqué second hand, yet still remained relevant. She attended conferences and everybody traded with Cuba. Many, even "First world" nations normalized relations with Cuba. Cuba was the first nation in Haiti after the earthquake.

The United States was essentially the last train out of the station to come to grips with Cuba. In similar fashion that Mr. Obama's mind perceived the utility of the **Affordable Care Act** and the impact it would have in helping Americans in the health care quandary, and his understanding of the hardships the Immigration initiative would alleviate; the President, after examining the evidence relating to the nation's Cuba policy, recognized its futility. In as much as the nation had downsized in many engines of its democracy, Mr. Obama chose to ditch this mill-stone cocoon around the American nation's neck. Flat-footed as Republicans generally are, Mr. Obama's Cuba Initiative caught them with their "drawers down." As such, the "Party of No's" stalwarts rushed to add their two cents of explaining how wrong the President's action really is but in fact, just as their "fools on errand" 43 Anti-Obamacare votes were, they're prepared to continue following the "ball and chain" Cuba Policy so unfit for the 21st century.

FREDERICK MONDERSON

In America, contending Republican aspirants began lining up to demonstrate their toughness and show how much more anti-Obama they could be. First Senator Marco Rubio, from his "supposed mantle of absolute wisdom" made unflattering remarks about Mr. Obama's decision. Next, Senator Ted Cruz of Texas joined the fray. Rubio was never grateful Mr. Obama now made it possible for him to visit his beloved Cuba. "Daddy Cruz," whose tree never fell far from the fruit, would never be thankful, for instead of "Sending Obama back to Kenya," the President now made it possible for him to visit his beloved fatherland. But, having "migrated," he would never return to Cuba even if Fidel stood ready to greet Papa Cruz! Most important, with Ted losing, "Papa's chance of sleeping in the Lincoln Bedroom" has become Nil.

It is interesting how President Obama, the first African-American President, sitting in "one pan in the scales of balance" outweighs an entire army of Republican operatives, thinkers, their backers, sycophants and a whole lot more. How unfortunate these folks have underestimated the intellectual fortitude, deliberative daring and punctilios messaging that undergirds Mr. Obama's work ethic and resulting successes. Even Mr. Obama is too modest to insist and demand, "Republicans, bring me giants instead!"

OBAMA THE JOURNEY COMPLETED - NEVER PROMISED A ROSE GARDEN

"On every front there are clear answers out there that can make this country stronger, but we're going to break through the fear and the frustration people are feeling. Our job is to make sure that even as we make progress, that we are also giving people a sense of hope and vision for the future." **Barack Obama**

Columbus Memorial stands before Union Station, Washington, DC.

FREDERICK MONDERSON

32. OBAMA AND NEW
CUBA POLICY
By
Dr. Fred Monderson

When the Obama - Cuba Comet to restore diplomatic relations and open an embassy in Havana streaked past, it left Republican rockets scrambling to just get a footing on its tail, but this in itself was nothing but streaks of melting ice. The significance of the move had global implications because it not only realigned Latin America relations heightened by the unpredictably creative capabilities of Mr. Obama's

OBAMA THE JOURNEY COMPLETED - NEVER PROMISED A ROSE GARDEN

vision and bold action, but it also signaled to the world his intentions of placing his nation in the forefront of future global developments and leadership. Actions of the "visionless at home" were understood and their anticipated response in support of a long-standing and failed Cuba Policy, terribly not in America's best interest was not unexpected. Cuba had long come of age, rapidly approaching "social security retirement" and Republican policy makers had failed to realize embargo and isolation were ineffective. This "ball and chain" mentality coupled with opposition to Obama was not only expected but was clear evidence of their bankrupt thinking in a new age. In the youthful age of the Cuban revolution there was a message of substance and symbolism in this action but with age this toothless tiger had lost all but its stripes and even its "dental implants" had lost its bite!

"With the changing economy, no one has lifetime employment. But community colleges provide lifetime employability." **Barack Obama**

The embargo and isolation did more for the Cuban Revolution than most will ever understand. Sure the associated action forced the Soviet Union to withdraw in the Cuban Missile Crisis; a dangerous and foolhardy power play, no doubt. Yet, and significantly, it demonstrated American tenacity, strength and resolve! More importantly, however, it did two unmistakably significant things for Cuba under Fidel Castro. Understandably, when "attacked" by a mighty power, especially from some 90 miles from its shores, the state became tremendously paranoid and restricted freedom of its citizens fearful of all suspicious behaviors. There is no doubt, external threats supporting internal anti-regime elements contributed to such restrictions. As such equally, the nation turned inward, making the most of its own capabilities, its natural resources, human and material. Much more far-reaching, it empowered the human mind to creatively explore all avenues of human progress fed on a bare-bones economic structure. Thus, as the nation became strong under strain, especially in the tumultuous 1960s and 1970s, Cuba began exporting its revolution through friendships and solidarity and social support by show of force in defense of other people's territorial integrity and sovereignty.

OBAMA THE JOURNEY COMPLETED - NEVER PROMISED A ROSE GARDEN

As "Third World" nations began wrestling with the challenges of the "First World" legacy of Colonialism, Imperialism, Neo-Colonialism; liberation struggles and aspirants to power began to take courage, for if Cuba could stand up to America, then they could fight to gain their freedoms. Into this melee Cuba found its "finest hour." Forging friendships with states as Libya and other emerging nations particularly in West, Central and Southern Africa, Cuba supported training liberation fighters, arming them and reintroducing them into "the bush" to fight for their freedom.

FREDERICK MONDERSON

As Ronald Reagan and Chester Crocker "pussy footed' with "constructive engagement" in South Africa certainly aided by the British government under Margaret Thatcher, both Mozambique under Samora Machel and Angola under Augstinho Neto exploded and detached themselves from Portugal. As if sensing the inevitable, South Africa intervened in Angola to aid Jonas Savimbi and threatened Luanda, Angola's capital. Who could forget that glorious cover of the *Africa Magazine* that depicted elements of a contingent of heavily armed "Cubans in Africa?" From then on it was all Fidel! We had allowed a puppet to become a master because of the embargo!

A master manipulator, a master propagandist as a master of oratory, Fidel Castro became famous for giving 6-hour speeches of which 5¾ were railings against the great dart-board to the north. And as he, by slight of voice, berated America, he tightened his grip at home indoctrinating an entire generation of Cubans to think differently outside the box about the wider world. As some have said, "We make dictators," we made Fidel by initially supporting and recognizing his

OBAMA THE JOURNEY COMPLETED - NEVER PROMISED A ROSE GARDEN

new government. We also made him innovate and grow in revolutionary conscious manhood which became a powerful symbol around the world.

Cuba founded its own medical and agricultural schools. It trained its people and offered free scholarship to deserving foreigners. It sent its goodwill doctors abroad to manage local hospitals and provide seriously wanting medical assistance. When disasters struck the Cubans were there first. Having established a weakened but effective system particularly because of the American Embargo and Isolation, which in fact, only America adhered to this since the "Enemy's enemy is a friend," the Cuban industry thrived among mischief makers.

FREDERICK MONDERSON

It may be argued; Cuba thrived more in the six years of the Obama administration than in any comparative period. It hosted conferences and attended conferences; it lent assistance to hurricane hit Caribbean nations; and most significantly it was the first to arrive in Haiti after the earthquake and the last to leave. Cuban doctors are in Africa fighting Ebola to this day.

Republican leadership was so married to the McConnell's "One term President" mandate and its ramifications they lost sight of the Cubans, Fidel and Raul, and their cadres. It's been said, if you assault a man's mother he will, in time, forgive you; but if you steal his money, he never forgets. The anti-Fidel "rabble" in Florida was really the Cuban privileged class who lost power, influence and their hold on the economy when Fidel dispossessed them. All America's attempts against Fidel and the Cubans in the Bay of Pigs fiasco, the assassination attempts, and the strategy to divorce him of his beard without his barber's consent were in vain. Impersonators now grew "Fidel's beard." Thus, all things considered, Cuba thrived within its sphere.

OBAMA THE JOURNEY COMPLETED - NEVER PROMISED A ROSE GARDEN

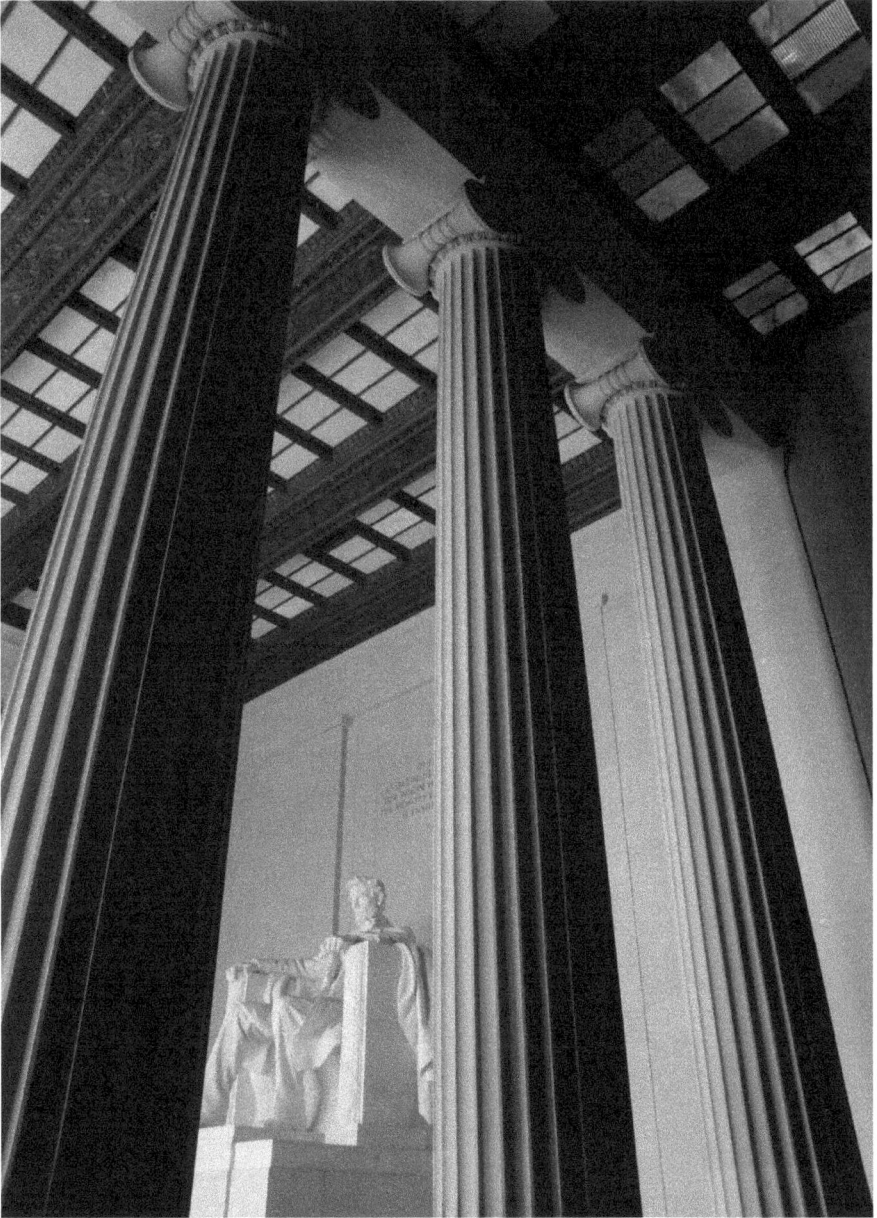

View of the Great Man seated from between the massive columns of his Temple.

FREDERICK MONDERSON

In his first campaign, Mr. Obama announced he is not opposed to talking to anyone, even Cubans. At Nelson Mandela's funeral, Mr. Obama paused and shook hands with Fidel's successor President Raul Castro. Who knows, Mr. Castro may have purposely been seated in that position for the encounter. The Republican uproar at home was instant and deafening. "He shook hands with the Devil!" This is what sets Mr. Obama apart from his critics who have been dubbed "dumb!" Can you imagine McConnell or Cruz in the same position, lifting their noses disdainfully and just sliding-by Mr. Castro? The next day world-wide, newspapers would mock America for being uncouth and arrogant at a globally solemn occasion.

Now, with all this as a back-drop, Mr. Obama announced his historic decision on Cuba by stating: "We will end an outdated approach that for decades has failed to advance our interests, and instead we will begin to normalize relations between our two countries and open an embassy in Havana, while the Cubans open one in Washington."

It is interesting how every time Mr. Obama unleashes one of those profound new domestic or foreign policy initiatives, Republicans rush to explain their opposition and offering poor excuses as an answer. Whether it's the Immigration issue, Opening to Cuba, the Asian Trade Pact, the Climate Change Agreement, even the Iran Nuclear deal, Republicans offered sorrowful and lame excuses in opposition. Meanwhile, these major accomplishments add significantly to the ever-expanding Obama legacy with yet, more, to come!

"After a century of striving, after a year of debate, after a historic vote, health care reform is no longer an unmet promise. It is the law of the land." **Barack Obama**

OBAMA THE JOURNEY COMPLETED - NEVER PROMISED A ROSE GARDEN

33. "GRINDING THE REPUBLICAN AXE"
By
Dr. Fred Monderson

Moments after President Obama announced his new Cuba Policy, Republican "axe-men" began grinding. We often tell young people not to join gangs because they ultimately become responsible for the many acts of the gang. It is debatable whether to characterize current Republican outlook and actions as equated with a "ship of fools" but whatever type of ship, foolish ideas seem to emanate there from. Leading Republican operatives in and outside government seem to operate in group-think mentality; it seems gang-like for they all gang-up on President Obama.

"There are patriots who opposed the war in Iraq and there are patriots who supported the war in Iraq. We are one people, all of us pledging allegiance to the stars and stripes, all of us defending the United States of America." **Barack Obama**

OBAMA THE JOURNEY COMPLETED - NEVER PROMISED A ROSE GARDEN

View of the Washington Memorial from within the Lincoln Memorial.

The first to challenge Mr. Obama's Cuba Policy announcement was Senator Marco Rubio (R. Fl.) who had unflattering things to say about the man and his position. As a member of the "Party of No" sailing that "ship," whatever it is, Mr. Rubio, in "group think" fashion mode remained unalterably committed to "Don't Mr. Obama's Dice!" That is, whatever the President says, he must respond in a negative manner. Thus, his negative and unflattering critique of this new Cuba Policy many have determined a wise move, a good thing, a major, major step forward, can probably be considered the Senator's first mistake on the road to 2016.

Here's a scenario! Let us suppose NASA launched a deep-space probe that nearly 60-years later made no contact, can we suppose we're searching in the wrong quadrant or location? Should we recall the craft and make a mid-course correction or continue in the same direction for another six decades that essentially reveals the folly of our policy?

At this stage in America's history, considering the Obama stamp of revamping the auto industry, invigorating the nation's economic and financial policy structures under Dodd/Frank, giving wings to Wall Street, incentivizing Research and Development of energy and mechanical structures, empowering Community Colleges to create a broad range of technical foundations to help mechanize the nation's thinking skills and innovative enterprises, reorganizing the military's fighting strategy and armaments in fleet-footed effectiveness and so much more that is essentially a firm foundation in guiding our nation's 21st Century war machine. These successes, in comparison should questions whether Speaker John Boehner and incoming Majority Leader Senator Mitch McConnell are really "good for America?" Sure they have new legislative authority but their "new wine in old wine-skins" mentality raises questions regarding the direction of their ship. Given the last years of their legislative behaviors even their questionable response to President Obama's new Cuba Policy and a slew of innovative and effective strategies, many could argue, it's time for "these fossils to become museum curios."

OBAMA THE JOURNEY COMPLETED - NEVER PROMISED A ROSE GARDEN

Senator Lindsey Graham is nothing but another equal at table aboard that ship dong donuts at sea. His caustic condemnation of the President is no less hostile than "Mac and Cheese" though he leads the "Lost Brigade" from behind! Chris Cillizza of *The Washington Post* pointed out Senator Mitch McConnell, among other things, has been around politics for nearly 60-years. It is interesting for nearly 60-years the U.S. Embargo and isolation of Cuba has not worked and this great mind has not seen this. Just as the many policies and procedures the President issued relative to the positive breakthrough listed above, Mr. McConnell saw them in a negative light and in similar manner he saw the Cuba initiative. A truly investigative reporter should ask Mr. McConnell that million dollar question put to so many other Republicans, "Can you think of one good thing Mr. Obama has done since he became President?" Given Mr. Obama's above 50 percent polling, a "NO" answer is truly foolish.

In by-gone days walking the dog meant you had a three-foot leash at your side. Today's leashes are some 20-25 feet. Some have argued, practically everyone is on a leash. Mr. McConnell, by virtue of his outrageous statement regarding "One term President" and that infamous "I got that Nigger in the White House" thumbs-up signal, placed him on a leash to deny Mr. Obama a "victory." Hence, on Cuba "He must cut his feet to fit the slipper" of objection to Obama!

Persons of inastute analytic vision may praise both Mr. McConnell and Mr. Boehner for recently funding the government for an entire year. Fact is, the elephants made donkeys of themselves the last time around. This time around they have gone to the other extreme, hoping to cut Obama off at the pass later. At that time, even with "Obamacare," given these great men's record of failure in the ring with Obama, now that some 16 million have registered for the Affordable Care Act's protections, Republicans will need "stilts to reach for challenge," all the while they waste the people's energy and expectations. There is something about the "Obama Mystique" that even when he is standing still, his opponents do or say the darnest things. The Republican big guns' response to Obama's initiative on Immigration and Cuba has been "We will not fund it!" Fact is, they have already funded it and by the end of the financial cycle these policies will have become so deep-rooted erasing their utility and significance will become so monumentally costly it will not be worthwhile. If they have not learnt anything with the Affordable Care

OBAMA THE JOURNEY COMPLETED - NEVER PROMISED A ROSE GARDEN

Act especially after nearly fifty failed attempts to scuttle Obama's signature legislative accomplishment, the fifty-million beneficiaries plus the forty-seven million who are watching and will vote their interest in 2016 equals a dilemma for Republicans.

The American eagle between the tips of two Ionic Capitals.

FREDERICK MONDERSON

OBAMA THE JOURNEY COMPLETED - NEVER PROMISED A ROSE GARDEN

FREDERICK MONDERSON

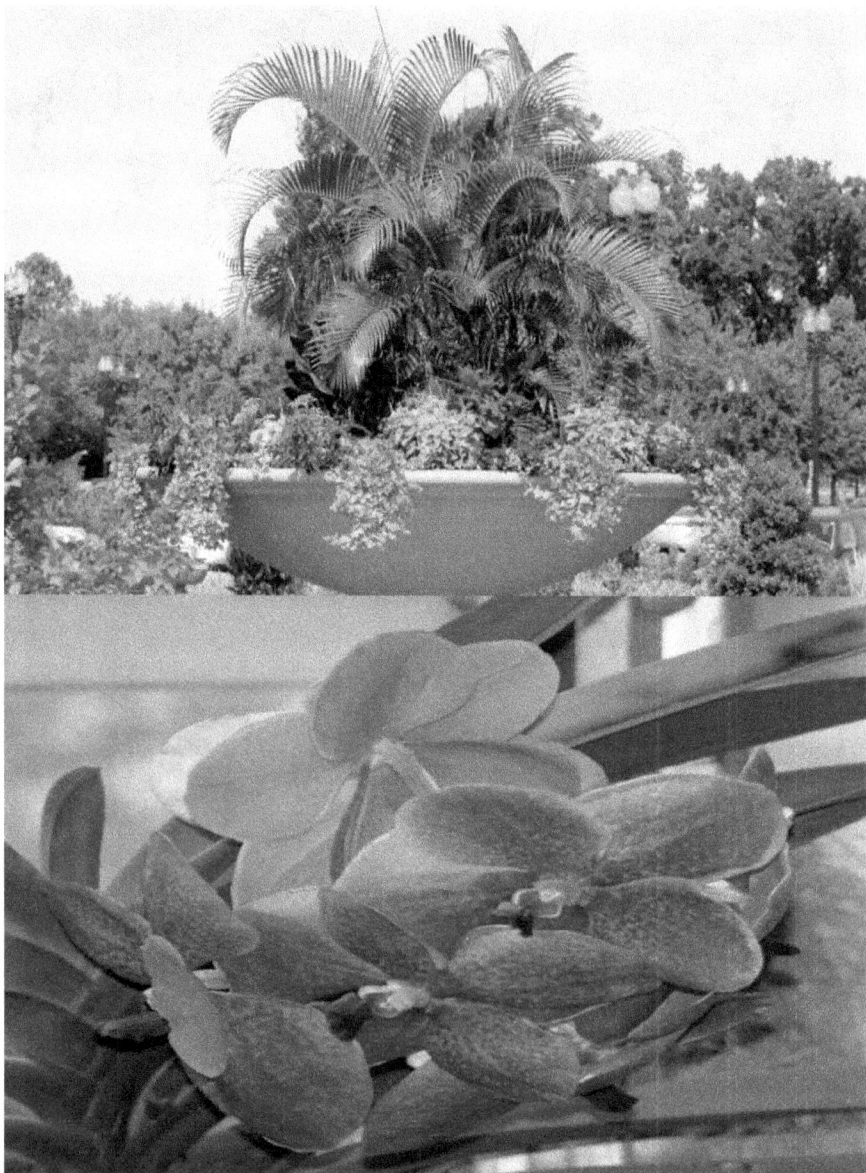

OBAMA THE JOURNEY COMPLETED - NEVER PROMISED A ROSE GARDEN

Panoramic view of Capitol Building from the Great Lawn.

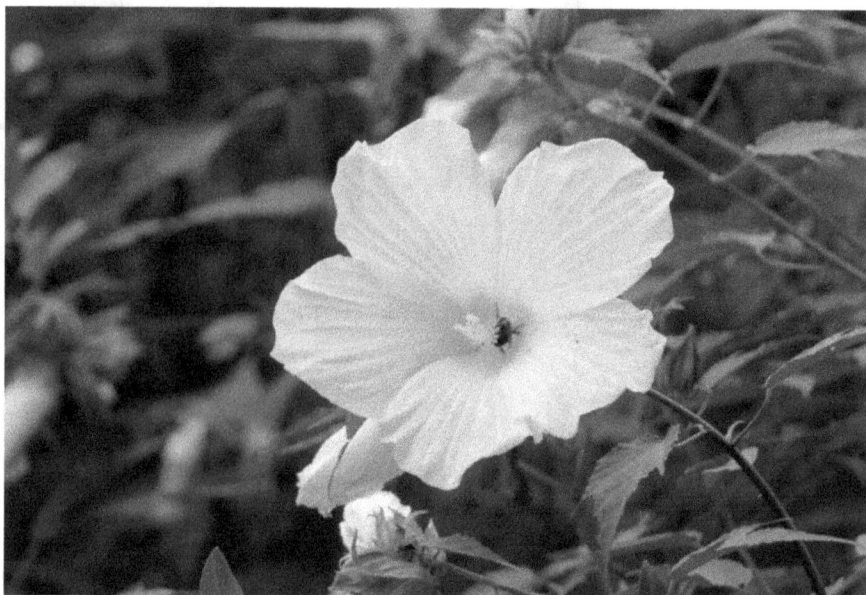

OBAMA THE JOURNEY COMPLETED - NEVER PROMISED A ROSE GARDEN

34. SALVATION THROUGH PAN-AFRICANISM
BY
DR. FRED MONDERSON

Across the globe, the African World is in disarray! Forces in opposition are escalating sentiments of division to suppress and control the aspirations and wealth of African people whether in Guyana where racial division is a fact; across the African continent where tribalism creates suspicion and division; and in local communities in America racists of all hues including militias, skinheads, even "Tea Party" types and associates racially stereotype as powerful an individual as President Obama, so what can we say of the average man. Gentrification is not only displacing many long in residence of local areas but with this trend a pejorative mentality pervades the behavior of some new residents fed by divisive elements emanating throughout the nation. Significantly, as many greats in Black perennial struggle for salvation through economic, political, education and social empowerment join the pantheon of revered ancestors because they came early, viz., Rev. Shutllesworth, Sonny Carson, Jitu Weusi, Bill Lynch, Queen Mother Moore, Malcolm X, Martin Luther King, Ossie Davis, Elombe Brathe, Maya Angelou, Ruby Dee, Et. Al., there is an ever-present need for a continued cadre of vibrant young leadership motivated by an active and effective philosophic orientation and *modus operandi* that will and continue to advance the cause of African peoples' salvation. Pan-Africanism is such a philosophic ideology. Pan-Africanism was born and nurtured in the cauldron of African people's struggles across chattel slavery, colonialism, imperialism, even Neo-Colonialism's exploitation and racism. It therefore gave birth to nationalist assertions in order to affirm and secure equality and dignity for African people wherever.

"Cutting the deficit by gutting our investments in innovation and education is like lightening an overloaded airplane by removing its engine. It may make you feel like you're flying high at first, but it won't take long before you feel the impact." **Barack Obama**

OBAMA THE JOURNEY COMPLETED - NEVER PROMISED A ROSE GARDEN

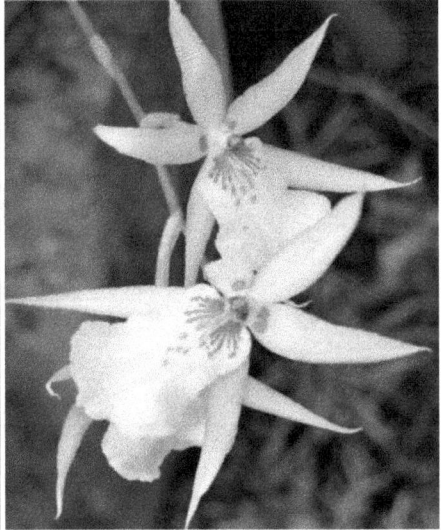

Viewing the 2014 Soccer World Championship in Brazil, it's clearly evident, that once European elitist sport has "gone African," where such soccer powerhouses as England, France, Germany, Netherlands, and especially South American teams, are manned by players whose ancestors are indigenous to the African continent. The unmistakable fact is; those teams' striking thrusts and threats are significantly African in representation!

Nevertheless, oftentimes viewing contemporary developments we see a unique phenomenon represented in map displays highlighting significant occurrences. In football, the various stadiums across the host nation Brazil stand out on such a representative map.

In that nation, there may possibly be 120 million people of African ancestry. This is the largest single number outside of the African continent. As such, it would be an important first-step if many Brazilians root for African teams taking the field to qualify as top contenders. Of course, we do not mean when their nation is playing, for then we saw the stands full of symbolic yellow and green Brazilian colors. After all and notwithstanding, enlightened Brazilian intellectuals have insisted, their people learn more about and appreciate their African heritage.

World War II Memorial of the conflict fought in the Atlantic and in the Pacific.

OBAMA THE JOURNEY COMPLETED - NEVER PROMISED A ROSE GARDEN

The notion of Pan-African consciousness was first articulated and championed by W.E.B. DuBois and Sylvester Williams in 1900 although it dates back to the efforts of Paul Cuffe, Martin Delaney, Henry Highland Garnett, Frederick Douglass, Sojourner Truth and Harriet Tubman, among many others. Booker T. Washington was a major Pan-Africanist player through his "Tuskegee Model" though he never got the recognition his efforts deserved. In the early decades of the 20th Century, Marcus Garvey was an ardent advocate for the unity of African people, at home and abroad, and thus founded the Universal Negro Improvement Association (**UNIA**) to advocate such a goal.

FREDERICK MONDERSON

OBAMA THE JOURNEY COMPLETED - NEVER PROMISED A ROSE GARDEN

Garvey came to America to meet Booker T. Washington who died just before his arrival in 1916, yet he continued the task of mobilizing and unifying African people under the banner of "**One People, One God, One Destiny**!" However, he was not alone in that era for besides Washington's Tuskegee Institute and the birth of the National Association for Advancement of Colored People as well as the National Urban League; these creative agencies' efforts have proved enduring institutions and testaments of constructive African unity and uplift movements through equally creative struggles. Then in 1919, DuBois convened the **First Pan-African Conference** in Paris contemporary with the **Versailles Peace Conference** concluding **World War One**. To contest the negative reaction to the conference from America and Great Britain especially, the latter quintessential imperialist and colonialist nation; DuBois appealed to Blaise Diagne, a Senegalese Delegate to the French Assembly during the tenure of Prime Minister Georges Clemenceau's government.

In this, Diagne was DuBois' "ace in the hole!" For, during the war, as the German military hammer pounded France, Clemenceau dispatched Diagne to West Africa to recruit Africans to fight their German enemy. He successfully recruited some 120,000 Africans who helped stem the German onslaught thereby rescuing France. In payback, Clemenceau simply said, "Go ahead, have the Conference, but keep it low key!" So once the go-ahead was given and venue secured, DuBois invited delegates from Europe, Africa, North and South America and the Caribbean. There the flames of a unifying global African consciousness had been lit! During the inter-war years (1919-1939) three such conferences were arranged as DuBois, aided by George Padmore and others remained active in the struggle. This struggle espoused the intent of Pan-African consciousness to combat the many years of systematic assaults upon the humanity and integrity of the African persona, long oppressed, at home and abroad.

FREDERICK MONDERSON

OBAMA THE JOURNEY COMPLETED - NEVER PROMISED A ROSE GARDEN

Africans from all over, particularly the colonial possessions on the continent and in the New World, fought to check German World War Two rampage in Europe, North Africa and among the Atlantic Ocean states and their sea traffic. At war's end in 1945, then an elder and somewhat tired DuBois turned over leadership of the Pan-African movement to a younger and more vigorous Kwame Nkrumah of Ghana who chaired the **Fifth Pan-African Conference** at Manchester. In that city, Fredrick Engels championed the Labor Movement, and so reception to the conference was more favored there. This time, the Pan-African movement had come of age, and so the next generation of leadership charted the movement with a mandate to decolonize Africa and the other colonial areas in the Caribbean. In America, desegregation of the Armed Forces following the War coupled with the on-going activism of such persons as A. Philip Randolph, Rev. Shutllesworth and legal eagles such as Thurgood Marshall, kept the flame burning in the desire to seriously free African people and uplift their status in all aspects of human relations in America and throughout the world!

World War II Memorial of the conflict fought in the Atlantic and in the Pacific.

As these delegates returned to their respective countries and began organizing their people to become more knowledgeable about colonial administration, organized labor and politics, a significant unifying idea was that of Pan-Africanism. The philosophy of Pan-Africanism essentially expressed; African people globally have been the victims of European and American political expansion, exploitation, racism and solely for the furtherance of these nations' elites' interests and privileges. In this climate, as people's consciousness evolved further animated by activism and unionization, the colonial powers began incarcerating leaders of the new movement seeking to free their land. While these setbacks may have been temporary, they actually further galvanized colonial peoples to seek their freedom. The "winds of change" had arrived.

OBAMA THE JOURNEY COMPLETED - NEVER PROMISED A ROSE GARDEN

FREDERICK MONDERSON

Nevertheless, within just over a decade of the **5th Pan-African Congress** of 1945, Kwame Nkrumah led Ghana to independence on March 6, 1957. With the colonial powers weakened by the war and the people united under a vibrant group of leaders, viz., Sekou Toure of Guinea; Namdi Azikwe of Nigeria; Jomo Kenyatta of Kenya; Gamal Abdel Nasser of Egypt; Tafawa Balewa of Nigeria; Et. Al., espousing an equally vibrant strategy, dominoes began to fall and African nations became independent enmasse; thereby becoming members of the United Nations simultaneously. In America, reaction against Blacks in general, nationalists, the Black Panthers, the Student Non-violent Coordinating Committee, the Republic of New Africa

OBAMA THE JOURNEY COMPLETED - NEVER PROMISED A ROSE GARDEN

and the Southern Christian Leadership Council under Rev. Joseph Lowery who pressed their case, protested, marched, used sit-ins, and encouraged economic boycotts while seeking political rights and educational and social advancement reaction against such demands for rights and equality, their actions drew condemnation on the world stage. All this occurred against a heightened and vehement backlash from persons seeking to "hold back the dawn" of human and equal as well as civil rights. This group was represented especially by Southern racists, foremost among whom was the segregationist George Wallace of Alabama, Sheriff "Bull Connor," and other nefarious allies in the North whose intent although unsuccessful was to hold back the dawn of rising aspirations and demands Americans be given their constitutional rights.

FREDERICK MONDERSON

OBAMA THE JOURNEY COMPLETED -
NEVER PROMISED A ROSE GARDEN

FREDERICK MONDERSON

The success of African and Latin-Caribbean-American nations in winning their independence and being seated at the United Nations in the 1950s and 1960s emboldened the Civil Rights Movement in this country. So much so, the reactionaries of "Bull Connors," the "White Citizens Council" and "Ku Klux Klan" terrorists demonstrated their inhumanity and unabashed racism against protesting African-American men, women and children. They used water cannons and dogs against protesters. The nation continued to be embarrassed on the world stage. There was, therefore a "push and pull," emergence of young and persistent leadership in Jesse Jackson, John Lewis, Stokeley Carmichael (Kwame Ture) and Rev. Abernathy, among others. Then there was the assassination of key figures in the struggle; and, government complicity in unscrupulous behaviors against its

OBAMA THE JOURNEY COMPLETED - NEVER PROMISED A ROSE GARDEN

citizens; nevertheless, hard won gains were accomplished. Just as the 1960s was the decade of African independence; concerted African-American struggles in coalition with progressives and sympathetic activists, in and out of government, especially the Kennedy brothers, brought about important gains in voting, housing, education and solidarity with Africa.

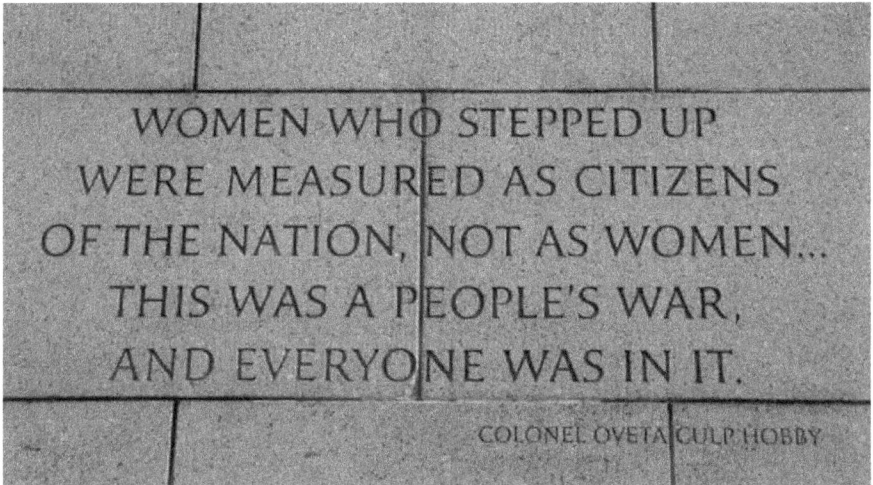

World War II Memorial of the conflict fought in the Atlantic and in the Pacific.

The historic 1954 *Brown v. Board of Education of Topeka, Kansas* Supreme Court ruling laid the foundation to desegregate the nation's school system, and the election of John Kennedy in 1960 started America down a "no-turn back" road of the "Great Society." The new philosophy and outlook Mr. Kennedy brought to the office was designed to transform the nation while looking to encourage its people to outdistance other nations in science and the various areas that measure global leadership. The President was naturally impressed with Dr. Martin Luther King's poor people's "March on Washington" in August 1963 that was actually the brainchild of A. Philip Randolph, longtime worker in the vineyards of social activism. He, Dr. King delivered his famous "I Have a Dream" speech which was really about jobs and the poor! However, within months President Kennedy was assassinated and his successor, Lyndon B. Johnson, in the interest of "continuity," launched his "Great Society Program" which was actually Kennedy's brainchild.

Surprisingly, the master politician, Lyndon Johnson, a Southerner from Texas, was able to cajole, "push and pull," "give and take" and his efforts bore fruit successfully in passage of the 1964 Civil Rights Bill. The next year, 1965, the Voting Rights Act was passed and then Malcolm X was assassinated. This was a major blow to Black-American nationalism. The Vietnam War was also a factor. Nevertheless, the struggle continued and by the end of the decade, Medgar Evers and Martin Luther King were also assassinated. Throughout, several acts of brutality were committed against the African-American community including more than 100 civil rights murders for which no one was brought to justice! Of course, in the southern "lynching states," for nearly a century after passage of the 13th Amendment outlawing slavery, these, by today's definitions, terrorists, lynched, killed, tarred and feathered, terrorized and intimidated African people and deprived them of society's protections and equal, human and civil rights guaranteed by the Constitution. Meanwhile, the Africans continued to express concern at the United Nations regarding the condition of their brothers and sisters in America.

OBAMA THE JOURNEY COMPLETED - NEVER PROMISED A ROSE GARDEN

FREDERICK MONDERSON

It is believed, that such behaviors continue today, often in clandestine actions, code words even coded statements. Nevertheless, as philosophic wisdom holds, "There are no permanent enemies, only permanent interests." Malcolm X, on the other hand, declared "History is a great teacher" and that we must learn about how other peoples addressed and solved their problems. As for example, without question, America was at war alongside Britain and France against Germany in World Wars One and Two. In these conflicts, untold numbers of American citizens were killed. Yet, as of today, June 22, 2014, on Fareed Zakaria's Sunday Program on CNN, in an interview with the German Minister of Defense, and in response to a question, she is quoted as saying, "We share the same values as America."

OBAMA THE JOURNEY COMPLETED - NEVER PROMISED A ROSE GARDEN

Therefore, that being so, and despite the war dead, the unmistakable fact is, if the above is true, then Africans worldwide, at home and abroad, should unite under the ideological philosophy of Pan-Africanism for this is a potent formula to strengthen African resolve and the only way the world will respect each and every one of Africa's sons and daughters!

"All of us take offense to anyone who reaps the rewards of living in America without taking on the responsibilities of living in America. And undocumented immigrants who desperately want to embrace those responsibilities see little option but to remain in the shadows, or risk their families being torn apart." **Barack Obama**

FREDERICK MONDERSON

35. CALLING OUT OBAMA!
By
Dr. Fred Monderson

The "Britisher," "Jihadi John," who murdered the American hostage Tim Foley, in stating **ISIL's** message called out Mr. Obama, which in itself is an affront and challenge! It was terrible that he committed an unspeakable horror but to specifically direct his invective towards "Obama" was a challenge that had to be met. However, we must first of all recognize the three-fold nature of this situation.

"If you were successful, somebody along the line gave you some help... Somebody helped to create this unbelievable American system that we have that allowed you to thrive. Somebody invested in roads and bridges. If you've got a business - you didn't build that. Somebody else made that happen." **Barack Obama**

First, **ISIL**, in seeking attention to their much lamented military action many have characterized as barbaric, needed to respond to

OBAMA THE JOURNEY COMPLETED - NEVER PROMISED A ROSE GARDEN

American Iraqi bombing in pushback enabling humanitarian assistance to Yazdis cornered on that Iraqi mountaintop. As bombings signaled America's repeated resolve in standing good and against tyranny and terrorism, Edmond Burke's universal admonition became more manifest. "The only thing necessary for evil to triumph is for good men to say or do nothing!" Thus, America's response to the siege was to bomb **ISIL's** targets in the vicinity signaling an act of good challenging evil.

Second, say what you will, but America is synonymous with championing the underdog and oppressed. This has become much more realistic when it comes to guarding and responding to the safety of its citizens facing harm abroad. Jim Foley, an American journalist, was captured by rebels some have labeled terrorists in Syria, more than two years ago. It is understandable, the dangers of being in harm's way in the middle of such a conflict. However, there is international law stating "Prisoners of Wars" should be treated humanely and this was expected regarding Mr. Foley. Well, the **ISIL** rebel did the unthinkable in beheading Mr. Foley. This unspeakable act sent shudders across the globe that, in this day and age; persons, in this case, terrorists, could act so inhumanly, and then especially boast of such in public.

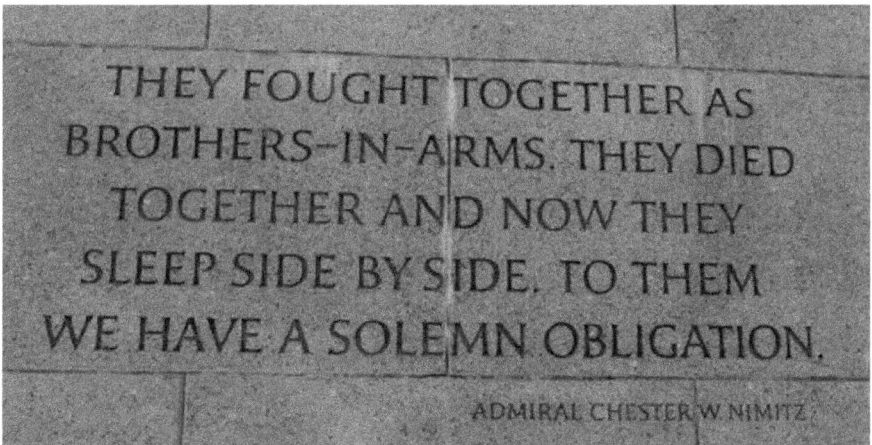

THEY FOUGHT TOGETHER AS BROTHERS-IN-ARMS. THEY DIED TOGETHER AND NOW THEY SLEEP SIDE BY SIDE. TO THEM WE HAVE A SOLEMN OBLIGATION.

ADMIRAL CHESTER W. NIMITZ

FREDERICK MONDERSON

Ok. So the **ISIL** terrorists have been rampaging across Iraq and Syria, pillaging, killing in murderous swaths and seizing territory. Then they beheaded Mr. Foley. In this final assault and insult, they called Mr. Obama's name as representative of the American people. Their spokesman "Jihadi John" spoke directly to Mr. Obama in a threatening tone. Reasonable people will acknowledge, Mr. Obama must respond having being called out. Most important, all those Navy men aboard the floating battleships, loading and dispatching attack fighters in unison, saw this assault not simply against the Commander-In-Chief, but equally against them as one with Obama.

OBAMA THE JOURNEY COMPLETED - NEVER PROMISED A ROSE GARDEN

Equally, this same steadfastness of will and persistence stood against Lieutenant Colonel Robert Maginnis who wrote an editorial critical of the President. A CNN program anchor asked Mr. Maginnis to explain his statement that "Mr. Obama lacked the testicular fortitude to attack **ISIL** at their bases in Syria!" This verbal assault was also against those said neb on battleships in the considered "Theater of Operation."

FREDERICK MONDERSON

Here again, we see evidence of the wherewithal Mr. Obama brought to the table as President, viz., a wonderfully active intellectual capacity grounded in an effective work ethic associates and assistants have characterized as "frighteningly well-prepared on all issues of concern." All this is enhanced by an exceptional team of advisers, military and civilian, who contribute various expert viewpoints on issues that enlighten and encourage Mr. Obama to arrive at the most optimum decision regarding any issue under study.

OBAMA THE JOURNEY COMPLETED - NEVER PROMISED A ROSE GARDEN

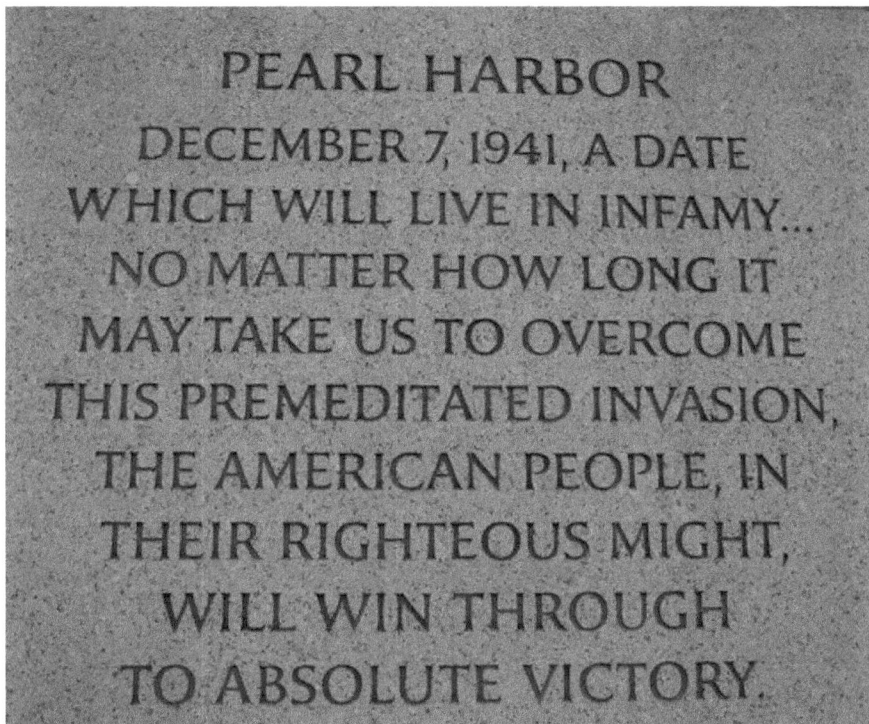

PEARL HARBOR
DECEMBER 7, 1941, A DATE
WHICH WILL LIVE IN INFAMY...
NO MATTER HOW LONG IT
MAY TAKE US TO OVERCOME
THIS PREMEDITATED INVASION,
THE AMERICAN PEOPLE, IN
THEIR RIGHTEOUS MIGHT,
WILL WIN THROUGH
TO ABSOLUTE VICTORY.

World War II Memorial of the conflict fought in the Atlantic and in the Pacific.

Mr. Obama has always demonstrated his thinking style is not one to rush to judgment but to deliberate all the pros and cons before arriving at a consensus and then final decision. However, in case of ISIL, as the United States of America Declaration of Independence insists, "After a long train of abuses," and if you add the personal touch the executioner added, the consequences should be expected. Add to this Mr. Maginnis' dare, tons of "bricks" or many hammers will descend on **ISIL**!

So, the President ordered surveillance over Syria to gather real-time information about **ISIL's** status. In some of General Clarke's comments, though critical at times, he stated: "The President ordered air reconnaissance to add to existing knowledge about **ISIL**." Here again is reinforced an aspect of Mr. Obama's thinking strategy. Make sure every step is on a firm foundation by studying all aspects of its ramifications. However, past experiences have taught Mr. Obama a great deal. President George Bush took a "go it alone attitude" against Saddam Hussein in Iraq in 2003 when the world admonished against such recklessness. This damaged the world's perception about America which Mr. Obama had to repair and reverse at the same time enabling him to learn many things.

Mr. Obama is not simply a passive thinker, for while he contemplates the "Syria scenario," he continues to pound **ISIL** movements in Iraq. All the while he strategizes to organize a coalition that will represent a broad consensus designed to eviscerate the "cancer" he spoke of. As caution rules his thinking, when pressed on Syria in a News Conference on Thursday August 28, 2914, Mr. Obama insisted he "did not have a strategy, yet!" He insisted this is because many, especially the press, had jumped ahead of him and were practically printing dynamics of his bombing strikes in Syria.

OBAMA THE JOURNEY COMPLETED - NEVER PROMISED A ROSE GARDEN

FREDERICK MONDERSON

Many quickly sought to characterize Mr. Obama as either weak or ineffective because he did not have a "Syrian strategy," but in clarification it became clear what he actually meant. As explained, his **ISIL** strategy was based on creation of a unified Iraqi government that was inclusive of significant elements of ethnic Iraqis. Once this is

OBAMA THE JOURNEY COMPLETED - NEVER PROMISED A ROSE GARDEN

achieved, there would be support for Iraqi forces in armaments and training. He seeks to engage regional governments to become involved because **ISIL** poses an even greater threat to them in the long run. He was working to engage global allies to support action against **ISIL** and then once these "ducks were lined up," he would consult Congress to authorize the use of more effective military force against **ISIL** in Iraq and then possibly in their home base in Syria.

FREDERICK MONDERSON

OBAMA THE JOURNEY COMPLETED - NEVER PROMISED A ROSE GARDEN

Men of vision reason, the President "does not want to tip his hand" for as many would tend to believe, **ISIL** strategists are also watching his press conferences. However, what the President is showing by his actions can be classed as follows.

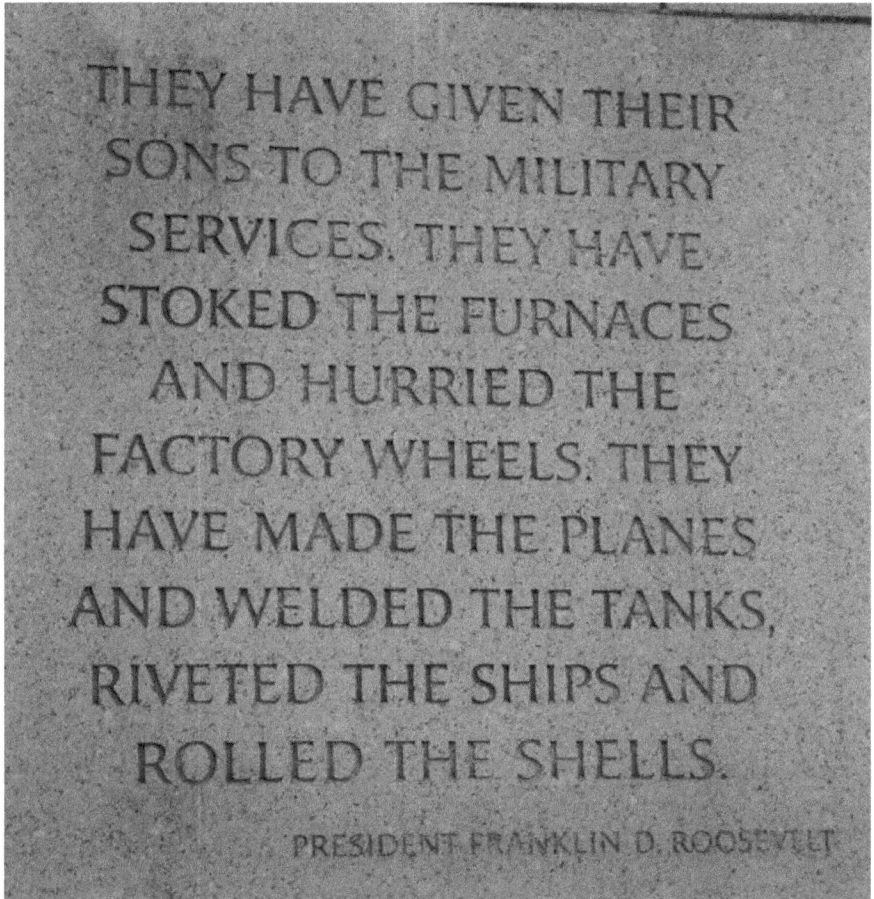

THEY HAVE GIVEN THEIR SONS TO THE MILITARY SERVICES. THEY HAVE STOKED THE FURNACES AND HURRIED THE FACTORY WHEELS. THEY HAVE MADE THE PLANES AND WELDED THE TANKS, RIVETED THE SHIPS AND ROLLED THE SHELLS.

PRESIDENT FRANKLIN D. ROOSEVELT

World War II Memorial of the conflict fought in the Atlantic and in the Pacific.

FREDERICK MONDERSON

1. The humility of the really powerful.

2. The integrity of a human being who respects the sanctity of human life which his critics do not have.

3. In his respect for human life, Mr. Obama is reluctant to risk the life of others without all legitimate considerations.

4. He recognizes Iraq is a sovereign nation and under international law recognizes America does not preclude the sovereignty of every other nation.

5. When it became clear Osama bin Laden had taken up residence in a sovereign nation he had the "Testicular Fortitude" to order military action that ended the life of the murderous mastermind, a feat which had eluded his predecessor other President.

6. The leader of Al Qaeda in Somalia, Al-Shabab, Mr. Ahmed Godane, long on Mr. Obama's radar and his resulting demise says much for planning and strategy, emphasizes Obama's "stick-to-it-ive-ness" which trumps the Colonel's contention.

7. Today, Somali Pirates are out of business because Mr. Obama has done his homework.

Perhaps when this is over, Lt. Colonel Maginnis will have the "testicular fortitude" to "eat crow" and admit sending Seal Team Six to pursue Osama bin Laden was indeed a courageous act as did the Somali surgical strike.

OBAMA THE JOURNEY COMPLETED - NEVER PROMISED A ROSE GARDEN

FREDERICK MONDERSON

Thus, Mr. Obama actions will not only address the Colonel's challenge but will answer the executioner's dare and punish him for his cruelty and upstart arrogance!

"No party has a monopoly on wisdom. No democracy works without compromise. But when Governor Romney and his allies in Congress tell us we can somehow lower our deficit by spending trillions more on new tax breaks for the wealthy - well, you do the math. I refuse to go along with that. And as long as I'm President, I never will."
Barack Obama

OBAMA THE JOURNEY COMPLETED - NEVER PROMISED A ROSE GARDEN

36. ARC OF THE MORAL UNIVERSE
By
Dr. Fred Monderson

Dr. Martin Luther King boldly exclaimed, "The arc of the moral universe is long, but it bends towards justice!"

At his 2005 Inaugural, the Republican President George W. Bush (No. 43) decried the prevalence of racism in the country up to that date, one hundred and fifty years after the Emancipation Proclamation and subsequently the Civil War Amendments. Through Jim Crow (1865-1890) legislation and practice, *Plessey v. Ferguson* (1896) being outlawed by *Brown v. Board of Education* (1954), the *Civil Rights Act* (1964) and the *Voting Rights Act* (1965) in response to the Civil Rights Movement all demonstrated advances in the American social order. The 1965 *Voting Rights Act* empowered African-Americans to gain political representation across the different states, culminating in the 2008 election of Barack Obama as the first African-American President. In response, the then Mayor of Newark, New Jersey, Cory Booker characterized Mr. Obama's election victory as ushering a new "post-racial America." Naturally, there was a difference of opinion on both sides of the issue, whether Black or White.

"We didn't become the most prosperous country in the world just by rewarding greed and recklessness. We didn't come this far by letting the special interests run wild. We didn't do it just by gambling and chasing paper profits on Wall Street. We built this country by making things, by producing goods we could sell." **Barack Obama**

Then along came Mr. Mitch McConnell (R. Kentucky), Minority Leader in the Democratic controlled Senate of the United States Congress. First, Mr. McConnell made a publicly advertised statement, "I intend to make Barack Obama a one-term president." This statement, Mr. Morgan Freeman, the actor, on Piers Morgan's CNN program, characterized as "blatantly racist!" Mr. McConnell's next ground-breaking and outrageous behavior was, after an important round of negotiations with the president, where bright-eyed and bushy tailed, smiling Mr. McConnell came forward to the camera and gave that now coded and infamous "thumbs up" signal to likeminded cohorts who were probably in the treasonous gathering. Observers with penetrating vision saw this for what it was; a signal to his handlers that "I got that Nigger in the White House!" Some five years later on October 6, 2013, in a big Front Page "write-up," *The New York Times* newspaper published a "big write-up" indicating in the run-up to the 2012 election, a group of influential Republicans and their backers met and strategized on how to deny Mr. Obama a second

OBAMA THE JOURNEY COMPLETED - NEVER PROMISED A ROSE GARDEN

term. The article named individuals and some 20 or more Republican affiliated Non-Governmental Organizations, many trained and training propaganda derivatives involved in propagandizing opposition to Mr. Obama's **Affordable Care Act** maliciously termed "Obamacare." Many characterized the gathering as a treasonous conspiracy to subvert the legally elected representative of the United States Government.

FREDERICK MONDERSON

Because Mr. Obama is an African-American who had the audacity to declare for the presidency, beat back his democratic challengers and be chosen to represent his party, a number of racial cross-currents began to emerge directed at this courageous individual. While Blacks accused him of "not being Black enough," Whites accused him of being "too Black!" No one ever accused the previous 43 American presidents of being too white! A whole flurry of activists mobilized to denounce Mr. Obama's quest. Republican propaganda helped foster notions Mr. Obama would change the Constitution and this fueled right-wing militias to purchase and stock up on enormous armaments for the coming "race riots" which, up to this date, have yet to materialize. Strange but, this same claim has been leveled against Hillary Clinton that she intends to change the Constitution and outlaw people's guns. This is just one recurring tool of the Republican playbook.

OBAMA THE JOURNEY COMPLETED - NEVER PROMISED A ROSE GARDEN

World War II Memorial of the conflict fought in the Atlantic and in the Pacific.

Some have called "Joe the Plumber" a "fraud" who accused Mr. Obama of promoting "socialism" and this garnered him enormous but short lived fame. "I can see Russia from my front porch," "Lipstick on a pig" Sarah Palin accused Mr. Obama of "Palling around with terrorists." Questions of his patriotism, ability to effectively lead and lack of foreign policy experience proved enormous capital for the Anti-Obamaites. Still, Mr. Obama forged ahead with an effective organizational strategy, a tremendous work ethic and an unfailing desire to be successful while not paying much attention to nay-Sayers. Along came the "Birther" movement with its queen and king Donald Trump on their "fools' errand" and while this emboldened anti-Obama forces, it also gave birth to the "Tea Party" formation. Through this entire parallel path, with Mitch McConnell's quest in full stride, Republicans benefitted tremendously. All the while, their "Party of No's" obstructionist agenda blocked every legislative effort by Mr. Obama designed to improve the condition and advance the cause of the American people. Meanwhile, Senator McConnell, having issued his charge set about plowing the path of opposition as part of the grand scheme we could come to learn of later.

Undaunted, President Obama continued to repair the faltering auto industry; lending money to banks and to bail out Wall Street; assessing the nation's crumbling infrastructure and providing for "shovel ready" jobs. Next Mr. Obama sought to overhaul the nation's economic and financial systems; express concern about the environment, energy supplies and laying great emphasis on research and development of future resources. Nevertheless, Republicans turned up the heat on the President. As a result, a climate of hatred and disrespect began to be encouraged against Mr. Obama. Surprisingly, as Republicans and their allies peppered Mr. Obama, they remained unmindful Edmund Burke wrote, "The only thing necessary for evil to triumph is for good men to do or say nothing." As such, this is what the higher echelon of Republican leadership did just that! Nothing!

OBAMA THE JOURNEY COMPLETED - NEVER PROMISED A ROSE GARDEN

Despite their failure to achieve anything but block the President's every move and falsely characterize the man and his work, they hood-winked the American people and so the Republicans made gains in the 2010 and 2014 mid-tern elections, which is not surprising as American election evidence has shown. Despite the vituperative Republican mischief, President Obama continued his efforts to scale down the wars in Iraq and Afghanistan, contend with Somali pirates and pursuit of Osama Bin Laden and his Al Qaeda affiliates. As this unfolded, Obama continued his responsibilities as Chief Executive and Commander-in-Chief. Meanwhile the Republicans convened, in a tunnel vision focus on how their new Congressional majority will hamstring Mr. Obama in the incoming Congress. Throughout it all, as Mr. Obama played it cool, in response to unfolding events, the Grand Jury decision happened.

The Arc of the Moral Universe swung back when people of goodwill, young and old, across all ethnic spectrums took to the streets in city after city, across the nation and world. It was clearly evident, the "Chickens had come home!" Republicans were caught off-guard. They said nothing and had nothing to say as the people staged numerous "Die-Ins" across the various cities and states. Young and old protested and demonstrated, chanting "Justice for Michael Brown," "I am Michael Brown" and "Hands-Up, Don't Shoot!" In New York City and as far away as California protesters chanted Eric Garner's last words, "I Can't breathe!" and "Justice for Eric Garner!" as well as "Black Lives Matter!" Prominent Athletes in the NFL and NBA joined the fray with "Hands Raised" in a "Hands Up, Don't Shoot" gesture.

World War II Memorial of the conflict fought in the Atlantic and in the Pacific.

Again, Republican, caught bent over with their pants below the knee and the people at their rear, are in a quandary. The hatred and disrespect they have sowed is now being called into question by young people who want an America free of racism and with justice for all. If, as some predict, this movement may last into next election, then the country may be transformed in more ways than one.

OBAMA THE JOURNEY COMPLETED - NEVER PROMISED A ROSE GARDEN

"In a world of complex threats, our security and leadership depends on all elements of our power - including strong and principled diplomacy." **Barack Obama**

FREDERICK MONDERSON

37. SHAMELESS "ANTE BELLUM" LEGISLATORS
By
Dr. Fred Monderson

As Speaker Boehner, Senator McConnell and others publicly flagellate President Obama accusing him of jeopardizing their children's future, they should be asked 'Are you teaching your children to be as reprehensible as you are?' 'Are you educating them on how to deal with the issue of racial hatred?' 'Will they continue to advocate superiority of white over black?' Unfortunately, these two men and others have presided over a climate of racial hatred and disrespectful treatment of President Obama, so that today formerly obscure lawmakers are emerging from the political woodwork to demonstrate that infamous Joe Wilson "You Lie" mentality. Now, seemingly individuals shamelessly acting like "Ante Bellum" legislators are championing sending the President to jail! Today

OBAMA THE JOURNEY COMPLETED - NEVER PROMISED A ROSE GARDEN

President Obama's poll ratings are very high and so we ask where these detractors are? Congratulations Speaker John, your people have descended to the sub-sewer of human indecency and have "damaged your foot," as the "chickens have indeed come home!" Sue the President and "fight Mr. Obama tooth and nail!" Don't you mean till you have no more teeth and there are no more nails! Point is, after such commendable circus performances, your people probably call and congratulate each other, and then sleep well believing they have done in "The Nigger in the White House." Meanwhile, Mr. Boehner, you like so many others have been retired to Republican "Old Folks Homes' Rocking Chairs," while Mr. Obama keeps carrying on!

"It was the labor movement that helped secure so much of what we take for granted today. The 40-hour work week, the minimum wage, family leave, health insurance, Social Security, Medicare, retirement plans. The cornerstones of the middle-class security all bear the union label." **Barack Obama**

Thanks to you guys, it is amazing how much of a laughing stock America has sunk into as if in a "barrel of crabs." When we tout the superiority of American democratic culture abroad, our political behavior seems hypocritical and emboldens our enemies who mimic Republican leaders in their propaganda repertoire. A credible question is 'Are we as weak as they profess; or, is it because Mr. Obama is a Black man, descendant of a race which has been enslaved, down-trodden and brutalized in this society?' Your arrogant blindness could never countenance where greatness lies. Are you aware of Count Volney who reminded all, "The people we enslave today are the founders of the arts and sciences that characterize our way of lives."

FREDERICK MONDERSON

World War II Memorial of the conflict fought in the Atlantic and in the Pacific.

Since "old ideas die hard," Republican behavior today is not much different from *Ante Bellum* days when slave owning legislators looked disdainfully upon, and harshly treated native born Blacks as this colony transformed itself through a revolution under the Articles of Confederation. Subsequently, the United States Constitution, viable though not perfect in its initial implementation requiring some 26 Amendments as the nation expanded; yet, is still considered a work in progress struggling to have rights guaranteed to Blacks not negated.

It is interesting how Mr. Jim Henson, the first President under the Articles of Confederation is for the most part not given his proper place in history as he guided the nation experiencing the initial pains of its birth, like Balthazar his race was perennially misrepresented. Have we forgotten America's first authentic hero and martyr, Crispus Attucks was a Black Man. This deafening silence, somewhat different in its recognition more intensely equates with the treatment meted out to the first African-American President of the Republic under the Constitution. Was Henson treated in similar fashion? Intermediate

OBAMA THE JOURNEY COMPLETED - NEVER PROMISED A ROSE GARDEN

between these two Black-American leaders, presidents and legislators either impugned or ignored the African-American, backbone of an emerging Republic who, up to today, fights its many wars that, in contradiction, protects individuals who today practice *"Ante Bellumism!"*

FREDERICK MONDERSON

First as unpaid laborers, then victims of share cropping crop lien, economic peonage, convict lease exploitation, and a largely ignored unemployed Black labor force as the nation progressed from agrarian through Industrial and Corporate Post-Computer age economy, continuing disrespect for Blacks has remained a premium mindset of influential members in the leadership of this nation. That is, regardless of Black persons academic and intellectual achievements and political standing; their intellectual, artistic, technological and overall creative contributions notwithstanding, even the lowest class White person seeks to manifest false and misleading tenets of "white supremacy."

Strangely, in a nation that takes pride in its history, as champions of liberalism, ethical and humanistic principles have remained, for the most part, silent on the significance and ramifications of important,

OBAMA THE JOURNEY COMPLETED - NEVER PROMISED A ROSE GARDEN

yet troubling, milestones in its national growth. Whether it was the **1787 Three Fifth Clause or Compromise** of the U.S. **Constitution**; the **1820 Missouri Compromise**; the **1850 Compromise**; the 1857 *Dred Scott Decision*; the "Grandfather Clause;" and the 1896 *Plessey v. Ferguson* decision, without question, merchants of discrimination and racial hatred, in contradiction, exploited and trampled upon these legislative milestones for political and or economic gain. Fortunately, some results of the Civil War sought to reinvigorate a semblance of humanity in the perception of America as a nation on a democratic mission. Sad to say, however, while Radical Republicans, not to be confused with others of the same genre today, championed the Black cause of equality and vote resulting in the 13th, 14th, and 15th Amendments to the Constitution, the defeated and disaffected South struggled and re-emerged, thanks to the **Compromise of 1877** that ended Reconstruction. This legislative betrayal in vengeance, gave birth to, and emboldened, the **Ku Klux Klan**, **Knights of the White Camellia**, the **Jayhawkers,** the **White Brotherhood**, the **Black Horse Cavalry**, who used whippings, maimings, and even murder to keep Blacks from the polls. Norman Hodges' *Black History* (Monarch Press (1971) 1974: 136) tells of South Carolina's racist Senator Ben Tillman" who "sum up" the white South's determination to deprive Blacks of their vote in this blatant statement to the Congress: 'We have done our level best. We have scratched our heads to find out how we could eliminate the last one of them (Black voters). We stuffed ballot boxes. We *shot* them. We are not ashamed of it." No wonder at Jim DeMint's and Joe Wilson's behavior, they continue in the tradition of that eminent South Carolinian.

Finally the White Citizens Council, ultimately ushered in White Primaries, with the intent of further curtailing the Black vote. These actions galvanized their true nature as acts of terrorism materialized against African-Americans through terrible acts of lynchings, tar and feathering, disrespect, intimidation, killings, trickery and denial of political expression. Caught in the throes of gushing wealth as the nation entered the industrial age and expanded across the North-American continent, the federal government ignored the plight of its most vulnerable and authentic citizens. Odious racist groups such as the Klan became the face of America!

Amidst Jim Crow and other forms of terrorism, promoting economic and social advantages and white privilege in the Southern "Lynching States," Teddy Roosevelt charged up San Juan Hill with "Blacks watching his back." Still, these warriors got no respect for their heroism. Confronted by racial riots at home, they were first to be sent abroad to "Save the World for Democracy" in 1917. Having fought abroad and return home fighting, Republicans abandoned these supporters who instantly became Democrats and changed American political history. In an age of "New Deal," African-Americans were still generally ignored in the labor force until A. Philip Randolph threatened to March on Washington! In government acquiescence, job offers became more real and the armed forces became desegregated during World War Two.

OBAMA THE JOURNEY COMPLETED - NEVER PROMISED A ROSE GARDEN

World War II Memorial of the conflict fought in the Atlantic and in the Pacific.

The 1954 *Brown v. Board* decision simply antagonized the hornets' nest of racial oppression which in turn spawned the Civil Rights Movement where Black men and women challenged the might of American racial prejudice that enabled Bull Connor to demonstrate "his finest hour." The "1963 March on Washington" was to address the need for jobs and the plight of the poor, Black and White! As events unfolded, the Black Community paid a heavy price in leadership and suffering to achieve the Civil Rights and Voting Rights Acts and their protections in the 1960s and beyond.

Today, every one of those hard-fought for gains are challenged and being eroded as Republicans re-emerge in the political leadership in state houses across the nation as they did in the post-Reconstruction era. The fight to remove Blacks from Congress, post-Civil War joblessness, the inequity of share-cropping and political marginalization, gerrymandering under political chicanery as well as denial of voting rights through all manner of schemes were ongoing. Today, the same type of trickery and chicanery warns us that we must be constantly on guard against members of the Republican Party who have exchanged white sheets and hoods for business suits and esquire titles. A Christian line asks 'Where were you when they crucified our Lord?' The answer, "I was under my sheet and hood!" Where else? Clearly, much of this is occurring under the cloak of blatantly false propaganda designed to mislead the gullible.

For example, on Saturday, November 22, 2014, **National Action Network** South Brooklyn Chapter with Queenie Huling presiding sponsored an **Affordable Care Act** "Obamacare" Open Enrollment Forum at the Coney Island Branch Public Library. New York State Assemblyman (D-46) Alex Brook-Krasny mentioned a Kaiser Family Foundation Study indicating "60 percent of Republicans support the 6-most important clauses on Obamacare." Strange they support Affordable Care Act but object to Obamacare! Asked if they supported expanding pre-existing conditions, they responded yes. Did they support carrying children up to age 26? Yes! Did they support Obamacare, no! The pending contradiction is, if the Republicans now in the Congressional majority repeal Obamacare, as they have long tried to do, will they retain those provisions which benefit their constituencies. If they do, then this is indeed hypocrisy of the highest order and the highest form of political chicanery.

Despite what Republicans may propagandize about Obama-Care, President Obama is a visionary who realized the need, since 60 percent of bankruptcies occur because of health care costs. This lack of insurance coverage more particularly affected people of color and immigrants as well as poor whites who are not exempt from the debilitating challenges of health care costs.

OBAMA THE JOURNEY COMPLETED - NEVER PROMISED A ROSE GARDEN

World War II Memorial of the conflict fought in the Atlantic and in the Pacific.

According to the New York State Health Care Navigator Pierre Devaud, who works for the Brooklyn Chamber of Commerce, another Republican misrepresentation is that the Affordable Care Act is government insurance but it is not. It is private insurance! The measure, falsely dubbed "Obamacare," yet provides ten essential health benefits ensuring quality and affordable access to health care to all those who are covered. This means a lot to poor folks.

Wide-ranging, with some ninety plans to choose from, in 2013, one million New Yorkers registered for this program. Many are eligible to qualify for some subsidy to assist their payment. In several Southern States, legislators prevent their constituencies from accessing these benefits! For example, a single individual making $46,000.00 or less per year is eligible for financial assistance to offset the costs as well as a family of four making $96,000.00 or less.

FREDERICK MONDERSON

OBAMA THE JOURNEY COMPLETED - NEVER PROMISED A ROSE GARDEN

All this is complicated but you have to hand it to Republicans who have emerged as masters of deception and misrepresentation to hoodwink those folks who are in their base. However, try as they may, the little men can never tie Gulliver because not only are his moves legal, his credibility unblemished, his work ethic unmatched and his humanity unparalleled. Mr. Obama is a cut above the opposition. That is, all the opposition combined!

FREDERICK MONDERSON

Iconic image of America's foundation on the cornice of the Capitol Building.

"And we have done more in the two and a half years that I've been in here than the previous 43 Presidents to uphold that principle, whether it's ending 'don't ask, don't tell,' making sure that gay and lesbian partners can visit each other in hospitals, making sure that federal benefits can be provided to same-sex couples." **Barack Obama**

OBAMA THE JOURNEY COMPLETED - NEVER PROMISED A ROSE GARDEN

38. NO TO REPUBLICAN BULLYING!

By

Dr. Fred Monderson

Everyone is familiar, from the inception of his Presidency, Republicans, not simply leaders but even obscure politicians and young upstarts have made a career, and however, short it has been, in defaming, bullying and disrespecting Mr. Obama. Some GOP lawmakers of whom you never heard because they have been irrelevant like Rep. King, not the New Yorker, who came out against President Obama's immigration stand, have and are now trying to impress the world with self-assumed political acumen, knowledge about current issues and electability of which they are actually ignorant. They wish to impress their fans how much they have "stood up" to Mr. Obama. Perhaps it was Rick Santorum who in recent years had coined the phrase, "Poison the well" and now Republicans are trying to pin this label on the President because he has issued an Executive Order on Immigration. Given "big money" problems, viz., health care insurance, immigration, bank collapse, auto industry woes, a lacerated economy bleeding untold millions of jobs, Osama bin Laden running wild with two concurrent wars, the nation's infrastructure in shambles and Republicans purposely incapacitated, then Barack Obama is forced to act decisively as he has done despite the "Party of No" "Fighting him tooth and nail." Such behavior required bold action by the President on issues such as Immigration Reform as he has demonstrated through the issuance of Executive Action.

"One of the great strengths of the United States is... we have a very large Christian population - we do not consider ourselves a Christian nation or a Jewish nation or a Muslim nation. We consider ourselves a nation of citizens who are bound by ideals and a set of values."
Barack Obama

Some time ago, in frustrated exasperation from observing Republican treatment of the President, that famous New York Knickerbocker Spike Lee asked, "When will Mr. Obama take off the gloves?" In response to Republican behavior which tried to reduce Mr. Obama to as Denzel Washington said in the movie "Inside Man," where he was in an almost vulnerable position!

OBAMA THE JOURNEY COMPLETED - NEVER PROMISED A ROSE GARDEN

World War II Memorial of the conflict fought in the Atlantic and in the Pacific.

The President consistently tried to work with Republicans whose mantra of "No" has earned them the deserved "Obstructionist" title. Those two famed "One term" and "98 percent" lawmakers, Mr. McConnell and Boehner respectively, could certainly have been numbered in that "Republican conspiratorial gathering" mentioned in *The New York Times* and were also principals in the obstructionist movement which finally hoodwinked the American voting public such that the Republican right-wing gained full control of Congress in the 2014 Mid-term Election. By completing the portrait caricature of Mr. Obama, as the earlier defamers Michele Bachmann, "Joe the Plumber," "You Lie" Joe Wilson, "Stupid" Senator Charles Grassley, "Waterloo" Jim DeMint, Issa and Chavetz, and the many others intoxicated from drinking the toxic tea of racial fear and inherent hatred including even "Palling around with terrorists," "Lipstick on a Pig" Sarah Palin still gazing at Russia from her front porch, have disparaged the President. There is an old adage which holds that "Politicians are liars and cheats" who can be bought. They hypocritically kiss babies then steal their lollipops. Their goals in life are to get elected and then re-elected; and they will say anything to further this aim. Let us not forget, it was Rick Santorum, a Republican, who said, "Anything gets said in a campaign." This Republicans do very well.

OBAMA THE JOURNEY COMPLETED - NEVER PROMISED A ROSE GARDEN

Central to that hue and cry has been: Mr. Obama is an unpatriotic socialist, too Black, not a citizen, lying about his place of birth and to quote "Daddy Cruz," we should "send Obama back to Kenya!" As all of this unfolded a "Light Colonel" in Republican leadership does not have the simple intelligence to realize and admit "Mr. Obama is a decent and knowledgeable, highly educated individual as well as the loving head of a family. Full of empathy as a humanitarian;" this is all because they are too busy fighting him "tooth and nail." Using the threat of "being sued" and "impeached," they have played the "stunt card." In fact, Mr. Obama is doing such an excellent job as Chief Executive; it is evident that he has rescued the nation from the economic quagmiric ditch into which Republicans under George Bush, Dick Chaney, Et. Al. drove the country. We must remain vigilant that history does not repeat itself in this behavior under this newest Republican Congressional leadership.

FREDERICK MONDERSON

OBAMA THE JOURNEY COMPLETED - NEVER PROMISED A ROSE GARDEN

Let's face it; it's stupid to assume that Mr. Obama, a highly intelligent Constitutional scholar, very well versed in the history of the office he now serves in and equally armed with a battalion of lawyers would propose illegal measures and or acts in an unlawful manner. As President he must certainly know how far his position allows him to act on behalf of the American people and those living within our nation's shores. If we care so much for one American being victimized abroad, can we care less for 50 million lacking health care protections and others who wallow in poverty? Are we so insensitive towards 5 million within our shores who generally do the low paying manual jobs which many Americans frown upon? Even much more important, functioning in an environment rife with racial prejudice and hatred, Mr. Obama certainly realizes as a Black man that he is and would be subjected to the most rigorous scrutiny and this would surely shape his behavior. As we await his biographical tell all book, one has to wonder how he will characterize the "B" and "C" political actors whom he has encountered in recent years.

Most observers will admit, as Malcolm X reminded us: "History is a good teacher," and when later scholars scrutinize this "Obama Age" they will probably admit it was also an age of prejudice and disrespectful by "two bit hustlers" and "chiselers" not yet caught but whose opportunistic intents didn't really consider the public good. So, after "a long train of abuse" Mr. Obama "tightened his belt," donned his armament, expressed, "Damn the torpedoes, full speed ahead" and walked into the street on immigration reform. There he called out Republicans to "Pass a Bill!"

Gold Stars, each one representing 100,000 lives lost in the conflict as represented in the World War II Memorial of the conflict fought in the Atlantic and in the Pacific.

OBAMA THE JOURNEY COMPLETED - NEVER PROMISED A ROSE GARDEN

Perhaps some Baptist preacher can ask incoming Senate Majority Leader Mitch McConnell and Speaker John Boehner, "What is the value to a man if he gains the world but loses his soul?" They should also ask this of Donald Trump. Then again, there's only one truly "Soul" Brother in American leadership. This is Barack Hussein Obama, 44th President of the United States of America.

FREDERICK MONDERSON

"I've got two daughters; 9 years old and 6 years old. I am going to teach them first of all about values and morals. But if they make a mistake, I don't want them punished with a baby." **Barack Obama**

OBAMA THE JOURNEY COMPLETED - NEVER PROMISED A ROSE GARDEN

39. NEWT! RUNNING DOWN OBAMA!
By
Dr. Fred Monderson

Former Republican House Speaker Newt Gingrich wears his "Obama hatred" badge unabashedly. Appearing on Candy Crowley's CNN program "State of the Union," in view of current complexities facing President Obama, Mr. Gingrich expressly stated the President's "behavior" is "now cowardly." Shameful that days after the surgical strike that killed the Al Qaeda-linked Somali Al Shabab leader Ahmed Abdi Godane, Mr. Gingrich would make the above statement rather than rush to congratulate Mr. Obama for dispatching one of America's notorious enemies. As such, a number of attendant factors involving Mr. Gingrich need be addressed.

First, either Mr. Gingrich did not get the "E-mail" about Mr. Godame's demise because he is out of the loop in such briefings, which the news reported on endlessly; or, he speaks without thinking!

Thus, no longer a force in Presidential politics, Mr. Gingrich wants to show he can still challenge Mr. Obama, hence his outlandish remarks.

"Why can't I just eat my waffle?" **Barack Obama**

Second, as a presidential candidate, albeit a loser, Newt's fluffy ego was stoked when often referred to as "the smartest guy in the room." Now, coming up against another who is demonstrably superior intellectually and politically, Mr. Gingrich demonstrates the envious "fox and the grapes" pathology. So Mr. Gingrich questions everything the President says or does in these challenging times as his Republican colleagues have done and as he accentuates the negative, he gives America's enemies ideas.

Third, all career politicians especially at the Federal level, ultimately aspire to be President. As Speaker of the House of Representatives and by virtue of the line of Presidential Succession, Newt stood "two heartbeats" away from being President. Ever since, Newt Gingrich has sought the Presidency unsuccessfully but he is caught in a contradicting maelstrom. He is a Republican, a member of the "Party of No" and certainly aboard Senator Mitch McConnell's "I intend to make Barack Obama a one-term president" bandwagon. However, even when doing his best, he falls short.

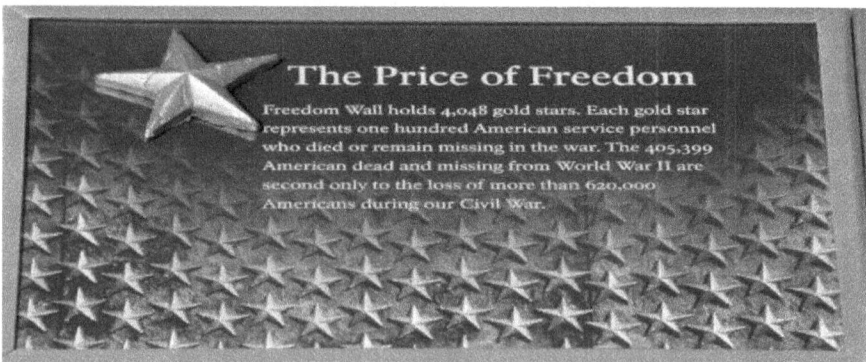

The Price of Freedom

Freedom Wall holds 4,048 gold stars. Each gold star represents one hundred American service personnel who died or remain missing in the war. The 405,399 American dead and missing from World War II are second only to the loss of more than 620,000 Americans during our Civil War.

The "Price of Freedom" in World War II Memorial of the conflict fought in the Atlantic and in the Pacific.

OBAMA THE JOURNEY COMPLETED - NEVER PROMISED A ROSE GARDEN

Fourth, Mr. Gingrich is from Georgia, a southern and "one of the lynching states." Georgia was among the states voting against Mr. Obama in both the 2008 and 2012 presidential elections. It would be nice to know all Georgians are not like Newt!

FREDERICK MONDERSON

Granted Newt Gingrich is not as smart as Barack Obama, evident in the 2-0 score in the presidential quest. However, "Newt is slick, not Vaseline-like but axle-grease slick." Notwithstanding, while he harbors presidential aspirations he does not want to appear as virulently anti-Obamaites as McConnell, Palin, Cruz, etc., who see Mr. Obama as the "Nigger in the White House" and out of his place. This list does not exclude contradictory "Nigger Lover" Jim DeMint who "likes the President" but wants to create his "Waterloo!"

Fifth, former National Security Adviser and Secretary of State Condoleezza Rice once exclaimed, "The view from the Oval Office desk is very different from what many believe." However, smart as Newt is supposed to be, Mr. Gingrich chooses to continuously lambast Mr. Obama because as a member of those who sought the presidency

OBAMA THE JOURNEY COMPLETED - NEVER PROMISED A ROSE GARDEN

and lost, he seems to follow a puppeteer's agenda. In this charade, he continuously seems to manifest an ante-bellum mentality so characteristic of Southern slave norms that saw the "Negro as inferior to Whites" in the "natural order" and their descendants continue to reinforce that false "white supremacy ideology" in the "social order" today. Mr. Newt Gingrich must also know, unless he is working vigorously and actively to change or remedy that racist mindset, he continues and helps perpetuate such and he most assuredly is numbered therein.

FREDERICK MONDERSON

Sixth, as *The New York Times* reported on October 6, 2013, a number of high-ranking Republican politicians and operatives met contemporary with the 2012 presidential election and strategized on how to obstruct Mr. Obama's re-election and his legislative and Executive Agenda. Big names such as former Attorney General, under Ronald Reagan, Ed Meese as well as leaders of some 20 Non-Government Organizations were mentioned as planning, training and executing a propaganda campaign under the guise of "educating" but in fact "mis-educating" the public about Affordable Care Act dynamics. In such an enormous agenda of concern to all Republicans it stands to reason the entire "Who's Who" would either be involved or briefed! Otherwise, they are not leaders but "wet-paper bags." Then, given they walk, talk and quack like all other Republican ducks, they cannot publicly negatively and similarly boast they were in that

OBAMA THE JOURNEY COMPLETED - NEVER PROMISED A ROSE GARDEN

room strategizing against Mr. Obama. Some have examined and characterized this behavior as treason, certainly sedition! Given Senator Mitch McConnell's classic racist statement regarding President Obama following events of January 2009, many observers theorized about such a gathering that gave McConnell's his marching orders. However, with no taped recordings of a roll-call, it simply remained suspended in thin air. However, in the now famous "Thumbs Up" after that first serious financial standoff, many agree Mr. McConnell was signaling his handlers and fellow conspirators. Nevertheless, in the debt-ceiling standoff that closed-down Congress, when Speaker Boehner exclaimed "We got 98 percent of what we wanted," the question is 'who was the "We" interest being served?' However, and again, in as much as *The Times* is the paper of record, its revelation provides the dots linking the 2012 to the 2008 behavior aimed at subverting Mr. Obama's legislative agenda from the beginning as the President's opponents manufactured and sustained a climate of hatred and disrespect for the "Nigger in the White House" It seems hard to deny, the objective of 2012 was same as 2008. If Mr. Ed Meese was a principal in 2012, most likely he was so in 2008. Thus, it seems reasonable to suppose any Republican leader not involved supports that Reagan 11th Republican Commandment mantra!

FREDERICK MONDERSON

New York part of the World War II Memorial of the conflict fought in the Atlantic and in the Pacific.

Equally, because he is a significant Republican operative, Mr. Gingrich cannot, even if he did, deny knowledge of and participation in the treasonous behavior. That being the case, Mr. Gingrich and the plotters should be arrested and put on trial for plotting against the legally constituted United States government headed by President Obama.

OBAMA THE JOURNEY COMPLETED - NEVER PROMISED A ROSE GARDEN

Seventh, those who think like Mr. Gingrich expects Mr. Obama to advise them about his strategies for this or that issue and are sadly mistaken. Unfortunately, Mr. Gingrich does not realize Republican behavior towards Mr. Obama pits them in the "enemy camp" so why should he inform them of anything given they are obstructionist by conviction and blatantly disrespectful by disposition and it is not inconsistent they would "leak" whatever to embarrass the Democratic President.

Eighth, when it comes to a strategy for dealing with **ISIL**, a state of continuing affairs Mr. Obama did not create but inherited, while Mr. Gingrich may claim to know its true ramifications; his denial of circumstances in its origin also affects his assessment of strategy and tactics to combat it.

FREDERICK MONDERSON

OBAMA THE JOURNEY COMPLETED - NEVER PROMISED A ROSE GARDEN

Ninth, as complex as the **ISIL** situation is, it needed the President's comprehensive approach, viz., insistence on a broad-based, multi-ethnic government in a post-Malaki Iraq; move to support, train and strengthen the Iraqi forces, Kurds and others in Syria; creation of a coalition of the willing who will assist in their respective areas of expertise; creation of a regional Middle-Eastern coalition of threatened states dispelling the "Crusader" myth; and with this arrangement satisfied, then requesting Congressional authorization to further pound **ISIL** in Iraq and Syria while insisting no American boots or combat soldiers be placed on the ground, except Special Operations groups to lend their expertise in training and to exploit targets of opportunity are all complexities Mr. Gingrich missed, despite his "smartest guy in the room" folly.

Tenth, perhaps one day, after a refresher course, Mr. Gingrich will come to recognize the dynamic nature of Commander-In-Chief President Barack Obama, a thinker and theorist, who keep besting all his Republican pals.

FREDERICK MONDERSON

"America is the student who defies the odds to become the first in a family to go to college - the citizen who defies the cynics and goes out there and votes - the young person who comes out of the shadows to demand the right to dream. That's what America is about." **Barack Obama**

OBAMA THE JOURNEY COMPLETED - NEVER PROMISED A ROSE GARDEN

40. HANDS UP!
By
Dr. Fred Monderson

It started a long time ago, this "Hands Up" salute when strangers, whether on horseback or walking, encountered each other, in a signal "I'm friendly and not hostile!" This became the origin of the salute. Sometimes one or even two hands were raised in this salutation. However, over the years the "hands up" salute changed to one, especially a waving hand; and two as a gesture of surrender showing the person has no armament that could threaten the other person. As times and circumstances changed, we saw prisoners-of-wars being led with their hands up, signaling surrender. Conversely, in sports arenas today we see fans doing "The Wave" which is a multitudinous hands-up wave in sequential motion, around the stadium. However, the first meaningfully significant hands raised in protest is traceable to the 1964 Olympics when amidst the Civil Rights struggle in America, two Black American athletes raised their fist in symbolic protest as the American Anthem was being played to show solidarity with the unfolding struggle at home. These heroes paid a price for this daring as the society Black-listed, ostracized and sought to forget them. Suffer, like heroes, they did, but the symbolism of their actions emboldened the civil rights movement in those days of their most haunting and memorable challenges. Thenceforth the raised fist symbolized demands for Black Power and a defiance in face of unjust authority.

"I want to reform the tax code so that it's simple, fair, and asks the wealthiest households to pay higher taxes on incomes over $250,000 - the same rate we had when Bill Clinton was president; the same rate we had when our economy created nearly 23 million new jobs, the biggest surplus in history, and a lot of millionaires to boot." **Barack Obama**

Subsequently, the raised fist thereafter became a symbol of resistance worldwide!

Modern dark days of the killing of Black men and women by police, civilians, even psychologically wounded Blacks, the raised fist became part of the repertoire of demonstrating groups across the country by persons of different persuasions fed up by the senseless killings. President Obama described such behaviors as "not who we really are."

Interesting, however, such a statement by President Obama has both domestic and international implications. When Mr. Obama succeeded to the Presidency in 2008, in the eyes of the wider world, even among

OBAMA THE JOURNEY COMPLETED - NEVER PROMISED A ROSE GARDEN

friends and certainly our enemies, America had sunk to the status of a "tin-horn banana republic" of bankrupt morals and questionable leadership. As such, and supported by some of the best minds the nation could muster, Mr. Obama effectively changed the world's view of this nation, halted its economic, financial and infrastructure decline, while researching and developing strategies to create a clearer vision for the nation's future. Who would have believed the nature of the "enemy lurking within?"

World War II Memorial of the conflict fought in the Atlantic and in the Pacific.

Today the Republican Party controls both Houses of the United States Congress having made additional and significant gains in the recent 2014 Mid-Term election. Many believe the nation does not really favor Republicans but voted against Democrats, who, despite their loss are still better regarded than Republicans who have been silent on Ferguson and may still again drive the car into the ditch as they did previously before being rescued by Barack Obama. Thus, Republicans may fumble the ball again.

FREDERICK MONDERSON

OBAMA THE JOURNEY COMPLETED - NEVER PROMISED A ROSE GARDEN

Nevertheless, in protest against unconscionable behaviors towards Americans, be they Black, White, Brown, or even Yellow or Purple, citizens in good conscience will continue to utilize the hands-up gesture to show disapproval of such behavior. As recent chants of "Hands Up. Don't Shoot;" were constants of street protests, they were not simply protesting these recent deaths but also calling attention to militarization throughout the national landscape.

FREDERICK MONDERSON

"If we choose to keep those tax breaks for millionaires and billionaires, if we choose to keep a tax break for corporate jet owners, if we choose to keep tax breaks for oil and gas companies that are making hundreds of billions of dollars, then that means we've got to cut some kids off from getting a college scholarship." **Barack Obama**

OBAMA THE JOURNEY COMPLETED - NEVER PROMISED A ROSE GARDEN

41. THAT MISSOURI COMPROMISE
By
Dr. Fred Monderson

Contrasting the actions of the Chief Executive when Missouri first became an item of significance and how President Obama responded to the current situation says much about both views of the issues and sadly, though things change how very much they remain the same. James Monroe was president when the Missouri Compromise became an issue of historical, political and moral significance and his impact

433

seemed minimal since he was probably planning colonization in Liberia, West Africa. On the other hand, after Ferguson exploded, President Obama directly intervened by sending a high level delegation to investigate and act. Now, as the community in Ferguson, Missouri awaited the Grand Jury decision on whether to indict Officer Darren Wilson for the killing of the unarmed teenager Michael Brown and in anticipation Governor Nixon declared a state of emergency in readiness of unlawful behavior; a young rapper and activist remarked to CNN Anchor Don Lemon, covering developments, "The racism of white supremacy is in the DNA of this state." This belief, therefore, dictates a look at some aspects of the nation's history particularly from the *de jure* and *de facto* mindset, set in motion by the Missouri Compromise of 1820; a significant milestone in the question of slavery and subsequently inequality of Blacks in the nation now famously or infamously characterized by events set in motion by the State of Missouri, the "Show Me State!"

"My task over the last two years hasn't just been to stop the bleeding. My task has also been to try to figure out how do we address some of the structural problems in the economy that have prevented more Googles from being created." **Barack Obama**

The Missouri Compromise was an important development in the legislative history of the new American Republic coming as it did in **aftermath of the War of 1812** which ended in 1815 and the beginning of **Internal Improvements** as the **Industrial Revolution** began to take hold in America. That year of 1820, with the **Compromise of 1787** or "Three-fifths Clause" as a backdrop designed to appease the "slave holding Southern states;" efforts to occupy and exploit the vast tracts of land acquired in the **Louisiana Purchase**, the future of enslaved Blacks in American was bleak at best! The dynamics unleashed in the **Cotton Gin revolution of 1793** conflicted with the shortcomings stemming from **outlawing the Slave Trade in 1808** then the labor

OBAMA THE JOURNEY COMPLETED - NEVER PROMISED A ROSE GARDEN

demands and wealth aspirations of plantation owners mounted and they demanded much from legislatures and protective forces. In Florida, generally under Spanish rule, the Seminole nation (Native Americans) had long been a place of refuge for runaway Blacks which was a source of irritation for slave-holding elements. So General Andrew Jackson was dispatched with a force to cross over to Florida and punish Seminoles for their acts of mercy in aiding runaways. This occurred in 1818 and if you add the creation of horrendous "slave farms" producing dreaded "**coffles of slaves**" chained and restrained in the most barbaric manner, this signaled Black lives within and outside the United States was not worth much, except as a commodity to a heartless, get rich slave owner class. After all, the entire "New World" seemed an enormous plantation where professing Christian White men, guided by the Bible, practiced the most inhuman crime against humanity lasting for centuries, extracting free labor at a brutal cost.

FREDERICK MONDERSON

OBAMA THE JOURNEY COMPLETED - NEVER PROMISED A ROSE GARDEN

Thus, the historic **Missouri Compromise of 1820** was accepted to achieve political balance by admitting into the Union one Slave State, Missouri; and one Free State, Maine. Harold G. Syrell in *American Historical Documents* (New York: Barnes and Noble, (1960) 1965: 177) explained it best in the following statement. "Missouri, part of the Louisiana Purchase, applied for admission to the union as a slave state in 1819. At the time there was an equal number of Slave and Free States, and neither wished the balance to be changed in favor of the other. James Tallmadge, a representative from New York, offered an amendment to the enabling act that would have gradually eliminated slavery in Missouri. The act as amended passed in the House but failed in the Senate. Meanwhile in December, 1819, Maine applied for admission as a free state. In the Senate the two admission bills were combined and were finally accepted by the House after the addition of a compromise amendment, introduced by Senator Jesse B. Thomas of Illinois. In November, 1820, when Missouri's constitution was submitted to Congress, it contained a clause unacceptable to the antislavery groups. Henry Clay, then, formulated a satisfactory compromise proposal, which was adopted on March 2, 1821."

FREDERICK MONDERSON

Constance Baker Motley, in an Introduction to "The Legal Status of the Negro in the United States" in John P. Davis' *The American Negro Reference Book* (Englewood Cliffs, New Jersey: Prentice Hall, Inc., 1964: 484) discussed the case involving Dred Scott and its impact on the status of enslaved Africans in America languishing on the altar of the Missouri Compromise of 1820. Ms. Motley writes: "In 1857 in the momentous Dred Scott case, nine members of the Supreme Court reviewed, at length, the prior and then current legal status of Negroes in the United States. At that time, most Negroes were slaves. Some had been freed by their masters in accordance with the legal procedures established by the law of the slaveholding states; others had likewise purchased their freedom. Dred Scott had been a slave in Missouri. In 1834 he had been taken by his master, an army surgeon, into the free state of Illinois. Subsequently, he was taken to the territory which is now Minnesota. There slavery was prohibited by the **Missouri Compromise of 1820**. In 1838 Scott was returned

OBAMA THE JOURNEY COMPLETED - NEVER PROMISED A ROSE GARDEN

to Missouri and later sold to another army surgeon. In 1853 Scott brought suit in a Federal court in Missouri claiming to be a free man. His claim was that he had become free upon being taken into free territory and consequently remained free upon his return to Missouri." It is to be noted, the many years he was languishing as a slave in an institution where untold millions were supplying free labor generating a significant portion of the nation's wealth!

FREDERICK MONDERSON

That is to say, for example, no one knows how long he had been a slave before 1834, most probably born a slave. Then the 1853 suit settled in 1857 had to be denied his freedom, if we accept 50 years as a slave this is a long time. **The 1965 Voting Rights Act turned 50 years in 2015; the 1963 March on Washington turned 50 in 2013; and the Cooperative Republic of Guyana which gained its independence in May, 1966 turns 50 years old in 2016.** This is a long time. It was a long time to be a slave. Equally, to conceive of millions and millions of people consigned to servitude and providing free labor in a heatless and brutal institution as **chattel slavery** is a phenomenon difficult to conceive; but this the American oppressor mindlessly perpetuated for nearly four hundred years. **Now what can these racists and these militias tell any Black man in America today**! No wonder today it is difficult for him to conceive of a Blackman as his equal, Christian beliefs, notwithstanding; for he remained mired emotionally and psychologically in the same filthy pit he consigned the enslaved African. If we use the aftermath of Dylan Roof massacre at Mother Emanuel Church in South Carolina where the victims' families forgave the killer to very early jettison that enormous guilt of hatred; the slave master is still trapped by the ghastly ghost of the inhuman malady, he constructed and perpetuated in the hellish slave system from which he benefitted enormously.

As a reminder, the story is told of a blind white man who went to a prize fight. He had an interpreter who gave him blow by blow commentary. As the fight waged into the late rounds he enquired of his commentator. What's happening now; to which the answer was, "The White Guy has the Black Guy down." "The Black Guy down? Keep him down, for when the Black man raises, hell raises!"

FREDERICK MONDERSON

However, as this courageous writer and activist continued, she noted: "The New York citizen who claimed to be his master defended on the ground, among others, that Scott could not bring suit in a Federal court because he was not a citizen of Missouri. Scott had just lost a suit on his claim to freedom in Missouri courts. The New York master asserted the Federal court would have jurisdiction of the suit only if Scott could show diversity jurisdiction, i.e., a suit by a citizen of one state against a citizen of another. Thus two questions required resolution: first, whether Scott was a citizen of Missouri, and second, whether Scott had been freed by being taken into free territory. The latter question involved a determination whether Congress had the power under the constitution to prohibit slavery in the territories, thus making Scott a free man in Minnesota. Chief Justice Taney's adverse conclusions on these questions were concurred in by the majority. He held Congress did not have power to prohibit slavery and consequently the Missouri Compromise was unconstitutional. He held Scott was still a slave because the highest court of the state of Missouri had held in Scott's case when it was before it that under the law of that state a master did not lose his property right in his slave by taking him to a free state like Illinois." Which, as stated above, "the legal procedures established by the law of the slave holding states" would have prevented Scott from being free and thus having no rights?

World War II Memorial of the conflict fought in the Atlantic and in the Pacific.

The tipping point in that famous Supreme Court Case *of Dred Scott v. Sanford* of 1857, Chief Justice Taney ruled: "Can a negro [sic] whose ancestors were imported into this country, and sold as slaves, become a member of the political community formed and brought into existence by the Constitution of the United States, and as such become entitled to all rights, privileges, and immunities, guaranteed by that instrument to the citizens? One of which rights is the privilege of suing in a court of the United States in the cases specified in the Constitution....The only matter in issue before the Court therefore, is, whether the descendants of such slaves, when they shall be emancipated, or who are born of parents who had become free before their birth, are citizens of a State, in the sense in which the word 'citizen' is used in the Constitution of the United States.'"

OBAMA THE JOURNEY COMPLETED - NEVER PROMISED A ROSE GARDEN

Thus, Ms. Motley rightly concluded, "Taney ruled that Negroes were not citizens within the contemplation of the Constitution. He based this on what he claimed to be the Negro's legal status throughout the civilized world at the time of the adoption of the Constitution. This status was a non-citizenship status, and he said, 'so far inferior, that they [the Negroes] had no rights which a white man was bound to respect." Given that the civilized world created and perpetuated a barbaric system of inhumanity of man towards man; yet, being born within the boundaries of the nation ought to have been enough. Such a situation later became law under the 14th Amendment to the Constitution, but the Court seemed to be favoring the planter class who benefitted from denying Africans those protections citizenship conferred. Notwithstanding, even when the Civil War Amendments conferred this right, it was often ignored and denied. In some respects, the oppressor tends to bend the law, and to ignore and suppress these rights. Again, legislation does not mean enforcement, effective enforcement.

Nevertheless, it goes to show, "This view of the Negro's legal status at the time of the adoption of the Constitution was disputed by the dissenting justices. One dissenting justice found that: 'At the time of the ratification of the Articles of Confederation [which preceded the Constitution], all free native born inhabitants of the states of New Hampshire, Massachusetts, New York, New Jersey, and North Carolina, though descended from African slaves, were not only citizens of those States, but such of them as had the other necessary qualifications possessed the franchise of electors on equal terms with other citizens."

Given what is stated, does the Roger Taney, planter class mentality still pervade in its many guises today? Consider what was done to President Obama, the answer is yes!

OBAMA THE JOURNEY COMPLETED - NEVER PROMISED A ROSE GARDEN

"This is the moment when we must build on the wealth that open markets have created, and share its benefits more equitably. Trade has been a cornerstone of our growth and global development. But we will not be able to sustain this growth if it favors the few, and not the many." **Barack Obama**

FREDERICK MONDERSON

42. MARCH ON WASHINGTON
By
Dr. Fred Monderson

Saying "**We're not anti-Police, we're anti-Police Brutality**" Reverend Al Sharpton explained at the National Action Network's weekly rally in Harlem, on December 6, 2014, "Why we're going to March on Washington, December 13," is to seek justice, to eliminate the smog of injustice in the air and force Congress to repair the broken Grand Jury system that miserably failed Black victims seeking justice. Many are disappointed in the Grand Jury System that seems manipulated in a conflict of interest scenario that exonerates

OBAMA THE JOURNEY COMPLETED - NEVER PROMISED A ROSE GARDEN

police officers who should at least be indicted for the killing of Blacks!" Hopefully legislation will address this national problem.

"Fixing a broken immigration system. Protecting our kids from gun violence. Equal pay for equal work, paid leave, raising the minimum wage. All these things still matter to hardworking families; they are still the right thing to do; and I will not let up until they get done."
Barack Obama

Speaker after speaker spoke of the "sin and iniquity in the form of injustice being perpetrated against young Black men" and why "the campaign for justice must continue through marches." The speakers referenced the Civil Rights Movements' marches that brought about the **Civil Rights Acts of 1964** and the **Voting Rights Act of 1965**. To this they emphasized the significance and effectiveness of the Montgomery Bus Boycott. Quoting Dr. King that "the moral arm of the universe is long but it bends towards justice" the cry was "the issue is not simply civil but human rights." All insisted, "we must demonstrate dignity and perseverance in this movement until righteousness rolls down like a mighty stream; yet, being mindful that change only takes place when you look in the face of injustice and force unbiased federal oversight."

FREDERICK MONDERSON

World War II Memorial of the conflict fought in the Atlantic and in the Pacific.

Realizing, citizens from all over the country came together to address recent Grand Jury rulings, Congress must hold hearings and pass laws to protect citizens' rights. Thus, the legislative branch must step in. "The people must not be run like hamsters on single issues" they cried. Strategists and decision makers must connect all the cases as a sort of "class action," and they mentioned, among such cases those of Eric Garner, Michael Brown, and Tamir Rice. "We must put the cases together to show police violence as we did in linking Rosa Parks with the Mississippi Freedom Riders and CORE and Dr. King cooperating for legislative relief."

OBAMA THE JOURNEY COMPLETED - NEVER PROMISED A ROSE GARDEN

FREDERICK MONDERSON

The mother of Eric Garner thanked all, saying "You have stood with me from the beginning. I felt proud, to see people standing for my son. That makes my heart overflow with joy. Keep on doing what you're doing, but do it in peace." Esau Garner, his wife, was "overwhelmed" at the people's response. She spoke of the "gentle giant" and that this does not fully explain the wonderful man he was! She was elated people were saying, "Mrs. Garner we're marching for you!" Thus, she insisted, "Keep fighting this fight to get justice!" His daughter Emerald offered, "I must shout out the young people. Do it peacefully!"

Equally, addressing the Press that has not been kind to him, Rev. Sharpton insisted he never got any "kick back" from any of the fights he has been in. All he wanted and wants is justice! He reminded "I have TV and Radio contracts and any kickbacks would jeopardize my livelihood!"

Joining the Reverend at the rally and in an Academy Award presentation, legal eagle Attorney Benjamin Crump eloquently made

OBAMA THE JOURNEY COMPLETED - NEVER PROMISED A ROSE GARDEN

the case of "Why we are going to March on Washington!" Mr. Crump first of all thanked and congratulated Rev. Al Sharpton for "always answering the bell, whether the camera is there or not, he is there when it is not popular." Praising his fellow lawyers Jonathan Moore and Michael Hardy for their stalwart role in quest of justice, he praised "Young people who stood up!" and indicated the National Bar Association, the largest African American organization of lawyers, stands behind Rev. Sharpton and this movement. Then he recognized "Eric Garner inspired and galvanized young people who crafted their own slogans," which the marchers chanted: "Hands Up, Don't Shoot;" and "I Can't Breathe;" "Black Lives Matter;" "I am Michael Brown;" and "Justice for Michael Brown!"

Next Mr. Crump explained his "Theory of the case!" because "the system needs to be indicted!" He insisted, "The system is what breaks our hearts." He decried the "closeness in time" of the killings of Eric Garner, Michael Brown, Tamir Rice and pointed to the symbolism and seemingly inherent conflict of interest, "Even Stevie Wonder could see," when a local Prosecutor must investigate a local police officer. Calling Ferguson "a fraud" he advised, "We must be specific. It's about chess not checkers!"

FREDERICK MONDERSON

NATIONAL SOCIETY
DAUGHTERS OF THE
AMERICAN REVOLUTION
☆ ☆ ☆
MEMORIAL CONTINENTAL
HALL

He then proposed a precedence by which he questioned Ferguson! That is, for 30 years the Prosecutor has been presenting cases to the Grand Jury. All of a sudden he changed his strategy!

OBAMA THE JOURNEY COMPLETED - NEVER PROMISED A ROSE GARDEN

World War II Memorial of the conflict fought in the Atlantic and in the Pacific.

Mr. Crump insisted the audience see what he termed "attempts to demonize young Black men" because as he pointed out, "Police officers are hired to protect and serve the community," but what you get is "Police protection for police and Police enforcement for Black victims." Searching for precedence he stated, "In 1982 the Supreme Court ruled, 'not to allow a suspect to testify!'" So for 30 years the Ferguson District Attorney presented to the Grand Jury but did not allow any suspects to testify. "All of a sudden he wants to be fair," and in presenting to the Grand Jury, allows the suspect, Darren Wilson, to testify. He therefore asked, "Had he not been fair for 30 years?" His view of "police demonizing young Black men" is seen, first, where Officer Wilson compared his encounter with Michael Brown as "Hulk Hogan to a 5-year old." Then he pointed out how they use the terms "Supporters for Officer Wilson" but "Protesters for Michael Brown and Eric Garner!" Then again, three seconds after the police arrived he shot Tamir Rice, yet he claims he told him to put down the gun three times. With Eric Garner they tried to play up he was arrested previously and that he was selling "loose cigarettes" which he was not doing at that time.

Vowing "Due Process" for Michael Brown, Eric Garner and Tamir Rice, Mr. Crump quoted former Supreme Court Justice Thurgood Marshall that "the Constitution guarantees the same equal rights to a Black, uneducated, poor, mother who gives birth in Mississippi to an affluent, educated, wealthy, white mother born anywhere in the United States. That is what being born in this country means."

Rev. Sharpton reminded all the National Action Network will provide free buses at different locations across the five boroughs but those interested must sign up for a seat. Go to National Action Network.Net or call and add your name. Buses will leave about 5:00 AM Saturday, December 13, 2014, to rendezvous at Pennsylvania Avenue and 13th Street.

"There are millions of Americans outside Washington who are tired of stale political arguments and are moving this country forward. They believe, and I believe, that here in America, our success should depend not on accident of birth, but the strength of our work ethic and the scope of our dreams." **Barack Obama**

OBAMA THE JOURNEY COMPLETED - NEVER PROMISED A ROSE GARDEN

43. THE WHITE HOUSE CONTRADICTION

By

Dr. Fred Monderson

I was in D.C. on Sunday, August 17, 2014 about 5:00 pm walking on 15th Street and made the turn at the Treasury Department building to enter the rear "White House Street Plaza." Alongside Lafayette Park, Capitol Police vehicles approached the corner barriers with lights flashing and sirens blaring. Approaching the classic White House viewing location; I saw a Secret Service agent and his dog whiz by. Nearby in the street a Baptist preacher was wailing about "the King of Kings;" the "144,000;" "Preparing for death and heaven and hell;" "Corruption in the American system of government;" and much more could be seen and heard.

"I just want to go through Central Park and watch folks passing by. Spend the whole day watching people. I miss that." **Barack Obama**

As we got closer to the fence for the customary photographs, there stood a compelling contradiction! A white male, naked except for a pair of short-shorts with tattooed writings on his chest and back, was facing the fence and White House. In apparent glee, he stood there jerking his middle finger unendingly. He did seem to have companions nearby. As onlookers gazed in disbelief the fellow continued his weird behavior. This, then, was the contradiction plain and simple! Why? But first!

The law enforcement interest was generated by the appearance and continued behavior of this individual as the Secret Service and Capitol Police observed his shameless behavior. They sent in the "dogs" to detect at least, whether he was on or had drugs in his possession. This was probably the only way to remove this citizen since in expressing his First Amendment Rights of Free Speech, there was no explosive threat. The police could only stand helpless but vigilantly observing this vivid example of "white trash" jubilantly thrusting his middle finger skyward thereby sending an obscene message to the White House and its occupants.

OBAMA THE JOURNEY COMPLETED - NEVER PROMISED A ROSE GARDEN

As to why! This is a shameless desecration of the nation's most sacred space. This lower-class crass behavior is a continuum of the climate of disrespect engendered against President Obama and his family, and more important, the Office of the Presidency! Now, as to the preacher working up frenzy; this is not unusual. This is "church" in the street! The other protesters, one about nuclear proliferation had been long-standing beside Lafayette Park with its floral decoration and Jackson and his canon on guard behind. Another gentleman sat in the street playing a recording of former President Jimmy Carter explaining the pros and cons of the Arab-Israeli conflict. Both protests, however, were peaceful and civilized, unlike the other lewd demonstration.

World War II Memorial of the conflict fought in the Atlantic and in the Pacific.

Hypothetically speaking, foreign visitors, of whom there were many, observing this "freak show," were amazed that such behavior could be directed towards the White House and its occupants. However, the problem manifesting here today is not with "a roach thinking he is an

OBAMA THE JOURNEY COMPLETED - NEVER PROMISED A ROSE GARDEN

eagle" but "a whales acting as minion." What we have witnessed in recent years is a climate of disrespect for President Obama created by high level government officials, senators, governors, important people and the press. These supposedly responsible leaders have shamelessly created a climate of hatred for President Obama and his family that we, the people, must never forget. Often we are reminded that a given officer or uniform philosophically represents the value of a given social institution. So, for example, when we respect the policeman, we respect both the uniform and the philosophical principle of law and order which they both symbolize.

FREDERICK MONDERSON

Mr. Obama did not inherit his political position. He happened to be the son of an African father who married a White-American female from Kansas; both of whom were of modest means. Nevertheless, the hatred for Mr. Obama really stems from the hatred against his father for marrying a white female! Visit the Jefferson Building of the Library of Congress. Notice how images depict the white female as pristine, the epitome of female beauty! That this African chose to marry, not live unmarried, to the beautiful lady meant nothing to these individuals who by their practice of hatred for others really betray their true pathological selves. Such hatred is also most malignant for persons in interracial marriage; especially if the male partner is Black.

On Mr. Obama's part, through hard work, competence, resilience, of tremendous fortitude, organizational skills and tenacity, he won the Presidency of the United States. In the history of this nation and the millions who have lived and died on these shores, only 43 white men previously accomplished this feat. Less than half did it twice and one, four times, because of prevailing circumstances during World War II.

OBAMA THE JOURNEY COMPLETED - NEVER PROMISED A ROSE GARDEN

Most people believe that the Presidency of the United States is a hallowed institution that also makes the individual inhabiting the position and sacred space, special. Thus, like the Officer and the uniform, both must be respected. As such, any behavior that impugns the man sullies the institution. Therefore, the crass attitudes and behaviors of the mud-slingers at Obama; those who throw stones to break the window; speak volumes not of noble souls' magnanimous actions but men of vile temperaments and questionable character.

In Meridian Park in Washington, DC, a statue sits as a memorial to President John Buchannan with an inscription that reads: "He walked on the mountain tops of the law." Such a tribute says much for this gentleman, certainly attesting to a noble spirit. Today evidence of elegance of mind and nobility of spirit are missing in that "City on the Hill" of Washington, D.C. However, these are behavioral hallmarks of President Barack Hussein Obama.

For centuries there has been a certain kind of behavior which was called psychosexual pathology. Today its "intellectual, cultural and ethnic heritage envy," that has become pathological. This behavior involves attacking a work ethic that is creative and successfully superior which generates the venomous hatred we see directed toward Mr. Obama as President heading the most powerful nation on earth. The disgusting behavior of the citizen referenced above was motivated by the behaviors of the many winners of the "Little Man" award who created that climate of contempt.

463

FREDERICK MONDERSON

First and foremost, Mitch McConnell (R. Kentucky): One has to wonder how the people of "The Great State" of Kentucky could countenance the continued petty behavior. John Boehner, the Speaker

OBAMA THE JOURNEY COMPLETED - NEVER PROMISED A ROSE GARDEN

of the U.S. House of Representatives who disrespected Mr. Obama; placed in a barrel of aspiring presidential contenders these would all be considered losers who sought or would have sought the position Mr. Obama so successfully captured, twice. Then we have "Waterloo" Jim De Mint, formerly (R. South Carolina); Donald Trump, disgracefully seeking a birth certificate and college transcript, as if he did not have such a one for himself; "You Lie" Joe Wilson (R. South Carolina); "Gangster Government," "God told me to run," Michele Bachmann; "a fraud" Senator Ted Cruz; "Poison the Well" Rick Santorum; "Lipstick on a pig" Sarah Palin; "Healthcare is Slavery" Benjamin Carson; and last but not least, John McCain, privy to this and more, yet his open attempts to demean Obama did not preclude him from trying to become President of the United States!

Some have accused Senator McCain of milking his "Hero" name for nearly half a century. Yet, comparatively out of nowhere "Po Boy" Obama was elected twice mostly through masterly organizing his assets and relentlessly pursuing his objective.

We cannot forget malicious psycho/spiritual lepers and powerful commentators like Charles Krauthammer, Michael Goodwin, and other sick minions, particularly Rush Limbaugh and Sean Hannity, all of whom possess and use malevolent vocabularies devoid of any respectful terminology when it comes to their commentary on Mr. Obama. Certainly constructive criticisms are always welcome from honest critics. But destructively malicious commentary and blatant denial of any of Mr. Obama's accomplishments are behaviors unworthy of responsible men in such high positions.

FREDERICK MONDERSON

OBAMA THE JOURNEY COMPLETED - NEVER PROMISED A ROSE GARDEN

Somehow they all manifest a Ron Paul reflection on George W. Bush moment, for when asked, "Can you name one good thing President Obama has done?" That "liberal" paragon of virtue, Ron Paul, thought "looong" and "haaard" and honestly confessed, "I can't think of anything good Mr. Obama has done!" Jesse Jackson once insisted, "Stay out of the bushes!" Mr. Paul did not and stole a phrase and mentality from George Bush though Mr. Paul turned that phrase on its head, but with the same useless and misleading meaning!

Now, if these "respectable" individuals could so disparage Mr. Obama, they certainly provide incentive and justification for "bottom of the barrel types" to vent as this fellow did in front of the White House. Strange that this individual felt justified in his highly disrespectful conduct. Obviously, given Mr. Obama has been subject to more threats, vilification and derision than any other President, a very dangerous climate and in which sinister behaviors including doing bodily harm to the nation's leader by some hate-filled lunatic is a real possibility. Nonetheless, the superior intellect and noble spirit which Mr. Obama embodies impels his critics to expose their deep fear and hatred of the Black man who occupies the White House!

FREDERICK MONDERSON

"What I believe is that marriage is between a man and a woman, but what I also believe is that we have an obligation to make sure that gays and lesbians have the rights of citizenship that afford them visitations to hospitals, that allow them to be, to transfer property between partners, to make certain that they're not discriminated on the job."
Barack Obama

OBAMA THE JOURNEY COMPLETED - NEVER PROMISED A ROSE GARDEN

44. GETTING IT WRONG!
By
Dr. Fred Monderson

We must ask ourselves 'Did the Ferguson, Missouri, Grand Jury get it wrong purposely?' Mindful that, when the jury acquitted O.J. Simpson, then found him guilty the second time, White America cried foul and was then elated. When the jury acquitted Robert Blake the consensus was, the system worked! So too when George Zimmerman was acquitted. Given the old adage, "A Prosecutor could indict a ham sandwich," even the most in-astute individuals easily discerned the top individual presiding over the Michael Brown death investigation

FREDERICK MONDERSON

lost the opportunity to bring charges against Officer Darren Wilson. Whether this was intentional or simply unprofessional raises a number of questions as events further unfolded particularly following the officer's interview with ABC's George Stephanopoulos. His answers to the questions of the reporter, his cool demeanor and his un-remorsefulness seem he was "thoroughly lawyered up!" These factors lead people to distrust the process and conclude the Grand Jury got it wrong! This deduction is certainly a credible proposition. Given the Black-Law-enforcement climate in Ferguson, many believe the outcome was purposely orchestrated!

"As a nuclear power - as the only nuclear power to have used a nuclear weapon - the United States has a moral responsibility to act."
Barack Obama

Several observers believed the District Attorney, of St. Louis County, Robert McCulloh should have reclused himself from the case because of a perceived conflict of interest. Back in the 1970s, while a cop, his father was killed by an African-American man. So, as he grew, Mr. McCulloh aspired to become a District Attorney rather than a cop. What drove him into this position is open to speculation.

Particulars of Michael Brown's killing are pretty well-known showing for months citizens descended on Ferguson joining residents to protest the horrible tragedy. As events unfolded, they painted a picture of life in Ferguson, Missouri, influenced by local law practice. First, citizens complain, though they comprise some 65 percent of the population they are under-represented in law enforcement and all facets of local government impacting their lives daily. Second, unemployment numbers are extremely high. Third, citizens complain of excessive and high handed police behavior to keep Blacks in line and to raise revenue. So much so, a coercive attitude pervades the Ferguson environment. Thus, the killing of Michael Brown, in their view, was not simply unjustified and highlights a pattern of behavior but more importantly it was the last straw that broke Ferguson's back! This generated an extended protest movement questioning factors regarding life in Ferguson and the need to set standards to impact life in the future.

OBAMA THE JOURNEY COMPLETED - NEVER PROMISED A ROSE GARDEN

FREDERICK MONDERSON

After the Grand Jury declined to indict Officer Darren Wilson, a White officer; for killing Michael Brown, a Black teen; while commentators' scrutiny focused on the failure to adhere to protocol in evidence collection, many rejected the claim Ferguson did not possess the professional apparatus compared to New York or Los Angeles Police Departments with more professional processing standards. However, in assessing the police show of force in their response to initial demonstrations attention began focusing on the quantity and quality of armaments police deployed to face the local community. The position of one sniper, in particular, with scope and "the whole nine yards" focused on his role! Army General Honore of Katrina fame, would have said, "This is America not Iraq," and the response is excessive!

OBAMA THE JOURNEY COMPLETED - NEVER PROMISED A ROSE GARDEN

FREDERICK MONDERSON

After the Grand Jury was convened and projected to last some months before their decision was reached, residents began a vigil of protest demanding justice for Michael Brown. They created a chant "Hands Up, Don't Shoot!" and "I am Michael Brown." Many people came to Ferguson to show support for the residents who felt the protest was justified. Politicians, entertainers, civil rights activists, local organizers, clergy, all came and the press reported daily from the scene. In an unprecedented move President Obama spoke out on Ferguson and sent Attorney General Eric Holder who met with the Brown family being visited by Trayvon Martin's mother and Sean Bell's mother, a young man killed by police, and a young man desperately wanting to be a policeman! Say what you will, law enforcement's insensitivity and rash behavior is killing Black men across the country!

World War II Memorial of the conflict fought in the Atlantic and in the Pacific.

474

OBAMA THE JOURNEY COMPLETED - NEVER PROMISED A ROSE GARDEN

Waiting from August through November, many applauded the young people of Ferguson who were reported as organizing, strategizing, registering people to vote, all becoming more civic and politically astute to thenceforth involve themselves in decision-making in their area. Despite this, no one envisioned the grand scheme behind the process seemingly to shield the police officer. Given Ferguson behavior as Matt Apuzzo reported in *The New York Times*, there were "stories of the police abusing suspects, disproportionately stopping Black residents and using tickets in Black neighborhoods as a way to raise money;" it is not unreasonable to believe "the fix was in for Officer Wilson in from day one!" As an example, in the movie **Fruitvale Station**, on the platform where a young man was shot, the first, tall, officer aggressive and seemingly inhumane behavior reflected a climate of hostility in which the young officer felt comfortable shooting the Black man.

Thus, some argued, the prosecutor's conduct was questionable from the inception. Rather than indict "the ham sandwich" he passed the buck to the Grand Jury so as not to be blamed for the outcome, for which he was, as events showed! Many thought the outcome was purposely engineered. This veteran District Attorney overwhelmed an exhausted Grand Jury to examine tons of testimony and data knowing Thanksgiving was coming! Rather than rake Darren Wilson over an intense fireplace, disrespectful of Ferguson residents in the first place; the District Attorney betrayed them by grilling eye-witnesses to focus on inconsistencies in their testimony and elaborated this as if *they*, not Wilson, had committed the killing. Imagine focusing some 40 times on the teenager smoked marijuana instead of the dozen or so shots Wilson fired. Thus, a number of commentators called the DA's behavior throughout unprofessional, a sham process, laced with injustice.

FREDERICK MONDERSON

OBABA THE JOURNEY COMPLETED - NEVER PROMISED A ROSE GARDEN

After an initial notification that a Grand Jury decision was reached, tension was allowed to build up. The Brown family was not properly notified, and releasing the results under cover of night was probably designed to ignite uncontrolled behavior and so "blame the victim!" Lieut.-General Honore of "Katrina fame," often a commentator on CNN, criticized the timing of the release citing military strategies at night to overwhelm the enemy in Iraq and Afghanistan. The General wanted daylight to challenge unwanted behaviors. We know detectives don't serve warrants at the beginning but the end of night, for good reason!

One of the extreme criticisms of police handling of the killing was letting the body of Michael Brown be exposed for some four hours in the sun which was "to preserve the crime scene." Forensic pathologist Cyril Wecht protested the revelation. He noted, "Measurements and photographs were needed to be taken." As it also turned out, the chain of custody was flawed. No measurements of the crime scene were actually made; no photographs were taken because the photographer had no workable battery; though there was a struggle at the car where 2 shots were fired, no tests were done to determine if Michael Brown's blood was on officer Wilson's gun; and in processing officer Wilson in custody when questioned after the shooting, no recordings or notes were made of his testimony. Was this a standard practice or only in this case? No record was made of blood on the officer's hands nor was he fingerprinted. More important, he was allowed to check his gun into the evidence bag.

All these factors question the DA's behavior, the process and just as Darren Wilson resigned; so too should the DA McCulloh.

"What Washington needs is adult supervision." **Barack Obama**

FREDERICK MONDERSON

45.   THE OBAMA LEGACY II
By
Dr. Fred Monderson

Just before the 2014 mid-term election season began, a high ranking Democratic senator was asked to define the Obama Legacy in which she responded, "It has not yet been written." What she actually meant, "Mr. Obama is making his list, checking it twice, crossing his eyes and dotting his tees, while being mindful of those who have been naughty." Then came the 'shellacking' of 2014 and 'talking heads,' 'pseudo-pundits' and certainly Republicans particularly "Tea Partyers" began singing Mr. Obama's "swan song," even christening him "Lame Duck!" To their great surprise, whether while from pontificating about Mr. Obama's leadership demise or distracted in a drunken euphoric party of his political legacy, Republicans were

OBAMA THE JOURNEY COMPLETED - NEVER PROMISED A ROSE GARDEN

caught unawares as he sprang to life by issuing his Immigration Executive Action and Cuba Initiative. So much so, though Republicans will enter the 114th Congress in control of both Houses of Congress, they are left holding the bag as Mr. Obama triumphantly rides into the realm of history as one of the greatest presidents this nation has ever had. Notwithstanding, the seeming ungrateful and fickle-mindedness of the American people, no matter how you wash their dirty linen, every 8-12 years they clean house and change party leadership. This is an unintended consequence of a viable system.

"So long as I'm Commander-in-Chief, we will sustain the strongest military the world has ever known. When you take off the uniform, we will serve you as well as you've served us - because no one who fights for this country should have to fight for a job, or a roof over their head, or the care that they need when they come home."
Barack Obama

After all, this is what Mr. Paul Krugman had said some time ago, that "Mr. Obama is the greatest American President ever." This assessment came before the Asian Trade deal, his immigration initiative, the Cuban major, major move forward and the Iran Nuclear Deal. Add to this, Mr. Obama's visit to Cuba in March, he could probably cross over from Miami to Havana. Yet, who knows, who was paying attention. Nevertheless, the forgiving nature of the American people dictates they eventually rehabilitate those initially proscribed. Much more important, young as he is, with his compounded wisdom and having proved a master of navigating Republican minefields, not only is Mr. Obama immune to their "dirty pool" but his cue stick is full of "English" and this can prove to be very interesting for decades to come. Given that one man can become a majority and given the sum total of his assets, Mr. Obama can probably remake and change the social and political direction of the nation in ways he could not while in the White House.

FREDERICK MONDERSON

OBAMA THE JOURNEY COMPLETED - NEVER PROMISED A ROSE GARDEN

The White House viewed from Lafayette Park with General Jackson on point.

Astute commentators and persons of penetrating vision certainly acknowledge Mr. Obama's legacy has been long in the making. Today, in the pugilistic business, most fights are 10 or 12 rounds, but in the classic contest, "Frazier-Ali," for example, 15 rounds were the norm. In that long contest Mr. Obama, while "still standing" at the final bell, will show he has taken hits and returned more with even greater ferocity and though his opponents may celebrate their pyrrhic mid-term election victories even they will acknowledge Obama was a formidable opponent.

FREDERICK MONDERSON

World War II Memorial of the conflict fought in the Atlantic and in the Pacific.

A cursory look at Mr. Obama's legacy will reveal, given circumstances as they unfolded, a photograph or two should suffice but not the chapter and verses more rightly volumes that recount the many episodes in a distinguished career. First and most significant, Mr. Obama did not commit ethically or morally reprehensible acts and as such this category is out. However, using a baseball analogy, we are reminded statistically, if a batter hits the ball three times out of ten times at bat, he is considered a 300-hitter and headed to the Hall of Fame.

In viewing Mr. Obama's legacy, a number of factors can be considered, viz., What he did positively; What he did negatively;

OBAMA THE JOURNEY COMPLETED - NEVER PROMISED A ROSE GARDEN

What was done to him; How he handled negativity directed towards him; What he brought in terms of decision making strategies; and, "How Americans benefitted from his leadership" and "How Americas' enemies," domestic and foreign, feared in the "Age of Obama." In sum, the record will show, Mr. Obama has stamped his imprint not only on America but significantly on the world stage, that despite the partisan naysayers and their directed negativity, at home, even abroad, considering where the nation was upon his arrival, all that has transpired where he leaves it upon his tenure's end, there is no question his legacy is strong, firm and indelible. That erstwhile adviser to Presidents, David Gergen, in commentary when discussing Mr. Obama's accomplishments in the economy especially on how Wall Street is doing could still caustically respond, "Yes, but a lot of people are still doing terribly."

FREDERICK MONDERSON

How fickle-minded people, commentators especially are for they forget how far the nation has traveled from that road-side ditch! Practically all the parts of that vehicle have been changed and retooled. That is, battery, rims, tires, doors, seats, coolant systems, air conditioning and heat, gas tank, fuel system flushed and cleaned, lights - fore and aft housings cleaned and with new bulbs. Mr. Obama even opened a new sun-roof. Fact is, this President re-tooled the whole system in creating a new foundation geared to the future by revamping the financial and economic realms; exploring new considerations about energy, the environment, infrastructure; even streamlining the armed forces, over-hauling responsibilities for Veterans' care; put new and greater emphasis on the nation's education; put a new face on the Nation's foreign policy and put terrorists and other "bad boys" on notice, America will remain unrelenting in pursuit to bring you to justice. All this was instituted without help from Republicans who continuously functioned as obstructionists along the way!

OBAMA THE JOURNEY COMPLETED - NEVER PROMISED A ROSE GARDEN

In response, here's a scenario. A graffiti artist inundates a wall with his colorful handiwork and a clean-up crew is assigned to erase all evidence of the saturation. This is not an easy task. Now, see this in human-societal interaction, given the state of the nation when Mr. Obama won the Presidency. The economy was in shambles loosing 500,000 to 800,000 jobs per month for the longest. Banks were in disarray. Wall Street had plummeted to some 6500, the Auto Industry had lost its market share, the jobs of "first responders" were on the chopping block, the nation's infrastructure was in shambles and then only people making money were the gun merchants supplying the war effort in Iraq and Afghanistan. At a past Al Smith Dinner, former President George W. Bush jokingly described these and similar entities, "They call you the wealthy, I call you my base." Nothing has changed!

In addition, the price of imported gas was more than four dollars per gallon. Today that is halved. Not much has changed even though the car remained in the ditch; George Bush's base became the Republican base and the wealth gap expanded as the poor grappled with health care costs and a bleak future. However, latest records show the economy has improved tremendously, jobs were added, wages were up and more people have risen out of poverty.

FREDERICK MONDERSON

World War II Memorial of the conflict fought in the Atlantic and in the Pacific.

OBAMA THE JOURNEY COMPLETED - NEVER PROMISED A ROSE GARDEN

FREDERICK MONDERSON

Mr. Obama set about strategizing on how to deal effectively with the wars in Iraq and Afghanistan, reform the nation's economic and financial system, securing "first responders" jobs, bailing out the auto industry, and despite stiff opposition he rescued banks and Wall Street. Offering incentives for clean energy initiatives, revamping education standards and providing security for teachers' jobs while emphasizing the important role of Community Colleges and encouraging parents to return to school, were certainly futuristic thinking. Laws were made to ensure equality of women in the work place and the long delayed discrimination against Black Farmers was settled, though it took some time for them to be compensated. Interesting, Mr. Obama did not single out Black-Americans for special

OBAMA THE JOURNEY COMPLETED - NEVER PROMISED A ROSE GARDEN

favors lest it be said he was a "Black" rather than American President. While campaign rhetoric haggled with white unemployment rates at 8-10 percent, Black rates were double. Black youth unemployment rates were, some estimated, at a staggering high of 40-50 percent. These people were certainly not premier in Mr. Gergen's account! They were long forgotten, especially during the two terms under George Bush and Republican leadership of the nation.

FREDERICK MONDERSON

Unrelenting in the hunt for Osama bin-Laden and Somali Pirates; the shenanigans of Iran and North Korea; and the heavy burden of the Presidency; Mr. Obama bore all like Atlas holding up the globe! As a racist seed germ mistakenly dubbed then for "Tea Party" manifested, equally racist militias were armed to teeth in preparation for their manufactured "race war." Racist propaganda, a climate of disrespect and threats to the President's safety mounted. The Secret Service realized they could not lose this one! Pleasing their handlers, Mitch McConnell and John Boehner exposed their dirty drawers and the world stood in awed astonishment over American sanctimoniousness that threatened the hard won gains of the Civil Rights and Voting Rights protections.

OBAMA THE JOURNEY COMPLETED - NEVER PROMISED A ROSE GARDEN

Meanwhile Obama took his hits from left and right yet continued to counter punch in steering the ship of state into clear futuristic waters. In his most challenging period, even Democrats relished in the "Iscariot" and "Petrine" syndromes especially that woman candidate from Georgia who could not even demonstrate simple testicular fortitude or "balls" to announce "she voted with Obama!" Georgians actually voted against her character not Mr. Obama's policies.

Thus, the Obama Legacy, sweltering on the battlefield for America's especial benefits and having to contend with an opposition that is really the enemy, as many have prophesied, for a long time to come, we may not have another president, Black or White, like Mr. Barack Obama!

"We can't get to the $4 trillion in savings that we need by just cutting the 12 percent of the budget that pays for things like medical research and education funding and food inspectors and the weather service. And we can't just do it by making seniors pay more for Medicare."
Barack Obama

491

46. STILL FIGHTING "TOOTH AND NAIL!"
By
Dr. Fred Monderson

The arch villain, seeking to crack the safe in the Nakatone Towers building, in Bruce Willis' movie **Die Hard**, at that pivotal time said to his fellow "exceptional" thieves, "You ask for a miracle and I give

OBAMA THE JOURNEY COMPLETED - NEVER PROMISED A ROSE GARDEN

you the FBI!" In the run-up to the 2014 Mid-term elections and amidst the misguided and also false propaganda underwritten by wealthy backers of the "Party of No," and tremendously unmindful of now realized realities of the nation's economic and financial health, voters were encouraged to pray for relief from the President's policies. Lo and behold, though the American electorate may have looked to the heavens, it is difficult to see divine intervention in the election results. A popular prophetic refrain, "Be careful of what you pray for, you may get it," characterized this period. Thus, the nation got Republican control of Congress, elevating Senator Mitch McConnell to the position of Senate Majority Leader and retaining Representative John Boehner as Speaker of the House. Only time will tell if the American people's prayers were answered from "above or below!"

"So while an incredible amount of progress has been made, on this fifth anniversary, I wanted to come here and tell the people of this city directly: My administration is going to stand with you - and fight alongside you - until the job is done. Until New Orleans is all the way back, all the way." **Barack Obama**

Certain truths are immutable! Chief among these, "Leopards and Dalmatians never lose their spots, nor do tigers their stripes!" Equally, there seems no abatement of Speaker Boehner's pledge to "fight President Obama tooth and nail!"

FREDERICK MONDERSON

As we saw at that iconic moment in American government tradition, where on January 20th, the President gave the State of the Union Address to the entire Congress "save one," as one would expect a

OBAMA THE JOURNEY COMPLETED - NEVER PROMISED A ROSE GARDEN

show of solidarity and unity of purpose particularly in an age of camera floodlights, expectations run high, particularly when the world tunes in to this important occasion to gauge America's path, certainly for the coming year. In that case we expect certain decorum particularly from those directly behind, the Speaker and Vice-President, as the President delivers his message.

To Mr. Obama's right, the viewer's left, we saw Vice-President Joe Biden in "snap, crackle, and pop" mode contrasted with Speaker Boehner's somber, sniffling, nose blowing, "sour pus" facial expression. Of course, you would expect the opposing party members to be parsimonious in their applause and standing ovations. To this we add "heckles," no matter how seeming inoffensive or certainly not the more blatant disrespect of a "You Lie" Joe Wilson outburst. But these are out of the glare of the camera and not easily discernible. It is expected Speaker Boehner would be dressed in his "Sunday best," viz., well-tailored suit, matching tie and handkerchief, and probably even his "church shoes." However, you don't expect "T-shirt and dungaree" behavior in these circumstances, certainly not a "Representative Issa facial expression," so much in need of a make-over.

FREDERICK MONDERSON

World War II Memorial of the conflict fought in the Atlantic and in the Pacific.

Ok. So the Speaker was "under the weather" evident from his "teenagers make dumb decisions," mannerism. What is interesting, however, the next day Mr. Boehner emerged in his usual immaculate outfit, "chip as a Jay bird," and announces he will invite the Israeli Prime Minister Benjamin Netanyahu to address a Joint Session of Congress! Mr. Boehner must have "taken 2 Excedrin tablets" that evening clearing up his "Post nasal-drip syndrome," thus enabling his healthy appearance the next day.

The content and importance of Mr. Netanyahu's message, notwithstanding, in view of Mr. Boehner's display, concerned citizens will observe the Speaker for sure, as an item, to determine if he will stand and applaud continuously, beam delightfully at the Prime Minister's presentation or sit sorrowfully, making sour faces, sniffling, blowing his nose and so forth! Perhaps Mr. Boehner will indeed "take 2 Excedrin tablets" prior to preclude his malady and be

OBAMA THE JOURNEY COMPLETED - NEVER PROMISED A ROSE GARDEN

on his "best behavior." Then again, several options of perception are presented.

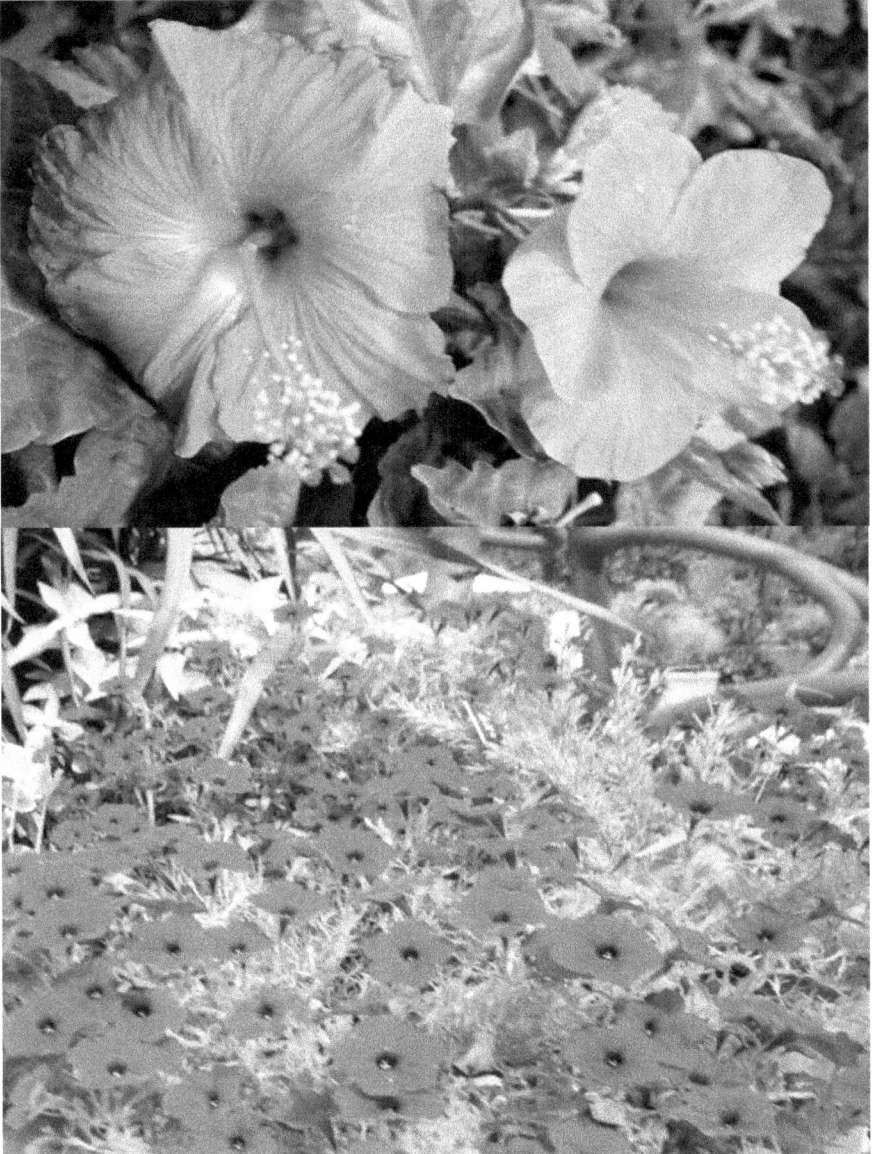

FREDERICK MONDERSON

(1)   In his "ill-considered decision," to quote Adam Schiff (D) of the House Intelligence Committee, the Speaker has shown more respect for a foreign head of state than his President. Of course, as we saw, with the world and the nation's attention focused on the Entrance to the House Chamber, the Sergeant of Arms did not announce Putin, Chavez, Kim Jon IL, or Ahmanedjad, or even Benjamin Netanyahu, he simply said, "Mr. Speaker, the President of the United States." In this arena, at this time of the announcement, the American people placed the Speaker's name before the Chief Executive, the Chief Legislator, Chief Diplomat, and Commander-In-Chief expecting, at least, "Second Year Graduate Student" behavior rather than that of a "Sixth-Grade Middle School student" just learning the ropes!

Irrespective of party affiliation, Mr. Boehner is our Speaker, and that position is not a partisan fiefdom belonging to Republicans. The Republican Party is simply charged with getting the job done for all the American people, not really to favor one group of people over another. All this is clear evidence, Speaker Boehner, as the congressional "right flank" of his Party's grand "Stop Obama" strategy is still "Fighting the President tooth and nail!" Now, not being able to "cut the Obama mustard," he has stepped out of the fiery kitchen.

(2)   In times of ancient tales, Knights of the Round Table were fighters, gallant and men of honor and high ideals. Having defeated an enemy who had fought well, the victorious knight would salute his vanquished foe, even show mercy! We now know such magnanimity is not a Boehner character trait. However, one-character trait Mr. Boehner seriously lacks is the ongoing ability to recognize, not only is Mr. Obama first among equals among the Knights at Table who "won both his campaigns," he is a highly astute, politically savvy operative seasoned by 6-years of Republican obstructionism and possessing an extraordinary ability to counter the machinations of the army of Lilliputians Boehner and McConnell lead, amassing on his perimeter, wondering if Obama will "fire on the rebels'" encampment.

OBAMA THE JOURNEY COMPLETED - NEVER PROMISED A ROSE GARDEN

FREDERICK MONDERSON

(3)   Equally, never mind the Speaker's disregard for protocol and his venture into the delicate world of international diplomacy by injecting partisanship in foreign policy, Former Republican Utah Governor and Ambassador to China John Huntsman commenting on this "mistake by the Speaker" also pointed out it, "also affected the Head of State to Head of State relationship." Nevertheless, Speaker Boehner may probably learn "some of the best laid plans sometimes go awry." Equally, history has shown, and Mr. Boehner may one day learn, the ancient Egyptian nobleman and social prophet Ptahhotep admonished, "Do not be arrogant because of thy learning" and in this case, "power."   Given such displays as indicative of the New Republican status quo, the American people may continue to pray "come 2016" that Republican "tooth and nail" may be beaten into ploughshares for the next farmers!

Tupac's album was entitled, "All Eyes on Me," but this time all eyes will be on Speaker John Boehner to gauge his behavior in the way forward and at the Address of the Israeli Prime Minister!

"And I will do everything that I can as long as I am President of the United States to remind the American people that we are one nation under God, and we may call that God different names but we remain one nation." **Barack Obama**

OBAMA THE JOURNEY COMPLETED - NEVER PROMISED A ROSE GARDEN

47. "THE UNBELIEVERS"

By

Dr. Fred Monderson

This is not about "Their Unbelievers" but it is about "Our Unbelievers" whom the columnist Paul Krugman so eloquently and factually identified and critiqued in his piece entitled "Voodoo Time Machine" in *The New York Times* of Friday, January 9, 2015, p. 23. Here is a man, Mr. Krugman, a scholar, an intellectual of the highest order who has not simply sung praises of President Obama, but importantly, over the years has had the vision to recognize and the tenacity to point out the significant accomplishments the Obama Administration has achieved. He equally and rightfully recognized not only have Republicans blocked every meaningful legislative initiative the President proposed but those, through political skill and Presidential pulpit cajoling representing significant progress was made in furthering the interests of the American people; but, Republicans nevertheless missed these successes. In modern parlance, "They never got those e-mails!"

Witnesses to the two terms of President Obama's Administration and even "a blind man" can discern the nation has made enormous progress in furthering the best interests of the American Republic, at home and abroad. But Republicans in their "Parallel Universe" understandably deny these accomplishments and where possible still claim responsibility for all that is good and beneficial. Clearly, these "Brothers from Another Planet," like bloodhounds with their noses to the ground, cannot see the clear waters and reflecting blue skies Mr. Obama has sailed the ship of state into in his futuristic visionary construct. Nor have Republicans recognized the fields Mr. Obama plowed with their flowering greenery and prodigious fruitfulness promising many predictable harvests he will reap and bequeath his successors.

OBAMA THE JOURNEY COMPLETED - NEVER PROMISED A ROSE GARDEN

Bishop T.D. Jakes put it another way!

A tortoise was ambling along and came upon a giraffe feeding upon the luxurious greenery amidst the clear Blue skies and fresh air circulating above. Looking skyward and hailing the fortunate ruminant the tortoise asked, "How's it going?" Looking downward the giraffe responded, "Great! It's like Heaven up here! Nothing but luxuriant shrub and clean air amidst a blue sky creating a wonderful view with great promise! How about you?"

Sadly, and seeming dejected, the tortoise responded, "It's like hell down here! All I see is garbage. The air is foul and people keep stepping on me!"

"How sad" the giraffe responded, "you should step up a few notches and enjoy this luxurious foliage!"

FREDERICK MONDERSON

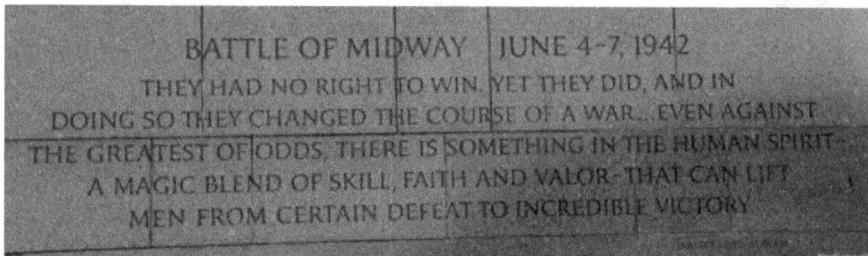

BATTLE OF MIDWAY   JUNE 4-7, 1942
THEY HAD NO RIGHT TO WIN. YET THEY DID, AND IN
DOING SO THEY CHANGED THE COURSE OF A WAR...EVEN AGAINST
THE GREATEST OF ODDS, THERE IS SOMETHING IN THE HUMAN SPIRIT-
A MAGIC BLEND OF SKILL, FAITH AND VALOR- THAT CAN LIFT
MEN FROM CERTAIN DEFEAT TO INCREDIBLE VICTORY

Fact is; both parties gave honest appraisals of their situation and view. From his skyward vantage point, the giraffe could see nothing but a positive, clear and refreshingly promising future. Down on earth, the tortoise's vision is clouded and stultified from seeing nothing but trash and wallowing in the foul odor of negativity. Unfortunately, these Republicans; as we know, "Leopards cannot change their spots;" while Republicans unquestionably having the Obama giraffe towering over their heads, should, to quote Hillary Rodham Clinton, "Get out of the gutter!"

So, Mr. Paul Krugman particularly identified some "bloodhounds" with their noses to the ground, a posture some may call foolish! Fortune has now favored these men, positioning them at the pinnacle of the American political structure, controlling both Houses of one third of the American government; but alas, a record precedes their ascent.

Given a fraction of the obstruction Mr. Obama experienced, Mr. Krugman's indictment questions Republicans' ability to govern in a manner beneficial to the broad masses of the American people. Equally, their misguided determination to roll back Obama's legislative policies and executive actions also seeking to benefit their wealthy 1% base, questions the notion of objective leadership on their part.

OBAMA THE JOURNEY COMPLETED - NEVER PROMISED A ROSE GARDEN

FREDERICK MONDERSON

Let's look at some features of his indicting critique:

(1)   The author mentions Mitch McConnell is claiming incoming Republican leadership for the nation's economic growth now in process.

OBAMA THE JOURNEY COMPLETED - NEVER PROMISED A ROSE GARDEN

(2)   While Republicans chastised "Obamacare" in the Pre - and Roll-out stages, particularly the "glitches;" in the positive turn around, some have cried foul, as Senator John Barraso of Wyoming let loose, "They are cooking the books." Can you imagine, President Obama, a leader of impeccable credentials, possessing a clear, conscionable view of history, as soon as he steps down, would have to shamefacedly back-peddle, saying, to Quote Richard Nixon apologetically, "I am not a crook!"

(3)   Paul Ryan, in response to the current successes of the Affordable Care Act, charged, "The law will collapse on its own weight!" The question is; will this new Chairman of the House and Ways Committee, after his party has tried more than four dozen times to gut "Obamacare," will he put his weight behind such efforts "to fix something that works?" Has he not heard of, "If it works don't fix it!" Of course, Mr. Ryan is a "special," and I don't want to say, "Basket" "case." Mr. Krugman wrote, "Speaking of Mr. Ryan: almost four years have passed since he and many others in his party lambasted Ben Bernanke then the Chairman of the Federal Reserve for policies

that they claimed would lead to higher inflation and debase the dollar. The inflation never materialized, and the dollar proceeded to strengthen, but Mr. Ryan gave no sign of having been chastened - and many Conservatives including favorite intellectuals like Niall Ferguson of Harvard became 'inflation truthers,' insisting that the government is hiding price rises. Can you do that in an open society? What of the Freedom of Information seekers with their "Hubble-like" intrusion, have they found the price rises? Are they still searching, as the Westerners are probably still looking for "Prester John" in Africa!

OBAMA THE JOURNEY COMPLETED - NEVER PROMISED A ROSE GARDEN

Next, Mr. Krugman points to "Climate Change" citing 2014 as the hottest year yet! Still, Senator James Inhofe now heading an Environmental Committee thinks, "all the science in this field is a liberal hoax." This "Brother from Another Planet" would not know climate change, if, as E.F. Hutton would say, "It arrived, slapped him on the bottom, and said I'm here!" However and prophetically, Mr. Krugman sounds the alarm, "Congress is now controlled by men who never acknowledge error, let alone learn from their mistakes.'

Three such mistakes can be referenced here!

(1)   The treasonous conspiracy among high ranking Republicans, and who knows, while not many individual names were mentioned in *The New York Times* article of October 6, 2013, but by virtue of their

509

seniority to hold such Chairmanships today, must have participated in, certainly known of and accented to Mitch McConnell's marching orders, "To make Barack Obama a one-term President!" Certainly no Republican worth his "salt" said, "Stop the madness;" or, it is that Republicans are all madmen. After all, all madmen think everyone else is mad but themselves! Instead of Senator McConnell giving that now infamous "Thumbs Up" signal, he should have been doing the "Perp Walk" in front of a Federal Judge for treason or certainly sedition. While Paul Krugman goes on to conclude a brilliant article by stating, "We can't have meaningful cooperation when we can't agree on reality, when even establishment figures in the Republican Party believe that facts have a liberal bias!"

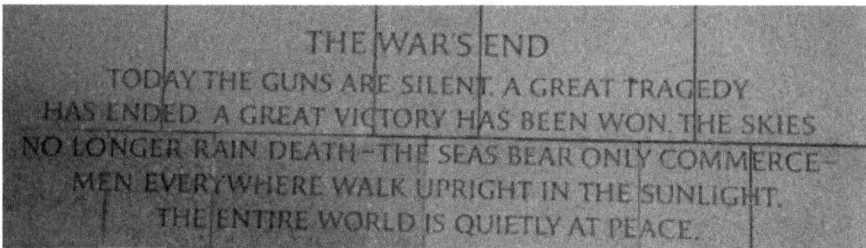

THE WAR'S END
TODAY THE GUNS ARE SILENT. A GREAT TRAGEDY HAS ENDED. A GREAT VICTORY HAS BEEN WON. THE SKIES NO LONGER RAIN DEATH – THE SEAS BEAR ONLY COMMERCE – MEN EVERYWHERE WALK UPRIGHT IN THE SUNLIGHT. THE ENTIRE WORLD IS QUIETLY AT PEACE.

One fact among many is that this party's base has not simply been brainwashed, it's been "Republican washed" through misguided propaganda, falsity, juggling and suppressing the facts, helped by listening to Fox News, Rush Limbaugh, Hannity and other such syncopates. It's like these people are in a "Parallel Universe" and their thinking and actions can affect America's future. Fact is, if they remove the plugs Mr. Obama inserted in the leaky ship he inherited, we may end up marooned on some remote island in the stratosphere in their party's fairy tale "Parallel Universe."

"I believe in American exceptionalism, just as I suspect that the Brits believe in British exceptionalism and the Greeks believe in Greek exceptionalism. **Barack Obama**

OBAMA THE JOURNEY COMPLETED - NEVER PROMISED A ROSE GARDEN

48. "HIS FINEST HOUR!"
By
Dr. Fred Monderson

It has been argued, "If you can manage the devil in his House, you're good at what you do!" President Obama is good at what he does and he will get the opportunity Tuesday January 20, 2015 to demonstrate such when he delivers this year's State of the Union Address. This, his sixth such address will be different in many ways. That is, this is the first time in his Presidency Republican control both House and Senate, the actual third of the National Government. It also represents the starting point of the last two years of his administration when

Republicans, based on past history, have championed seeming to bully the master of the "Bully Pulpit."

"I can make a firm pledge, under my plan, no family making less than $250,000 a year will see any form of tax increase. Not your income tax, not your payroll tax, not your capital gains taxes, not any of your taxes." **Barack Obama**

Given Senate Majority Leader Mitch McConnell's and House Speaker John Boehner's challenges to Mr. Obama's legislative agenda, then as the majority party in the Legislative Branch of government, Mr. Obama is fully aware of the kind of reception Republicans will give him. Statisticians will count the number of applauses of his speech and particular individuals who will be doing such. For six years Republicans have undermined every legislative initiative the President has proposed to the Congress. In addition, the avalanche of racial hatred Republicans have helped generate and encouraged under camouflage in disrespect they have either initiated or encouraged through proxies and lunatics with the same objective in mind, has been of one Mantra, "Stop Obama," irrespective! Naturally this "fool's errand" has failed. However, and having endured their unrelenting attacks and obstructionism, Mr. Obama has long recognized and confessed, "Politics is a contact sport!" Even more important, whenever the tables are turned, how strange these masters of "Dirty Pool" are the first to cry "Foul!" All this has reinforced the President's work ethic regarding, "How to work smarter not harder!" As such, we know "When the going gets tough, the tough gets going!" Now, having resided in the White House for some six years, never mind all the "commotion outside" and still be able to boast of the many accomplishments he has achieved, Mr. Obama has certainly demonstrated "brains over Republican brawn!" Thus, to have outfoxed, outsmarted, out-maneuvered the heavy-weight might of the Republican Party, even the most slanted assessment must still give Mr. Obama enough credit to "out-coyote" such focused ill-intent assaults, some say because of his race. But the extraordinary talents of this extraordinary individual, perhaps the last great American President; Mr. Obama certainly knows what he is up against. A lesser man, in fear and trembling, would probably have cancelled the State

OBAMA THE JOURNEY COMPLETED - NEVER PROMISED A ROSE GARDEN

of the Union Address this year. Instead, he is more confident, more prepared, and undergirded by his many accomplishments, he is probably more emboldened and looking forward to the "Big Dance." He is probably more confident than General Sherman "Marching through Georgia," though not with the same destructive mentality.

FREDERICK MONDERSON

Certainly knowing the players, he can look into the "Whites of their eyes" and perhaps telepathically communicate to the principal haters, "I know what you did over the past several years; I know what you have been planning; I know what you have in mind; and I know what you have in store for me after this and my next and last Address in this Chamber!" How interesting it is to await Mr. Obama's next book, perhaps entitled, "How I beat the Republican Game Plan!" There he can name names and give credit for each nefarious action to its respective perpetrator.

Imagine as he delivers his state of the Union Address, proclaiming the "Union strong," even if challenged, and at each pause nod at "Stupid Grassley;" into the television to "You Lie Wilson" now at home; perhaps in the gallery above at "Waterloo DeMint;" into the television audience to "The Donald" enquiring "How's that 'Birther' thing going?" Most assuredly he will seek out "One term President" Mitch McConnell in the Senate section of the Members of Congress. Not to be overlooked the man sitting behind him, Speaker Boehner who

OBAMA THE JOURNEY COMPLETED - NEVER PROMISED A ROSE GARDEN

"boasted how he **robbed** Mr. Obama," and 'We got 98% of what we wanted' in negotiations. But Mr. Obama is not like that. He is a straight shooter who confidently affirmed, "The shadow of crisis is past, the State of the Union is Strong!"

John Podhoretz, one of those Republican apologists and "attack dogs" who constantly portray Mr. Obama in a negative light in the *New York Post* entitled "O's Tween Fantasy" put it best. "The state of the economy is indeed strong, because even if you're just talking in relative terms, what nation on this planet is in better shape than ours? Europe remains in crisis. China is slowing down dramatically and arresting thousands. Russia is a tinpot empire. In Japan more people expired last year that were born - a wildly dangerous death spiral. Here, our economy is actually growing, oil prices are falling, consumer confidence is rising and if you have a 401 (K) you're finally back to feeling pretty good about it due to the stock market explosion." As the president said in his Address, "That was good news, people;" but he numbered more than the apologist. Yes, unbelievable as it is, if nothing changes between today and the end of his Presidency, he could still boast of leaving the country in better shape than he found it, despite Republican negativity and lack of cooperation through purposeful obstructionism, a fostered climate of disrespect and fermented racial hatred, as they tried to deny Americans their basic constitutional rights as voting and other protections; all from the highest levels of the United States government.

Nevertheless, in expounding the high road and even seeking greater bipartisan cooperation, President Obama emphasized great confidence in his Cuba policy; Russia's growing insecurity, massive gains against terrorists and echoing a call for tax overhaul nip and tuck, crime, challenges to education and lauding positive gains in the Affordable Care Act, "Obamacare," enhanced registration. Now approaching 11 million, far above the 7 million initially predicted.

Mr. Obama boasted of having rebuilt the economy on a new foundation; lower gas prices and reduced dependence on foreign oil have been "**God Send**;" advocated paid sick leave for workers and underscored women's rights to equal wages as men; praising laws to strengthen domestic Unions to give all Americans a voice and enable skills upgrade through free community college education. Veterans also came in for their share of consideration as it relates to jobs and health care, a free and open Internet, encouragement for creating jobs in America and greater emphasis on science, technology and research and development.

Now, ask that paragon of liberal virtues, eve his mal-clone Rick Santorum, "Can you name one good thing President Obama has done?" We know their "No" answer and it's not surprising because of the "Old Guy" "never converted on the road to Damascus!" However, in case of Santorum, he may still be grappling or trying to bail his "poison well!"

OBAMA THE JOURNEY COMPLETED - NEVER PROMISED A ROSE GARDEN

"The Bush Administration's failure to be consistently involved in helping Israel achieve peace with the Palestinians has been both wrong for our friendship with Israel, as well as badly damaging to our standing in the Arab world." **Barack Obama**

FREDERICK MONDERSON

49.　　PIPELINE WISE, INFRASTRUCTURE FOOLISH

By

Dr. Fred Monderson

Driving along the highway where Brooklyn-Queens Expressway (NY) intersects along the Belt Parkway going east, it's plain to see the work being done to repair the deplorable roadway also known as I-287. Added to this, a bridge collapsed in New Jersey and the ordering of hurried inspections to the several thousand such structures across that state, is symptomatic of the problem across the 50-states of this nation. In his recently delivered State of the Union Address, President Barack Obama drew attention to this problem as part of

OBAMA THE JOURNEY COMPLETED - NEVER PROMISED A ROSE GARDEN

general infrastructure deterioration. Here he emphasized Republican incessant emphasis on the Keystone Pipeline, ignoring the significance of infrastructure repair or replacement along the nation's roadway, rails, ports, bridges, airports, tunnels and the many jobs potentially they provide to strengthen the economy as opposed to the measly, some would say, 35 permanent jobs Senator Charles Schumer mentions the pipeline will provide.

"But do I think that our actions in anyway violate the War Powers Resolution, the answer is no." **Barack Obama**

For six years, a popular refrain has been, "If Obama favors it, then Republicans oppose it." That is, the foolish policy is, prevent "An Obama win" at all costs! As such, every initiative President Obama has proposed to Congress, Republicans, especially in Control of the House of Representatives, in "group think" mode and "like lemmings," have lined up to say "No to Obama!" Imagine, whatever proposal the Chief Executive initiates, by saying "No," Republicans affirm it is not good for the country! An interesting and "hot out of the oven" issue surfaced when President Obama requested congressional authorization to declare war against **ISIL** (**ISIS**). When the question was put to Senator Lindsey Graham (R. N.C) he instantly declared, "I will vote for it!"

For six years the Senator could not see eye to eye and vote favorably to support any measure of the President but all of a sudden he would support a War Resolution. Recognizing that war is costly, requiring great financial outlay in armaments, tanks, bullets, weapons, artillery, aircraft jets and helicopters, desert terrain vehicles, and most important American lives, Mr. Graham all of a sudden is in step with the President. No one can deny the danger posed by **ISIL** but this move is not about benevolence, humanitarianism; it is about financial outlay and profits of war! It will also be interesting to see how many of the Senator's Republican colleagues, will see this as a "good Obama policy," that paradoxically "gives Obama a win!"

FREDERICK MONDERSON

OBAMA THE JOURNEY COMPLETED - NEVER PROMISED A ROSE GARDEN

It is not unexpected Speaker John Boehner will support and expedite a vote on this resolution. Imagine, the Speaker of the House of Representatives representing the people of the United States not simply the Republican base, what a change! Again, at a historically important time as the State of the Union Address when the President of the United States addresses Congress and the American people and the world are both watching, rather than manifest a sedate, dignified, intelligent and attentive posture, the Speaker sits behind the President sniffling, sneezing, and rolling his eyes, wearing a sour expression! This "child-like action" is not befitting a person in such a key, responsible position with such tremendous visibility.

521

FREDERICK MONDERSON

Let us suppose, Mr. Boehner had the sniffles; which is a natural malady. For sure, it did not begin at 9:00 PM on January 20, when the Sergeant of Arm announced, "Mr. Speaker, the President of the United States!" So he calls up his doctor, "Let me have 2 Excedrin tablets to stop this sniffling before I take the stage behind the President" rather than appear as a fidgeting Middle School student outclassed in his position. To his right, the counter-weight, Vice-President Joe Biden appeared so majestic, dignified and attentive with a pleasing smile. That is, Joe Biden as a "well-cooked steak" and John Boehner as a "chicken in the rough!"

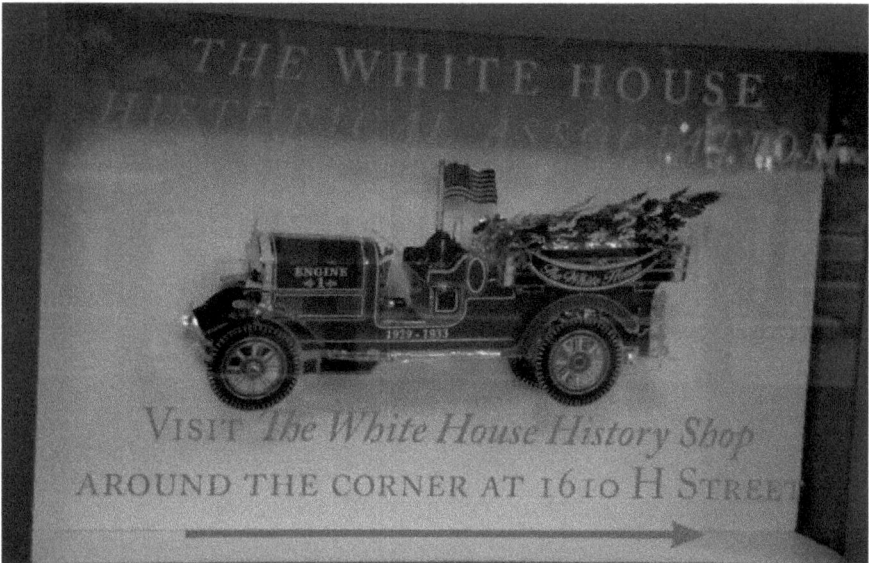

Oh yes, so at the Roulette Table of this important issue, Republican put all their chips on Red unmindful of the actor Wesley Snipes admonition in the movie **Passenger 57**, "Always bet on black!" That is, they value the Keystone Pipeline much more than a Jobs Bill that will benefit all of America, people and landscape; as it employs millions putting these people back onto the tax roll, benefitting families who shop at grocery and clothing stores, plan for their kid's education, pay doctor bills, buy new cars, gas at the pump, take a vacation after work gets into full swing and even put away a little for

OBAMA THE JOURNEY COMPLETED - NEVER PROMISED A ROSE GARDEN

retirement. Even more important, this type of action and outlay strengthens the nation's heartland.

FREDERICK MONDERSON

Some have argued; the Keystone Pipeline only transits American terrain with the potential to unleash environmental harm which is really to bring Canadian oil to an Atlantic port for sale abroad, perhaps Asia, specifically China. This is more significant, for while this project may one day have long-time American significance, at a time when world oil is in a glut, prices are down, the global economy is in down-turn from declining oil prices, to place such great emphasis on the pipeline at the expense of a national Jobs Bill, seems not a wise Republican decision which is not surprising given the rays of Mr. Obama's brilliance which continues to affect, perhaps temporarily blind the vision and thinking of his opponents.

Much ink has been spilt on the pros and cons of the benefits of the Keystone Pipeline. Some myths explored in *Huffington Post* include, the "competitive advantage in processing compared to foreign refiners;" that "traditional sources of heavy crude are declining;" that "the US will need to import oil to meet its domestic demand for decades;" questions regarding "the number of jobs that will be

OBAMA THE JOURNEY COMPLETED - NEVER PROMISED A ROSE GARDEN

created;" whether "declining gas prices will benefit American consumers;" whether "native Americans" are getting a fair share; and whether it is "cost effective for producers in light of falling oil prices."

FREDERICK MONDERSON

All this notwithstanding, as the nation's Chief Executive and Chief Legislator, we must seek to understand the President's objection to the feasibility of the project. Given the prevailing view from a Republican perspective, "if Obama favors it, then it's bad;" thus, we must recognize and ask, if Republicans favor it especially so intensely weak, does the President have a better perspective in addition to the Power of the Veto? Nevertheless, if in total all Republican eyes are on the President, we need to know and remember; his eyes are on the well-being and welfare of the American people.

"I don't think marriage is a civil right, but I think that being able to transfer property is a civil right." **Barack Obama**

OBAMA THE JOURNEY COMPLETED - NEVER PROMISED A ROSE GARDEN

50.   "FOOLS" ON "Errands"
By
Dr. Fred Monderson

It has been often said, "If you keep doing the same things you will get the same results." Someone should tell the Republicans who now control both Houses of Congress of this wise maxim. On the issue of the Keystone Pipeline, President Obama, as Chief Executive and Chief Legislator found fault with the measure and promised to veto it. He even compromised and suggested, if corrected from its present state, he would consider it more seriously, but there is an even bigger problem with the pipeline that the President's experts discovered the Obama-Republican clash, and the issue of jobs. During the State of the Union Address, Mr. Obama urged the New Congress to pass a **Jobs Bill** that would, principally, address the problems of the nation's crumbling infrastructure such as rails, roads, bridges, ports, etc., and he contrasted the benefits of such a bill against "one pipeline" which seem more than reasonable.

"I think same sex couples should be able to get married." **Barack Obama**

Republicans in Congress, bullied by the emergent "Tea Party" movement had set a list of priorities they would enact if they were successful in the 2014 mid-term election. As fate, perhaps, misguided or misinformed, would have it, Republican "thumped" Democrats. Succeeding to control of both "Houses of Congress" and emboldened by their good fortune of largesse from the American public, "victims" of a sordid portrait of President Obama the Republican propaganda artists had painted, the new power began sharpening their "long knives" and "checking their list" perhaps more than once.

OBAMA THE JOURNEY COMPLETED - NEVER PROMISED A ROSE GARDEN

Unmindful of the President's veto threat, Republicans passed the Keystone Pipeline bill. Their claim, the pipeline as "their jobs bill" would provide "thousands of jobs," while Senator Charles Schumer (D. NY) responded it will provide "only 35 permanent jobs." Thus, it makes one wonder, "In that 'Washington Desert' who is manufacturing 'snow Jobs?'" Another question enquiring minds want answered is "What is the true nature of this new Republican mandate?"

Decrying American voting apathy in past elections and especially in this 2014 mid-term, it's been revealed only 36 percent of the electorate participated. In view of Republican gains and if we give them a 55 to 45 or 60 to 40 advantage, that means their mandate based on the turnout is not that overwhelming, despite Hillary Clinton's wisdom, "A win is a win!" The interesting thing is; Republicans seem not for the general welfare but only their base. However, as Chief Executive as the Constitution states the President's job is to promote the "general welfare." That is, the President's job is to determine what is beneficial to the broad masses of the American people. That is why among the broad repertoire of his tools, the veto is important. More perceptively he has to think more of the 99 percent than the 1 percent, which the Republicans do wonderfully well in reverse.

Now, there are two principal types of veto, the "Pocket Veto" and the "Regular Veto." The "Pocket Veto" is a "backdoor" way of saying no to a bill, while the "Regular Veto" is a more confrontational rejection.

Everyone has seen the history of Republican behavior towards the Obama administration has been a sordid experiment in American government hypocrisy and chicanery. Powerful individuals from the highest levels of the American government have prosecuted and helped sustain an offensive climate of disrespect and racial hatred towards Mr. Obama, particularly because of his race. What is even more sinister, according to the "father of the Republican Party" Abraham Lincoln, "Silence in the expression of wrong doing creates culpability on the part of such onlookers?" Because a seeming fundamental tenet of Republican political behavior, "group think" or "law of the pack," no Republican leader of stature has visibly taken a

OBAMA THE JOURNEY COMPLETED - NEVER PROMISED A ROSE GARDEN

stand against the racial crucifixion of Mr. Obama, especially and in view of the excellent performance of his responsibility as President and Chief Executive. That is to say, persons such as Senator Mitch McConnell, Speaker John Boehner, Sarah Palin, Michele Bachmann, Joe Wilson and even Donald Trump have risen not simply to their highest level of incompetence but to their grossest levels of despicable and chicane behavior, disrespect as elected officials and purported leaders.

General Ulysses Grant on guard in front of the Capitol Building.

FREDERICK MONDERSON

OBAMA THE JOURNEY COMPLETED - NEVER PROMISED A ROSE GARDEN

After having passed the Keystone Pipeline bill, Republicans announced they will next focus on the Affordable Care Act, they have derisively named "Obamacare. The "blind leading the blind," Mitch McConnell and John Boehner are not simply persistent but we can probably say, "foolish." The proverbial "ship of fools" Republicans are piloting have voted to repeal "Obamacare" some 50 times. They are now trying to achieve the half-century mark. While history will record the **Affordable Care Act** as Mr. Obama's signature legislative accomplishment, those analytic appraisals of the last two Congresses characterizing Mr. Obama's second term will be highlighted by this monumental Republican failure to truly assess Barack Obama as a political opponent but more particularly expose Republican chicanery and deceitfulness. Even more important, when

FREDERICK MONDERSON

"Obamacare" was first being rolled-out a threshold of seven million registrants was projected to make the system functionally cost effective. Despite the negativity first propagated about the new health care provision, the supposed economic costs to taxpayers, that it was a government program and not actually private, and especially the initial "glitches" in the "roll-out," the Republican predicted gloom never materialized. Currently, enrollment is fast approaching 11 million! Thus far demonstrated callous Republican behavior, even though many Republican controlled states' political apparatus have prevented eligible citizens from enrolling in this health care offer, they are still threatening to eviscerate the health care protections of the 11 million Americans, while their party members line up to drink from the one billion dollars promised in the Koch brothers trough for the 2016 election.

OBAMA THE JOURNEY COMPLETED - NEVER PROMISED A ROSE GARDEN

FREDERICK MONDERSON

The sad reality, however, with scalpel in hand, President Obama is waiting in that big White House Oval Office Desk to circumcise the bill once it lands on his desk!

In *American Government* by Robert C. Bone, (New York: Barnes and Noble, 1977: 74-75) pointed out: "Perhaps the most effective influence the President possesses over legislative actions is not mentioned in Article II. This is the veto power provided by Article I, Section 7, which deals with congressional legislation. Such a power had long been possessed by the British ruler but Hamilton pointed out in *The Federalist* (No. 69), a classic commentary on the Constitution, rather than an 'absolute negative' the President has only a 'qualified negative' over legislative actions. This is so because Congress, by a two thirds vote in both houses, can pass legislation over a presidential veto."

OBAMA THE JOURNEY COMPLETED - NEVER PROMISED A ROSE GARDEN

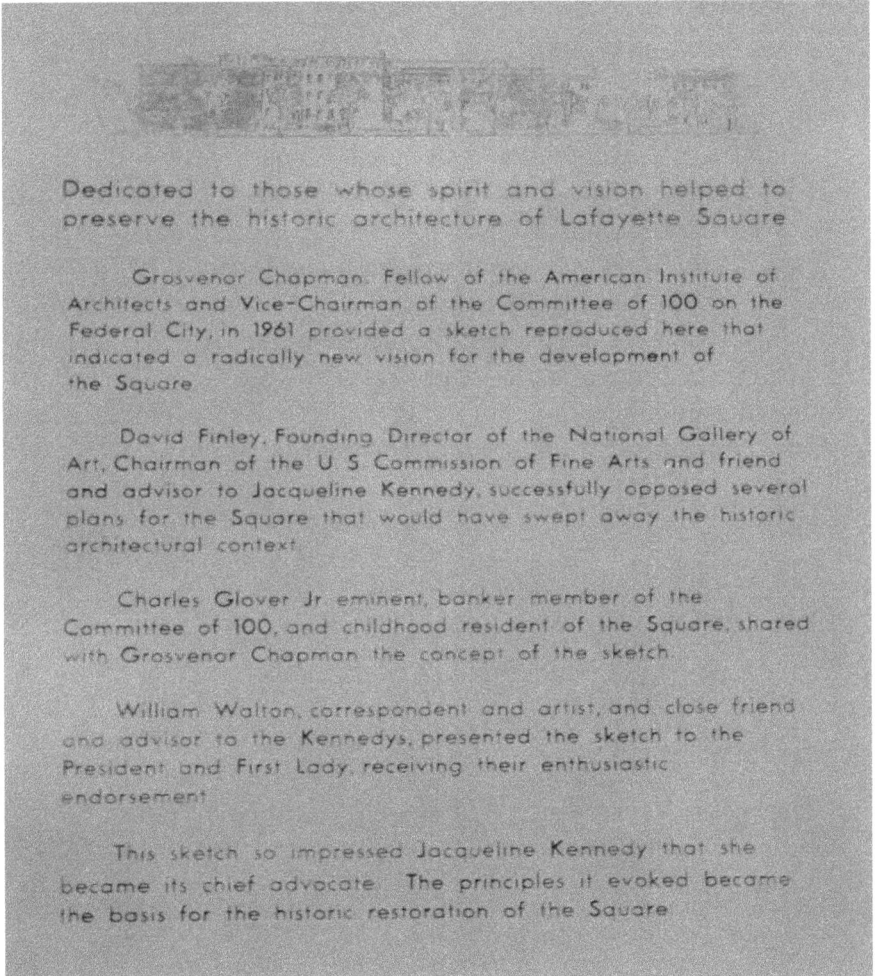

Dedicated to those whose spirit and vision helped to preserve the historic architecture of Lafayette Square

Grosvenor Chapman, Fellow of the American Institute of Architects and Vice-Chairman of the Committee of 100 on the Federal City, in 1961 provided a sketch reproduced here that indicated a radically new vision for the development of the Square.

David Finley, Founding Director of the National Gallery of Art, Chairman of the U.S. Commission of Fine Arts and friend and advisor to Jacqueline Kennedy, successfully opposed several plans for the Square that would have swept away the historic architectural context.

Charles Glover Jr. eminent, banker member of the Committee of 100, and childhood resident of the Square, shared with Grosvenor Chapman the concept of the sketch.

William Walton, correspondent and artist, and close friend and advisor to the Kennedys, presented the sketch to the President and First Lady, receiving their enthusiastic endorsement.

This sketch so impressed Jacqueline Kennedy that she became its chief advocate. The principles it evoked became the basis for the historic restoration of the Square.

Jack C. Plano and Milton Greenberg in *The American Political Dictionary* (eighth Edition) (New York: Holt, Rinehart and Winston, Inc., 1989: 183-84) equally describes the veto as: "A legislative power vested in a chief executive to return a bill unsigned to the legislative body with reasons of his objections. The Constitution provides that every bill, both public and private, that passes the House and the Senate must be sent to the President before it becomes law. When the President receives a bill, he may: (1) sign it, whereupon it becomes law; (2) not sign it, whereupon it becomes law after ten congressional working days; (3) veto it, and send it back to the house of its origin; or (4) not sign it, whereupon if Congress adjourns within ten days the bill is killed (pocket veto). The President vetoes a bill by writing "veto" (I forbid) across the face of the bill; he then sends it back to Congress with a message setting forth his objections. Congress may amend the bill according to the President's demands and then re-pass it, or it may reject the President's objections and override the veto by re-passing the bill with a two-thirds roll-call vote of those present and voting in each house. Finally, the President's veto may be sustained, which occurs more often than a direct override of the veto."

OBAMA THE JOURNEY COMPLETED - NEVER PROMISED A ROSE GARDEN

Again, explaining the significance of the veto Plano and Greenberg write: "Presidents employed the veto power infrequently and with great caution until the post-Civil War administration of Andrew Johnson. Since 1865, the veto power has been used with increasing vigor by most presidents; Grover Cleveland, with 414 regular and pocket vetoes, and Franklin Roosevelt, with 631, has been its most persistent users. The scope of the veto power has also expanded since 1865. The earlier view that the veto should be used to block unconstitutional or technically imperfect laws has been supplemented by its employment to express disapproval of any kind. Although the veto is merely suspensive in effect, few vetoes are overridden by Congress, since if one-third plus one of the members voting in either house support the President's view, the veto prevails. The threat of the veto can also be used effectively by a chief executive to shape and change legislation while it is still in the hands of the legislature."

The story is told of political opposition in the Ivory Coast, West Africa, against President Houphey Boingy. One demonstrating gathering assembled chanting "Down with Boingy," and decided to "march on the Presidential Palace!" Along the way, excitement reached fever pitch, exhortations were uttered until they reached their destination massing in front of the Palace gates. They even demanded the President come out and speak. Answering, in his brief address to the agitated gathering Mr. Boingy simply said, "Say what you want, I am what you have!" In the American political democratic system, until 2016 Mr. Obama is all the Republicans have and thanks to the veto and their inability to override with scalpel in hand he will be "shearing the sheep!"

OBAMA THE JOURNEY COMPLETED - NEVER PROMISED A ROSE GARDEN

FREDERICK MONDERSON

The sad thing about the Obama-Republican saga, as the "Lilliputians struggle to tie-down Gulliver," they remain unmindful of the illuminated record of their behavior towards a decent yet thinking individual; a man of high character and nobility of spirit. That is, Mr. Obama knows all the players; he has experienced everything including the kitchen sink they threw at him; has effectively "out-think" their greatest minds; and still holds them to a standstill. Still, as this drama unfolds, the public is forced to enquire, 'What manner of man is this?' For, as an example, like the Duracell Bunny; Mr. Obama "takes a licking and keeps on ticking," towards 2016 and beyond. He never misses a beat in his responsibility despite unprecedented Republican obstruction along the way.

"I will continue to believe that Israel's security is paramount."
Barack Obama

542

OBAMA THE JOURNEY COMPLETED - NEVER PROMISED A ROSE GARDEN

51. SLAVES, MASTERS AND SECURITY
By
Dr. Fred Monderson

Sure, there is a police organization in New York called "100 Blacks in Law Enforcement Who Care" and there may very well be similar groups across the country, but they are few. Most Black Police officers who fill this category with a function possess a sense of community in pursuing their calling as public servants committed to protecting their community but also caring about how they go about such a business. One such policeman Witherspoon confessed; in twenty years of service, not once did he pull his service revolver. However, across the country, for the most part, Black Police Officers serve as minorities ethnically and numerically, but are yet constrained within a "Blue Wall of Silence." Still, strange enough, when some are in forefront of vigorously policing, they sadly also resolutely brutalize! I'm reminded of the "House Negro" in the movie **Django Unchained**.

"I'm a Christian by choice." **Barack Obama**

Notwithstanding, the great many officers, mostly white, who serve consciously are also constrained by the "few bad apples" who spoil their barrel disregarding the honor of the profession and the fact "Black Lives Matter." Nevertheless, all function within psychological mindsets sanctioned by legal precedence sanctioned under *ante-bellum* legislation that held the Black Man in contempt. *Ipso Facto*, and in serviced to the ante-bellum cultural norm that falsely claimed "Blacks were, and are, inferior in both the natural and social order." As such, law enforcement functionality that grew out of an empowered "slave catchers" ideology and operationalization empowered through **Black Codes**, was designed to protect property at all costs and so viewed Black Men especially as chattel and so disregarded their humanity in serving the interests of the "business class" who not only subjugated the unfortunates but when they revolted or ran away, these "rough riders" only saw color and ran roughshod over them disregarding whether they were enslaved or free.

OBAMA THE JOURNEY COMPLETED - NEVER PROMISED A ROSE GARDEN

When the saga of Ferguson unfolded a young Missouri activist reminded "Slavery is in the DNA of this state!" Equally, it can be argued, the ideology, personality and make-up of the slave catchers' DNA seem transmitted into the veins of many current law enforcement officers as evident in the wanton police killing of unarmed Black men from not too distant Trayvon Martin through the recently killed Freddie Gray. To understand how we got here, however, history provides a clear road map from the brutality of the overseer, through the rapaciousness of the slave catcher and into the need for law and order that disregarded the humanity of the Black image in executing the need to protect property even though the Black was regarded as property under the system of chattel slavery, a phenomenon that lasted for centuries.

FREDERICK MONDERSON

OBAMA THE JOURNEY COMPLETED - NEVER PROMISED A ROSE GARDEN

736

JACKSON PLACE

Regardless of arguments for origins and dynamics of New World Slave Trade and Slavery unmistakably, Europeans and those morphing into Americans saw Africa lose "some 100 Million Africans" from the continent to engineer the transformation of the New World through a system relying on the process of Plantation Slavery. In response to an old adage, "You can take the horse to water but you can't make him drink!" to this Teddy Cubia responded, "If you work that beast unending he will get thirsty and must drink!" Thus, in the reversal of science undergone by the African from a "Happy-Go-Lucky-Freeman" to a captured and degraded piece of property engineered through legally sanctioned and harsh chattel slavery, was born an enforcement mechanism of cruelty designed to reduce into subservience and forced into unpaid labor, an African spirit dehumanized by supposedly god-fearing Christian white men who orchestrated a regimen "To make them stand in fear!" of the white man, that is!

Now, having suffered through the "long night" of the first two centuries of that inhuman ordeal of captivity, the promised light of the **Declaration of Independence** and the freedoms of the **Constitution** were nothing but dim candles flickering in a windswept storm. While the art of compromise for political appeasement elevated the enslaved African from the depths of the "animal kingdom" to "three-fifths" of a man, the demands of cotton fueling economic progress, unconscionable "southern gentlemen" were confronted with the contradiction of freedom's aspirations and slavery's hopelessness. So repression in *de jure* and *de facto* garb, having enlisted the nation's slickest legal minds who crafted **Black Codes** that empowered an enforcement mechanism of slave catching along the nation's by-ways, this phenomenon worked in conjunction with the overseer's brutal mentality on the plantation.

OBAMA THE JOURNEY COMPLETED - NEVER PROMISED A ROSE GARDEN

FREDERICK MONDERSON

As the slave world turned, protection of the African spirit, his family, his future was a far cry from government responsibility. Thus, the **Willie Smiths** and terror groups with the same objective in mind evolved a disregard for Black lives engineered by the slave catchers' whip, strategies and tactics and much of this undergirded by emerging law enforcement practices. In the mix of a lynching mentality, disregard for the humanity of Blacks, envy toward his humaneness despite his trials and tribulations and when one flavors all this with a

OBAMA THE JOURNEY COMPLETED - NEVER PROMISED A ROSE GARDEN

lot of Jim Crowism, a little "separate and unequal," two cups of racist white supremacy ideology, lack of jobs, poor housing and inadequate education, threats and intimidation, lynchings, and most important, lack of protections that open doors to inequality before the law that translates into injustice towards the "fly in buttermilk."

Interestingly enough, though liberal elements may protest mildly, the "old money" and their progeny sanction the protection apparatus for fear of "Black uprisings" in the form of Denmark Vesey and Nat Turner even Malcolm X and Martin Luther King who threaten a social order in itself tottering under a yoke of inequality and struggling on the verge in need for vigorous social challenge. In a nation that has fought many wars at home and abroad and knowing the consequences of such destruction has nevertheless empowered domestic law enforcement with the most devastating armaments ostensibly to keep the peace, becomes a menace on this nation's sacred grounds. Yet, the citizenry, not being fully apprised of this machinery is left to feel the brunt of its culpability.

FREDERICK MONDERSON

When an event such as Ferguson unfolds and local government deploys such lethal war machinery to face down its citizenry, observers are forced to ask who is really the enemy.

Recall the TV glimpse of Koreans firing their weapons from roof tops into rioting looters after the Rodney King verdict. Has anyone wondered whether these individuals were licensed to carry. In Baltimore, after the now infamous night of looting and burning, the next day another glimpse after the governor had declared a state of emergency, a line of military Humvees backed by several thousand national guardsmen and other law enforcement personnel took center stage. These too were deployed against citizens seeking to secure redress for wrong committed against the poor unfortunates.

OBAMA THE JOURNEY COMPLETED - NEVER PROMISED A ROSE GARDEN

In decoding the American social environment, a latent disregard for Black life has led to many deaths; Jesse Jackson gave a number of 110, at the hands of law enforcement, White and Black police officers. Recently an activist gave a number of 500 for 2016 so far, but this number seem very high. The "party line" justification for such killings or deaths is that the "officers were in fear of their lives" from "Negroes with Guns" even though these young men, were, for the most part, unarmed. This behavior, scrutinized through the benefits of technology that is, the video, the camera, the cell phone has moved the people to a new sense of activism because contrary to denial and false justification of wrongful police action, there is a third eye looking on at developing situations.

FREDERICK MONDERSON

One such recording made known the Rodney King beating; another filmed the Eric Garner homicide; execution of Tamir Rice is still another that clocked the rapidity with which the officer shot his weapon after arrival on the scene; shooting of Michael Brown; and who knows what truly happened to Freddie Gray! Unfortunately George Zimmerman got a pass in killing Trayvon Martin but we later see his deeper pathological maladies in run-in with the law. Let us not go into Eleanor Bumpers, Dorismond, Amadou Diallo, but Jesse Jackson's reminder is that there were at least 110 such incidents of fatalities and this may be nearer the truth than the activist account quoted above.

"I'm a warrior for the middle class." **Barack Obama**

52. DEFENDING A MYTH!
By
Dr. Fred Monderson

On Monday June 22, Congressman James Clyburn (D. SC), appearing on Wolf Blitzer's **Situation Room** was interviewed regarding Governor Nikki Haley bi-partisan support and statement regarding removal of the Confederate flag from the grounds of the South Carolina State Capitol in which he praised this "idea whose time has come!" It is interesting that just prior Mr. Blitzer had interviewed a gentleman of the League of the South in which he went on and on about the virtuous defense of the flag because of the 100,000 South

OBAMA THE JOURNEY COMPLETED - NEVER PROMISED A ROSE GARDEN

Carolinians who died fighting an invader under that flag. Mature, he still seemed nervous, "defending the seeming indefensible!"

"I've been fighting with Acorn, alongside Acorn, on issues you care about, my entire career." **Barack Obama**

Nevertheless, in his response to "Blitz," Mr. Clyburn explained his researched understanding regarding the Confederate flag. First, he reminded this flag did not come from the battlefield at the end of Civil War hostilities. He did indicate the current Confederate Flag was hoisted in opposition and response to progress made during the Civil Rights Movement of the 1960s. Even more significant, he correctly identified the Confederate Flag not as belonging to South Carolina but Tennessee as created by General Forest Beckford, founder of the Ku Klux Klan. The version flying in South Carolina was actually that of West-Virginia. Thus, theirs is truly "Defense of a Myth!" He went on to explain the people defending the flag did not even know their own history! Fact is, "they did not know they did not know!"

However, this idea of defense of a myth is not new. In fact, down through recorded history, people, not necessarily misguided, but they have, through circumstances and cultural custom, been inculcated in defense of a myth and such resulting way of life. And, as "practice makes perfect" and "repetition is the bane of learning," these individuals became psychologically ingrained in believing their myriad bits the whole of reality. As such, if we examine myths in historical perspective we would realize Mr. Clyburn's subjects are subscribing to beliefs in which they stand as the majority of one, or, perhaps a small sum.

FREDERICK MONDERSON

First, even though there are problems of reality as portrayed in the movie **Ten Commandments** starring Charleston Heston and Yul Brynner, a scene in the movie depicts King Seti I of the 19th Egyptian Dynasty, when confronted with the prospects of a "Messiah" instructed his son and ultimately successor, the next Rameses II, "If it is a myth bring it to me in a bottle. If it is a man, bring him in chains!" This admonition began events throughout history where myths have sustained people, led them falsely in beliefs and been stanchly defended. Sometimes it led the wrong way at the fork in the road!

OBAMA THE JOURNEY COMPLETED - NEVER PROMISED A ROSE GARDEN

The story of the Donation of Constantine is another of those fascinating but intriguing historical documents involved in an issue of great controversy. Purportedly put to analytic scrutiny because it's an extant document justifying certain types of actions, problems were observed in its wording. Accordingly, Roman Emperor Constantine was on the verge of a major battle and the night before he had a dream involving a bishop's miter and other religious symbolism. Successful in the next day's battle, he attributed his success to divine intervention and as a result ended persecution of Christians and accepted Christianity as an official religion within the Roman Empire. In good faith, he convened the **Council of Nicea** in 325 when a great many bishops were summoned to prepare the way for the church going forward. As such, to create a unified front and solidify the magnanimous developments, the Emperor ceded great tracts of land to the church and produced a document, a deed that became the "Donation of Constantine." Held in great reverence, some 800 years later, linguists and other scholars, examining this prized document were alarmed it was forged, a fake, possessing no legitimacy!

FREDERICK MONDERSON

What these sleuths were able to ascertain, there were words and phrases in the document that were not "invented" at the time of its issuance. That is to say, linguistically speaking as is evident, new words and phrases are added to language every day and others, by virtue of not being used, are dropped. A good example explaining this phenomenon is best understood in the following analogy. Let us, for argument sake say, we have a document written in 1920 after the Versailles Peace Conference of 1919. Sometime in the 1970s a popular phrase "Where's the beef?" appears in a TV commercial. Given this is a later creation, to have it appear in an earlier document when it was "not yet coined" or in use tells scholars it's a later insertion and so, the authenticity of the document becomes questioned and it is deemed a forgery. This is what happened in the case of the **Donation of Constantine**.

OBAMA THE JOURNEY COMPLETED - NEVER PROMISED A ROSE GARDEN

In the emergence of that "superior, Western, European mental capacity," a great number of historical falsifications were perpetuated to the detriment of many people and cultures. Even more important, science especially was led in the wrong direction for the longest until meticulous scholarship, *al be it* too late to prove the forgery; and, sad to say, the people concerned or benefitting from the hoax remain vociferously committed to proclaiming and defending the stated situation. A good example of this is the Piltdown Hoax. Hence, we could end up with Mr. Clyburn's "Defense of a Myth!"

FREDERICK MONDERSON

In the great religious swindle denying African involvement and playing a significant role in the formative efforts to establish Christianity, untold energy was expended omitting the influence of Africans as church fathers and popes. We know in the classical world, "everything African was African!" However, within the modern mind influenced by the falsity of white supremacy, even when the person, through historical evidence, was proven to be born in Africa, the spurious argument held, "Yes, he was born in Africa but of European parentage!" Undoubtedly, while this denial is more modern than ancient, it's been part of the overall methodology and strategy not only to contribute to the myth of white supremacy; that is, elevating white and denigrating black; but it has caused untold psychological damage on the one hand and fooled many people on the other. The issue with the fathers of the church, notwithstanding, the case of Priscian is another prime example. This North African born individual dominated all forms of western grammatical structure for more than 1200 years. Born in the 7th Century, he wrote and taught in Europe all aspects of grammar with only minor adjustments being made to his method as late as the end of the 19th Century. Still, little is known of the man as an African and the significance of his work and this is considered a major historical distortion.

OBAMA THE JOURNEY COMPLETED - NEVER PROMISED A ROSE GARDEN

FREDERICK MONDERSON

The "Myth of Prester John" is significant for the African and resources of Africa. It is a well-known fact, just prior to Columbus' voyages of discovery to the New World, Portuguese explorers Bartholomew Dias and Vasco Da Gama began explorations southward along the West African coast. As prospects for riches, trade and otherwise, the "Myth of Prester John" was sometime created possessing end of the rainbow attractions of adventurous integrity and promises of wealth as rewards. The myth held, Prester John was considered a white, Christian, king ruling a kingdom peopled by savage Africans. And so, adventurers of every hue and cry set out to find this individual. Well, they came searching; missionaries wearing religious garb as the first wave of imperialist colonizers, then traders, consuls and soldiers. Before long, while still searching for the king, "spheres of influence" were created, trade encouraged, land concessions secured and consuls sent to protect the missionaries and traders. To aid these, soldiers were sent to protect the consuls who in turn recruited locals to form "frontier forces" commanded by white officers whose role was to establish law and order. Naturally, these locals became spies breaking down their own cultural norms and acted as interpreters and so dramatic changes took place.

In all of this, there emerged propaganda labeled Africans as "killing and eating the white man." As Prof. John Clarke more correctly reminded, "We invited the white man to lunch and we became the meal." Or, even the insight offered by King Menelik II of Ethiopia who defeated the Italians at the Battle of Adowa in 1896. "I know the strategy of European governments," he explained. "First they send missionaries, then consuls, then soldiers to protect them both." Or, even more as Jomo Kenyatta wrote in his book *Facing Mount Kenya*, "When the missionaries came, they taught us to close our eyes and pray. When we opened our eyes we were holding the Bible and they the land." In similar fashion, the Bible Study Group at "Mother Emanuel Church" invited young Dylann Roof into their religious circle and the killer committed the most unspeakable act. So, some have argued, in as much as Prester John was not found there may very well be individuals still searching the bushes of Africa for him.

FREDERICK MONDERSON

The "Myths of the Phantom and Tarzan" got much traction from that astute English mind, where Edgar Burroughs, etc., fabricated superhuman white individuals overcoming and outwitting untold numbers of Africans and as Hollywood got in the act we laughed heartily in movie theaters as Africans caricatured reinforced the "Cigar Store African" image. Even Calypsonian Mighty Sparrow sang how British Education Minister Cutridge's curriculum was intended "to create comedians" among the children in the British colonial areas.

That assiduous European mind, quick to explore and exploit every situation, offered all forms of rationalizations for the Slave Trade. Starting with African culture being different from that of Europe; Noah's curse condemns Africans to "obey your masters;" the Slave Trade was just that, instead widely believed robbery; Africans sold their brothers into slavery; trans-shipment was not that bad, they arrived refreshed and ready for New World sale; instead of the physical and psychological brutalities of the Middle Passage experience where they were plied with skin oils and fed a last hot meal before being sold upon arrival in the New World; "tight packing" and "loose packing" demands of the Triangle Trade justified expected profit margin; the terror of separation and fears of an unknown future; all in preparation "To Make Them Stand in Fear" of the white man! Slavery was good for the African, who had not Christianity rescue him he would have stagnated in Savage Africa. These arguments never considered Africans of Ethiopia were converted long before Christianity came to Europe. In fact, had it not been for the African Church Fathers, Christianity would not have made it this far.

OBAMA THE JOURNEY COMPLETED - NEVER PROMISED A ROSE GARDEN

A similar not too different case headlined the *News of the World* newspaper some 15 years ago. A By-line read, "Scientists discover the Home of Queen of Sheba, in Nigeria." Lo and behold, the centerfold showed the image of a white woman, despite the fact the Queen's famous words were "I am Black and comely!" Ivan Van Sertima argued if that was possible, then the Queen's empire may have stretched across the belt of Central Africa, from east to west. This meant her empire was many times the size of Solomon's tiny country. Nevertheless, that an Editor could publish such a false photograph is an equally significant hallmark of distortion to defend a myth.

FREDERICK MONDERSON

The "Myth of a Caucasian Egypt" is one of those contemporary issues strangling this aspect of African history because for most of the 19th and 20th Centuries, unchallenged interpretation of the evidence has created a false, ossified belief. Without question fathers of the foundation of Egyptological archaeology, linguistics, and anthropology did exceptional work of reclamation, analysis and identification and interpretation. However, since these were humans, and there was no Diop as critic, mistakes were made in interpretation of the data. This has been shown many times over that the existential data contradicts the symbolic representation. But, ideas gone abroad are difficult to recall particularly since they were ingrained in an era of white supremacy chauvinism and imperialism's clamor then their falsity became engraved in the minds and psyche of both perpetrators and their victims. That is also why "Moderns" as Derry, Emery, and Wortham could claim "The Egyptians are Caucasians." That is why also, such scholars as Elliot Smith, even C.G. Seligman's *Races of Africa* could claim Caucasian penetration not simply in the Delta but very far into Nubia. Conversely and in contradiction, David O'Connor could pronounce, "The Egyptians were not white," William Arnett in *Evidence for the Development of Hieroglyphs in Southern Upper Egypt* could assert, "While Dr. Diop proved the Egyptians were not Caucasians, the bones could not prove they were Negroes (Black)." Yet, despite Arnett giving only half a loaf, Diop did provide tremendous evidence to prove "Africa in Egypt" and "Egypt in Africa." Nevertheless, the Myth lives on of a Caucasian Egypt.

OBAMA THE JOURNEY COMPLETED - NEVER PROMISED A ROSE GARDEN

FREDERICK MONDERSON

The "Myth that Africans never contributed much to American culture" not only flies in the face of reason but insidiously questions the role of the fundamental pillars of music, sports, even entertainment, more particularly, the importance of religiosity, compassion, healing and the power of prayer on behalf of America and its leaders are without question among this nation's valuable and cherished resources. Black scientists and inventors and their inventions, mathematicians, and much more are not only undercounted but were omitted and denied their significant contribution to American academic and scientific progress for much of the 19th and 20th Centuries. Even more important, for the last 50 years, school science texts across the curriculum, have totally ignored the Black Scientist, underscoring the myth while justifying falsity in American education providing the necessity for a curriculum of inclusion.

OBAMA THE JOURNEY COMPLETED - NEVER PROMISED A ROSE GARDEN

Today the "Myth of the Confederate Flag" seems to be dissipating as smoke in open air. Across the nation, not simply citizens but state houses with links to the flag are now experiencing a groundswell to distance themselves from the odious atmosphere now revealed in association with the flag. A glaring irony was pictured on Wednesday, June 24th 2015, when the Caisson carrying Reverend Clementa Pinckney to "Lay in State" in the State Capital building, passed the Confederate flag fluttering in the wind. Meanwhile, many were gathered nearby chanting, "Take it down!" However, and because of the legislative maneuvering involved, in a clever ruse, an important South Carolina legislator proposed, for the Reverend's funeral, "We could take the flag down to clean it!"

HARRY S. TRUMAN SCHOLARSHIP FOUNDATION

It is a sad tragedy throughout the continued progress of America, lives were lost, suffering ensued, perpetrators of evil acts have, for the most part, gone unpunished and remain unrepentant having committed untold terrorist acts against Black Americans. Nevertheless, whatever may be said by the nefarious, some have branded racist, bigoted, inconsiderate, evil, the magnanimous humanity of African-Americans

571

FREDERICK MONDERSON

un-measurable commitment to religious tenets of love, forgiveness and commiseration for fellow man are significant anchors proudly buoying the American ship of state boosting the Red, White and Blue flag's image among the nearly 20 modern nations comprising the human family.

Despite what may be said of the Founding Fathers' creative efforts, had African-Americans not applied their tremendous virtuous and spiritual potency, the American ship of state may have sunk a long time ago.

"In America, there's a failure to appreciate Europe's leading role in the world." **Barack Obama**

OBAMA THE JOURNEY COMPLETED - NEVER PROMISED A ROSE GARDEN

53. OBAMA - GREATEST PRESIDENT EVER!
By
Dr. Fred Monderson

Sometime ago, the Noble winner in economics and *The New York Times* columnist, Jack Krugman dubbed Barack Obama the greatest American President ever. At that time, still in the throes of the "Birther

Queen's" and Donald Trump's "Birther Movement;" following Mitch McConnell's "I intend to make Barack Obama a one-term President" and his flashing that infamous "I got the Nigger in the White House" thumbs up signal; despite such outlandish behaviors, Mr. Obama remained focused on his responsibilities as leader of the nation and first African-American President. Then there was Speaker John Boehner's disrespecting the President; all, while Mr. Obama was vigorously challenging the nation's economic quagmire of bank failures and Wall Street collapse he inherited. The auto industry was profusely losing market share to foreign competitors was bailed out despite great resistance from Republicans in Congress. Unemployment rates were escalating rapidly affecting the tax base of federal, state and local governments; the housing industry was in great disarray with rising foreclosures, and new building starts slowed dramatically; yet, and instead, Republicans single-mindedly focused on efforts so Mr. Obama would be denied "a win" as they lambasted him. Nevertheless, and while "first responders" stood nervously with their heads on the chopping block across the nation, not only did he relieve their anxiety, but simultaneously the President struggled to find the right formula in his military strategy. And so, with two wars raging in Iraq and Afghanistan and Somali pirates on the rampage; one man, Barack Obama, stood tenaciously as an island, "being shot at by friendlies" as he aimed to combat unfriendly forces.

"No one is pro-abortion." **Barack Obama**

Mr. Krugman's assessment, for as a Noble Laureate, he has a "special eye" to observe and see things normal humans are unable to notice, thus, with no end in sight to their enmity, as Mr. Obama persevered in the talk at hand, demonstrating great flexibility in efforts to prosecute the nation's business despite Tea Party every effort to embarrass the man, Mr. Krugman made his assessment. This is despite Republicans vigorously seeking to endanger his legislative agenda and legacy in their unrelenting efforts, especially, to repeal the **Affordable Care Act** misnomered "Obamacare." Equally, their refusal to pass the President's jobs bill while simultaneously contributing to and encouraging a climate of racial bigotry, hatred and disrespect, such actions were a green light to miscreants and not only threatened execution of his responsibilities but unquestionably enabled escalating threats to Mr. Obama's and his family's life and limb, that further encouraged militias and home grown terrorists to brazenly spout their divisively threatening rhetoric. Lacerate this with Donald Trump's "Birther movement" indicates how Mr. Obama walked a bed of fire coals.

When men of questionable integrity, intellectual and moral fortitude would fold under such trying circumstances, not only did Mr. Obama keep his cool providing effective leadership but he remained level-headed, assessing every situation, fighting on several fronts, and thus began to prove very effective as a Chief Executive, Commander-In-Chief and First Diplomat. And as if, justifying Mr. Krugman's assessment, very much like John Paul Jones, the President signaled his aggressive opponents, "I have not yet begun to fight." All the while, the rabid underbelly of Republican animus designed to embarrass the President caused the world to wonder at their ingratitude and "anti-Americanism" practiced at home

Nonetheless, in operationalizing his effective work ethic, Mr. Obama stood to boast, "Still I Rise." Concomitantly, he boldly asserted, "We think one way in a tunnel vision. We must change how we think!" Conceptually he shifted the nation's moral and philosophical compass of seeing and doing things. "Blind Republicans" never thought of or saw this. Objection to that old way of seeing "only white men in leadership and decision making positions" was a major reason opponents threw the kitchen sink at Mr. Obama. Nevertheless, man of great intellect, profound faith in doing-right by honest humanity, perhaps his divine inspiration stemming from a belief in an awesome especially Christian, god enabled him to forge ahead against actions from the caustic likes of Representative Darrell Issa and Jason Chaffetz as well as Senator Grassley.

FREDERICK MONDERSON

Yet, through a successful mud-slinging campaign and reveling in their misguided glee, the 2010 mid-term election happened! All of a sudden Republicans hunkered down and now in control of the House of Representatives, "Repeal of Obamacare" was revisited for the fiftieth time while these legislators arrogantly refused to move the President's legislative agenda, jobs bill, etc. Fact is, they have nothing credible to replace the health care measure with. Meanwhile, across the nation, Republican controlled state houses gerrymandered and put in place efforts to disfranchise Blacks, seniors and the poor, for on the one hand they demanded "State Id" and on the other they closed state DMV Id processing centers, among other measures. Ex-convicts who had served their sentences and paid their debt to society were subject to continued chicanery from Republican playbooks. In response, amidst all this, President Obama deployed his primary weapon consisting of a disarming smile, effective electronic campaigning and appeals to young voters, who, for the most part realized the nation's path they must ultimately travel was strewn with difficulties. However, hope was in the air, for, very evident his economic and financial policies began working and he evolved to acceptance of same sex-marriage though he was pilloried for not supporting the "Defense of Marriage Act." In addition, he was more considerate of

OBAMA THE JOURNEY COMPLETED - NEVER PROMISED A ROSE GARDEN

women, children, the working poor, even the middle class; all to contest and win the 2012 election.

FREDERICK MONDERSON

Now, with no more campaigns to run and not wanting to be considered a "lame duck" but more importantly having effectively put in place meaningful legislative, economic, financial, and administrative strategies to move the nation forward, the rewards came in an early harvest. Without a doubt, policy and tactical changes he instituted will change future American practice for the better. As was evident, first and most significant, when Mr. Obama succeeded to the Presidency, Wall Street's **DOW** languished at a stifling 6500. Today it surpassed 18,000. The housing slump was halted and new housing starts were showing recovery. With the auto industry profusely losing market share he encouraged their engineers to retool and, reengineer, and they rebounded with more efficient and stylish cars that proved tremendously attractive to American consumers and undoubtedly to foreign buyers as well. Through attractive incentives and offers of other strategic challenges, educators and educational institutions reinvented the teaching and learning experiment to make American

OBAMA THE JOURNEY COMPLETED - NEVER PROMISED A ROSE GARDEN

education more competitive in a fast-changing world, these efforts were tremendously helpful. Further, while encouraging greater domestic energy exploration to lessen reliance on foreign supplies, cautiously guarding the environment, Mr. Obama insisted technical scientist make more effective and efficient "mousetraps," such as longer lasting and more efficient batteries as well as attempting to promote improvement of various clean energy sources. All the while, he was changing the world's opinions and attitudes towards America seriously tarnished in President Bush's and Republican's "Go it Alone" push into Iraq after the attack on the World Trade Center and subsequent invasion of Afghanistan.

Many would agree America would probably have felt uncomfortable having Donald Trump, Ted Cruz, Rick Santorum, Newt Gingrich, Rick Perry, certainly not Sarah Palin or Michele Bachmann, representing them at Nelson Mandela's funeral. In his effort, "Star Obama" did wonderfully well. After all, Edmund Burke reminded us, "Little Minds and Empire go ill together."

FREDERICK MONDERSON

However, while Republicans were fiddling in the morass of "Obamacare Repeal" and other useless sour grapes destructive engagements, President Obama was busy crafting "Race to the Top" and initiating "My Brother's Keeper." Having taken lumps in regards the "Beer Summit" fiasco, we see a repeat of such treatment in his "Trayvon Martin" pronouncement that nevertheless and subsequently witnessed the mindset and behavioral tendency that created Erick Garner, Michael Brown, Tamir Rice, Coleman, and other similar incidents that gave birth to the "I Can't Breathe;" "Black Lives Matter;" and "Hands Up, Don't Shoot" Movements spawning demonstration in cities across the nation and worldwide. Dumfounded and shameless, Republicans remained conspicuously silent, lest the marchers detect their true inhumanity and hypocrisy.

OBAMA THE JOURNEY COMPLETED - NEVER PROMISED A ROSE GARDEN

CARNEGIE ENDOWMENT
FOR INTERNATIONAL PEACE
700 JACKSON PLACE
HAS BEEN DESIGNATED
A
NATIONAL HISTORIC LANDMARK
THIS SITE POSSESSES NATIONAL SIGNIFICANCE
IN COMMEMORATING THE HISTORY OF THE
UNITED STATES OF AMERICA
NATIONAL PARK SERVICE
1974
FROM 1910 TO 1948 IT SERVED AS THE FIRST
HEADQUARTERS OF THE CARNEGIE
ENDOWMENT FOR INTERNATIONAL PEACE.
IT WAS ENDOWED BY ANDREW CARNEGIE
TO "HASTEN THE ABOLITION OF
INTERNATIONAL WAR."

THE TOWNHOUSE WAS BUILT IN 1860 FOR
DR. PETER PARKER FOUNDER OF MEDICAL
MISSIONS IN CHINA WHO OCCUPIED THE
BUILDING 1861-1888. HE WAS THE U.S.
MINISTER TO CHINA 1855-57.

THE BUREAU OF PAN AMERICAN REPUBLICS,
WHICH WAS THE FORERUNNER OF THE
PAN AMERICAN UNION, WAS HOUSED HERE 1888-1908.

GENERAL SERVICES ADMINISTRATION
1976

Strange enough and miles beyond, Mr. Krugman's "spot on assessment," the biggest slap in the face to Republicans was when that active mind of Mr. Obama recognized our nation's Cuba Policy was not working. Thus, he promised to abandon the 50-year ineffective embargo, remove Cuba from a list of states considered sponsoring terrorism, establish full diplomatic relations and open an embassy in

FREDERICK MONDERSON

Havana with reciprocating privileges for Cuba in Washington, D.C. This move infuriated Ted Cruz and Marco Rubio especially, in view of their hurried and wishy-washy negative commentary on Mr. Obama's actions in regards Cuba, we see the "grown-up boys" in them. Or, as Ben E. King has sang, "Young boy," in them.

Several Presidents have had setbacks with Immigration Reform. However, in a bold Executive Action, Mr. Obama granted relief from deportation for immigrant kids brought here by their illegal parents while they were young. Some were given an opportunity to get a college education or joint the military as they awaited Congressional action to address the immigration problem. To this date, Congress has refused to effectively craft a comprehensive Immigration Policy, nor

OBAMA THE JOURNEY COMPLETED - NEVER PROMISED A ROSE GARDEN

address the immigrant kids' dilemma even though many are now serving in the military.

With his "Mojo Working" and in an attempt to get every possible success added to his legacy, first he had some setbacks and finally the Asian Trade Bill passed Congress which complemented reports of an improved economy. Meanwhile, a racist nut sporting the Confederate flag entered the "Mother Emanuel Church" in Charleston, South Carolina, and after sitting through one-hour of Bible Study, killed 9 people and wounded several others. In the Eulogy of the Church's Pastor, among those killed, President Obama delivered a moving speech on race where there was "Not a Dry Eye" in church and perhaps among many watching on TV. The President's compassionate speech, carried live on CNN, coupled with the emotional outpouring of Christian forgiveness expressed by those tragically wounded and the families of those killed in the Sanctuary made many people, young and old, black and white, realize the racist pathology of this nation is not what they want for the future. It is certainly not the fires Donald Trum0p is stoking. And we are reminded, as the President said, "A flag did not kill those people!" It is a racist ideology alive and well generally supported by high echelon Republicans and their allies in government and public and private life across the country as adamantly demonstrated against the President and now against the humble citizenry. It is said, when the enemy is self-destructing say or do nothing, just watch. This then is what America's enemies, especially the "domestic ones" perhaps prayed for but also began doing.

FREDERICK MONDERSON

OBAMA THE JOURNEY COMPLETED - NEVER PROMISED A ROSE GARDEN

Ten years ago in 2005, at his Second Inauguration Address, President George Bush decried functioning racism in the American social and political culture to this date. Now, after the Charleston shooting there was no better opportune time to address the scourge. Thus, President Obama was able, because of the power of his intellect and nobility of his spirit, to make Americans wonder about the racial cancer eating away at the conscience and body politic of this nation because this stands to endanger its future. When Republicans speak of the future of their kids, yet they rally to Donald Trump banner described as not just a George Wallace type but worse, we ask who is dividing America and endangering their children's future?

FREDERICK MONDERSON

Who could forget the disappointment expressed by Michele Bachmann, who confessed to being in the "Chamber" when Chief Justice John Roberts, in the majority, ruled against the Republican litigants seeking to eviscerate the Affordable Care Act? In that nauseating umpteenth experience, and then again the Supreme Court ruled in favor of Mr. Obama's Health Care legislation and so the President exclaimed, "The Affordable Care Act is here to stay."

Other than a lukewarm recognition of the capture and killing of Osama bin Laden, there has never been an Obama Bill, Executive Order, legislative initiative and policy decisions, foreign and domestic, or public statement that "Republicans, in Tea Party clothing," could like. Thus, and naturally, there has been a negative Republican reaction to every initiative or effort of President Obama. As such, whether it's his Iraq, Afghanistan or **ISIL** strategy, or, in the Iran-Nuclear negotiations Republicans have again taken President Obama to task, accusing him of not simply selling but giving away the farm to the Mullahs. They have, however, been unmindful, in addition to the United States several other nations are partners and signatories to the same agreement with Iran.

Nonetheless, the most pertinent question one should ask, given all the obstacles placed in his path, that he had to overcome, did President Obama do the right thing for the American people? Has he cemented a legacy worthy of Mr. Krugman's assessment that "Barack Obama is the greatest American President ever?!" It is not easy to establish that yardstick but given the animus and obstacles strewn in his path, "If we think of him as white" his credits do fit the bill!

May I also point out, his home-run ideas, viz., Cuba Policy, the Iran Nuclear Deal, the Asian Trade bill; all came after Mr. Krugman's pointed and correct assessment.

586

OBAMA THE JOURNEY COMPLETED - NEVER PROMISED A ROSE GARDEN

"The fact that my 15 minutes of fame has extended a little longer than 15 minutes is somewhat surprising to me and completely baffling to my wife." **Barack Obama**

54.   BORN A ... Democrat or Republican
By
Dr. Fred Monderson

For the longest political diehards have exclaimed, "I was born a Democrat/Republican" and one could not sway their party affiliation and intransigence. Now in the 2016 political climate two candidates seeking their party's nomination for the Presidency are making waves forcing observers to determine whether they are "born again" or opportunistic show-man/show-woman hoping to hoodwink the voting public? As a lifelong democrat who has only voted for one party, I am concerned Donald Trump has been making controversial statements for the longest. More recently, however, his hounding Barack Obama

OBAMA THE JOURNEY COMPLETED - NEVER PROMISED A ROSE GARDEN

over his birth certificate and college transcript has caused some to question Mr. Trump's sincerity and sanity, even declare his shenanigans not presidential but simply to promote his business enterprises. Yet, in the 2016 Republican campaign, many are supporting much of his outlandish rhetoric. As a reminder, who could forget the long, dusty and false road Trump took this nation down with his "Birther" charade nonsense, despite judicial and official recognition of the legality of Mr. Obama's birth?

"The Middle East is obviously an issue that has plagued the region for centuries." **Barack Obama**

In the heyday of the Republican 2008 and 2012 Presidential campaigns, Newt Gingrich was often classed as "the brightest guy in the room." Still, he was unsuccessful in these two presidential tries. Not so with the truly "brightest guy in the room," Barack Obama. We know Mr. Obama graduated from Columbia University and Harvard Law School. That makes him a top notch intellectual and even more significant a Black One! He was elected President of the Harvard Law Review. Some have argued with these credentials Ivy League School graduate go to Wall Street and make big bucks. Mr. Obama, with more of a sense of "give back" and greater degree of concern for humanity, compassion and faith in doing good; chose to work for a church, not as a preacher, but a social advocate. Thus, he became a Community Organizer and with a desire to be more impactful through legislation that addresses social inequities, he became State Senator and finally a Federal Senator.

Given the opportunity, a clear thinking young mind spoke with great passion at the 2004 Democratic National Convention. Within four years, the first term Senator from Illinois declared for and won the U.S. Presidency, becoming the first African-American to do so. However, finding his "Birther" strategy not working, Mr. Trump demanded to see President Obama's college transcript! Imagine, after all that this Black man has been able to achieve, this entertainment showman besmirched a man of great integrity, a family man who was married only once to beautiful Michelle, and important, became President of the United States. However, in the eyes of many, Donald Trump was actually besmirching Donald Trump!

Marquis de Lafayette in Lafayette Park being handed the sword by his female revolutionary counterpart.

OBAMA THE JOURNEY COMPLETED - NEVER PROMISED A ROSE GARDEN

Equally too and across the aisle, Bernie Sanders, an Independent, is running for President on the Democratic line in a challenge to Hillary Clinton. The interesting thing is; like Donald Trump he is making strides in the polls; still, she is well-ahead of him. However, having only voted Democratic, I'm forced to examine and question whether Mr. Sanders is an opportunist, moving between parties when it is most convenient. Donald Trump, on the other hand, was first a Democrat who switched party and is now a Republican. Thus, we have two crossovers or can we call them flip and flops; you choose who is who.

As a businessman of some stature, Mr. Trump probably made donations to both Republican and Democratic candidates, sort of "hedging his bets" in furtherance of his business interests. Nevertheless, and this aside, rather than keep a "low profile" in a constructive campaign the circus master-showman so characteristic of Mr. Trump's behavior, caused the New York *Daily News* to label him "Bozo the Clown!" While he has "fired" many, sued a few, strange he has not challenged the *News* for calling him a clown and worse. Has he truly accepted this designation?

Now, in 2015 as the 2016 Republican Presidential Campaign unfolds, Mr. Trump is again making public waves. He purportedly read a news article and in response; according to some, he insulted Mexicans by saying many of them are rapists as he tried to draw attention to a porous border and its effect on immigration and the nation's policy in this respect. Again, he insisted "I will build a wall and Mexico will pay for it." Subsequently Ted Cruz, in copycat style insisted, "I will build a wall and get Donald Trump to pay for it." The general consensus is this is not how political aspirants approach this issue. As a result, Univision, a Spanish TV station, which airs the Miss Universe Contest, hosted and in many respects is owned by Mr. Trump, opted out for his hostility towards Hispanics whose vote Republicans would like to cultivate. He responded and threatened to sue Univision for cancelling his show. Then he reported they were very apologetic the next day. The price tag of his suit is $500m. While this may be so, NBC announced they too will cancel the show, but he did not respond to them in similar fashion. Mr. Trump is the first Presidential candidate who has threatened to sue practically everyone, from "Pillar to Post!"

Having announced his Presidential aspirations, Mr. Trump began rising to second place in polls among New Hampshire voters, the first to hold a primary. That is, after his second place showing in the Iowa Caucus behind Ted Cruz. There, he stands behind Jeb Bush, and among some 14 declared Republican candidates, reduced from 17. In response, the Republican Party soon realized a credible candidate is not only embarrassing them but also alienating the significant Hispanic constituency. As such, his Republican competitors began expressing differing views on his statement and especially his "not walking it back." Now, using a random killing in San Francisco he doubled down to reinforce and justify his statement that Mexicans are drug dealers, "rapists" and so on.

OBAMA THE JOURNEY COMPLETED - NEVER PROMISED A ROSE GARDEN

Jeb Bush, the former Republican Governor of Florida and heir to the Bush Dynasty of Presidents, explained, "Trump is wrong on this. His statement inflames and excites." Rick Perry, Governor of Texas, equally believed, "Trump does not represent the Republican Party." On the other hand, Senator Ted Cruz of Texas was emphatic, "I like Trump. He is bold and brash and that is good." However, Mr. Cruz would level caustic and inflammatory accusations against Mr. Trump. Meanwhile, Chris Christie, Republican Governor of New Jersey stated plainly, "Trump's comments are not appropriate." Yet, he too would endorse Donald Trump. Mike Huckabee, on the other hand, wants to sit on the fence by not criticizing Trump. Even former New York Republican Governor George Pataki emphatically felt, "It is not appropriate to demonize people from Mexico."

Many will agree Donald Trump does not have to make loud statements to gain name recognition. His failed "Birther" charade and other antics have certainly benefitted him and his business, in this respect. Bernie Sanders, on the other hand, may have caucused with Democrats in the Senate but he is not a true democrat. Thus, though he proposes to have a good idea to raise new revenue, in his criticism of Wall Street. Hillary Clinton has to keep an eye on him but not feel threatened. After all, her many years as a true Democrat in service to this nation coupled with being a woman are powerful assets and whose time has probably come. Even more, she is comp0etent and the most experienced of the two main candidates.

OBAMA THE JOURNEY COMPLETED - NEVER PROMISED A ROSE GARDEN

Nevertheless, while Republicans may favor the true Republican Bush, there's also no reason why democrats may not favor a favorite daughter. Senator Sanders calls her "the establishment candidate" because all the democratic senators favor her over him. They must know something!

"There's not a liberal America and a conservative America - there's the United States of America." **Barack Obama**

FREDERICK MONDERSON

55.   THE POWER OF WOMAN!
By
Dr. Fred Monderson

Today the decision to remove the Confederate Flag from the South Carolina State Capitol grounds by Governor Nikki Haley signaled "a great day in South Carolina." But seriously, it is difficult to find another day of such significance in the South where the universal soul of humanity could class this as a joyous occasion. Nevertheless, the flag will now be taken down along with its pole, given due honors, and deposited in a South Carolina military history museum where the Civil War conflict's end 150-years ago will be most adequately remembered. However, we must never forget Malcolm X did remind

OBAMA THE JOURNEY COMPLETED - NEVER PROMISED A ROSE GARDEN

us, "History is a good teacher," not simply because it focuses on a single event but most important it can reflect the span of time for purposes of constructive study.

"We all remember Abraham Lincoln as the leader who saved our Union. Founder of the Republican Party." **Barack Obama**

Speaking of history, we need be reminded also, while today Governor Nikki Haley is a hero or heroine, that new found fame is recent making her "born again" because from her lips, a year ago, this action would not have been possible and certainly not from her efforts. Nonetheless, in signing the new bill the governor paid tribute to the "martyred 9," and reserved a "Pen from the signing" for each of the victims of Charleston's Mother Emanuel Baptist Church whose catastrophic end proved the catalyst to begin the consideration and debate that, at times proved contentious with many lawmakers voicing the historical significance and "heritage" of the flag as southern resistance to "tyranny." Underscoring this behavior, some lawmakers received oral and written death threats because the light in their humanity, especially in commiseration with the massacre victims, condemned the repugnance of the symbolism of South Carolina flying the Confederate flag. For example, an article in *The New York Times* entitled "State House Oratory Reflects South Carolina's Division Over Rebel Flag," Thursday, July 9, 2015, p. 1, 15, the author quotes Weldon Hammond, 76, a Black South Carolinian who was "involved in anti-segregation protests in the early 1960s, and spent hours Wednesday in the front row of the House gallery with his wife, Loretta, hoping to see a change that to him was too long in coming," and explained: "'It is an insult and a hurt, especially when they say that flag is about heritage. It is definitely something that for all my life we've been trying to disinherit.'" Equally significant, Jerry Govan (D) a South Carolina State Representative saw the flag as a symbol of "hate, viciousness, racism and white supremacy."

The Black residents of that state, long the victims of slavery and resulting racial discrimination, have always felt victimized by this

597

FREDERICK MONDERSON

symbol of "white supremacy" they see flying proudly on lands belonging to all South Carolina citizens. However, one voice in opposition that stood out remarkably well, a descendant of the Confederate President Jefferson Davis rose to the occasion in that august chamber and made a profound and impassioned plea for removal of the flag, identifying it as a symbol of "hate" and "racism." That is, correctly critical of "heritage" in this instance, Representative Jenny Anderson Horne, a Republican, emotionally exhorted the body as opposition and delaying tactics took hold, by saying, "The people of Charleston deserve swift and immediate removal of that flag from these grounds. I cannot believe that we do not have the heart in this body to do something meaningful." Still, as the man said, "It was long in coming."

OBAMA THE JOURNEY COMPLETED - NEVER PROMISED A ROSE GARDEN

That emotional filled voice, "speaking truth to power" may have made the difference in swaying the vote, but it also signaled the awesome "Power of Woman" committed to bringing effective "change for good into the world." But, truly speaking that profound expression of conscience on behalf of advancing the cause of humanity is not germane to a single race. In many respects, the Black Woman has been so engaged, whether as mother, divinity, ruler or religious worshipper. That powerful significance of womanhood from ancient times first exemplified in **Lucy** or **Denk Nesh** (6 million years ago); then **Eve**, of the African Plains some 250,000 years ago, and importantly as the ancient Egyptians reminded us, the female species not only carried the divine essence but were also goddesses who enabled and empowered females of royal blood to transmit that special divine spark unto the Pharaoh as king making him a divinity on earth. This phenomenon weighed significantly when, in his critique of a "Caucasian ancient Egyptian," Cheikh Anta Diop in *The African Origins of Civilization: Myth or Reality* argued for African matriarchy over Caucasian or European patriarchy and emphasizing the significance of matrilineal over patrilineal descent in that ancient African land. Equally and important, these Black women as indispensable human specimens and both their **Pygmy** or **Twa** people and offspring, have been victimized through death, harsh treatment, social ostracism all were experiencing the horrors of having loved ones subject to the terror of beatings, hangings, tar and feathers and murder. They have been restrained by mechanical devices, even having their elderly men called "**boy**," and having to defer to others because of their race and untold times been victimized within New World Slavery. Many met untimely death over the centuries of slavery, even after freedom and guarantees of the Civil War Amendments. Nonetheless, while Governor Haley and Representative Horne must be remembered for their bold and courageous stance in face of racial bigotry masquerading as historic and cultural pride, the future needs to know how we got to this epoch-making moment and the role the Black Woman of yesteryear played in that continuously unfolding historical drama often named the American, Black, experience.

From the foundation of America the Black Woman has been an essential lynchpin in the growth and development of this nation. After all, she had equal representation aboard slave ships bound for plantation servitude in the New World and America. It stands to reason she fought kidnappers on the African coast; endured the stench and humiliation in the Cape Coast castles holding areas; been sexually and otherwise assaulted in those dungeons and aboard slave ships even in front of her man; been psychologically abused, disrespected and even more so, in seeing her man physically and emotionally abused and psychologically disfigured as they both endured the Middle Passage's and Triangular Trade's unbelievable horrors. As Malcolm X, that veritable fount of modern and insightful wisdom, put it: "We did not land on Plymouth Rock, Plymouth Rock landed on us!"

OBAMA THE JOURNEY COMPLETED - NEVER PROMISED A ROSE GARDEN

Thus, in the entirety of that long train of abuse, the Black Woman was subject to all the physical and emotional agonies the Black Man was a victim of. Most important, it's on record slave-catchers and slave-dealers mostly took the youngest and most beautiful African Woman of child-bearing age they could find to further their financial and commercial interests. On board slave ships during the Atlantic journey African women were unduly even when chained. Upon arrival, let's not talk about the agonies of family separation; significantly the beautiful Black Woman was victimized through being examined naked in public by licentious traders and perspective buyers; then leering overseers played their part on the plantation; and finally by the masters and their sons whose sexual desires were unrestrained making her "a victim of sex on demand" and the emotional cruelty such a condition created. She did full-time duty in the cotton and cane fields.

FREDERICK MONDERSON

Who could countenance the humiliation of Black men having their intended wife "sampled" the night before their wedding? Just as significant, in the TV Series, "Fight against Slavery" narrated by Ruby Dee in the 1970s during the Bi-Centennial era, an interesting scene is vividly remembered. A young Englishwoman arrived on a plantation in the West Indies. As she was being escorted by a planter, the braggart tried to impress the young woman about his sexual prowess. Essentially stated, he "wanted to de-flower a young slave virgin for every year he lived" and had been true to his word. Modestly, she asked, "Well, how old are you?" In that broad, boastful smile the braggart responded, "I am now 65 years old!" You do the math!

This type of wanton and unrestrained and laviscious behavior as they made them "Stand in Fear" is a miniscule example of the "cage of sexual tyranny" the African, Black Woman, endured throughout the period of both Slave Trade and Slavery. Without question, though this particular instance occurred on the West India Plantations, it was by no means restricted to that region. Following British Abolition of the Slave Trade in 1807, America outlawed the trade in 1808. This important development came after a 20-year period of political

OBAMA THE JOURNEY COMPLETED - NEVER PROMISED A ROSE GARDEN

contention as lawmakers throughout the Union debated the economic feasibility to outlaw American involvement in the Slave Trade. In that 1787-1788 "age of constitutional development" after independence, the slave holding South, and South Carolina as a principal slave owning and slave trading state, were adamant about political representation for membership in the new Union. Hence the consensus arrived at was the "Three-fifths Clause" or "Three-fifths Compromise" where "5 Black Men were counted for 3 White Men." Comparatively speaking, when today, White Women argue they are worth 70 cents to the White Man's dollar, we first of all must wonder how much the Black Women as Harriet, Diana and Sandy were worth. Even more important, there is no way to gauge what the Black Woman was worth in 1808, not as a contributor to society but as property, or more properly, chattel.

Nevertheless, in outlawing the Atlantic Slave Trade, an "Internal Slave Trade" developed in the "Deep South," very much the "lynching states," where "Slave Farms" subjected the Black Woman to the most inhuman factory-like sexual breeding practices. Many were given a choice, "Make so many children and the master will free you!" One woman is on record of producing 36 children for her master and still she died a slave. President Thomas Jefferson did not free his concubine sally Hemmings and her children upon his death. Naturally each child represented more wealth for the master on the plantation or in that lucrative "Slave Market" brought there in "Slave Coffles" to be sold at "Slave auctions" especially in such areas as Charleston, South Carolina, one of the biggest slave markets in all the land!

Given every form of mistreatment the Black Man was subject to, the Black woman was a part of; whether in the "House" or in the "Field," the Black Woman was not only engaged in productive laboring but remained an object of admiration and potential seizure by Black men, White men, overseers, owners, or just passing merchants looking to be amused by a defenseless female. However, while the moral suasion of the "Slave Community" was a check on the Black Male's sexual appetite, no such checks applied to White lust.

603

FREDERICK MONDERSON

Marquis de Lafayette (above) and General Kosciusko (below) in Lafayette Park in front of the White House.

Nonetheless and despite the obstacles and psychologically trauma endured, the Black woman stood by her man, raised a family, sought an education, struggled to contribute to society whether as cook, domestic nurse, poet, abolitionist, teacher, scientist, doctor, medical nurse, lawyer, judge, revolutionary, Underground Railroad Conductor, and even preacher. In that journey, the faith, fortitude and humanity of the Black woman, especially the praying ones, proved to

OBAMA THE JOURNEY COMPLETED - NEVER PROMISED A ROSE GARDEN

be a source of strength in an exceptionally moving experience that lasted for centuries. However, what makes the Charleston Massacre so insidiously different, six of the nine were women, slain "On their knees praying to their god!" Throughout history, even the most barbaric conquerors often said to the vanquished, "My god or death!" Never, "Let me kill you while you're praying!" Now, enduring the racist depravity of which the Charleston shooter was guilty of and the racial hatred the South Carolina Representative denounced in the House Chamber for its viciousness and racism; the most profound act was that of the survivors' families magnanimously forgiving the assailant because they were god-fearing, in the divine element when executed and full of love for humanity. In some respects, Murlie Evers, Coretta Scott King and Betty Shabazz experienced that "sudden death" shock Clementa Pinckney's wife experienced as did so many Black mothers whose sons and husbands were murdered by racists and senseless violence, but lived on and resolved to work for good. While Fannie Lou Hamer did not experience the Black martyrdom resonating across the South especially in the Civil Rights era; however, representing the "Grassroots" in struggle, her good enlightenment was, like Harriet Tubman, to liberate the enslaved human body, spirit and mind. Still, these exemplary souls, meeting challenge after challenge and tragedy after tragedy, must have been "carried by God" confidently believing the Divine plans the destiny of us all. This magnanimity is what the racists will never understand.

FREDERICK MONDERSON

OBAMA THE JOURNEY COMPLETED - NEVER PROMISED A ROSE GARDEN

That outpouring of the good side of humanity's behavior so characteristic of the "Power of Woman" is what moved the world to wonder at the "mountain-top human spirit and behavior of the Black Woman" often for long held in scorn and ridicule. This extraordinary conscience of the human spirit inspired by the awesomeness of a benevolent, loving and inspiring god is what President Obama, a man of many words, having experienced that divine spark when he expressed "Faith in face of Doubt," and was able to recognize and expressed the divine workings so brilliantly in his Eulogy for Reverend Clementa Pinckney. There he recognized and praised that magnanimous gesture of forgiveness on part of the nine but especially those six Black women's families so injured, having lived within the racial turbulence of the Carolina Teacup. Their forgiving nature in wake of such a calamity not only surprised but gladdened the world of the good while clearing their conscience of the burden of hate as they looked to their god for guidance, comfort and inspiration in trying to soothe their unbelievable and collective grief.

FREDERICK MONDERSON

It is interesting, amidst that profound period of grief, those left to carry on, did not at short notice get an epiphany to forgive, it was inbred in their psyche and was an essential part of the armament that brought them and others of similar experience through the long night of "American slave and political captivity." Given that dark besmirched moment, the power of forgiveness not only shocked, yet impressed, the world community, but this action provided that soothing peace achieved along the stairway heavenward towards the divine, all practicing religions persons go to church, mosque and temple, week after week, seeking, yet few find.

"We proved that we are still a people capable of doing big things and tackling our biggest challenges." **Barack Obama**

OBAMA THE JOURNEY COMPLETED - NEVER PROMISED A ROSE GARDEN

56.   THE SCOURGE OF
RACIAL HATRED
By
Dr. Fred Monderson

As a student of the esteemed Professor Dr. Leonard James at New York City Technical College of the City University of New York, Brooklyn, among hundreds, perhaps thousands, we were taught a **Methodology of History** very different from the usual. Not foremost the question of when something happened but what happened, how it happened, why it happened and last but not least, when it happened. There were also other variables such as the ability to make **Critical Comparative Historical Analyses** and the role such factors as **Internal and External** developments play in creating outcomes that are favorable or unfavorable.

FREDERICK MONDERSON

"What do you think a stimulus is? It's spending - that's the whole point! Seriously." **Barack Obama**

One such ingredient as part of the Methodology, Internal and External, can be applied to a discussion of the question of racism in America, today an issue many believe needs attention but never gets. Many will agree; decisions of great significance need a point, place or time of departure in order to arrive at a satisfactory conclusion or answer to the question under study. In that case, the External and Internal components of the Methodology can be applied to the phenomenon of recent events in Charleston, South Carolina. Interesting, the tragedy of Charleston raised the issue of "heritage" and its dynamics relatively manifested in history, hate and racism. Many will agree upon purported harmony among citizens, while in fact, deep-seated racism simmers beneath a sheer veneer full of ugly puss, and if pricked can easily explode. That is to say, heritage should truly be considered on both sides of the racial equation.

Sad to say, the Charleston Church martyrs proved a catalyst and drove a number of subsequent developments to the surface, chief of which were the viciousness of the church massacre with intent to incite a race war; the realization, even a "holy place" is not immune from such violence; a profound and true belief in the goodness of God and the forgiving nature of the "victims;" the bold and courageous vision to recognize the existence of prevalent racism and hatred masquerading as heritage and the actions to speak out against such harmful negativity; a realization, removal of the Confederate Flag was not only easy but soothing; and most important, this entire phenomena may only be the "tip of the Iceberg." As such, it must be urgently addressed to help America shed the shackles of this devastating "psychological ball and chain" that stifles its moral compass especially in all its prevalence across the South.

OBAMA THE JOURNEY COMPLETED - NEVER PROMISED A ROSE GARDEN

Strange, but this boiling cauldron is not really new and can be easily traced in a series of developments emerging from as late as 2008, even if we, in this respect not give much attention to the previous age through which the foundation of all this rests. From the time Barack Obama declared for the Presidency, in 2008, the scab of American racism was pricked and slowly but profusely it began oozing the puss of a sin that has long stained the conscience of this nation. Winning the Presidency, all manner of opposition declared in response to a Black man leading the nation. From militias who began arming to the teeth for a race war fabricated in their own minds and belabored to impressionable youth and seasoned racists alike; to Dylann Roof following in this putrid path seven years later who massacred in and stained a holy place, was actually a race-war misfiring dud, unable to spark that mischievous intent; and from an Arizona Christian pastor who prayed for Barack Obama's death to "Rev. Daddy Cruz" who wanted to "Send Obama back to Kenya," but when Obama offered him Cuba, he declined. Then we had Mitch McConnell who failed to "make Obama a one-term president" and "Waterloo DeMint" who surrendered his seat, to "You Lie" Wilson and "Stupid" Senator Charles Grassley who could only languish while President Obama won twice in the Supreme Court. We could only conclude across that wide spectrum of anti-Obama and anti-Black sentiments many "South Carolina Flag Syndromes" of "hate" and "racism" stands camouflaged in business suits across the nation, drenched in perfumes to cover the stench of racial hatred they today yet harbor.

OBAMA THE JOURNEY COMPLETED - NEVER PROMISED A ROSE GARDEN

In the 2012 Presidential Election all the Southern or "Lynching" states voted for Mitch Romney but ostensibly they voted against the Black guy. These slave owning Confederate or rebel states could not countenance, given their history, of being on a "Black man's plantation." However, it was more than that and it can be argued, the unforgiving nature of losing the Civil War, giving birth to the Ku Klux Klan ideology and practice of lynching and terrorism of Black folk, denial of due process and the right to vote and hold office in a climate of "Jim Crow" and "separate and unequal," celebrating the White Citizens Council and resultant "White Primaries" and equally having discrimination, terror and joblessness as its hallmarks, such actions and intents reflect a fiery hatred not easily quenched even with the passage of time. Hence, the hatred and racism the South Carolina legislators identified in association with the Confederate flag is a well-camouflaged fact, abounding denials, notwithstanding.

Given that ideas and practices masked as beliefs and heritage are extremely difficult to surrender and given all of the above, and the fact a good man such as Mr. Obama could not win a Southern state, then the "Carolina Syndrome" is effectively masked and deep seated as especially represented in the 2012 vote. We could thus argue it is still with us, again, despite denials.

Recently *The New York Times* featured an article about a Southern legal eagle who documented some 3,953 lynchings and racial killings across much of this nation's landmass from the period of 1877 to 1850. The gentleman vowed to memorialize these "Heritage Sites" with a marker. Equally, and given such cultural markers will blemish a lily-white topography, resistance in the "Carolina Confederate Mold" is expected but the nation must confront the problem.

Granted some business entities, in activism, have raised the issue of divesting from states publicly promoting the "Confederate Brand," the first and most profound question that arises becomes, "Is this an economic epiphany or a moral obligation?" If the first; then it is a strategic decision to forestall the consequences of an economic boycott of such a state? If the latter, it is a realization on the part of some to divest of the racial albatross this baggage of heritage brings at a time when the consequences exert a stiff penalty in moral and material payments. Second, "With slave trade and slavery, 19th Century racial terrorism and 20th Century lynchings among other unspeakable acts," "Do residents who live in the potential marker site states have the courage, strength, conviction even wisdom to forgive, themselves, for that history of unspeakable acts?"

Therefore, still more questions can be posed, given the legacy of slavery and resistance and the prevalence of a Confederate culture across the South, which after all, was a defense of slavery. Thus, the first question is, "Must there be another horrendous act before hate loses?" Rodney King asked pointedly, "Can we all get along?" Should the old legacy of hatred, terrorism and racism remain in the closet and trotted out ever-so-often? The contradiction is, young people want a united country with equality for all given there are so many, internally and externally, who envy and plot against the goodness of this nation as represented by the forgiving nature of the victims of the Charleston Massacre who refused to be chained to tit-for-tat hatred.

OBAMA THE JOURNEY COMPLETED - NEVER PROMISED A ROSE GARDEN

The irony is; this is a praying nation so "Do we have the courage to confront the malady" allowing the force of change to emanate from within "our Christian values and institutions?" "Can we truly teach multiculturalism in our schools?" "How do our practices and teachings affect the young who long for a tranquil future?" To address the myriad problems, we must move beyond and address the inequality that has plagued our nation for the longest. That is rich over poor; white over black; man over woman; war hawks over peace doves; rural versus urban; employed and unemployed for as Lincoln admonished, "A house divided against itself cannot stand." It should not be only when catastrophe strike does the nation come together for a minute. Americans are thought to be able to do anything but "Can these physicians heal themselves?"

Then again, contrary to misguided beliefs that though Africans are a god-fearing, praying and forgiving people we are by no means cowards. Aristotle made the contradictory mistake in ancient times when in his work *Physiognomonica* he declared "Egyptians and Ethiopians are cowards because they are black!" What the great scientist did do first is affirm the ancient Egyptians and Ethiopians were Black Africans. Second, and unfortunately, he misjudged the martial prowess of the Back man evident from the many wars they fought down through the ages especially in America's wars at home and abroad.

Internecine warfare for the burgeoning wealth of the Nile Valley; Narmer's Unification to inaugurate Dynastic rule, Old Kingdom pharaohs represented as smiting the Bedouin at Serabit el Khadem; Mentuhotep II pacifying and uniting the land to establish the Middle Kingdom; Senusert establishing his boundary at Egypt's southern border in Nubia during the 12th Dynasty; Sekenenra-Tao unleashing a protracted 50-year war of liberation in the 17th Dynasty and his sons Kamose and Ahmose expelling the Hyksos, finally founding the 18th Dynasty and New Kingdom. Whether Amenhotep I, Thutmose I's efforts or Thutmose III's brilliant military strategy on the Plains of Megiddo; Rameses II dominating at Kadesh; Merenptah, "My country, right or wrong;" Rameses III against the "Peoples of the Sea;" the Ethiopians Khasta, Piankhi, Shabaka, Shabataka and Taharka in conquest and incorporation of Egypt with their capital established at Thebes and their struggles in Palestine, all happened before "Alexander the Great." Then there was Hamilcar, Hasdrubal and Hannibal Barca challenging the Roman Empire; the Haitians at the Revolutionary War Battle of Savannah; the Buffalo Soldiers on the American Plains; Samori Toure against the French in West Africa; Yaa Asantewaa against the British in Ghana; Shaka Zulu against the Boers in South Africa; and one could ask the Italians about losing the Battle of Adowa in 1896. Let us not forget Blaise Diagne recruiting 100,000 West Africans to stem German obliteration of French manhood in World War I; Black Americans Charging up San Juan Hill protecting Teddy Roosevelt's "Rough Riders" and Black Americans overseas fighting "to save the world for democracy." Haile Selassie stood against the Second Italian coming; the Tuskegee Airmen fought and flew brilliantly in World War II; the feared Black soldier in Vietnam and our boys in the Gulf, Afghanistan and Iraq are remarkable examples of modern Black military prowess. We cannot

OBAMA THE JOURNEY COMPLETED - NEVER PROMISED A ROSE GARDEN

also forget the thousands of Black Veterans buried in the Brooklyn Navy Yard including Samuel Carson who ran away from South Carolina slavery, joined the US Navy, fought and died in the Mexican War, and now has been repatriated to Ghana, West Africa. He opened the "Door of Return" to Africa so long closed against the "Door of No Return" dating back centuries.

Thus, the malicious should know we would rather pray than fight; remaining fully aware that Machiavelli admonished, "Any man who wishes to make a profession of Goodness must naturally come to grips with many who are not good. Thus, he must learn how to be good and not good and use and not use this knowledge as the situation warrants." As we continue to pray, we continue to pray the situation does not warrant such a response.

FREDERICK MONDERSON

Therefore, Americans must girdle themselves in a forgiving mold reminiscent of the "Charleston martyrs' families" and work for the betterment of the nation, not the narrow racially motivated and stained self-interest of those who wish to divide and devastate the nation. In every respect, the old labor movement's admonition "United We Stand, Divided We Fall" should be our watchword as we face the future particularly in view of the many futuristic policies and practices put in place by President Obama and the variety of challenges America face now and in the future.

"A mother deserves a day off to care for a sick child or sick parent without running into hardship - and you know what, a father does, too. It's time to do away with workplace policies that belong in a 'Mad Men' episode." **Barack Obama**

OBAMA THE JOURNEY COMPLETED - NEVER PROMISED A ROSE GARDEN

57. PRESIDENT OBAMA IN AFRICA I
By
Dr. Fred Monderson

After successfully attending a Summit establishing a new chapter in American-Russian relations, then on to Italy for a G-8 Economic Conference where he and the First Family had an audience with Pope Benedict, President Obama arrived in Ghana, West Africa, for a one-day visit charged with more significance and electricity than that of all past Presidents combined who have visited Africa. To recall, as a Senator from Illinois, Barack Obama visited Kenya, his father's homeland, which provided a tremendous welcome to this "Son of a son." In glaring appreciation, Elders dressed Obama in the traditional garb and this provided a firestorm of accusations in the 2008 Presidential Elections at home as opponents sought to paint him wrongfully as a Muslim among many things. However, this time as the first African American President, rather than return to his "roots" in Kenya, President Obama chose Ghana because of its symbolism as a thriving and vibrant democracy, evident from a recent election and peaceful transfer of power.

"Al Qaeda is still a threat. We cannot pretend somehow that because Barack Hussein Obama got elected as president, suddenly everything is going to be OK." **Barack Obama**

In a historic address to the Ghanaian Parliament, carried by CNN and equally broadcast across the African continent, Mr. Obama was pragmatic, stuck to his guns and delivered a "tough love" speech outlining America's new relationship with African nations. He emphasized the single and unmistakable fact, "we must start with the simple premise that Africa's future is up to Africans" and recognizing Europe's imperial role on the continent insisted, "a colonial map that made little sense bred conflict and the West has often approached Africa as a patron, rather than a partner, but the West is not responsible for the destruction of the Zimbabwean economy over the last decade, or wars in which children are enlisted as combatants." No, but the West was responsible for centuries of rape and pillage of the African landmass, population and minerals and other resources, just as they were responsible for efforts to pacify Africa after Partition on paper at the Berlin Conference of 1884-85. They were certainly responsible for the realities of Neo-colonialism that threatened the newly independent nations as they struggled to stay truly independent.

Five hundred years after the discovery of the Americas and the subsequent efforts to conquer this hemisphere, the European Slave Trade in Africans, and resultant plantation slavery with the psychological and physical emasculation of the victims of such barbarism, we see the legacy of slavery still functioning institutionally in many guises even though we have crossed the bridge to the next century. This forces us to remember that (in this emerging great nation of America); the English colonials under Britain fought the French, in the French and Indian Wars (1756-1763) and fought the British in the War of Independence (1776-1783). "Runaway Slave" Samuel Carson fought in the Mexican War (1844-45). Prior to this the

OBAMA THE JOURNEY COMPLETED - NEVER PROMISED A ROSE GARDEN

new nation had fought the British in the War of 1812. There is no need to mention the Civil War (1860-1865). Then we fought the Spanish in the Spanish American War (1898-1900); the Germans and their allies in World War I (1914-1918) though we practically entered the conflict in 1917; again, the Germans, Italians and Japan in World War II (1939) entering that conflict on December 7, 1941; the Korean War (1950-1953); and against the Chinese, Russians and their allies in the "anti-Communist Cold War." Yet again, particularly the Russians, who have atomic weapons, probably still aimed at us today that can devastate this nation, the citizens of these countries can all come to these shores, mostly "blend in with the population," and with some effort particularly aided by their cultural organizations, begin moving up the social ladder towards realization of the "American Dream." That is citizenship! However, the ravages and devastation of slavery and its legacy still identifies sons and daughters of Africa in America and make us victims of racism that was born out of the dehumanizing experience.

FREDERICK MONDERSON

Therefore, we need to never forget as we ended the Twentieth Century and crossed the bridge to the Twenty-First Century; it was W.E.B. DuBois who said the question of the "color bar" would dominate these past hundred years. In many ways this has not changed. Thus, all people must move away from this odious conception and practice that is very much alive and well in the world in today's 21st Century! Providing an example, Fordham in *Geography of African Affairs* (1965: 58-59) recounted how Africans worldwide are viewed in the most disdainful manner, by supplying an example that indicated, "As late as 1928 a distinguished Englishman" could write, "The Negroes of Tropical Africa specialized in their isolation and stagnation in utter savagery. They may even have been drifting away from the human standard back towards the brute when migratory impulses drew the Caucasian, the world's redeemer, to enter Tropical Africa ... mingle his blood with that of the pristine negroes and raise the mental status

OBAMA THE JOURNEY COMPLETED - NEVER PROMISED A ROSE GARDEN

of these dark skinned, wooly haired, prognathous retrograded men ...."
He failed to remark all this happened after the slave trade and efforts
to plant Christianity in Africa that served as cover to exploit and ship
its natural and mineral resources to Europe.

He continued (1965: 59) to describe the odious behavior stating:
"Echoes of this attitude were still to be heard in the British House of
Lords in 1961" when he quoted Lord Barbizon of Tara, on March 23,
1961, in *Hansard* Vol. 229, No. 57, Cols. 1277-9. This respectable
Englishman went on to explain, "As I went to it [the United Nations]
I really got the impression that there was a convention of nigger
minstrels going on ... the Commonwealth is a piebald set-up, and a
pie-bald set-up is a poor form of organization that will never last." Of
course, while the above is certainly biased at least, that is not to say,
some of our people have not progressed despite difficult odds among
purposely orchestrated restraints, in their struggles with and without
bootstraps.

FREDERICK MONDERSON

OBAMA THE JOURNEY COMPLETED - NEVER PROMISED A ROSE GARDEN

However, as we celebrated another Martin Luther King Birthday and head towards Black History Month way back in February, 1998, the voices of such commentators as Julian Bond, Kwame Mfume, Leonard Jeffries, Tony Martin, Sonny Carson and a whole host of others, all pointed to the disparities and difficulties of high unemployment, police brutality, racial discrimination, poverty, lack of proper medical care, drug infestation, crime, poor education, etc., that plague Black and other minority communities. Such an odious legacy is principally because of the African heritage of Black people that seems anathema to many in this nation and abroad in some Western European nations. Even though we now have a Black President whose term in office is winding down, many people still harbor odious sentiments towards him and other Blacks, perhaps it is particularly because of the color of their skin. But it must be remembered, Black people paid the ultimate sacrifice to build America, and we intend to earn our place at the table of this nation, under the philosophic and humanistic banner believing in the fatherhood of God and the brotherhood of man. However, in the current political climate as Donald Trump and his fanatical followers subscribe to an ever-increasing climate of racial hatred particularly cultivated in Mr. Trump's "Birther" movement escapade, African people in America must reflect upon and draw from their history especially in this nation cultivating resolve from the most positive experiences to meet the challenges of the next "seven projected lean years."

With that, we need to understand the social and psychological dynamics of the forced removal of Africans, called the Atlantic Slave Trade which began soon after the Portuguese landed in West Africa in 1441. That year, a trickle of Africans was first taken to Lisbon, Portugal. Lloyd (1972: 51) has shown how early contacts made by the Portuguese along the West African coast were beginning to clear the way for the later onslaught. "In 1434 Portuguese ships passed Cape Bojador in Mauretania; by 1475 Fernando Po had been reached, and in 1483 Portuguese sailors visited the capital of Benin, probably the most highly organized coastal kingdom at this period. The Portuguese were impressed by it and established a trading port at Ughoton (Gwatto) in 1486, but their main attention was directed to the Gold Coast with its more valuable exports; the castle of San Jorge da Mina was erected at Elmina in 1482. Gold apart, the West African coast offered little to attract European trade until the discovery of the Americas provided a demand for slaves."

However, from 1485 onward we witness a number of significant events in Europe. First there was the unification of Spain and the defeat of the Moors at the fall of Granada and then in 1492 Columbus' expedition got underway. Decades thereafter, Africans began to be shipped to the Americas to cultivate plantation culture. By the end of the century, plantations were producing sugar cane and derivative products particularly in the British West Indies, e.g., Barbados and Trinidad; Slavery came after 1814 to Cape Town, South Africa; and after the Dutch in Guiana now Guyana, enslaved Africans were harnessed to exploit this sweet product with its derivative industries,

OBAMA THE JOURNEY COMPLETED - NEVER PROMISED A ROSE GARDEN

strange enough, that began to transform industry through jobs and infrastructure development in Europe.

The beginnings of the ghastly experiment is best explained by Iliffe (1995: 127-128) who wrote: "The Atlantic slave trade began in 1441 when a young Portuguese sea-captain Antam Goncalvez kidnapped a man and woman on the Western Saharan coast to please his employer, Prince Henry-the-Navigator - successfully, for Goncalvez was knighted. Four years later the Portuguese built a fort on Arguin Island, off the Mauritanian coast, from which to purchase slaves and, more particularly, gold, which was especially scarce at this time. After failing in 1415 to capture the gold trade by occupying Ceuta on the Moroccan coast, Portuguese mariners groped down the West African coast towards the gold sources. Arguin was designed to lure gold caravans away from the journey to Morocco. Yet slaves were not merely by-products, for a lively market in African slaves had existed since the mid-fourteenth century in southern Europe, where labor was scarce after the Black Death and slavery had survived since Roman times in domestic service and pockets of intensive agriculture, especially the production of sugar, which Europeans had learned from Muslims during the Crusade. As sugar plantation spread westwards through the Mediterranean to Atlantic islands like Maderia and eventually to the Americas, they depended increasingly on slave labor. The Atlantic slave trade was largely a response to their demand."

FREDERICK MONDERSON

OBAMA THE JOURNEY COMPLETED - NEVER PROMISED A ROSE GARDEN

Significantly, by 1505 or thereabouts, exploration of the newly discovered "new world" had become ingrained. The result was systematic and widespread destruction of indigenous cultures, viz., the Incas, Mayas, Aztecs, Tainos, etc., that were flourishing in this hemisphere. Commenting on the people who followed Columbus into North, Central and South America at the end of Fifteenth Century, Basil Davidson (1996: 202) explained: "These others, who were Spanish soldiers and adventurers, ruined the [native] American peoples whom they found. Their intention was not trade, but loot; not peace, but war; not partnership, but enslavement. They fell upon these lands with greed and the fury of destruction. And the [native] American peoples, unlike the Africans, were unable to defend themselves. Being at an earlier stage of social and technical development than the Africans, they fell easy victims to Spanish violence. Along the coast of Guinea, the Portuguese and other Europeans had begun by trying their hand at violence. But they had given that up. The Africans they met were too strong for them. In the Americas it was different."

Even further, Davidson (1996: 203) continued: "There was terrible destruction of the 'Indians,' the name that was mistakenly given by these raiders to the native-born American people. A Spanish report of 1518, only twenty-six years after the first voyage of Columbus across the Atlantic, says that when the island of Cuba was discovered it was reckoned to contain more than a million 'Indians,' but today their number does not exceed 11,000. And judging from what has happened, there will be none of them left in three or four years' time, unless some remedy is applied."

That unfortunate state of affairs, forced Bishop Bartholomew De Las Casas to petition the papacy. He requested that Africans be brought into the Americas for labor purposes, to replace the rapidly disappearing indigenous population. Losing the battle to "save the Indians," he unleashed an even greater tragedy that lasted for centuries, and claimed many, many more lives. This stain on humanity's integrity was Europe's Slave Trade in Africans to America.

The Age of Exploration created new opportunities for discovery and transformation of the new lands introduced to European by Columbus and the other explorers, for which they sought official sanction. The "Papal division of the world in 1492" gave half to Portugal and the other half to Spain, Christian nations and ardent defenders of their religion and the Papacy. Two years later in 1494, the demarcation was enshrined in the Treaty of Tordesillas, moving the boundary line 300-leagues to the West. The first official pronouncement gave most of the New World to Spain. The pronouncement was changed once Portugal complained in which they were awarded a foothold in South American that became Brazil, today the largest country in South America. As such, this Papal beneficence prohibited the Spanish from involvement in the trade in enslaved persons from Africa. The Portuguese, however, did have a free hand there. Iliffe (1995: 130) continued, recounting: "The first West African slaves went mainly to Portugal, then to Maderia, and then to Sao Tome. Direct shipments from Africa to the Americas began in 1532. As European and African diseases destroyed the Amerindian peoples, African slaves replaced them, because Africans alone were available in the required numbers, and then were cheaper than white indentured laborers, and they had the unique degree of immunity to both European and African diseases which came from living in the tropical periphery of the Old World." It's also been argued, there were no organized and sufficiently powerful African nation to challenge the Europeans and defend the African people. There were a few powerful tribes so disposed, but these were "local."

By the late sixteenth century nearly 80 per cent of all exported West African slaves went to the Americas, especially to Brazil, where plantation sugar took root during the 1540s.

The Spanish *Hacienda Treaty* was agreed to in 1713. Whom-so-ever held it had permission to supply the Spanish possessions in America with enslaved persons from Africa. In fact, Moore and Dunbar (1968: 110) have written: "The British took a leading part in this trade from

OBAMA THE JOURNEY COMPLETED - NEVER PROMISED A ROSE GARDEN

the middle of the seventeenth century, with the development of the plantation colonies. New impetus was given when at the *Peace of Utrecht* in 1713 [Britain] obtained the Asiento." This Spanish contract was to supply cargo to and from the New World. For the African victims involved, this dreaded official instrument, yet, provoked many wars at sea among slaving European nations. Dreaded, in the sense that, the Spanish could not get slaves in Africa, so they had them brought to their New World plantation. For Africans, it provided death and hopelessness of Slave Trade committed to supplying an institution of Slavery. Oliver and Fage (1970: 120) have argued that Spanish territory was very lucrative; for "The early Spanish colonies there had been supplied with African slaves, mainly through the Portuguese, from about 1510. But it was not until the competitive irruption into the West Indies of the Dutch, French and English in the seventeenth century, when there was a rapidly growing European demand for sugar - a crop making heavy demands on labor - that the transatlantic slave trade began to dominate European activities in West Africa. Compared with an estimate of some [275,000 Negro slaves landed overseas by 1600, Author's italics.] the seventeenth-century figure is thought to be about 1,340,000; the figures of the eighteenth and nineteenth centuries seem to have been about 6,050,000 and 1,900,000 respectively. The new development ousted the Portuguese from the Gold Coast. For a short time, the trans-Atlantic trade was almost a Dutch monopoly, but their success provoked English and French hostility, and by the eighteenth century it was the traders of these two nations who were the principal competitors in the international trade, thought the Portuguese continued with a private slave trade of their own, from Angola and San Tome to Brazil. In terms of the trade alone, victory went to Britain. By the end of the eighteenth century her ships were carrying nearly half the slaves taken to America." Two things can be deduced from the above quote. The first is "Negro slaves landed overseas by 1600." The most important term is LANDED and this did not terminate then but continued throughout the duration. Second, a more accurate figure of the totality of the Slave Trade's cost to Africa, according to W.E.B. Dubois was 100 million souls lost!

FREDERICK MONDERSON

Entrance to the United States Botanical Gardens, Washington D.C.

OBAMA THE JOURNEY COMPLETED - NEVER PROMISED A ROSE GARDEN

And so it continued for centuries until the trade and institution was finally ended in Brazil in 1888. But that is not to say, though scholars have mentioned the Portuguese, English, French and Dutch, that these were the only nations involved. We must remember colonial America was also an active participant in Slave Trade development. This systematic and undeniable holocaust, which Merimba Ani termed the **GREAT MAAFA**, provided an inexhaustible supply of free labor required by slave trading nations then transforming the American landscape. Those other nations involved included the Brandenbergers or Germans, the Danes, and Swedes. Still, though not involved in carrying Africans to the "new world," the Spanish, because of the needs of empire, helped maintain a system of slavery in America, for three centuries after Columbus, that encouraged the perpetuation of this ghastly free and cruel labor-supply phenomenon.

From the Atlantic Slave Trade's inception, it would appear that few of the traders worried or were concerned about carrying capacity conditions aboard their ships. As a result, the terms "tight packers" and "loose packers" came to characterize how enslaved Africans were transported to the Americas.

Again, as Malcolm X's penetrating insight revealed, "We did not land on Plymouth Rock, Plymouth Rock landed on us;" this unfolding and escalated drama and resulting harsh treatment promised nothing but death, hopeless melancholy and despair. The resulting psychological damage to the African persona remains untold to this day.

Relative to mortality and in view of this situation, in 1788 and again in 1792, the House of Commons of the British Parliament conducted inquiries regarding the Slave Trade. They found that "persons transported from Africa to the West Indies are kidnapped, solely for the purpose of selling them to the traders." Alexander Falconbridge (1788: 13), a surgeon in the Slave Trade, had written there is "great reason to believe that most of the Negroes shipped from the coast of Africa are kidnapped." Sold to European slavers, the enslaved Africans faced a difficult journey. It took some fifty-two days to cross the Atlantic from Africa to America. At times the voyage was longer. However, it was seldom shorter!

In this harrowing experience, a constant problem of the Slave Trade was overcrowding. The famous slave ship **BROOKES**, out of Liverpool, sailed to the West Coast of Africa in 1783. This 320-ton frigate was built without forecastle and pierced for 20 guns yet enabled every available square foot of the vessel to be used to store its human cargo. *Minutes of the Evidence on the Slave Trade to Parliament* (1789: 43) indicated calculations were made of the men's room, boys' room, women's room, the gun-room, cabin, half-deck and a number of platforms.

A. Stuart-Brown (1932: 48-49) described some carrying logistics of this famous vessel: "The slaves were lodged on the lower deck, the men in a room 46 feet by 25 feet 4 inches and 5 feet 8 inches high, the women in a smaller room 28 feet 6 inches by 23 feet 6 inches and the boy's room was 13 feet 9 inches by 25 feet."

In one instance, this slaving ship spent 10 months on the coast and collected 609 captive Africans. Those who boarded first experienced the horrors of "holding" before the "Middle Passage" began.

Dr. Thomas Trotter, the **BROOKES'** surgeon, according to *Evidence of Robert Stokes Esq., Before the Select Committee of the House of Lords* in 1849, reported "seeing Africans all over the ship." In testimony to the *Committee of Parliament*, Stokes (1849: 5) described his observations on the ship and stated the "slaves in the passage was so crowded below, it is impossible to walk through them without treading on them." These conditions existed in the "pre-regulation period" when "tight packers" was the rule. "Tight packers" meant purchase and carry as many enslaved persons without concern about safety and mortality. Some ships carried as many as 800 persons. Imagine! In the Frontispiece of this same source, Charles Fox, an abolitionist had insisted: "True humanity consists not in a squeamish ear; it consists not in staring or shrinking at tales such as these, but in a disposition of heart to relieve misery. True humanity

634

OBAMA THE JOURNEY COMPLETED - NEVER PROMISED A ROSE GARDEN

appertains rather to the mind than to the nerves, and prompts men to use real and active endeavors to execute the measures which it suggests."

After regulation in 1789, the **BROOKES** was restricted to carry only 454 enslaved Africans. The ship was still crowded with 450 aboard. One could only wonder how it managed to transport 609. After regulation, "loose packing" or carry fewer based on ship's tonnage, helped reduce the mortality rate of captives and crew aboard this and many other British slavers. While in this essay the British example is often used, the practice applied for colonial America and other slave-trading European nations, making Britain the "best of a bad lot." Some have disagreed and believe they were the worst during the 1700s-1800s. Fact is, while the British ultimately sought regulation this was not a pre-requisite of other nations. Generally, business operated on the conscience of the monetary unit whether pound, frank, mark, or dollar and as such, the stark inhumanity of the trade victimized and physically dehumanized the African man, woman and child with long lasting social and psychological implications.

According to *An Historical Account of the Liverpool African Slave Trade* (1884: iii) there was an old saying in the City of Liverpool: "Get slaves honestly, if you can, and if you cannot get them honestly, get them!" Of course, a colleague of mine, Stanley Simpson, reviewing this comment asked: "What is meant by the term 'honestly' in this context during the 1700s?" Does it mean pay first for the merchandise? Or, pay a good price for what you got. If so, what would be the true value of a human being? That is the question. In fact, it forces one to wonder what is the true value of an African man, woman or child, then as well as today? When objective observers and commentators apply this context to the present state of relations among victimized people, it does not matter if persons are killed by their own or by others, a human life should not be regarded as being without value. That is why for the last 30 years an underlying theme of every Black Solidarity Day has been: "No (Black) one should die at the hands of another." This was Sonny Carson's idea and should apply equally today across this nation, whether in Chicago, New York, or Los Angeles!

In those Atlantic slave trade times, in the principal British trading city of Liverpool and elsewhere, it was a popular belief, notes *Historical Account....* (1884: 14) that:

OBAMA THE JOURNEY COMPLETED - NEVER PROMISED A ROSE GARDEN

"Slavery was right; it was supported by the Bible, and strenuously advocated by the clergy of the time; as well as the politicians. They asserted it was divine right that the blacks were of an inferior race and were to be bought and sold by the white man, with his brand on them.... How many crimes have been committed in the name of the book?" Perhaps, however, it was not in the name of the Book but in the name of profits! Nevertheless, though the mentality of that time has changed, its operational handle in today's reckoning and environment has evolved from a "Jump Suit" to "Business attire" reinforced with the Esquire title.

We are told further in the same source (1884: 16) of George Franklin Cook, tragedian, who was born April 17, 1756 and died September 26, 1812. While drunk at a performance in the Liverpool Theater, he is quoted as saying to his critics: "I have not come here to be insulted by a set of wretches, of which every brick in your infernal town is cemented with an African's blood."   We are also informed in *Edinburgh Review* (1908: 26), the "chief center of the African trade Liverpool, [was] remarkable in the commercial history of the United Kingdom." Even further, the same source, *Edinburgh Review* (1908: 33) states: "Of all English communities, Liverpool derived the most wealth from the debasing trade." More, in the *Illustrated London News* (1957: 18), we are again reminded of descriptions of the city's investment in the Slave Trade as an "impressive array of commercial institutions, banking houses, insurance companies, trading associations and produce exchanges." In addition, *Illustrated London News* (1957: 18) informs further, "Liverpool merchants performed a variety of economic functions incorporating the means for financing and insuring the commodities they bought and sold, and controlling the ships which carried the commodities overseas." Still more, that the "Liverpool merchant body exerted a powerful influence over Parliament through the Liverpool Parliamentary Office." This was probably because the prosperity of the port was tied to the import of raw cotton, sugar, wheat, flour, rum, and tobacco, and to the export of cotton piece goods, woolens, salt, coal, iron products, chemicals, glass

637

and soap. However, this profit motive notwithstanding, things have an uncanny way of working themselves out, for there were individuals whose conscience and high moral standards dictated that they resist and challenge this plague perpetuated by their countrymen. One such instance can be cited of James Fox, an abolitionist quoted as saying during the English Parliament's attempt to regulate the Slave Trade, that: "There can be no regulation of robbery and murder."

We know the Atlantic Slave Trade began after Bishop De Las Casas sought papal approval to ship Africans to the Americas to save lives of Amerindians. This is underscored by Foxburn (1932: 56) who explained: "Las Casas, ... saw no harm in subjecting African Negroes to the treatment from which he sought earnestly to save the aborigines of the new world." However, some have argued that de Las Casas thought this the lesser of two evils. Perhaps he never thought it would escalate as it did. Yet, and arguably, the trade was continued under religious sanction through the belief that Africans were not Christians, not Europeans, had an "exotic culture" and easily definable by skin color. Therefore, official policy held it was okay to enslave them. Thereafter, in 1562-63, Sir John Hawkins, the first Englishman to trade in enslaved Africans, sailed to Africa in the slave ship *Solomon*. Two years later in 1564-65, he sailed in the slave ship *Jesus*, blazing a trail for his countrymen.

Harris (1972: 72-73) has made the case, "it was a combination of European attitudes about blacks and the demand for cheap labor that sired the Atlantic slave trade and New World black slavery." When the Portuguese arrived in Africa they began seizing Africans to take to Europe as 'curiosity pieces,' at which time it was confirmed, a "new land had been reached." The early African victims were honored in Portugal, taught Portuguese, and used as informants and guides for future Portuguese voyages to Africa.

OBAMA THE JOURNEY COMPLETED - NEVER PROMISED A ROSE GARDEN

However, as the number of Africans increased in Lisbon they gradually were relegated to menial tasks, and by the middle of the fifteenth century, a lively trade in African labor (slaves) evolved. Thus, even before the Americas were settled by Europeans, Europe witnessed the development of black slavery, especially in Portugal, Spain, Italy, and Sicily. It has been estimated, for example, that between 1458 and 1460, from 700 to 800 slaves were exported annually from Africa to Europe, with an estimate of 35,000 for 1450-1500.

Some authorities have calculated that from 50,000 to 100,000 Africans were taken to Europe during the whole course of the trade. Whatever the numbers, the point to emphasize here is that a half century prior to their settlement in the Americas, many Europeans (especially the inhabitants of Spain and Portugal, the two countries that spearheaded American settlement) had become accustomed to the enslavement of the Africans.

Yet, and conversely, from the middle of the 18th century, a religious conviction motivated men of good will to lead the fight to outlaw the slave trade. In Britain, many important abolitionists were involved including Granville Sharpe, Thomas Clarkson, Charles Fox, Wilberforce, Macaulay, and the Reverend John Newton, a reformed slave dealer. Reverend Newton authored the hymn "How Sweet the Name of Jesus Sounds," after a religious conversion, while aboard a slave ship he operated off the coast of West Africa.

In 1849, evidence was presented by Robert Stokes before the *Committee of the House of Lords*, as previously stated. This body, following inquiries of six decades earlier, reflected on the high mortality rate of English seamen in the trade before regulation. Their results revealed the following percentage of mortality rates: 50, 20, 20, 30, 33, 25, 30 and 50. This showed an average of 32 per cent death rate for seamen on board some English slavers. Well, if the slavers were experiencing such high rates of mortality given they had the ability to be mobile, a chance for exercise, fresh air and perhaps better food, imagine what it was among their cargo denied the above and exposed to other unimaginable horrors!

John Latimer (1893: 474-75) in *The Annals of Bristol in the 18th Century* recounted the view of "one captain from the port of the slave trade who did not deserve long ago to be hanged."

Slaving methods of procuring sailors were notorious. In the slaving business, these seamen were: "Dreadfully ill-treated .... drugged with liquor until impotent to offer resistance... sailors ... encouraged to run into debt, and then offered the alternative of a slaving voyage or a goal [jail] ... never permitted to read the articles they signed on entering a ship, and by the insertion in these documents of iniquitous clauses.... wages in the slave trade (30 s per month) though nominally high, were actually higher in other trades."

Nonetheless, in his *Essay on the Impolicy of the Slave Trade*, Thomas Clarkson (1785: 35) mentioned the "difficulty of procuring seamen for the slave trade is well known at the ports where it is carried on." Again, Clarkson (1788: 57) notes, "in the year 1786, 1,125 seamen will be found upon the dead list in consequence of this execrable trade." That same year Clarkson (1788: 60) recalled, among West India Seamen, "1470 deserted or were discharged.... Only 610 seamen out of the whole number deserted or were discharged yet found their way out of the colonies;... that 860 yet remain to be accounted for in the expenditure of the year 1786." These figures, reinforced the view that mortality rates were high aboard these frigates of death, and, once tricked, sailors seemed to want to get out of the business themselves. Still, and also important, not all sailors were shanghaied and money was being made by the investors, whose mantra was "Buy low, sell high!" Imagine!

FREDERICK MONDERSON

More importantly, however, was the high incidence of deaths among the Africans, victimized in this Atlantic Slave Trade's forced migration, being the subject of centuries of psychological and physical assaults that was transmitted through the emotional and affected DNA

OBAMA THE JOURNEY COMPLETED - NEVER PROMISED A ROSE GARDEN

gene pool for generation after generation. In 1788, Clarkson called for "Efficiency of Regulation of the Slave Trade" because of its effects on both victims in the trade, Africans and Europeans. He supplied particularly interesting data on the subject of mortality. In his evidence, sailors' testimony show regarding slaving escapades, "we purchased 350 slaves and buried 61; in a second voyage, in the same ship, we purchased 350, and buried 200; and in ... we purchased 370 and buried 100 .... We purchased 700 slaves and lost 250 ... we purchased 300, out of which we buried 17 ... 350 were purchased, and 25 were lost as before.... about 500 were purchased, and 150 buried."

Most deaths were due to overcrowding and the inhumanly intolerable conditions of the voyage. Practically, the physical, emotional and psychological cruelties of slavers were significant factors Africans had to reckon with. Victimizers also became victims of conditions they themselves created.

In the end, the African personality, emotional, physical, psychological, was denuded and broken from this horrible experience. Or, as the Afrocentrists would say, the Africans were "detached, isolated, de-centered." Arriving in the West Indies the African was again debased. There, a final merciless legislative act transformed him into chattel or property. For example, *Report of the Lords' Committee of Council...* 1789, Part III, in Jamaica, states slaves were considered as property as indicated Anno 1696 Act 38: XL.... "That no slave shall be free by becoming Christian; and for payment of debts and legacies, all slaves shall be deemed and taken as all other goods and chattels are in the hands of executors or administrators;... all children of slaves, born in the possession of tenant for life or years, shall remain or revert."

Again, in Jamaica, Anno 1719, Act 67: V ..., "no Negro, mulatto, or Indian slave shall hire themselves out to work, either ashore or on board any ship or vessel, boat, ferry, canoe ... every such slave so offending, shall be whipped at the discretion of any magistrate in the parish or precinct where such slave or slaves shall offer themselves for hire."

In Barbados, slaves were also considered as property, for according to Act No. 94 of April 29, 1668, the "Negro slaves of this island shall be real estate .... all Negro slaves, in all courts of judicature and other places within this island, shall be held, taken, and adjudged to be estate real ... and shall descend unto the heirs and widow of any person dying intestate."

Again, in Barbados, January 1672, Act No. 178 was considered, "A declarative Act upon the act making Negroes real estate" and "that Negroes shall be deemed real estate and not chattels ... Negroes may be sued for and recovered by action personal ... Negroes continue chattel for the payment of debts."

Even further, on August 8, 1688, Act No. 329 states, "where any Negro or other slave ... shall suffer death then shall such justices and freeholders, colonels and field officers who adjudged such Negro or other slave to suffer death, immediately after sentence thereof given inquire by the best means they are able of the value of such Negro or other slave, in which value they shall not exceed the sum of five and twenty pound sterling .... tempt or persuade any Negroes or other slaves to leave their masters and mistresses ... adjudged to pay the master of the said Negro or other slave five and twenty pounds."

On November 28, 1705, Act No. 516 read, "... for all Negroes and other slaves that shall be imported to this island and landed there, an importation or duty shall be paid, that the merchant or merchants ... pay into the treasurer of this island ... five shillings current money for each and every Negro or other slave imported, whether male or female, young or old ...."

Finally, a *Supplemental Act* was passed on February 7, 1715, No. 593 that read as follows: "Be it therefore enacted ... that no Negroes or other slaves whatsoever, which shall for the future be once imported into this island shall be exempted from paying the duty of five

OBAMA THE JOURNEY COMPLETED - NEVER PROMISED A ROSE GARDEN

shillings a head, but such only which shall be within 48 hours exported in the same ship or vessel."

Therefore, the psycho social ramifications of the centuries' old experience seemed to, and still, so significantly plague the survivors of the greatest of all tragedies, that Prof. (Donna Richards) Merimba Ani of Hunter College called **The Maafa** or "Great Enslavement" as "the basis of the Western World's Economic Development on the Backs of African people!"

Now, when President Obama referred to "mismanagement of the Zimbabwean economy" let us not forget the history that underlay the independence of that nation and the resistance to its independence that were instrumental in forcing President Mugabe into that direction of Zimbabwean financial hopelessness.

FREDERICK MONDERSON

58. PRESIDENT OBAMA IN AFRICA II
BY
Dr. Fred Monderson

It is interesting how President Barack Obama visited Africa at different times to make two of his most significant addresses outside of the Continental United States. His Address in Egypt at Cairo University was designed to start a conversation, open a dialogue of mutual respect, mutual dignity "with the Muslim world." His speech at the Ghanaian Parliament in Accra was crafted to send a message to Africa and the world of America's intent to more closely engage the continent of his ancestral heritage. More particularly, to the African nations and their rulers, he insisted the will, interests and future of their people, their greatest resources, must be paramount if Africa is to emerge and play the significant role in world events that it is truly capable of. Recognizing China and other nations are making trade and investment headway in Africa, last year again Mr. Obama visited his father's homeland, Kenya; this time as President; and then on to Ethiopia, acknowledging the ancient nation state and its strategic East

OBAMA THE JOURNEY COMPLETED - NEVER PROMISED A ROSE GARDEN

African location as an ally in the Middle Eastern conundrum and also then reinforced its ties with Egypt.

"America and Islam are not exclusive and need not be in competition. Instead, they overlap, and share common principles of justice and progress, tolerance and the dignity of all human beings." **Barack Obama**

Yes, Egypt is in North Africa, it has always been there. Importantly, of all African nations, Egypt benefits most from the potency of the geographical detritus impregnated in the life giving Nile River flowing from inner Africa. The potentialities of cultural effluence from time immemorial has enriched, energized and revitalized that nation and its people in all aspects of their existence.

Ghana, in West Africa, is pivotal in the historical development of modern Africa for a number of reasons, and thus, was an ideal location for President Obama to make his first trip and historic address. The name Ghana piggybacks on the first of three medieval empires of Ghana, Mali and Songhai, which dominated Middle African history. This name was very significant in influencing modern Ghana's march to independence in 1957 and the symbolism it represented in Kwame Nkrumah's vision of an independent and united continental economic, cultural and social African government, shedding the shackles of colonialism.

In the dreaded Slave Trade, Ghana became a principal trans-shipment point for enslaved Africans being forcefully embarked to New World plantation slavery. Elmira Castle, in Ghana, is one of many lining the West African coast where European marauders, in the age of "naked Imperialism" used their enormous canon power to fight off Atlantic competitors and when turned around, terrorized the surrounding countryside in their insidious effort to marshal, accumulate, house, and ship Africans through the "Door of no return," to a life, unknown to the African, yet unspeakable horrors awaiting far away.

FREDERICK MONDERSON

It is interesting that President Clinton visited Ghana in the last years of his tenure and was shown in a photograph looking through the "Door of No Return." The same may be said for President Obama. The important question, however, is whether the guides informed these two Presidents "an American activist named Sonny 'Abubadika' Carson" reinterred his ancestor Samuel Carson, a US Navy Veteran of the War with Mexico (1845) here in Ghana, on August 1, 1998, creating the "Door of Return" as this historic even inaugurated the First Emancipation Festival. Now he is buried alongside a Jamaican slave named Crystal at Assin Manso, beside the river where the captives took their last bath before being shipped through the same and infamous "Door of No Return." In a significant and historic move, Mr. Carson had formed "The Bones Committee" comprising Dr. Fred Monderson (Chairman), Cherise Maloney (Member) and two dozen others who met two or three times per week for two years to strategize over a series of events that ultimately repatriated Mr. Samuel Carson and opened the "Door of Return" so African-Americans can visit the site as pilgrimage and connect with their ancestral roots through Ghana, as springboard to similar searches elsewhere in Africa. The guide's follow up question to Mr. Obama then should have been, "Would you like to see the site of African American Pilgrimage at Assin Manso?" Naturally, this never materialized particularly for security reasons.

OBAMA THE JOURNEY COMPLETED - NEVER PROMISED A ROSE GARDEN

America was essentially founded as a Christian nation and in that searing crucible, many un-Christian acts, such as the horrors associated with the Slave Trade and Institution of Slavery were perpetuated against African people for centuries. In an age when people struggled with government to declare the Universal Rights of

FREDERICK MONDERSON

Man and issue the American Declaration of Independence, boasting of life, liberty and the pursuit of happiness as god given rights, African people were denied much these universal principles were intended to achieve. Yet, in the religious contradiction in its founding principles, America struggled to evolve a level of tolerance so that through good works the American "melting pot" would come to accept in its mix, Baptists, African Zionists, Moravians, Anglicans, Jehovah's Witnesses, Catholics, Jews, Muslims and atheists, all being allowed to practice their beliefs or non-beliefs, peacefully, in a society respecting religious tolerance.

Upon his arrival in Cairo, Egypt, Mr. Obama, true to his campaign promises, wanted to dispel the myth that America was at war with Islam, Muslims. This is because of the recent history of events that led to the war on terrorism and subsequent developments that saw Americans fighting in Iraq and Afghanistan, and equally, seeming to ignore the fundamentals of the Arab-Israeli conflict which is fueled by the Palestinian-Israeli issue. Currently Americans are fighting in Syria, advising in Somali against Al-Shabab; in Nigeria against Boko Haram; and in search of the elusive "Army of God" in Central Africa. So, therefore, in his initial greeting to the audience at the Cairo University and to Muslims worldwide tuned in to the young American President who promised fundamental change in American relations with Islam and the world; he therefore began with the greeting "Salaam-Wali-Kom" to which the response was "Wali-Kom-Salaam," not only from the live audience, but one could imagine hearing it through the TV sets and radios emanating from the worldwide listening audience. He had struck a positively sensitive nerve in this initial and fundamental show of respect. Thus, he could say, "I bring you peace from Muslims in my country" and, having Muslim forebears himself, he had broken the ice! Today Donald Trump's calling card, to which he has recounted many, is "No Muslim Adherents Welcome" to these shores. Foolishly, the sweet music and fine wine served by this Pied Piper has drunken many who may in return be banned from the territories with one quarter of the world's population whether for trade, tourism or even to visit family "back home"

OBAMA THE JOURNEY COMPLETED - NEVER PROMISED A ROSE GARDEN

Seeking to defuse the time of tension, and being "proud to carry the good will of the American people," he reflected on the "historical conflict" rather than cooperation colonialism had generated between the Arab/Muslim world and the West, and particularly America. Thus, Mr. Obama wanted to create a new beginning in America's relations. Significantly, as a student of history he emphasized that Islam has always been a part of American history and that American-Muslims have enriched American history. Then he went on to boast of "civilization's debt to Islam."

Here Mr. Obama spoke of a "partnership based on what Islam is, not what it isn't." He also sought to make it clear "America is not the crude stereotype of a self-interested empire" and that it's been shaped by events and people who contributed much to shape its creed, "Out of Many, One."

Here again he emphasized, "Let there be no doubt, Islam is a part of America," and that "words alone cannot meet the needs of our people." Equally, with that astute historical perception, he stated clearly as a remindful warning to so many, at home and abroad, "Any world order that elevates one nation or group over another will inevitably fail." Perhaps the "Trumps" will learn a thing or two from this history lesson. Here he particularly referenced and spoke against the issue of "violent extremism in all its forms" and that "America will relentlessly confront all extremism which poses a grave threat to our security." It can be reasoned he meant domestic and foreign terrorism. Reiterating the now known fact, President Obama pointed out, "Al Qaeda killed over 3000 people on 9/11" and America in response "partnered with a coalition of 46 nations" to which "Afghanistan demonstrates Americas goals and our need for better relationship." However, unlike the rapid withdrawal from Iraq and the devastating consequences, Mr. Obama has promised to retain a significant American military presence in Afghanistan.

Next Mr. Obama dealt with the "Palestinian-Israeli issue" and emphasized his early dispatch of an envoy to the region, the

651

recognition of a "two state' solution "and the need to end the construction of settlements," all while reiterating and reassuring "America's commitment to Israel" and the need to guarantee its "safe and inviolate borders." This issue, however, has been an intractable one; given so many forces impact the conflict between two peoples, Israeli and Palestinian.

OBAMA THE JOURNEY COMPLETED - NEVER PROMISED A ROSE GARDEN

By the time he ended, commentators agreed this was the "most powerful and most persuasive speech of any President to the Muslim world." They further pointed to Mr. Obama's "emphasis on soft power rather than hard power," and that this represented an "important shift in America's relations with the Muslim world." Commentators again believed, in this respect he had gained "enormous political capital around the world."

President Obama treated "any attempt to deny the Holocaust ever occurred as criminal behavior." He cited his great uncle, Charles Payne of the 89th Infantry Division, who was an eyewitness in liberating one of the death camps, Again, like Mr. Obama, "the New York activist Sonny Carson's uncle was a member of one of the first Black units to liberate one of the death camps." At a later date, after a visit to Russia, the President arrived in Ghana, West Africa, and addressed the Ghanaian Parliament in a message carried continent-wide. The essential message of his address is that Africa's future is in Africa's hands. "Africa does not need a strong man; it needs strong institutions;" and that Africa's "ruling elites have not thought of re-investing in the well-being of the masses" of its people, its greatest asset.

Critics wondered why the President chose Ghana instead of Kenya, land of his paternal heritage. Clearly, as Secretary of State Hillary Clinton would later indicate, corruption is rife in Kenya and thus this would have been an unlikely venue for the President to have given such an important speech. However, the stated reason why Ghana was chosen is that it has a functioning democracy with easy transfer of power as evident recently following the last election. Notwithstanding this reality, the role of the military cannot be overlooked, some scholars have argued with "foreign interference" in overthrow of Prime Minister Kwame Nkrumah, Ghana's first elected leader and the names Adjai, Achaempong, and finally Jerry Rawlins, who, incidentally was in the audience, is recognized as part of Ghana's troubling past image of "Neo-colonialist" activism. Now, Mr. Obama,

653

in his ultimate visit to Kenya before moving on to Ethiopia decried the "Myth of the Strong man" who is the only one who could keep the nation safe. To this he reminded; "Africa needs strong institutions not strong men!" To many long-in-service-politicians he implored, "Retire, you're already rich," referring to their "raiding the cookie jar" of the national treasury, rather than training young leadership to move the nation forward.

President Obama, nevertheless, seemed to be building upon the little publicized initiatives in Africa begun by Presidents Clinton and Bush. In America's catch up in Africa, President Obama hoped to challenge major nations such as China who have been making investment inroads on the continent rich in natural resources. China, for its part, has a significant head start since the days of building the Tan-Zam railroad free of charge and having been an active supporter in the struggles against Apartheid in South Africa, Rhodesia and South-West Africa (Namibia). Mr. Obama, on the other hand, because of his African-American heritage, this appears helpful for his new initiatives of bringing Africa into the hub of global commerce. In addition, terrorist infiltration of the African continent and East African ports as naval operational points for military action in the Middle East and Pacific, are issues that drives America's new interest in the long neglected Africa continent. However, he could not emphasize this new involvement without speaking out against corruption, nepotism, mismanagement and inefficiency in Africa as well as the disruptive nature of civil wars and lack of fundamental respect for the rights of Africa's citizens. It is a conundrum that Africa is a resource powerhouse, yet its people are economically impoverished and not well served. This is the theme he emphasized in both Kenya and Ethiopia.

The practical and diplomatic side of his visit over, the President began an emotional tour of the slave dungeons with his wife, children and mother-in-law, as Anderson Cooper of CNN reported on July 18, 2009. The President thought this was a "powerful moment for me, Michelle and the girls." As he toured the slave castle dungeons and looked through the "Door of No Return" he equated it with his trip with Eli Wiesel to Buchenwald, a Holocaust site and felt "as if the

OBAMA THE JOURNEY COMPLETED - NEVER PROMISED A ROSE GARDEN

walls could talk" painting and creating a profound, shocking experience.

FREDERICK MONDERSON

Acknowledging his wife Michelle as a descendant of slaves, Mr. Obama declared "people were willing to degrade others if they appeared different." Realizing a church was in the castle's yard, President Obama reflected, "Slave merchants may have loved their children and gone to that church above the dungeon."

Taken below to the "Door of No Return," he muttered, "Through this door the journey of the African-American began" and expressed "profound sorrow must have been felt as people were hauled off to the great unknown." Dr. DeGruy in commentary revealed, these African victims "experienced profound emotional feelings from sorrow to rage."

The CNN Program's Host, Anderson Cooper of **AC 360**, mentioned "12-40 million people were forced to make the Middle Passage." This is somewhat inconsistent with conservative traditional doctrinal beliefs that 12-15 million were actually transshipped. In fact, W.E.B. DuBois in his 1896 Harvard PHD Thesis *The African Slave Trade to America* - 1638-1888 gives a figure of "100 million souls lost to Africa."

These figures included dead and dying in the kidnappings and march to the shore, on shore in the holding pens and those thrown overboard in the trans-shipment. Let us not forget, March 9, 1732 when 132 slaves were thrown alive overboard in three sets and the ship's owners had the audacity to file for insurance coverage under a clause as "perils of the sea."

The dead and dying on shore was a significant factor in the equation. First of all, we were reminded by President Obama that the slave trade was "very, very big business controlled by royal families of Europe." Let us not also forget, New England merchants built ships and their seamen provided slaves for southern plantation owners. Also, New England merchants established a price of "140 gallons of rum for 1 male African; 120 gallons of rum for 1 female African; and 90 gallons of Rum for 1 pre-puberty female." We could also add the employment opportunities in boat building and ancillary trades as painters, barrel makers, makers of metal hoops that bind barrels, etc. Not to omit the metal fetters that binds the African captives en-route to be slaves on "New World" plantations.

It is clear, profit motives required strict rules and punishments that were harsh and deadly; all designed to make examples of slaves; or as Terence Stampp in *The Peculiar Institution* indicated in a chapter "To Make Them Stand in Fear!" All manner of owner actions were designed to instill fear and trepidation among the slave lot. Among the many tools of intimidation used by perpetrators of the system in addition to a wide range of restraining devices, in vicinity of the "Door of No Return" were female slave dungeons and punishment cells in the slave castles. In the female slave dungeons, 150 women were packed in a single room. This was really eerie. The punishment cell was a death sentence for those about to die. With no ventilation, lighting, or relief facilities, the room contained a "foot thick of feces." The dungeon's odor coupled with the accumulated odor of feces, two centuries later is debilitating, imagine the psychological and emotional impact in the "fresh state" as the enslaved endured, some praying for death or "escape" through the "Door of No Return." From these horrible beginnings stem the historical disadvantages and misadventures African people in the Americas were victims of, for a long period of time. Yet, in the centuries long voyage of human degradation the African was forgiving same as the victims of historic Mother Emanuel Church in South Carolina who forgave the killer Dylan Roof executioner of 9 parishioners during a Bible Study session.

Out of the dungeon's hole, in the courtyard, President Obama reflected on his wife Michelle's slave roots. He spoke of her great, great, grand-father and great, great grand-mother Jim and Louisa Robinson who started in sprawling South Carolina, about 1850. These people were victims of, according to President Obama, "a terrible labor regime that was oppressive and created deep wound in our nation."

FREDERICK MONDERSON

For much of his presidency, descendants of these Bible thumping Christians have been less than kind to President Obama. Essentially, from Ghana on the West African Coast, to Slave Street in Georgetown, South Carolina, the slave experience and its legacy of racial discrimination has imprinted with long lasting emasculating implications on the psychological and emotional well-being of slavery's institutional victims, African Americans. South Carolina, home of Jim DeMint and Joe Wilson, was not only the largest slave port and market during the hey-day of the horrible trade and institution, right there in the middle of Jim Crow's shenanigans; and as late as recently Jesse Jackson criticized the state for having 36 state prisons and 1 state college. Nevertheless, as the 2016 presidential primary takes off, South Carolina is projected to play a major role as a "Southern Firewall." However, many will admit, Donald Trump seems to be going down that same vicious path and carrying many of similar dispositions staining America's hard won moral fiber.

OBAMA THE JOURNEY COMPLETED - NEVER PROMISED A ROSE GARDEN

Baron Von Steuben in Lafayette Park.

FREDERICK MONDERSON

Yet, when all is said and done, President Barack Obama's trip to North and West Africa was a double pointed stroke of genius. In Egypt he was able to deliver a strong message designed to improve America's relationship with the Muslim world and in Ghana, critique Africa's leadership, while outlining preconditions for American assistance and partnership were key. At the same time, he shined the light on a dark chapter on Western and American slave history experience. While this article does not seek to examine the relations of foreign companies in ownership, extraction and price setting for Africa's natural resources and raw materials, suffice to say Europe, America and the West still undermines that area's economic structure. In his trip to Kenya and Ethiopia the President not simply talked about security issues but he brought entrepreneurs, businessman and engineers to talk about helping develop Africa's hydroelectric and other forms of potential all with promises to encourage more economic investment across the continent. One thing is unmistaken; President Obama created tremendous goodwill for American investors in Africa. However, and let us not forget Obama has railed against the role of corruption among leadership that facilitates the resulting process of "under-development." Therefore, as a good faith broker, President Obama has focused on helping to level the playing field in Africa's relationships to create a reliable partnership that will be able to extend dependable cooperation as world events become more complex and America seeks more "true friends."

"And that means that no matter how we reform health care, we will keep this promise to the American people: If you like your doctor, you will be able to keep your doctor, period. If you like your health care plan, you'll be able to keep your health care plan, period. No one will take it away, no matter what." **Barack Obama**

OBAMA THE JOURNEY COMPLETED - NEVER PROMISED A ROSE GARDEN

59. DIVIDING THE COUNTRY
By
Dr. Fred Monderson

In response to a question regarding Marco Rubio's "Stumble" in the New Hampshire Republican Debate, Representative Jason Chavetz, (R. Utah) appearing on Wolf Blitzer's Situation Room repeated the tired pliant that "Obama is dividing the country." Like so many other Republican liars, if he is asked "Is Donald Trump dividing the country, he would probably say no!"

FREDERICK MONDERSON

Certainly within recent memory Republicans have unleashed the most aggressively creative attacks on Democratic candidates and office holders from their "win-no-matter-what" playbooks. Remember Willie Horton and Dukakis "soft on crime," or "Swift Boat" of John Kerry. Fast forward to 2012 the "soft on terror" label could not be leveled against Barack Obama since he had recently taken out Osama bin Laden, but everyone is familiar with the numerous accusations unleashed in 2008 before and after he won and assumed the Presidency. Thus, the notion of "Dividing the Country" may very well have been in the works as Obama traveled the path to the Presidency. That is, if we consider the reality expressed in the October 6, 2013 version of *The New York Times* article in which a treasonous gathering was discussed as planning to undermine the legally constituted U.S. Government under the leadership of Barack Obama we may very well see the fabricated lie of division. In that article, Ed Meese, Ronald Reagan's former Attorney General and an enumerated list of some 20 NGO leaders were identified as being part of the planning process to "Stop Obama." One of the prongs of the strategy was to train young Republican operatives to "educate the public" across the country about the negative aspects of the Affordable Care Act maliciously labeled "Obamacare." Many observers later slammed the disingenuous disinformation of this strategy as Republicans voted in Congress more than fifty times and the Supreme Court had to uphold two challenges before making "Obamacare here to stay."

"But if you - if what - the reports are true, what they're saying is, is that as a consequence of us getting 30 million additional people health care, at the margins that's going to increase our costs, we knew that."
Barack Obama

662

OBAMA THE JOURNEY COMPLETED - NEVER PROMISED A ROSE GARDEN

However, the question remains "who knew and when did they know of the campaign against Mr. Obama?" That is, such a massive broadside against the Presidency of the United States more than likely involved those in the highest echelons of the Republican Party, given the unanimous voting record of "No" against every measure of the President, legislative or otherwise. This means, all the senior "Anti-Obama Players" in and outside government must have known if not "signed on the dotted line." History and time will tell. Perhaps one day Assange and WikiLeaks will reveal this on the "Net."

Nevertheless, we must consider and give credit, for in the history and development of this country Blacks have been in-step with their shoulder to the wheel moving the nation forward. In that favored Progress we have seen 43 white men serve as President through which African-Americans stood mightily among the military ranks, defeating the enemy, being wounded, many died, in every war this nation has fought under the President as Commander-In-Chief. When today Barack Obama succeeded to that position an insidious underbelly of elements, mainly Republicans began painting him indiscriminately with a broad racist brush. Every conceivable name and accusation was in place in January 2009 when Mr. Obama took the oath of office.

OBAMA THE JOURNEY COMPLETED - NEVER PROMISED A ROSE GARDEN

FREDERICK MONDERSON

The consistent claim that Mr. Obama is dividing the nation has not been specific. Enquiring minds want to know, Is it rich and poor, democratic and Republican, Black and White, or along religious lines? It is interesting, one of the claims leveled against Mr. Obama, to this day, is that he is a Muslim. However, in the early days of his national prominence he was accused of sitting in the pew for 20 years listening to Rev. Jeremiah Wright, who happens to be a Christian minister. This is just one example of the contradictions in the Republican Anti-Obama arsenal. Even today, while Chris Christie could point out Marco Rubio's rehearsed 25-second anti-Obama tirade, he too, disingenuously stops short of criticizing the message as he killed the messenger. The fact is, every president and his administration has sought to put their stamp on the time duration of their term. More important, considering what he inherited as a Republican legacy, Mr. Obama has done more for this country than most even though he does not get the true and full credit for his efforts. Nevertheless, the keen observation of Paul Krugman that Mr. Obama is probably the "greatest American President" may very well be the truest and most sincere statement ever made.

Who could properly gauge the long reach of the "treasonous gathering" since from day one, Militia groups began escalating arms purchases in preparation for an imminent race war. Imagine if you will, "Blacks won the Presidency" and they will initiate race war! This is another of those contradictions all Republican aspirants to the office trumpet; being unmindful, the President's job is to protect the nation from foreign and domestic enemies. This certainly includes the enemies of rising unemployment; foreclosures; bank failures; a car industry ran into the ditch; crumbling infrastructure; teachers and first responders on the chopping block; the nation choking amidst the fog of air pollution; gas prices escalating at the pumps; this nation features prominent in Climate Change; and so on. All people across all spectrums of the nation were affected by these maladies and equally benefitted from the application of the prescription that addressed these problems.

John Kasich recounted his complain to Arnold Schwarzenegger that he was being "beaten-up by critics" and the Gubernator simply

666

OBAMA THE JOURNEY COMPLETED - NEVER PROMISED A ROSE GARDEN

responded, "Love the beatings." Republicans were upset Mr. Obama did not love the floggings they unleashed on him. He was more focused on his responsibilities than on the behaviors of racists perennially benefitting from white privilege.

FREDERICK MONDERSON

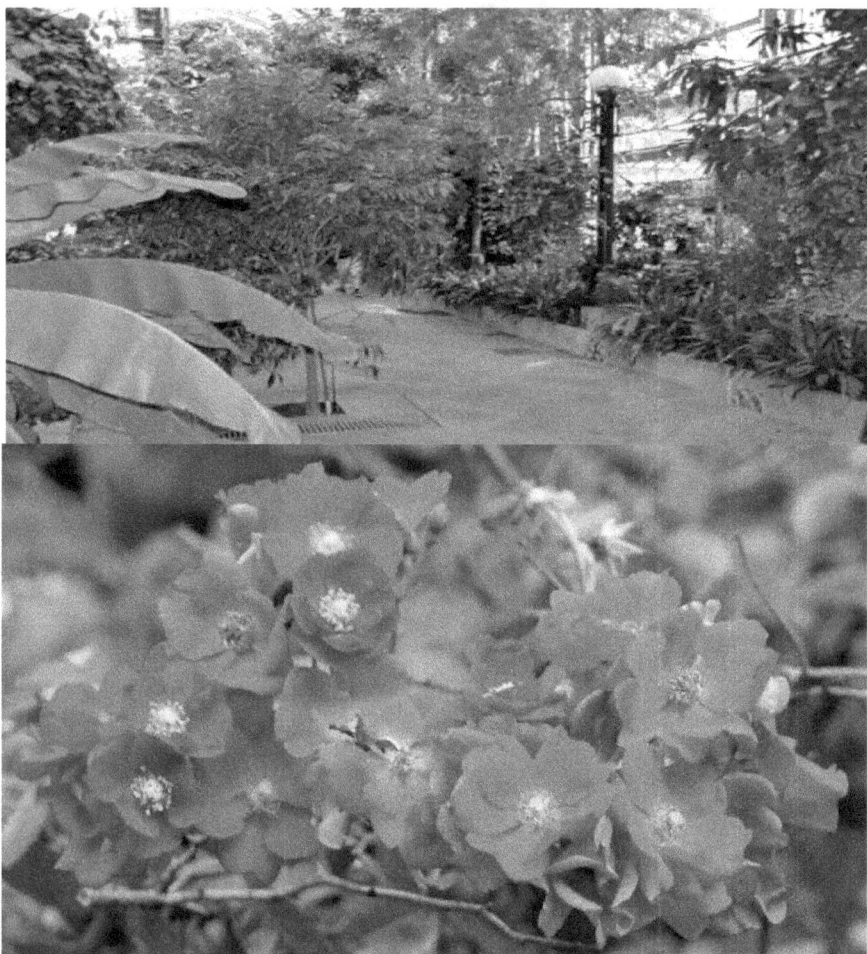

60.   BARACK OBAMA
RHETORIC AND REALITY
BY
Dr. Fred Monderson

It is a given, Barack Obama never "Loved the beatings" but he publicly admitted, "I know politics is a contact sport" and that "American politics is tough." Surprisingly, however, when we

OBARA THE JOURNEY COMPLETED - NEVER PROMISED A ROSE GARDEN

consider the rhetoric spewing in the current Presidential campaign, a number of important deductions become very apparent. First and foremost, the Republican front Runner Donald Trump has been tremendously outrageous in his brinkmanship posturing to quote Jeb Bush, former Florida governor, "Mr. Trump has been insulting his way to the Presidency." However, and equally alarmingly outrageous, his growing and equally outrageous band of followers rather than condemn his vile behavior have consistently been flocking to his clarion call and *Ipso Facto* goading him on, remindful of both is and their sourpussfullness. Second and most important, the office to which he now aspires has been so tarnished by Mr. Trump's as well as fellow Republicans' behaviors in recent years, it is certainly questionable as to their level of concern for the future of this nation. After all, these people are campaigning on plans to repeal not simply "Obamacare," but practically every meaningful measure Mr. Obama successfully implemented that did not have Republican support. That is, everything.

"But let me be perfectly clear, because I know you'll hear the same old claims that rolling back these tax breaks means a massive tax increase on the American people: if your family earns less than $250,000 a year, you will not see your taxes increased a single dime. I repeat: not one single dime." **Barack Obama**

Most observers would consider the above political posturing but the statement of then Senate Minority Leader Mitch McConnell "I intend to make Barack Obama a one term President," showed he had morally crossed the line. Morgan Freeman, the academy award winning actor, on CNN's Piers Morgan, blatantly stated it was racist! More important, however, coming as it did from within the halls of government, many agree Mr. McConnell had opened the floodgates of the rapidly escalating racism and disrespect Republicans and their supporters have heaped upon President Obama for the duration of practically two presidential terms.

FREDERICK MONDERSON

From the time of the original rollout of the Affordable Care Act the rhetoric was deafening and destructively vocal. These people operate from within the prism of "Win" or "Lose." Therefore, the grand strategy thus appeared, "Block every chance of a win for Obama!" This meant, block every meaningful measure he proposed but most important his signature health care accomplishment, the Affordable Care Act. The "Long knives" in Jim DeMint's "Waterloo;" Billy Crystal's "Go for the Jugular;" "Lipstick on a pig" Palin then accusing Mr. Obama of "Palling around with terrorists" and now responsible for her son's PTSD excuse for female abuse and refuses to accept this round of the war malady manifestation as a Republican administration creation. Then there was "Suing the President" and "Fighting Obama Tooth and Nail'" John Boehner, who is now probably playing "Bingo" in a retirement home. Therefore, every Republican candidate, those with or without a "Daddy" wants to abolish this law unmindful of the nearly 20 million who have signed up for the measure's health care protections.

Today we stand on the verge of an encore performance as the "War Hawks" prepare to re-take the helm of the Presidency, they so abused under Obama rule. Who could forget disgraceful "You Lie" Wilson or even "Stupid" Senator Charles Grassley who could not recognize a constitutional scholar if he came up to him as E.F. Hutton would say, He "Slapped him on the bottom and say, I'm here?" Then there's that "Light Colonel" who stooped so low as to examine, perhaps smell and question the President's "testicular fortitude" area.

Let us not forget "Daddy Cruz," banking on spending at least one night in the Lincoln bedroom demanding we "Send Obama back to Kenya," but too bad such a dream has faded thanks to Ted's failure.

"Joe the Plumber" and the "Queen Birther" had faded into oblivion like an imploding star while the "Birther King" Donald Trump and the new crop of rhetoricians have coined new shibboleths to continue the "dirty work." Meanwhile President Obama like the Teflon penny long in circulation still retains his luster as is evident in his more than fifty percent poll ratings, higher than the best Republican president Ronal Reagan.

It is interesting how the rules for white men differ to those that apply to Black men. For instance, while in the Dred Scott decision of 1957 Chief Justice Roger Taney ruled enslaved Africans were not men and could not bring suit in federal court. In time Mr. Obama, was elected to the presidency; yet, "the Donald" questioned Mr. Obama's birthright though the same court upheld it. However, today Ted Cruz is known to have been born in Canada to an American female yet eligibility to run for the Presidency is not questioned. Obama's mother was an American female, similar to Cruz's mother but while Cruz was, admittedly, born in Canada, Mr. Obama was admittedly born in Hawaii. Talk about Double standard. Even sillier, in Arnold's heyday as Governor of California, Republicans wanted to change the

FREDERICK MONDERSON

Constitution so he could run for President until we learn he was "With the maid." Too bad Mr. Obama was from Chicago, because if he had done an "Arnold" Southern racists would probably lynched Mr. Obama.

Who could forget when Mr. Obama referred to a female as "Sweetie" and the press and others had a field day vilifying the man? Now, Donald Trump talks "Pussy" and even, in his confessed sexual abuse by "Grab them by the Pussy;" "Bomb the shit out of ISIS" and much more, yet the Christian Right especially love him. "Pussy then" now "Pussy Grab" because he is a star and could engage in "Locker Room Talk."

OBAMA THE JOURNEY COMPLETED - NEVER PROMISED A ROSE GARDEN

Thus, we have to ask what is acceptable as presidential behavior. Has Obama so changed America they now settle for less?

We know Obama dispatched the "losers" McCain, Palin, Romney, Ryan, De Mint, Allen, Joe Wilson, and so many others thanks to strategic thinking, planning and execution, hallmarks of his focused and effective work ethic. Yet, he respects these "Unworthy opponents."

FREDERICK MONDERSON

"For more than four decades, the Libyan people have been ruled by a tyrant - Moammar Gaddafi. He has denied his people freedom, exploited their wealth, murdered opponents at home and abroad, and terrorized innocent people around the world - including Americans who were killed by Libyan agents." **Barack Obama**

OBAMA THE JOURNEY COMPLETED - NEVER PROMISED A ROSE GARDEN

61.   PO BEN CARSON!
By
Dr. Fred Monderson

The Republican presidential contender Ben Carson has been fading fast into oblivion which forces campaign watchers to question whether it's the man, his policies or lack thereof, or the other contenders, even the political party and its causes he so adamantly supports. At one point recently, he so challenged the Republican front-runner Donald Trump, almost eclipsing his lead in Iowa, Mr. Trump remarked flamboyantly, "The people of Iowa must be stupid to vote for Ben Carson." Seriously, there are a number of implications in this statement. Now, a serious problem of Donald Trump, he utters controversial statements that encourage equally controversial analyses to determine beyond the braggadocio and brinksmanship he projects, how insidious is his meaning and to whom is he sublimely speaking. However, the problem with Ben Carson on the other hand, is medically he is a genius; street wise he is an idiot. There was another Carson, Sonny; medically he was an idiot; street wise, he was a genius. In none of these categories Ben matched up to Sonny; but given his other baggage, one can easily recognize this comet as it fades into the oblivion in the great Republican political cosmic void. Today, he is on board Donald Trump's bandwagon and confronted with defending untold outrageous statements made by his candidate.

"I know that there are millions of Americans who are content with their health care coverage - they like their plan and, most importantly, they value their relationship with their doctor." **Barack Obama**

In his new political career, the retired Neurosurgeon Ben Carson came out like a new penny, but once in circulation, he became tarnished and quickly lost his "spring chicken" luster. Mr. Carson first took the stage speaking out on Republican issues and soon earned spokesman status. Caught up in the vortex of conservative, Republican and "Tea Party" stone-throwing, Mr. Carson publicly attacked President Obama, criticizing his Affordable Care Act law facetiously nicknamed "Obamacare" because that was the "flavor of the months." For such a bold move, calling "Obamacare worse than slavery," Mr. Carson had "arrived" and he was truly elevated by having his photograph engraved front page on the Heritage Foundation website. The next step was to declare for the Presidency as a Republican candidate. Unfortunately, there were 16 other candidates and there stood Dr. Carson among the contenders, proudly, as a "fly in buttermilk," and uttering the "right wing party line."

The cold, callous and calculated attack on President Obama's health care law was like burning an important bridge to his cultural heritage as a Black man. However, thinking Blacks were in synchrony with Jesse Jackson, when back in 2009 at Mr. Obama's Inauguration the Reverend declared, Mr. Obama is, "the best the Civil Rights movement has to offer." Now, imagine individuals as Donald Trump burning the airwaves with a distorted pliant, "Obama has not done

OBAMA THE JOURNEY COMPLETED - NEVER PROMISED A ROSE GARDEN

anything for the Blacks!" Conversely, one of his adamantly supporting converts blurted "Obama has done too much for the Blacks!" What a contradiction and one wonders whether the vast majority of this Pied Piper Trump's followers can untangle this complex yet distorted thought. However, astute Blacks never subscribed to the panacea that electing a Black man to the Presidency would solve many of the problems facing Black people in this country, since it never did with the 43 preceding white men who held the office. These same observers, analysts and commentators, from the inception have overlooked the spiritual and psychological warfare waged by the people Mr. Carson is now curled up in bed with, especially given his associates' way-laid the first African-American President of this great Republic.

Again, objective observers have taken note of and applauded Mr. Obama's many efforts to help Americans, not exclusively Blacks, in various forms as a jobs bill; rescuing the auto industry to maintain

American market share and equally save American jobs; bailing out banks tottering on the brink of bankruptcy; lending a hand to Wall Street financial wizards; passing of Dodd/Frank financial reform; seeking to infuse life into the housing industry drowning in foreclosure and stalled building construction starts; encouraging Silicon Valley to continue its creative breakthroughs; breaking ground in Research and Development in new and clean energy sources of a renewable nature; being more concerned about climate change; even encouraging mothers to return to college and seeking to emphasize community colleges as a vehicle to generate a more technically trained workforce to meet future needs and expectation of the nation. In all these initiatives, "The Blacks" benefitted relative to their proportion in the population as did the greater percentage even though the "Party of No" not only mined the field but blocked every initiative of the President. Today's revelation that the unemployment rate has dropped below the national rate to 5% and the Black rate has dropped below 10% is certainly good news. However, and fact is, Blacks were so far behind in job acquisition no matter how they fared in the new setting they still remained behind. Nevertheless, only Mr. Obama's vastly superior intellect, his tremendously focused and effective work ethic, aided, perhaps through divine intervention on behalf of the American people perhaps it was because Barack Obama stood at the helm of the ship of state that enabled America to still progress. Nonetheless, in this Christian land, the god all these pray to is the same god Republicans pray to; but as he listens he does not seem to hear their pliant, nor prayer of hypocrites who make every effort to derail the many benefits Blacks were to be given and received from an Obama Presidency empowered to benefit the nation.

Notwithstanding, as all this unfolded, not once did Mr. Carson raise a voice or finger in protest or in ethical condemnation as men of questionable aims and intent lambasted the President; some agree much of this was because of his race and tenacity to run, win, stand up and be counted, make policy, deliver the State of the Union Address, command the troops and represent the nation abroad alongside his beautiful wife and partner, the "Mighty Michelle."

OBAMA THE JOURNEY COMPLETED - NEVER PROMISED A ROSE GARDEN

As the various factions of the Republican Party labeled Mr. Obama, "Nigger," "Nigger in the White House," and given they associate Blackness with such degradation, not only did Mr. Carson not stand up for Mr. Obama, he probably felt, "He's a Nigger, but I'm not!" However, the Ethiopian Emperor Haile Selassie's 1936 dictum, "Today for me, Tomorrow for you!" may very well materialize in regard this contemporary Washington, D.C. political and racial scenario. In the current contest, while Mr. Carson may have started out as a cultural "nice boy" many soon realized he did not have the street smarts and the propensity for treachery proving so indispensable in the unfolding presidential and political party dynamics that now dominate Capitol Hill.

There is something about the Republican Party that seems to propagate an anti-Black posturing sentiment that despite the camouflaged masquerade, "sinister pies" seem baking in the inner chambers. A credible argument can be made if *The New York Times* article of October 6, 2013 is used as a penetrating example. Mr. Carson's love affair with the Heritage Foundation did not spring to life yesterday, and considered "a soldier," one wonders was he in the loop of the "Stop Obama" "treasonous gathering" in which some 20 NGOs including his Heritage Foundation organization as well as former Ronald Reagan Attorney General Ed Meese were mentioned as participants in planning and dispensing "disinformation" about Obamacare and other Obama policies. Was he purview to this "treasonous gathering" that sought to thwart the policies of the legally constituted U.S. government under an Obama Administration? As a legal and law enforcement issue, was Dr. Carson involved, was he knowledgeable of the action and intent, and if so, why did he not speak out or advocate for arrest and incarceration of those involved rather than encourage an "under the rug" solution.

Mr. Carson needs be reminded about the history of his political party. That is, from its Post-Civil War "Radical Republican" nomenclature; it's championing of the 13th, 14th, 15th Amendments as protections for the Freedmen; despite Black wholesale "Party of Lincoln" voting record until 1932 Blacks languished under "Jim Crow" laws that aided the KKK as an American institution. All helped facilitate Public lynchings, lack of jobs and even economic peonage under sharecropping tenant farming that stigmatized and limited Black political, social and economic advancement. This state of affairs forced Blacks to bolt the Republican Party in 1932 remaining loyal Democrats to this day; in response practically every conceivable "trick" and action has been used to disfranchise Blacks affecting their participation at the Ballot box coupled with a system of escalating incarceration wherein Blacks and other minorities comprise the greatest number of the US prison population. Yet, Dr. Carson said or did nothing. We must always remember as Edmund Burke believed, "The only thing necessary for evil to triumph is for good men to do or say nothing." By these precepts, given his deafening silence, the question then become, 'Is Dr. Carson a good man?'

As such then, and having served his purpose as a Republican "hit man" who failed miserably in denting President Obama's Teflon armor, Mr. Carson will probably go by way of the "Do Do Bird," but more especially like Michael Steele, Allen West, J.C. Watts, Alan Keyes, all hired "hatchet men" who failed miserably at their tasks and were fired or allowed to fade into the "black hole of Republican Party oblivion." The interesting realization, however, is the potency and leadership President Obama brought to his responsibility that not simply has aided America across the national landscape but equally vanquished so many Republicans of statue, he forced them into retirement or simply to have them "change their call numbers." In all this, Dr. Ben Carson simply stands in line to be another victim of the Obama political skill apparatus.

OBAMA THE JOURNEY COMPLETED - NEVER PROMISED A ROSE GARDEN

"I said that America's role would be limited; that we would not put ground troops into Libya; that we would focus our unique capabilities on the front end of the operation, and that we would transfer responsibility to our allies and partners." **Barack Obama**

FREDERICK MONDERSON

62.   RALLY AROUND BARACK!
By
Dr. Fred Monderson

"Time will tell" is full of merit and without a doubt; we must now "Rally around Barack" because he has proved he has earned the credits to certainly be considered one of the great Presidents of the United States of America, especially for this new century. Such a view is credible for a number of reasons including Mr. Obama's full-fledged grasping and grappling with the economic and domestic issues and handling the international challenges as they present

OBAMA THE JOURNEY COMPLETED - NEVER PROMISED A ROSE GARDEN

themselves. Unquestionably, despite all the negativism, he seems to be prevailing in his vision. However, unlike the woman at his town hall meeting who publicly criticized the President and he took it smiling while the *New York Post* and such ilks gave her unprecedented coverage, front page and all, because as an African-American she dared to call out the President; many supporters who understood the big picture never wavered in their support and such loyalty now seems to be paying just deserved rewards, as the merits of Barack Obama's strategy and unrelenting hard work ethic continues to unfold. As a matter of fact, while this appeal was first issued during the early years of his presidency, it is just as relevant today as he winds down his second term tenure. Thus, the appeal is just as relevant for his legacy and the significance of his experience and vigilance beyond his term in office.

"I think there are a whole host of things that are civil rights, and then there are other things - such as traditional marriage - that, I think, express a community's concern and regard for a particular institution." **Barack Obama**

Perhaps the farmer with his conception of the agricultural season requiring the process of tilling the field, planting the seeds, watering the ground, weeding the shoots and allowing the plants to bud, grow, develop and mature for the harvest could identify with the genuine efforts demonstrated by Mr. Obama. Opponents, competitors, critics and even "haters," on the other hand, have shown their true colors of contempt in the unrelenting attacks on Barack Obama from the time he demonstrated audacity to run for the Presidency of the United States. This bold move for a Black man to run for the Presidency and serve with distinction called into question a number of factors global observers used as a yardstick to evaluate the presumed state of America in the young century. Through his seven years as Head of State, Chief Legislator, Commander-In-Chief and "man of the people," Mr. Obama has shown a steady hand, not easily reaching where he himself questions his decisions.

FREDERICK MONDERSON

In wake of "opposition scorched earth" methods, the words of Edmund Burke in his *Reflections on the Revolution in France* (1792) that "The only thing necessary for evil to triumph is for good men to say nothing" rings true today, as it related to assaults on the integrity of the Senator and now President Barack Obama and for that matter the Office of the Presidency which he represents and upholds. When we reflect on the inhuman characterization of Barack Obama in the "birth of the Tea Party movement" and the unrelenting assaults on his human, civic and intellectual personality as represented by the actions of the "Birthers Movement's" king and queen one has to wonder about the deafening silence of those leaders, men of conscience, who claim to speak to and for America. Add to this the secretive treasonous gathering of high echelon Republican operatives and the bold and unmistaken confession of then Senate Minority leader Mitch McConnell, "I intend to make Barack Obama a one-term President," was starkly racist as Morgan Freeman boldly affirmed on CNN's Piers Morgan, such consistent actions paint a sad commentary about these practitioners.

Principal among questions stated and unstated were whether America was ready for a black President? This was answered in the most unquestionable fashion. Could a black effectively run such a major entity as the United States government? The successes he chalked up, answered in the affirmative. Was he sufficiently experienced to contend on the world stage as a major statesman? Consistently he remained in step with the major players on the world stage. Could his new face and voice change the world's image of America, particularly in view of its perception over the last decade or so? It certainly did; and, even more important "Could Barack Obama run a credible campaign to be elected President of the United States?" This he did twice! As demonstrated to all observers, the answer to the last question was the unleashing of a well-orchestrated surprise machine that snowballed in organizational sophistication as he took his opponents down a "dusty road," into the Presidency and the rest is known re-election history.

Pitfalls along the way included that nascent "Tea Party" movement in alliance with the Republican Party that vindictively characterized the

OBAMA THE JOURNEY COMPLETED - NEVER PROMISED A ROSE GARDEN

intelligent gentleman candidate Barack Obama who, is not only organizationally gifted but has remained glued with his "eyes on the prize," looking "straight ahead" and ignoring "Cat calls" while working feverishly at his task. Yet, Barack took no action towards such behaviors, as some clamored "we want our country back" because he is "not like us." Equally they thought he was "inexperienced" and even after being elected, he was soon "challenged" by various nation states' "bad boys."

All the while the President set out tackling the problems he inherited. Even more sinister, given the domestic and global mess bequeathed this new Chief Executive and Commander-in-Chief; the "Birthers" kept up their attacks. Black Republicans including Alan Keyes and the much publicized "black protester with guns" in Arizona whose church leader was "praying for Obama's death" were the most vocally sinister. Allen West was a sprinter who could not even finish the 100-yard dash. Notwithstanding the latter state of affairs, in view of the task ahead of impending economic, financial and fiscal collapse desperately in need on monetary regulation, a hemorrhaging job market, foreclosures, etc., and with international ideological competition escalating; to accuse the President of being unsuited for office was a blindsided attack that disrespected the institution of the Presidency and the man who held that office. Let us not forget the older attacks during the campaign of Mr. Obama of "not being a citizen," "unpatriotic," "too black," "not black enough," that he "forgot the name of a solder whose bracelet he wore" and to boot opponents rolled out "Joe the Plumber" who parroted a false notion that "Obama was a socialist." Yet, in time, the *New York Post*, in a political cartoon, showed Obama flushing "Joe the Plumber" down the bowl! Today in 2016 the electorate seems fickle attracted to socialist Bernie Sanders and bigoted Donald Trump.

Just as Obama's opponents could not honestly admit to the mess their Republican cohorts had created in the American economic, financial, international and political climate, even Mr. Obama did not, at first, comprehend the size of the mess he inherited. Nevertheless, he set about tracking and attacking the problems requiring banking and financial and economic reforms and regulation; as well as paying attention to problems of housing starts and foreclosures; expressing concerns about jobs, health care and educational reforms; and touting the need for energy independence through innovative research and development of wind energy, energy from the sun, and new forms of batteries, all designed to reduce the nation's dependence on foreign oil sources. Mr. Obama even supported an increase in domestic production. Couple this with the international situation, and the ramifications of two wars in Iraq and Afghanistan, as well as challenges posed by North Korea, Iran, the Middle East quagmire and the global threats of Al Qaeda and the potential of domestic terrorism, to not aid but tear down the President at this time was truly un-patriotic, un-American. Yet, but because it was done by Republicans hardly any voices of conscience spoke up. When Donald Trump criticized John McCain as not being a war hero many were blaringly upset. The President responded, "These same people remained silent when I was being abused and raked over a bed of coals." In response, to the many unfolding challenges, Mr. Obama pursued and nailed Osama bin-laden.

We cannot forget during and after the first and second campaigns, physical threats to Mr. Obama increased manifold as right wing groups stockpiled military hardware to combat a falsely perceived and publicized threat Mr. Obama represented. Still, many American "leaders of repute" said nothing though law enforcement agents tightened their scrutiny so as to ensure the president's safety. Added to this, the *New York Post* printed a political cartoon showing two policemen shooting the President disguised as an ape. This action stirred the irony of particularly Obama's Black supporters and many liberal whites across the nation never let the "birdcage floor mat" *New York Post* forget. Nevertheless, the President continued his tremendous efforts of fulfilling the functions of the many hats he wore.

Of course, the big assignments come to mind first: historic health insurance reform, even though he lost his biggest ally and champion

OBAMA THE JOURNEY COMPLETED - NEVER PROMISED A ROSE GARDEN

of this bill, Edward Kennedy. The **Affordable Care Act's** passage was designed to rein in the insurance companies and help control the cost of care for millions of Americans who had no health care coverage; Wall Street reform, which put in place the toughest consumer protections ever enabled that institution to recover and prosper; the question of passage of the bill to close Guantanamo Bay prison and the move to begin trials of those incarcerated there has remained a stumbling block the Republican controlled House of Representatives has refused to move on; and bringing an end to combat operations in Iraq, which brought more than 100,000 troops home has in some respects backfired as **ISIS** rose to prominence. However, while Mr. Obama's opponents often blame him for the Iraqi mess, they grossly underestimated the narrow-mindedness and failure of Nuri Alaki, the Iran lackey, who betrayed the high ideals of statesmanship by ignoring the value of significant elements in his nation.

Treachery is such that we must be constantly reminded, Chalaby mislead President Obama about Sadam's armaments that put Colin Powell in the hot seat at the United Nations.

FREDERICK MONDERSON

And there is so much more the Obama-Biden team helped achieve that is right now improving lives across this country:

The first act Mr. Obama passed as President was the Lilly Ledbetter Act giving women equal pay status as men.

The team passed the Recovery Act, which saved and created to date in cooperation with the private sector more than 15 million jobs, provided the largest middle-class tax cut in a generation, and made landmark investments in clean energy, infrastructure, and education. Today, these nearly 15 million private sector jobs created across the board during his presidency were hard won without Republican support since they refused to pass Mr. Obama's jobs bill.

The administration, in fairness, made critical investments in General Motors and Chrysler Corporation operational financing that saved

OBAMA THE JOURNEY COMPLETED - NEVER PROMISED A ROSE GARDEN

tens of thousands of jobs - and perhaps the companies - thus spurring revitalization of the American car industry which could have gone into oblivion. Instead this resulted in greater market share in the auto industry.

Obama's team wrote into law student loan and credit card reform, which ended the worst abuses of the banking industries and are making lending fair for American families.

The Barack Administration put two new Supreme Court justices on the bench - Sonia Sotomayor and Elena Kagan, who bring rich and diverse experiences to the Court and his re-election prepared the way for his Democratic successor as President to be able to add to choices on the Supreme Court. The potential of such an act irks many and has spurred much animosity towards the President's potential successors. There is talk of appointing Mr. Obama to the Supreme Court but given the domestic activist restrictions on such a position, his post-president grass-roots organizing may suffer a setback.

The Administration has begun to reset America's relationship with the international community, from the ratification of a new **START** nuclear arms treaty with Russia to the tough sanctions on Iran has forged a nuclear pact with that nation forestalling its nuclear ambitions. Thus, to strengthening America's long-term partnership with a struggling Iraq challenged by Isis and to his engaging China to rein in its close ally, North Korea bent on nuclear mischief. Mr. Obama set in motion a dialogue with Iran backed by a significant coalition of states vigorously negotiated by Secretary of State John Kerry resulting in Iranian concessions in the Iran-Nuclear Dead. However, though the world is satisfied with the deal, Mr. Obama's enemies vigorously oppose such an agreement.

The very thorny "Don't Ask, Don't Tell" legislation which was the right thing to do - not only because it makes the military stronger at a time when it needs to be the strongest, but because Americans are seeking military might with an abiding sense of justice. This and more were accomplished in a two-year period. Then Mr. Obama advocated and pushed for the protections and benefits same sex marriages and gay and lesbian unions were entitled to.

We do recognize the November mid-term elections of 2010 and 2014 saw Republicans regain the House of Representatives that sent a strong message to the President and the Democrats, that is, despite what has been done to turn things around; the country wants to go in a new direction. Yet, Republicans remain intractably opposed to Mr. Obama rather than cooperate for mutual benefit of the American people. Still, countering conventional wisdom by applying the great resources of his thinking economic and other forms of advisers particularly Paul Volker, as the economy began to improve, the President was able to wrangle a new tax-cut bill despite the lame-duck status of a Democratic Congress. Still, some have argued Republicans, despite their rhetoric about deficits are more interested in MONEY for their re-election.

Like everything else, "time does tell" and the ship of state, like the enormous battleship that it is, has slowly begun to turn and as things unfold, Mr. Obama's numbers have improved. This is because the recession is over, businesses are hiring, unemployment rates have dropped, housing starts have increased, Mr. Obama has insisted, having pulled the economy back from the brink, he wants to put it in overdrive and has proposed a number of measures to do so. With such efforts, the prospects of Mr. Obama's re-election were justified and he continued to work even harder in his second term despite total Republican control of Congress. Still, the "Party of No" has not successfully checked his creativity given the most recent and impressive accomplishments from the Cuban normalization move to the Asian Trade Deal to the Challenges he posed for Republicans.

While some have blamed the recent violent murders in Arizona on anti-Obama inspired rhetoric that seemed to motivate an unbalanced individual, the President went to Tucson to pay tribute to those victims and sent a powerful message of healing. Following the Paris Attack

OBAMA THE JOURNEY COMPLETED - NEVER PROMISED A ROSE GARDEN

and that in San Bernardino he sadly had to again console the nation. Some have hailed his reconciliatory message designed to heal and unite the nation, so much so, one of his harshest critics and credible opponents Senator John McCain, came out and praised Mr. Obama's healing words, while Condoleezza Rice, former Secretary of State on Pierce Morgan's new show remarked "Mr. Obama is a decent man and doing his best for this country." Therefore, it is time to "Rally around Barack" to show his detractors, supporters and the world, Mr. Obama is indeed a good man and has done his best to turn the nation around and help it recover from the quagmire of the last decade. And, with this we rally and stand behind Barack Obama!

"I think there are a whole host of things that are civil rights, and then there are other things - such as traditional marriage - that, I think, express a community's concern and regard for a particular institution." **Barack Obama**

FREDERICK MONDERSON

63.   THAT OBAMA LEGACY
By
Dr. Fred Monderson

Fresh from the significant agreement at the recent Climate Change Conference, reality dictates observers and history commentators consider Barack Obama's legacy constantly and positively unfolding as his presidential term winds down. No time in American history has the nation been more challenged than when Barack Obama captured the Presidency in 2008! Since, in assessing the times and the man, Noble Laureate Paul Krugman, writing in *The New York Times* declared Barack Obama "The Greatest American President Ever!" Naturally, both Mr. Krugman and President Obama were the subject of enormous "pushback" especially from Republicans, viz., right wing and media conservatives; "Tea Party" operatives in and out of

OBAMA THE JOURNEY COMPLETED - NEVER PROMISED A ROSE GARDEN

Congress; political operatives on a mission in the persons of then Senate Minority Leader Mitch McConnell's mandate aided by the efforts of House Speaker John Boehner; ex-Alaska Governor Sarah Palin; Representative Michele Bachmann; former Senator Jim DeMint; the disrespectful South Carolina Representative Joe Wilson, who, in the House during the President's State of the Union Address, in response to a statement blurted out, "You lie;" the Arizona Pastor "Praying for Obama's Death" and his misguided parishioner, the Black Protester with Guns, himself unable to understand the full dynamics of the issue and his role; to this we may add the late comers "Daddy Cruz" and his presidential contending son Senator Ted Cruz and of course there's the never to be forgotten Heritage Foundation's "Poster Boy" Dr. Benjamin Carson, the retired neurosurgeon.

"I will cut taxes - cut taxes - for 95 percent of all working families, because, in an economy like this, the last thing we should do is raise taxes on the middle class." **Barack Obama**

FREDERICK MONDERSON

As the subject of the assessment that Mr. Obama was, like Mohammed Ali, "the Greatest Ever," Mr. Krugman called it as he saw the reality and projection of the man, the burden of the office and how intellectually skillful he effectively carried forth his responsibilities. After all, to win a Noble prize means the individual possesses an extraordinary intellectual capacity and potential to assess fully the highest and most complex issues and what is higher than the responsibilities given the Presidency of the United States. President Obama, on the other hand, was vilified for more insidious reasons than piloting the ship of state successfully through the perilous waters in which he inherited the nation's mantle and into the calm seas and overhead blue skies wherein he sailed his craft. Yes! Today, when we observe the bigotry and racism spewing from lips such as Donald Trump, regarding Muslims, immigrants, Mexicans, women, how he views President Obama, Secretary of State John Kerry, Mrs. Hillary Clinton, etc., the manner in which not simply Trump's supporters among Republican Evangelical Christians and others, we ask, 'Are they Christians?' 'Do they speak for Jesus?' Or, 'are Trump and that brand of his supporters hypocritical opportunists?'

OBAMA THE JOURNEY COMPLETED - NEVER PROMISED A ROSE GARDEN

It is interesting, how none of the Republican candidates for the Presidency in 2016 has uttered a word regarding the unfolding Black social situation the Black Lives Matter movement keeps emphasizing across the nation. Mr. Carson has not uttered a word for or against, nor has the insulting Donald Trump. Perhaps it is because they have no intention to help, perhaps can't do anything about it; or, even more important, as the great visionary Malcolm X once recognized, "The nation is so evenly divided, polarized, the Black vote can make the difference between who goes to the White House and who goes to the dog house!" Therefore, "don't disturb the Black waters; perhaps they may not rise!" For, remember the story of the "blind white guy who went to see a championship boxing match!" He was accompanied by a guide who gave him blow-by-blow commentary as the fight unfolded. As the event waged into the late rounds, the blind man asked, "What's happening now." His commentator responded, "The White guy has the Black guy down!" "The Black guy's down? Keep him down, for when the Black man raises, hell raises!" Many should take note of this time-tested wisdom. However, with all the publicity Republicans are currently generating, this is hardly likely and the next election will certainly have to contend with the influence of the Obama legacy because the genii is now out of the bottle.

Very early, understanding the nature of the game he was a part of, Mr. Obama took the high road in stride regarding attacks on his person, simply exclaiming, "I know politics is a contact sport." However, when it came to attacks on his wife, he stared boldly into the camera and warned, "If you're watching, lay off my wife!" As with all unconscionable bullies, the stated message was well received. Important, instead of wilting under the huge climate of disrespect and racial hatred generated towards him because of his race, he continued to strategize and more effectively continued to rack up "wins" in areas that benefitted the broad masses of the American people.

First he proposed women, especially moms, return to college to develop skills needed in a changing economic environment he was moving the country towards. Then he emphasized a more upgraded role for community colleges. Recognizing that student loan is a problem for students and graduates, Mr. Obama directed efforts to help alleviate some of the burdens that keep accumulating. Financial and economic policies eased the job situation with many millions of new job hires impacting areas as Wall Street, empowering citizen to "Junk the Clunker" and purchase automobiles thereby increasing the industry's market share with the strategies carrying over into strengthening the President's position in securing favorable terms in the Asian Trade Agreement deal. In wake of the immigration reform issue for long stalled, President Obama issued an Executive Order easing the burden on undocumented youth brought to these shores when young by parents themselves undocumented, giving them an

OBAMA THE JOURNEY COMPLETED - NEVER PROMISED A ROSE GARDEN

opportunity to serve the nation in the military and the promises this patriotic act represented.

FREDERICK MONDERSON

"In fact, the best thing we could do on taxes for all Americans is to simplify the individual tax code. This will be a tough job, but members of both parties have expressed an interest in doing this, and I am prepared to join them." **Barack Obama**

OBAMA THE JOURNEY COMPLETED - NEVER PROMISED A ROSE GARDEN

64.   TRUMP AND OBAMA
BY
Dr. Fred Monderson

Donald Trump and President Obama see the world differently because of their responsibilities and interests. Mr. Obama sees the world from his position as President but more particularly as Commander-In-Chief, Chief Diplomat, Chief Legislator and leader of his political party and more important as an African American leading this great nation. The huge responsibilities that come with the many "Hats" the President wears are crafted by the notion of what Republican Condoleezza Rice, former Chief of Staff and Secretary of State exclaimed, "The world looks different in the view from behind the Oval Office desk." There is so much the President has to balance in executing his "Oath of Office" and equally maintaining diplomatic relations with most of the world's more than 190 nations. In these nations' representative visits to the White House to discuss relations, the contents are for the most part announced or an "Open Book."

"Let's be honest - tracking down, rounding up, and deporting millions of people isn't realistic. Anyone who suggests otherwise isn't being straight with you. It's also not who we are as Americans." **Barack Obama**

Mr. Trump on the other hand sees the world from behind the desk of Trump Tower No. 1 and No 2, and so on as a businessman. While Mr. Obama has to answer to the American people who elected him and the press who follow him, his every word is watched and carefully scrutinized, and at a cost he is held answerable to a multitude of constituencies and therefore must be wise in every respect; Mr. Trump answers to no one except his bank account manager, perhaps not even him or her. While Mr. Obama's every action is subject to legislative and judicial scrutiny, not least his constituency, the American people; as an insurgent, Mr. Trump is not so constrained and remains unrestrained in his speeches and behaviors as he continues to trumpet, "Make America Great Again."

If we begin by analyzing the two men's response to recent developments both at home and abroad, a stark contrast emerges. In Europe, especially, the night and day differences between the two outlooks becomes clearly evident. Of course, in this instance, these developments do not seek to underscore, as an example one man seeking the other's job.

OBAMA THE JOURNEY COMPLETED - NEVER PROMISED A ROSE GARDEN

Soldiers and Sailors Memorial entrancing the Capitol Building.

First, if we begin with the recent "Brexit" development, the **DOW** Jones Average "fell" nearly 600 points. Mr. Trump and similarly displeased pundits emphasized this significant one day loss on the stock market in the plunge from nearly18,000. Strange, but the 600 point was quickly regained and the **DOW** is again above 18,000. No one said much about the precipitous rise of the "market" from 6500 in 2008 just before Mr. Obama took over, to the historic high then hovering at 18,000. Thus, this stark contrast and the evident reality must remain clearly evident in every arena the two men are compared in. However, let readers not forget, the role of personality in the two views for, while Mr. Obama is open and looking positively outward, Mr. Trump is closed and seeming pessimistic in his rants against Muslims, women, Mexicans, Mr. McCain, Mr. Khan, the disabled, a federal judge and let's not forget his disparaging and demolishing Republican presidential contenders and constantly not to forget Mr. Obama himself. Calling Hillary Clinton the devil, even railing against the Republican establishment and many of its top echelon members who publicly and especially disfavor the man. Even more, to show empathy for the grief felt by families who have lost loved ones in the ongoing tragedy, we must focus on the man given his fool's errant "Birther" escapade that may today be dormant but not defunct.

Second, as head of the nation, in aftermath of every shooting that kills Americans on its soil, the President feels the pain and must commiserate with grieving families who clamor for gun ownership or purchaser controls, but more particularly responsible ownership and use of firearms. Mr. Trump and his Republican counterparts single-mindedly focus on the National Rifle Association's unequivocal insistence on the Second Amendment's right to bear arms guarantee regardless of any reckless behavior that results therefrom. Of significant note, however, the application of this pristine right is different from the Constitution's original enactment and the proliferation of weaponry given today's many dynamics of population, ethnic composition, business enterprises, size of the nation; the nature of foreign threats with gun ownership as a defensive mechanism and most important easy access to gun possession which has resulted in numberless killings and gun related criminal behavior. However, in their control of the House of Representatives especially since 2010 and 2014 Mid-term elections, the most Republicans do is "offer a moment of silence," following tragedy after tragedy, after

702

tragedy and the fundamental reality of gun violence remains a deadly reminder we must seek a responsible solution to gun violence and senseless killing. This is especially so when people under scrutiny for terrorist behavior even on a "No Fly List" can still find shelter under the Second Amendment.

The Supreme Court building.

Thomas Jefferson building of the Library of Congress.

Another remarkable issue of note is, classic gun owners possess arms from the time of the "Old West" and this is unmistaken. However, and as an example, in January 2009, when President Obama assumed his office, insidious propaganda held, "Obama wants to change the Constitution;" "Obama wants to take your guns;" "a race war is coming;" so, militias and the gun owners began or should I say, continued stockpiling arms and ammunition year after year. Thus, since and given guns never go out of style, "How many weapons can one person shoot at one time?" Or is it simply the sale of guns to benefit the gun industry's economic bottom line. Nonetheless, President Obama has to respond after each shooting but Trump and Republicans, avid supporters of the National Rifle Association and gun owners' rights, never do. Still, another case in point with much relevance, after the Orlando nightclub shooting, Mr. Trump insisted "If gun owners were 'carrying' in the club they would have been able to stop the madman who executed so many." Well, a Black man with a carry permit was recently shot in his car reaching for his identification in front of his wife with a child in the back seat. We still await justice for this "victim" with a permit!

Third, in seeking to execute and in response to the war on terrorism, Mr. Trump wants to impose a "complete and total ban on all Muslims entering the country." With some "pushback" this has been modified to "only Muslims coming from countries with known terrorists" actively engaged in such activities. Even more, he would reintroduce Water-boarding, go after terrorist families, even carpet bomb their places of operation. These potential policies have forced many high ranking and retired military personnel to question whether, the US military would obey such illegal practices and this can prompt a constitutional crisis. Nevertheless, the modified Terrorist "pushback" would now apply to "any country compromised by terrorism" which includes France and Germany, American allies. Heaven forbids a terror incident occurs in Britain, America's staunchest ally, then the proscription would apply there also or there is "no universal application" of this strategy. Logically then, the position seems somewhat ridiculous and not thoroughly thought out even though Mr. Trump's base supports it steadfastly. Another example in which this megalomaniac loyalty tarnishes the American Brand, Mr. Trump once

OBAMA THE JOURNEY COMPLETED - NEVER PROMISED A ROSE GARDEN

said, "If I stand on Fifth Avenue and shoot someone, I would not lose any votes." If so and such an action presents no consequences, Mr. Trump would be above the law for firing a weapon within city limits and the consequences of actually shooting someone, especially if unarmed, is still another and more serious matter.

A. Philip Randolph - Labor Leader.

FREDERICK MONDERSON

President Obama, who really understands the "big picture" acquired through eight years of high level security briefings and diplomatic

applications as the head of state recognizes such positions have "pushback" of global proportions. For instance, when an ally supports a country's position on an issue, they themselves have to relate to other countries with whom they have relations and who may disagree from which diplomatic complications can arise. Simply put, what may sound palatable to a few may have negative consequences for the many in response to any arrogant or not properly thought out behavior or strategy. We must never forget how a "go it alone" mode of conduct sullied the American image in the world community under George Bush as he led the nation into Iraq seeking Weapons of Mass Destruction (WMD).

Fourth, conventions are a time when political parties invite their members to come together, present and debate platform issues then crown their party's standard bearer to contest the Presidential Election sometimes 3-4 months later in November. This 2016 Presidential Election has been described as like no other. The Democratic and Republican campaigns to succeed Barack Obama as President have been exercises in stark contrast. It's interesting, both Donald Trump and Barack Obama ran against Hillary Clinton. However, while Barack Obama ran a resolutely civil campaign purely based on brains, Donald Trump waged his on brawn. While Obama's was civil, speaking on the issues of loss of jobs, deplorable condition of the housing industry, America's loss of face on the world stage, etc.; Trump's was uncivil spewing hatred, animus, bigotry, racism, even ignorance and lacking policies and programs of substance. As an African-American seeking the Office of the President, Barack Obama had to offer sound policies, economic, social, and educational and energy-wise which he delivered upon. All Mr. Trump wanted to do was "jail Hillary" and call her bad names, nothing but negativity that have won him disfavor with "Republicans of Note." Still, Mr. Obama wonders why Republicans such as John McCain, Paul Ryan, Mitch McConnell and others, while rejecting many of Mr. Trump's stated views, yet till endorse and support him. Their position seems, "No matter what, he's still our boy!" The sad commentary, some have expressed concern, given Mr. Trump's outlandish, bigoted, some say racist statements and his solid support among his base, there is an alarming realization of how many Americans share his questionable behavior and views. After all, in the outlandish statements he uttered Donald Trump was compared to dictators Hitler and Mussolini and many ultra-right wing, even Neo-Nazi groups in Europe particularly those objecting to "immigrants changing the face of their nation," but they also bring the potential for terrorist action. We can't lose sight of the fact many nationals of these nations fought for Isis in Syria then returned or plan to return home with a desire to further that cause of terror and mayhem. There is no question loose rhetoric and "gloom and doom" declarations of Donald Trump's stokes the cauldron upsetting even staunch Republicans.

Rochambeau in Lafayette Park.

Fifth, because Mr. Obama is a principled man, presided over a unified party, in 2008 and again in 2012, he was able to operationalize an orderly and constructive convention and with a tremendous work ethic he waged a successful campaign to become president twice. Mr. Trump, on the other hand, rode a bulldozer roughshod against a field of 16 others amidst an unusually rancorous climate of hate, insult, disrespect and speaking out of turn. As the RNC wound down, New

708

OBAMA THE JOURNEY COMPLETED - NEVER PROMISED A ROSE GARDEN

Jersey Federal Senator Corey Booker took to the airwaves to denounce the hate spewing out of the Republican Convention. Imagine Christian Conservatives behaving in a manner that savaged Hillary Clinton, perhaps forced the on-looking world to wonder if this behavior reflects the character and true nature of America, in which staunch and practicing Christians seem "going to hell in a hand-basket."

Sixth, the two men's spouses came under scrutiny in the manner in which they shared the spotlight with their husbands. In the 2008 campaign Michelle Obama, a potential First-Lady, proved a class act. So much so, "Mighty Michelle" became an effective fashionista ambassador and asset for Barack Obama and America on the world stage. Michelle is an attorney by trade who writes her own material while Melania has a hired speech writer. However, while she publicly claimed ownership for the Convention speech, another fell on her sword in claiming she is the culprit. Again, a good example of how the world pays attention to developments in America, Wednesday August 3, 2016, under the timeline, "Trump's Wife Melania's Photos Make A Splash," an English language Egyptian newspaper, quoting Monday's *New York Post*, expose of "Potential first lady, Melania Trump's naked 'Ménage a Trump," which "The picture shows a nude Melania being hugged by another nude woman as she is in bed." Even further, "On Sunday the Post ran a front page picture of a nude Melania with stones covering her breasts, under the title "The Ogle of Office." The Republican Presidential campaign appeared to shrug of the pictures. Trump's adviser told CNN Sunday that there was "Nothing to be embarrassed about with the pictures. She's a beautiful woman."

"The *New York Post* endorsed Trump for President in Mid-April, describing him at the time as "a potential superstar of vast promise, but making rookie mistakes." "Some wondered how conservative Evangelical Christians would react, while others wondered if Murdock, who also holds conservative views, had turned against Trump."

FREDERICK MONDERSON

In an interesting comparison, back in the day when Vanessa Williams, a beautiful African American woman won the Miss America pageant title, when similar nude photos surfaced, she was stripped of her crown. As a beauty queen, Miss America does not have the same influence as the first lady at home or even on the world stage particularly as she accompanies her husband on those important global summits. Remembering the "Shoe thrown at George Bush," one cannot fail to wonder how Mr. Trump will react at one of these high powered global gatherings when persons disparagingly comment on America's naked first lady.

OBAMA THE JOURNEY COMPLETED - NEVER PROMISED A ROSE GARDEN

The Republican Convention seemed to "savage" Hillary Clinton, "Put her in jail," was a constant chant and every effort to discredit her were made giving no consideration to her nearly four decades of public service. This contrast with Donald Trump, who as an "outsider," has done no public service for anyone but himself. Mr. Trump's children have painted him not simply as an angel but perhaps the "best thing since slice bread." Yet, more and more is coming to light about his character. Many will agree there were no specifics in how Mr. trump will seek to solve the many problems facing the nation such as "Isis," "Infrastructure repairs," "terrorism;" "Global Warming;" all except a hostile attitude towards Hillary Clinton. However, don't underestimate Bill Clinton who is always watching and planning.

The Democratic Convention, on the other hand, painted a picture of midday versus midnight contrasting Hillary Clinton and Donald

Trump respectively. The interesting comparison, however, the numerous social services Hillary Clinton was credited with performing over the many decades of service contrasts markedly with Trump's negatives, viz., not releasing his taxes; not paying people who worked for him; facing thousands of lawsuits for what appears a fraudulent Trump University "Scam;" never forgetting Mike Blumberg, as a new Yorker, "Who knows a scam when I see one;" his statements following the "Brexit" developments; then Mr. Trump's either silence or outspokenness on domestic gun violence is all disturbing. Pointedly stated, "I know" yet his supporters remain committed irrespective.

Realizing the pedestrian versus jet age differences between the cardboard cut-out and the finished oil painting of Hillary Clinton particularly when Mr. Trump played the "Russian Card" appealing to Mr. Putin to hack into the server of an American Secretary of State paints Mr. Trump as a President of questionable and potentially dangerous leadership. As such, we can probably paint Mr. Obama as an optimist; Mr. Trump as a pessimist. Mr. Obama sees the nation great and rising; Mr. Trump on the other hand, may have characterized as not simply pessimist, but as some have proclaimed racist, unsteady, demagogic, and most important "someone who should not have his hands on the nuclear trigger." Mr. Obama sees the nation as great and rising; Mr. Trump sees the nation in decline and he needs to "make it great again," at no matter what cost. Now, with the Republican and Democratic Conventions over, a number of surprising fallouts have raised eyebrows.

OBAMA THE JOURNEY COMPLETED - NEVER PROMISED A ROSE GARDEN

President Obama, on the other hand must maintain good relations with perhaps half the nations of the world who are Muslims all possessing a significant Muslim population. Many of the issues America presents at the United Nations and needs those nations' vote of support is tied to those cordial relations with these "Muslim nations." In the fight against Al Qaeda and Isis, though essentially in the Middle East, our nation needs the same Muslim support for ground troops, intelligence sharing and such things as forward bases, resupply routes and fly-over rights dictate a balanced and delicate approach to those nations whose citizens Mr. Trump wants to ban.

FREDERICK MONDERSON

Seventh, as a businessman whose book "The Art of the Deal" masquerade as the "Bible of Business" Mr. Trump wants to condemn and renegotiate every deal from the Trans-Pacific Partnership to the Iran Nuclear Agreement. Mr. Obama understands much effort goes into such agreements and that you can't use a gun or club to the head to get others to sign away their natural resources. In the 21st Century, we must realize it's a different playing field and negotiations need to be creatively constructed and fair.

As a loving husband, father of two beautiful daughters and no matter the claims, an effective President, Mr. Obama takes pride in having served at a critical time in the nation's history. His tenure was based on the realities of the day. As many "in the know" have indicated, Mr.

OBAMA THE JOURNEY COMPLETED - NEVER PROMISED A ROSE GARDEN

Trump's bluster and pronouncements are a cause for great concern. Thus, let us summarize some differences between the two men.

1.   His attack on a Gold Star Family prompting Senator John McCain, Speaker Paul Ryan and especially the Veterans of Foreign Wars to weigh in expressing disapproval of his behavior.

2.   His seeming bitter intent to support a challenger seeking to unseat the Speaker of the House form his Congressional Seat clearly signals disharmony in the Republican camp.

3.   The invitation to Mr. Putin to "Find Hillary Clinton's missing e-mails Mr. trump is asking the very people with whom he must sit across from. Such an action casts further light on Mr. Trump's unpredictability." US investigative agents blame Russian operatives for hacking into the DNC files.

4.   Mr. Obama, understands the full implications of the office, relative to foreign policy. The use of nuclear weapons; loggerheads with Military commanders; Mr. Trump saying he "knows more about ISIS than the generals;" the President has endorsed Hillary Clinton to succeed him not especially because she is a Democrat but more important Mr. Trump is unfit for the office and his erratic pronouncements make him a risky President and Commander-In-Chief.

5.   A number of retired Generals; especially because active duty general officers cannot publicly express political sentiments; officers are fearful as Commander-In-Chief, Mr. Trump may order the military to undertake water-boarding and other unconscionable and illegal, potentially criminal acts and this may pose a constitutional crisis if the military refuses.

6.   Supreme Court Justice Ruth Bader Ginsberg made the highly unusual criticism of Mr. Trump because she felt the need to speak out against him and his potential for nominating and appointing the

"wrong judges." Nevertheless, we have had 8 years of Obama on public display; Mr. Trump is yet to prove himself. As such, we can conclude much though these are just a summary of some differing issues between Mr. Obama and Mr. Trump people should be concerned about.

7. A decent husband, father that he is, Mr. Obama would not express vulgar thoughts about women as Mr. Trump has done, describing their private parts and aggressive behavior claiming this is "Locker Room Talk."

OBAMA THE JOURNEY COMPLETED - NEVER PROMISED A ROSE GARDEN

"It's time to fundamentally change the way that we do business in Washington. To help build a new foundation for the 21st century, we need to reform our government so that it is more efficient, more transparent, and more creative. That will demand new thinking and a new sense of responsibility for every dollar that is spent." **Barack Obama**